ALSO BY BRUCE LEVINE

Confederate Emancipation:
Southern Plans to Free and Arm Slaves during the Civil War

Half Slave and Half Free:
The Roots of Civil War

The Spirit of 1848:
German Immigrants, Labor Conflict, and the Coming of the Civil War

Who Built America? Working People and the Nation's Economy, Politics,
Culture, and Society (co-author)

Work and Society:
A Reader (co-editor)

The Fall *of the* House *of* Dixie

The FALL of the
HOUSE of DIXIE

The Civil War and the Social Revolution
That Transformed the South

BRUCE LEVINE

RANDOM HOUSE
NEW YORK

Published in the United States by Random House,
an imprint of The Random House Publishing Group,
a division of Random House, Inc., New York.

RANDOM HOUSE and colophon are registered trademarks of Random House, Inc.

Library of Congress Cataloging-in-Publication Data

Levine, Bruce
The fall of the house of Dixie : the Civil War and the
social revolution that transformed the South /
Bruce Levine.
p. cm
ISBN 978-1-4000-6703-9—ISBN 978-0-679-64535-1 (ebook)
1. Confederate States of America. 2. Confederate States of America—Social
conditions. 3. Confederate States of America—Economic conditions. 4. Slavery—Social
aspects—Southern States—History—19th century. 5. Slavery—Economic aspects—
Southern States—History—19th century. 6. Elite (Social sciences)—Southern States—
History—19th century. 7. United States—History—Civil War, 1861–1865—Social
aspects. 8. United States—History—Civil War, 1861–1865—Economic aspects. I. Title.
E487.L494 2013
973.7'13—dc23   2011048310

Printed in the United States of America on acid-free paper

www.atrandom.com

2 4 6 8 9 7 5 3 1

First Edition

Book design by Diane Hobbing

Title-page illustration: View of ruins, Richmond, from Main Street, looking down
Fourteenth Street, April 8, 1865 (The Library of Congress)

to Ruth Hoffman

Decades after the Civil War ended, Katherine Stone recalled the "gay, busy life" she had led at Brokenburn, her family's 1,200-acre plantation in prewar Louisiana. "There was always something going on—formal dining, informal 'spend the days,' evening parties, riding frolics," fox hunts. To make these and other diversions possible, Katherine remembered, her family had "quite a corps of servants to keep us well waited on," since naturally "no one expected to wait on himself." Each of Katherine's young brothers also "owned a little darkie in the quarters who would eventually become his body servant." And some 150 other slaves toiled in Brokenburn's cotton and sugarcane fields, "six days out of seven, week after week, month after month, year after year," generating the wealth that sustained the Stone family's life of "luxurious ease."

The war's outbreak in April 1861 augured the end of the Stone family's complacent idyll. The fighting between North and South, Katherine soon perceived, had "infected" her slaves with hope for a radical change in their condition. Some were becoming "lazy and disobedient" and "giving a lot of trouble" generally. One evening, as the Stones took the night air on the gallery of their plantation home, "a runaway Negro" darted past them. Though Katherine's brothers leaped to the pursuit, the desperate fugitive made good his escape. She and her neighbors began to worry that they were living "on a mine."

Seeking refuge from such anxieties, Katherine turned to the works of a popular southern author—Edgar Allan Poe. With her nerves already frayed, however, she decided to avoid "his most fearsome pieces." Perhaps she chose "The Fall of the House of Usher." Neither grisly nor filled with supernatural horrors, it might well have seemed a relatively safe distraction from the unsettling events of the day.

As that story begins, Poe's narrator pays a visit to an old friend, Roderick Usher, the scion of a "very ancient family" and current master of its imposing mansion. At first glance, the massive edifice "gave little token of instability." But its seeming solidity conceals "a barely perceptible fissure which, extending from the roof of the building in front, made its way down the wall in a zig-zag direction, until it became lost" in the foundation and the lake adjacent to it. After a while, the mansion's hidden structural fault begins to announce itself, at first in a "muffled reverberation," then in a mounting roar and powerful shudder. Finally, as the visitor watches in shock, that once barely discernible fissure gapes dramatically open, the walls tumble, and the august mansion collapses, burying its owner under the rubble. The surrounding lake's waters then close "sullenly and silently over the fragments of the 'House of Usher.'"

If Katherine Stone did choose to read this tale, it could hardly have offered her much comfort. She, too, resided in an imposing and outwardly sturdy structure—the House of Dixie, the slavery-based society of the American South. And hers, too, was already beginning to display deep fissures running through it. As the Civil War continued, those fissures would widen until the whole structure fell.

Contents

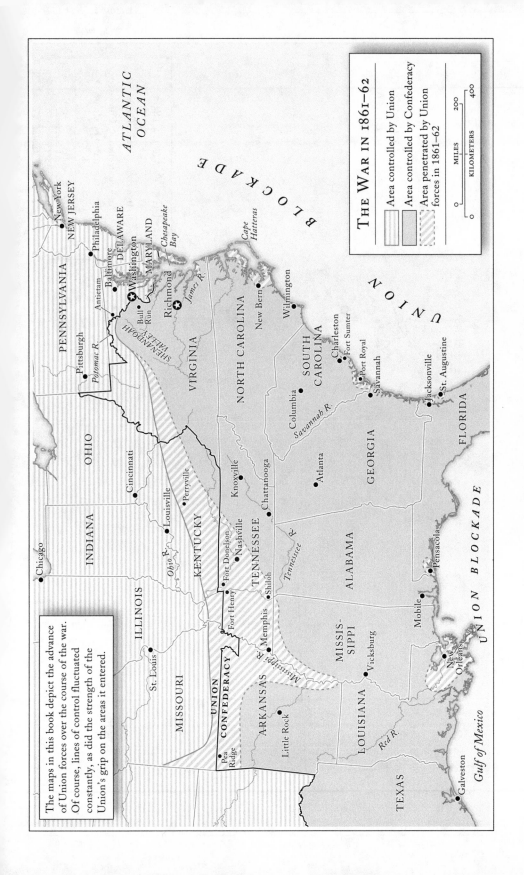

The maps in this book depict the advance of Union forces over the course of the war. Of course, lines of control fluctuated constantly, as did the strength of the Union's grip on the areas it entered.

THE WAR IN 1861–62

Area controlled by Union
Area controlled by Confederacy
Area penetrated by Union forces in 1861–62

MILES 0 200 400
KILOMETERS 0 200 400

ATLANTIC OCEAN

BLOCKADE

UNION

NEW JERSEY
New York
Philadelphia
PENNSYLVANIA
Pittsburgh
Baltimore
DELAWARE
MARYLAND
Washington
Chesapeake Bay
Antietam
Potomac R.
Bull Run
Richmond
James R.
Cape Hatteras
SHENANDOAH VALLEY
VIRGINIA
NORTH CAROLINA
New Bern
Wilmington
OHIO
Cincinnati
Louisville
Perryville
Knoxville
Chattanooga
Columbia
SOUTH CAROLINA
Charleston
Fort Sumter
Port Royal
Savannah
Savannah R.
Jacksonville
St. Augustine
INDIANA
Chicago
ILLINOIS
KENTUCKY
Ohio R.
Fort Donelson
Nashville
TENNESSEE
Shiloh
Tennessee R.
Fort Henry
Memphis
Mississippi R.
Atlanta
GEORGIA
ALABAMA
FLORIDA
Pensacola
Mobile
St. Louis
MISSOURI
UNION
CONFEDERACY
ARKANSAS
Little Rock
Pea Ridge
MISSIS-SIPPI
Vicksburg
LOUISIANA
Red R.
New Orleans
TEXAS
Galveston
Gulf of Mexico
UNION BLOCKADE

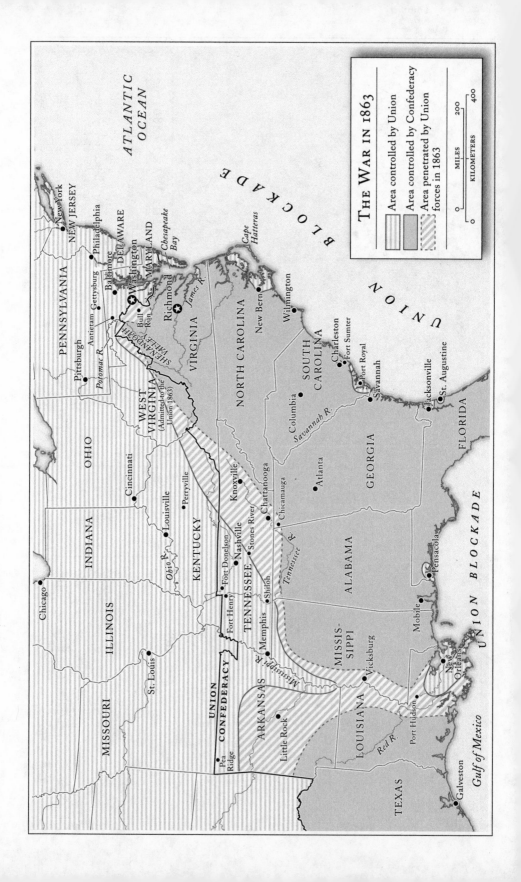

THE WAR IN 1863

Area controlled by Union

Area controlled by Confederacy

Area penetrated by Union forces in 1863

MILES   200   400
KILOMETERS

ATLANTIC OCEAN

UNION BLOCKADE

UNION BLOCKADE

NEW YORK
New York
NEW JERSEY
Philadelphia
DELAWARE
Baltimore
MARYLAND
Chesapeake Bay
Washington
PENNSYLVANIA
Antietam
Gettysburg
Pittsburgh
Potomac R.
Bull Run
Richmond
James R.
SHENANDOAH VALLEY
VIRGINIA
WEST VIRGINIA
(Admitted to the Union 1863)
Cape Hatteras
NORTH CAROLINA
New Bern
Wilmington
OHIO
Cincinnati
Perryville
Louisville
Knoxville
Chattanooga
Chicamauga
SOUTH CAROLINA
Columbia
Charleston
Fort Sumter
Port Royal
Savannah R.
Savannah
Jacksonville
St. Augustine
FLORIDA
INDIANA
Ohio R.
KENTUCKY
Fort Donelson
Nashville
Stones River
Shiloh
Tennessee R.
Atlanta
GEORGIA
Chicago
ILLINOIS
Fort Henry
TENNESSEE
Memphis
Mississippi R.
ALABAMA
MISSIS-SIPPI
Mobile
Pensacola
MISSOURI
St. Louis
UNION
CONFEDERACY
ARKANSAS
Little Rock
Pea Ridge
Vicksburg
LOUISIANA
Red R.
Port Hudson
New Orleans
TEXAS
Galveston
Gulf of Mexico
UNION BLOCKADE

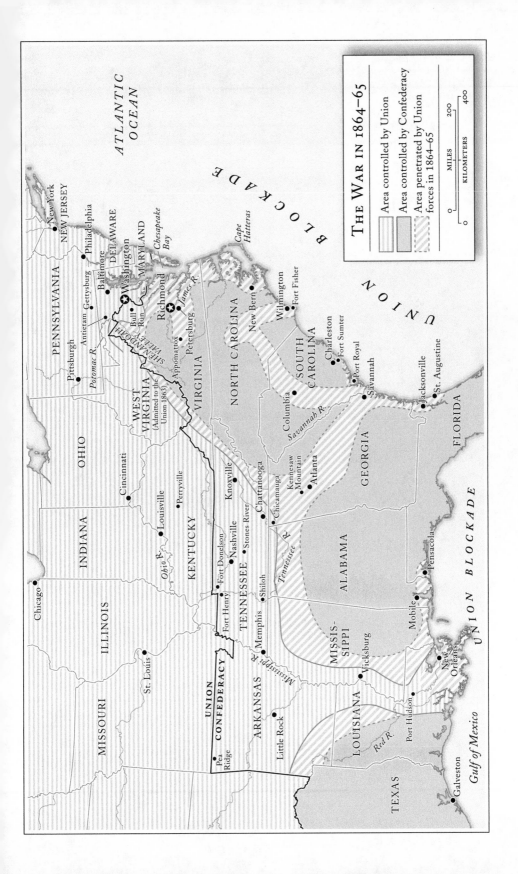

THE WAR IN 1864–65

Area controlled by Union
Area controlled by Confederacy
Area penetrated by Union forces in 1864–65

MILES
0   200   400
0
KILOMETERS

ATLANTIC OCEAN

BLOCKADE

UNION

NEW JERSEY
New York
Philadelphia
PENNSYLVANIA
Baltimore
DELAWARE
Pittsburgh
MARYLAND
Washington
Chesapeake Bay
Antietam
Gettysburg
Bull Run
Richmond
Cape Hatteras
Potomac R.
James R.
Petersburg
Appomattox
WEST VIRGINIA
(Admitted to the Union 1863)
SHENANDOAH VALLEY
VIRGINIA
New Bern
NORTH CAROLINA
Wilmington
Fort Fisher
OHIO
Cincinnati
Louisville
Perryville
Knoxville
Chattanooga
Columbia
SOUTH CAROLINA
Charleston
Fort Sumter
Port Royal
Savannah
Savannah R.
INDIANA
KENTUCKY
Ohio R.
Fort Donelson
Nashville
Stones River
Chickamauga
Kennesaw Mountain
Atlanta
GEORGIA
Jacksonville
St. Augustine
FLORIDA
Chicago
ILLINOIS
Fort Henry
TENNESSEE
Shiloh
Memphis
Tennessee R.
ALABAMA
Pensacola
Mobile
St. Louis
MISSOURI
UNION
CONFEDERACY
ARKANSAS
Mississippi R.
MISSISSIPPI
Vicksburg
New Orleans
Pea Ridge
Little Rock
LOUISIANA
Port Hudson
Red R.
Gulf of Mexico
TEXAS
Galveston
UNION BLOCKADE

Introduction

In the middle of the nineteenth century, southern writers and politicians boasted often—and with considerable justification—that their states were the richest, most socially stable, and most politically powerful in the United States as a whole. Southern farms and plantations yielded handsome profits to their owners, who were some of the wealthiest people in the country, and the southern elite had controlled all three branches of the federal government during most of its existence. At the root of all this economic and political power lay the institution of slavery—an institution that, as the former slave Frederick Douglass would later recall, then "seemed impregnable." Few could then have imagined, he noted, "that in less than ten years from that time, no master would wield a lash and no slave would clank a chain in the United States."[1]

But what almost no one foresaw in 1860 is exactly what came to pass. In Mark Twain's words, the Civil War and its aftermath "uprooted institutions that were centuries old, changed the politics of a people, transformed the social life of half the country."[2] The most important and dramatic of these transformations was the radical destruction of slavery. About one out of every three people in the South suddenly emerged from bondage into freedom, a change of such enormous significance and full of so many implications as almost to defy description.

For the South's ruling families, meanwhile, the war turned the world upside down. It stripped them of their privileged status and their most valuable property. It deprived them of the totalitarian power they had previously wielded over the men, women, and children who produced most of the South's great wealth. "The events of the last five years," a Memphis newspaper editor summarized in 1865, "have produced an entire revolution in the entire Southern country. The old arrangement of things is broken up."[3] The ex–Confederate general Richard Taylor lodged the same complaint that year. "Society has been completely changed by the war," he wrote. Even the stormy French Revolution of the previous century "did not produce a greater change in the 'Ancien Régime' than has this in our social life."[4] Abraham Lincoln applauded this "total revolution of labor" as "a new birth of freedom."[5] Black South Carolinians cheered this "mighty revolution which must affect the future destiny of the world."[6]

Even as it upended society in the South, the Civil War era transformed the shape of national politics in the United States as a whole. Beginning with Lincoln's election in 1860, it finally broke the southern elite's once-iron grip on the federal government and drove its leaders into the political wilderness. Into the offices that planters and their friends had previously occupied there now stepped northerners with very different values, priorities, and outlooks. These new men used their political might to encourage the growth and development of manufacturing, transportation, finance, and commerce and thereby sped the country's transformation into the economic colossus familiar to the late nineteenth and twentieth centuries. Under the hands of these same men, meanwhile, the post–Civil War federal government assumed key roles previously assigned to the states, including the power and the responsibility to safeguard the freedom and rights of the nation's citizens—citizens whose ranks now expanded to include millions of former slaves. Constitutional amendments adopted in the war's aftermath laid the legal basis for and pointed the way toward transforming the United States into a multiracial republic.

Relatively few people today are aware of just how all this happened. Although "the military movements connected with the Civil War are well known," a witness to those events commented decades afterward, "the great mass of American people know but little, and so think less" about the destruction of slavery and all that it entailed.[7] That observation holds true after the passage of another century and more.

The Fall of the House of Dixie was written to help fill that gaping hole in our collective memory. It traces the origins and development of America's "second revolution," explaining why it occurred and how it unfolded—especially how this great and terrible war undermined the economic, social, and political foundations of the old South, destroying human bondage and the storied world of the slaveholding elite. In recent years many scholarly books and articles have analyzed the Civil War's momentous consequences. But bookstore shelves allotted to the Civil War are to this day filled principally with detailed accounts of armies, officers, and the battles they fought, great and small. Nearly every major study of the Civil War as a whole—especially those aimed at a wide audience—continues to take the military story as its organizing principle and narrative spine.

The Fall of the House of Dixie by no means ignores that subject. The slave-based society of the American South required powerful blows to break it along its lines of internal stress. Union armies delivered those blows—blows that therefore make up a crucial part of the story told in this book. But the chapters that follow focus especially upon the transformation of that war from a conventional military conflict into a revolutionary struggle. And they emphasize the ways in which very different groups of people—slave owners, slaves, the great mass of slaveless southern whites, and both Union and Confederate soldiers, black as well as white—experienced and helped to bring about what one newspaper at the time called "the greatest social and political revolution of the age."[8]

The Fall *of the* House *of* Dixie

Chapter One

THE HOUSE OF DIXIE

The House of Dixie was an imposing thing indeed. On March 4, 1858, South Carolina planter and political leader James Henry Hammond rose on the floor of the U.S. Senate to emphasize the slave states' wealth, power, and solidity to northern colleagues who were then challenging some of their prerogatives.

One of the things that Hammond boasted of that day was the South's sheer physical size, which had grown greatly since the nation's founding. The number of southern slave states more than doubled over those years with the creation of Kentucky (in 1792), Tennessee (in 1796), Louisiana (in 1812), Mississippi (in 1817), Alabama (in 1819), Missouri (in 1821), Arkansas (in 1836), Florida (in 1845), and Texas (in 1845). "If we never acquire another foot of territory for the South," Hammond summarized, "look at her. Eight hundred and fifty thousand square miles. As large as Great Britain, France, Austria, Prussia, and Spain" combined. Here, surely, Hammond trumpeted, was "territory enough to make an empire" that might "rule the world."[1]

But the American South was more opulent and formidable than even its great size suggested. Of the more than twelve million souls who resided there, almost one out of every three was enslaved—owned outright by others.[2] As commodities that could be (and were) freely bought and sold, slaves themselves were immensely valuable. At prices quoted on the markets of the day, those nearly four million human beings were worth something like $3 billion—an immense sum, especially at that time, a sum that exceeded the value of all the farmland in all the states of the South, a sum fully three times as great as the construction costs of all the railroads that then ran throughout all of the United States.[3]

Still more important to southern wealth than even the enormous potential sale price of these human beings was the work that they could be made to perform. The efforts of slaves yielded more than half of all the South's tobacco; almost all of its sugar, rice, and hemp; and nine-tenths of its cotton.[4]

The last item on this list, cotton, was in aggregate the single most valuable commodity produced in the United States. It was a key raw material for the international Industrial Revolution and therefore of trans-Atlantic commerce. By 1860, in fact, the American South was producing two-thirds of all the commercially grown cotton in the world and about four-fifths of the cotton that Great Britain's mammoth textile industry consumed every year. The cotton trade was just as important to the national economy of the United States. The ubiquitous dirty-white bales that were hauled down to coastal wharves and there packed into the holds of big ships destined for European markets accounted for about half the value of all the United States' exports, as they had since the 1830s.

Small wonder, then, that most of the country's richest men lived in the slave states and that the nation's dozen wealthiest counties, per capita, were all located in the South.[5]

Slaves were by far the most valuable properties one could own in the southern states. But only a minority of white southerners (about one-fourth) owned human beings in 1860, and among those who did, the size of their property holding varied dramatically.[6]

The typical master owned between four and six slaves.[7] That much human property made him or her many times as prosperous as the average southern farmer but considerably less wealthy than those masters who owned at least twenty slaves, for whom the federal census bureau reserved the title of "planter."[8] Only one out of eight southern masters belonged to this group—some forty-six thousand in total. But as a group, they controlled more than half of all the South's slaves and an even larger share of its total agricultural wealth.[9]

Some planters were far richer than others. The true planter aristocracy embraced ten thousand families that owned fifty or more slaves apiece.[10] These were the people who, as the former North Carolina slave William Yancey later recalled, "gave shape to the government and tone to the society. They had the right of way in business and in politics."[11]

Among these people were Patrick M. Edmondston and his wife, Catherine Ann Devereux Edmondston, who owned two plantations in northeastern North Carolina.[12] Jefferson Thomas and Ella Gertrude Clanton Thomas owned Belmont, a plantation in east-central Georgia that by 1861 boasted ninety slaves.[13] In Virginia, Edmund Ruffin, a well-known agricultural innovator and a tireless exponent of slavery's merits, also claimed a place in this charmed circle. So did Robert E. Lee and his wife, Mary Fitzhugh Custis Lee. Both came from old Virginia planter families. Mary's father, George Washington Parke Custis, was one of the state's largest planters. He left the Lees one of his three plantations (Arlington) and sixty slaves to work it.[14]

About one in fifteen planter families enjoyed wealth that dwarfed the holdings of even the Ruffins, Lees, Edmondstons, and Thomases. Each of these three thousand or so families owned at least 100 slaves in 1860.[15] The family of Louisiana's Katherine Stone was one of these.[16] Twenty-five to thirty miles south of the Stones' Brokenburn plantation lay Davis Bend, a peninsula formed by the twists and turns of the Mississippi River. It contained Jefferson Davis's 1,800-acre cotton plantation, named Brierfield, and the 113 slaves who lived and labored on it.[17] Rev. Charles Colcock Jones, who spearheaded the campaign to bring a proslavery form of Christianity to southern bondspeople, owned 129 slaves on three plantations in coastal Georgia's Liberty County.[18] Robert Toombs, who became the Confederacy's first secretary of state, held 176 slaves and 2,200 acres of land in three counties.[19]

And even richer than *these* moneyed masters were about three hundred planters who each owned at least 250 people. One of them was Jefferson Davis's brother, Joseph; another was Howell Cobb, who at various times served as Georgia's governor, Speaker of the U.S. House of Representatives, and secretary of the Treasury, and went on to become the Speaker of the Confederacy's provisional Congress.[20] A third was James Henry Hammond. The son of a teacher and minor businessman who had married into the planter class, by 1860 he owned 338 people. Another South Carolinian, Robert Barnwell Rhett, Sr., published the fire-eating *Charleston Mercury;* Rhett owned at least two rice plantations and more than 400 slaves.[21] Other Palmetto State planters of comparable wealth included Colonel James Chesnut, Sr., master of the grand Mulberry plantation in Kershaw County. His son, James, Jr., sat successively in both houses of the U.S. Congress and later became a Confederate brigadier general and aide to Jefferson Davis.

At the very apex of the South's social pyramid stood about fifty southern planters, each of whom owned at least five hundred slaves. Some owned considerably more than that.[22] The richest planter in North Carolina was Thomas P. Devereux, the father of Catherine Devereux Edmondston, referred to earlier. He owned more than one thousand people.[23] Georgia's James Hamilton Couper owned fifteen hundred.[24]

In the words of North Carolina plantation mistress Gertrude Thomas, members of the planter elite enjoyed the "life of luxury and ease."[25] Many lived in homes that were palatial by the standards of their day. In eastern Virginia, John Armistead Selden presided over the venerable Westover plantation. Its mansion boasted a great hall, a dining room that regularly hosted more than fifty, a grand stairway, multiple fireplaces, a lush garden, and a lawn that carpeted the 150 feet between the mansion and the James River.[26] In Virginia's Chesapeake region, Richard Baylor's neoclassical mansion, Kinloch, boasted twenty-one rooms, eighteen fireplaces, four great halls, an imposing front portico, and an observation deck that overlooked the valley of the Rappahannock River.[27] James Hamilton Couper modeled his Hopeton plantation in Georgia on an Italian villa. Its main house was three stories tall and had twenty-three rooms, elegant gardens, and a grand staircase descending from the second-floor entranceway. Here, if anywhere, were the mansions celebrated in Hollywood's version of *Gone with the Wind*.

In some of the richest but more recently settled cotton-growing states, elite society was still too new and its members too preoccupied with assembling their slave workforces in 1860 to devote much time or money to elegance and ostentation. In northeastern Louisiana, for example, the Stone family was living in what its members considered a temporary dwelling on their Brokenburn plantation. It, too, was big, with long galleries and two great halls. But it was nothing compared with the structure they looked forward to building soon.[28]

Such "big houses" (as they were generally called) were not only grand; they were also furnished and filled "with everything that a hundred years or more of unlimited wealth could accumulate," much of it purchased in the North and in Europe. So noted the assiduous diarist Mary Boykin Chesnut, who was born into a prominent Mississippi planter family and who married James Chesnut, Jr.[29] In addition to their rural residences, many of the larger low-country planters also owned stately town houses in cities such as Charleston, Augusta, Savannah, Natchez, Mobile, and New Orleans. Those urban abodes commonly featured impressive gardens fronted by high walls and large iron gates, all of which spared owners the proximity to and shielded them from the gaze of less privileged passersby.

In their free time, families like the Stones of Louisiana always had "something going on" (as Katherine put it). They entertained themselves with hunting, boating regattas, and horse races (using slave oarsmen and slave jockeys), lavish dinner parties, and balls. They summered at northern spas in Saratoga Springs, Cape May, Niagara Falls, Newport, and Montreal and at southern resorts such as Biloxi, Pass Christian, and the springs of western Virginia.

The southern states of the Union contained the nation's least developed school system. But the planters' children wanted for few educational advantages. Private tutors provided individual instruction. Daughters attended elite female academies. Sons went off to colleges in the South, in the North, and in Europe.[30] A leisurely and luxurious "grand tour" of Europe often followed college, allowing future leaders of the southern elite to bathe in the high culture of the Old World.

At least as impressive as their sheer wealth and personal comfort was the slave masters' political might. Robert E. Lee's wartime aide-de-camp, Colonel Charles Marshall, later recalled "the controlling influence" that "the owners of slaves" enjoyed "in the management of affairs in the Southern States."[31] In the capitals of nearly every state that would go on to join the Confederacy, slave masters occupied at least half the legislative seats in 1860. In Alabama, Mississippi, and North Carolina, more than a third of those seats belonged to full-fledged planters. In South Carolina, planters claimed not a third but more than half of those positions.[32]

But the masters' writ ran far beyond the confines of their own states. They also exercised tremendous power over the United States as a whole, and they had done so for generations. James Henry Hammond put it bluntly in his Senate speech of 1858. "We, the slaveholders of the South, took our country in her infancy," led it to independence, and have since then continued "ruling her for sixty out of the seventy years of her existence." Since the Revolution, in fact, nearly all the occupants of the White House had been either slave masters (George Washington, Thomas Jefferson, James Madison, James Monroe, Andrew Jackson, John Tyler, James Polk, and Zachary Taylor) or the allies and advocates of masters (Martin Van Buren, Millard Fillmore, Franklin Pierce, and James Buchanan). The same kind of men consistently controlled both the U.S. Congress and the Supreme Court.[33]

The masters used all this political power to secure and extend the economic system that gave them their wealth, authority, and comfort— a system squarely based on slave labor. The South's four million slaves formed the core of its laboring population. "They are the source in large measure of our living, and comprise our wealth," the Georgia planter and Presbyterian minister Charles Colcock Jones reminded his fellow churchmen in 1861. Slaves and the profits that their labor yielded paid for "our education, our food, and clothing, and our dwellings, and a thousand comforts of life that crowd our happy homes." They also performed many other vital kinds of labor: From the slave quarters came "our boatmen . . . on the waters; our mechanics and artisans to build our houses, to work in many trades; . . . they prepare our food, and wait about our tables and our persons, and keep the house."[34]

As Jones noted, slaves toiled in all sectors of the southern society and economy. Some worked in the region's relatively small urban economy, in workshops, factories, and a variety of commercial establishments. Others labored as household servants in the masters' homes in town or country or as artisans of various kinds on their farms and plantations. But the great majority, perhaps three-quarters, worked the land. As Jones put it, they were "our agriculturalists to subdue our forests, to sow, and cultivate, and reap our land; without whom no team is started, no plough is run, no spade, nor hoe, nor axe is driven."[35] The 1860 census estimated that one in every ten slaves cultivated tobacco (centered in parts of Virginia, Kentucky, Tennessee, and Missouri), another one in ten raised sugar, rice, or hemp (in Virginia, Louisiana, Mississippi, Georgia, and South Carolina). And more than half worked in the cotton fields (especially in South Carolina, Georgia, Alabama, Mississippi, and Louisiana).

Katherine Stone noted some of the characteristics of slave labor that made it most attractive to landowners anxious to turn a profit. Slaves could be made to perform especially heavy, intensive, and continuous work in return for just "the bare necessities of life." James Henry Hammond accounted for slavery's importance in just those terms in a well-known open letter to British abolitionist Thomas Clarkson. *Only* slaves, Hammond held, could be made to work as hard while costing the landowner so little. People who enjoyed the right to protest, resist, or simply refuse such terms would never tolerate such conditions.[36]

The South's slaves worked very hard indeed. It was "no uncommon thing," Katherine Stone remembered, for the more productive slaves in her family's cotton fields to pick "five or six hundred pounds each day for maybe a week at a time."[37] That was almost three times as much cotton as agricultural workers would pick after slavery was abolished.

What was the secret of this enormous prewar cornucopia? How did masters manage to get so much work out of their human property? Perhaps, Stone suggested, the answer was to be found in the pleasure that slaves found in their work. "The Negroes really seemed to like the cotton picking most of all," she later mused. And spurring that enthusiasm, Stone presumed, were the "prizes" awarded to the most productive—"money for the men and gay dresses for the women."[38]

Some masters did offer modest rewards (what modern economic historians would call "positive incentives") to encourage the hardest, fastest, and most continuous work. But masters did not have enough confidence in the persuasive power of these incentives to depend upon them alone.[39] Field workers disinclined to chase after such prizes (just like those who tried but fell short) soon encountered "negative incentives"—especially the whips with which masters and supervisors inflicted "stripes" upon their bodies. In fact, the regular application of that kind of violence accounted for much of slavery's extraordinary output. When some South Carolina masters wished to gift one another on special occasions, they gave cowhide whips.[40]

The northern traveler Frederick Law Olmsted witnessed this form of what masters called "slave management" in action one day. He was touring a plantation on horseback in the company of its overseer. As the two men rode along, they saw a black girl apparently trying to avoid her assigned tasks. The overseer promptly dismounted and "struck her thirty or forty blows across the shoulder with his tough, flexible, 'raw-hide' whip," Olmsted recorded. "At every stroke the girl cringed and exclaimed, 'Yes, sir!' or 'Ah, sir!' or 'Please, sir!'" Unsatisfied that the young woman had yet learned her lesson, the overseer made her pull up her dress and lie down on the ground facing skyward. He then "continued to flog her with the raw-hide, across her naked loins and thighs, with as much strength as before." As he beat her, she lay "writhing, groveling, and screaming, 'Oh, don't, sir! Oh, please stop, master! Please, sir! Please, sir! Oh, that's enough, master! Oh, Lord! Oh, master, master! Oh, God, master, do stop! Oh, God, master! Oh, God, master!'"

Unable to watch any longer, Olmsted spurred his horse away from the scene—though the sound of whip lashes, screams, and finally "choking, sobbing, spasmodic groans" continued to fill his ears. The overseer then caught up with his guest. Laughing at Olmsted's squeamishness, he explained that the offending young woman had tried "to cheat me out of a day's work." But, the aghast visitor asked, "Was it necessary to punish her so severely?" "Oh yes, sir," the overseer replied between additional chuckles. "If I hadn't, she would have done the same thing again to-morrow, and half the people on the plantation would have followed her example. . . . They'd never do any work at all if they were not afraid of being whipped."[41]

Olmsted supposed that the scene he had just witnessed was a common one, and in that he was quite correct. "It is true," South Carolina lawyer and political leader William Harper readily acknowledged in an often-reprinted essay, "that the Slave is driven to labor by stripes." And why? The answer was simplicity itself: because that was "the best method of punishment."[42] Daniel Hundley was a proud southern lawyer and writer who would eventually become a staunch Confederate.

But even he complained in 1860 about the increasing number of money-hungry planters that he saw around him. On the farms and plantations of such men, he wrote, "the crack of his whip is heard early, and the crack of the same is heard late, and the weary backs of his bondmen and his bondwomen are bowed to the ground with over-tasking and over-toil, and yet his heart is still unsatisfied; for he grasps after more and more, and cries to the fainting slave: 'Another pound of money, dog, or I take a pound of flesh!' "[43]

Hundley was anxious to attribute such conduct to only the greediest and cruelest masters. In fact, however, cracking whips and piercing cries were heard throughout the South. Robert E. Lee liked to think of himself as a humane owner. But he could react as fiercely as any other when his power and authority were challenged. In 1859, three of Lee's slaves—Wesley Norris, his sister, and a cousin named Mary—attempted to escape from the Arlington plantation. Recaptured in Maryland, the unfortunate people were jailed there for two weeks and then delivered back into Lee's hands. Promising to teach them a lesson they would not soon forget, Lee had them taken to the barn, stripped to the waist, and whipped between twenty and fifty times each on their bare flesh by a local constable named Dick Williams. As the punishment proceeded, Wesley Norris later related, Lee "stood by, and frequently enjoined Williams to 'lay it on well,' " which he did.[44]

Masters recognized clearly that legally free field laborers could not be worked as hard or forced to submit to such treatment. At the very least, they would simply abandon plantation labor. But flight was only one of the specters haunting the planters' imaginations. Almost equally daunting was the thought of what legally free workers might do if they remained in the fields. William Harper dared his readers to "imagine an extensive rice or cotton plantation cultivated by free laborers who might perhaps strike for an increase of wages, at a season when the neglect of a few days would ensure the destruction of the whole crop." Harper's own imagination, he confessed, was not up to that challenge. After all, he asked, "What planter would venture to carry on his operations under such circumstances?"[45] Without slavery, Harper therefore concluded, the plantation system would simply collapse, reducing the southern elite to "utter poverty and misery" and spreading "dissolution" throughout the land.[46]

The slaves' centrality to southern prosperity did encourage masters to keep their field hands alive, if possible—and therefore to provide them, as Katherine Stone recalled, with at least "the bare necessities of life." But with a sharp eye on the bottom line, as Stone also acknowledged, masters gave most of their poorly sheltered, coarsely clothed, and badly nourished human property little "hope of more" than that.[47]

This set of opposing impulses—one aimed at keeping slaves at least minimally fit, the other preoccupied with reducing the cost of their maintenance—governed the health of slaves. Masters profited when slaves became parents, so masters encouraged their slaves to have children. When Catherine Edmondston's slave Vinyard delivered a male child, her mistress was delighted. "If the child lives I intend to bring him up as a table servant, have him in [service] by the time he can walk and talk & never let him be rusty."[48] James Henry Hammond was deeply disappointed when his slave Anny delivered a stillborn child. "Bad luck," he grumbled about that loss of a hoped-for asset—a loss the more bitter because during the last months of her pregnancy Anny had "not earned her salt."[49]

Anny's tragedy was by no means unusual. The intensive labor that slave women performed, the unhealthy locales in which many plantations sat, the minimal quantity and quality of food, clothing, and shelter provided to slaves—all these things took a high toll. Throughout the South, one out of every three children born into slavery died before reaching his or her first birthday; a white infant's chance of surviving was twice as good.[50] Conditions were even harsher in the rice and sugar districts of South Carolina, Georgia, and Louisiana. On some sugar plantations, more than half of all slaves died during childhood.[51] In the rice districts, two-thirds of all slave children died before reaching the age of sixteen. At Gowrie, one of Charles Manigault's rice plantations, nine of every ten children suffered that fate.[52]

Slave owners commonly claimed to be paternalistic Christian masters. They used their power, they said, to improve the lives not only of themselves but of their dependents, black as well as white. James Henry Hammond and other champions of slavery thus claimed that masters made black families much stronger and more cohesive than they would have been in freedom.

In fact, however, masters broke up slave families all the time, tearing wives away from husbands and children away from parents as they sold off individual family members to slave traders or to other masters. Sometimes masters did this because they needed money. Slaves also found themselves sold as punishment, because they (or someone else in their family) had earned the master's displeasure. And when a master died, heirs and creditors divided the deceased's slaves among themselves like any other form of property, breaking up families as they saw fit. That is what happened, for example, when Katherine Stone's uncle died of a fever in 1861. One heir received a woman named Sydney and her younger children. Sydney's older children, however, went to another heir. This, Katherine acknowledged in her diary, was "a great grief" to Sydney and her family. Stone quickly added that it was also "a distress to us." But the masters' regret did not prevent the division from proceeding.[53]

The geographical expansion and migration that produced the states of the lower South tore apart an enormous number of slave families. Because the U.S. Congress had outlawed any further importation of slaves from Africa in 1808, slaves for the new states had to come from the old ones. Between 1820 and 1860, an average of two hundred thousand slaves were transported *every decade* from the more northerly situated slave states to those farther south and west.[54] Other people were sold in large numbers from one part of the cotton kingdom to another. Most reached their destinations in "coffles," long lines of men, women, and children (ranging in number from thirty to forty upward into the hundreds) who were roped, manacled, or chained together and marched on foot over their long journeys.[55]

Great numbers of them had first been separated from their parents, spouses, or children, never to lay eyes on their families again. Thomas Rutling was born into slavery in Tennessee in the 1850s. His earliest memory was of his mother being sold and sent away from him when he was still a small child. He remembered that "she kissed me and bade me good by, and how she cried when they led her away." The last word that Thomas ever heard about his mother was that her new owner had whipped her "till she was almost dead."[56] The master of a Georgia woman sold her away from her baby in order to pay a gambling debt. The distraught mother could not sleep at night. "Every time I shut my

eyes I hear my baby cry, 'Take me wid you mamma; take me wid you!'
I put my fingers in my ears, but all the time I hear him just the same,
crying, 'Take me wid you, mammy; take me wid you!' "[57]

In North Carolina, the planter Joseph Thomas purchased a man
named Sam from a slave trader. Thomas subsequently passed Sam on
to his son and daughter-in-law, Jefferson and Gertrude. Subsequent
sales then tore Sam's family apart. He watched helplessly as his daughter was sold away from him, just as that daughter later suffered her
children being taken from her. Hearing about all this from Sam, Gertrude Thomas found it "really interesting." She coped with whatever
distress it may have caused her by repeating one of the shibboleths dear
to southern masters. People like Sam and his daughter, Gertrude assured herself, could cope with the serial destruction of their families
more easily because "fortunately for them the Negro is a cheerful
being."[58] And, anyway, whites commonly claimed, neither black men
nor black women had strong parental feelings toward their offspring.

Just as masters congratulated themselves on shoring up slave families, so did they boast of the respect they showed for family integrity
and spousal and parental rights. When slavery's critics accused them of
taking sexual advantage of their chattels, slave owners huffily dismissed
the charges. Among southern whites, James Henry Hammond insisted,
"there are fewer cases of divorce, separation, . . . seduction, rape and
bastardy" than among any other population of the same size. "A decided proof" of the masters' admirable sexual restraint, he added, was
the fact that "very few mulattoes are reared on our plantations."[59]

Hammond's claim makes his own conduct especially instructive. Six
years before he published those proud words, Hammond purchased
eighteen-year-old Sally Johnson and her year-old daughter Louisa.
Hammond first took Sally to his bed and then, years later, took Louisa
as well. Hammond's son Harry followed suit. In time, both Louisa and
Sally bore Hammond's (or his son's) children, and those children, too,
as a matter of course, became Hammond family property. The elder
Hammond counseled the younger not to sell either of those youngsters.
Slaves of "my own blood," he felt, should be owned by none "but my
own blood." But neither did he free them. No, he announced; "slavery
in the family will be their happiest earthly condition."[60]

Hammond's case was especially repulsive and hypocritical, but it
was only an extreme example of a prevalent practice. Frederick Doug-

lass's father was his mother's master—and, therefore, his own master as well. Gertrude Thomas was sure that both her father and her husband had sired children by slave women.[61] Plantation mistress Mary Chesnut believed that her father-in-law had done the same thing. "Our men," she confided to her diary, "seem to think themselves patterns—models of husbands and fathers." But in reality, "like the patriarchs of old" they "live all in one house with their wives and their concubines," and "the Mulattoes one sees in every family exactly resemble the white children."[62] Judge Samuel S. Boyd, a prominent member of the Natchez district's elite, for many years kept a slave mistress named Virginia, with whom he fathered three children, all of whom became his property. To avoid a possible scandal, Boyd eventually arranged to have Virginia and the children sent off to Texas for sale. Perhaps naïvely, Virginia expressed shock that "the father of my children" had so easily decided "to sell his own offspring yes his own flesh and blood."[63]

Such conduct was clearly no secret to women of the slave-owning class. Many deeply resented it for undermining their own status in both their families and society at large. But that resentment led nearly none of them to oppose slavery itself, because it provided the basis for their own wealth, comfort, and social station. Many southern men turned a blind eye to the same kind of conduct among relatives and neighbors. Others, including Rev. Charles Colcock Jones and Robert Toombs, acknowledged that their society displayed some blemishes. They insisted, however, that those blemishes revealed nothing fundamentally unhealthy about the institution of slavery. They were only reminders that the South's "peculiar institution," like all others known to history, was administered by human beings—and humans were, of course, imperfect, fallible creatures.

The solution, they said, therefore lay not in wholesale emancipation but in introducing specific reforms. Enlightened individuals would simply explain patiently to excessively harsh, hard-hearted, or careless masters the error of their ways. Meanwhile, wise legislators would enact a few necessary changes in the law, some of which would protect slaves against gratuitous cruelty. Others would allow slaves greater liberty to participate in Christian religious life or repeal fear-inspired prohibitions against teaching slaves to read and write. Still others would forbid the forcible breakup of slaves' families.

None of these changes, said the would-be reformers, would undermine, much less abolish, slavery itself. On the contrary, they continued, these laws would strengthen the ties binding slaves to masters. They would, Robert Toombs declared, prove "wise, proper, and humane" while transforming "the institution of slavery as it exists among us" in no basic way.[64]

But reality, it turned out, made it difficult to impose even such limited reforms. Although some laws defined the wanton killing of a slave as murder, for example, it proved almost impossible to convict a master of that crime. As for physical punishment of a slave short of murder, well, who could precisely point to the boundary between whipping that was necessary and proper and whipping that was excessive? Even most who thought they could do that were loath to interfere in the relations between other masters and their slaves.

Similarly, while many masters professed a general aversion to breaking up slave families, very few were prepared to rule it out absolutely—much less ban the practice legally. The freedom to sell any slave at any time to anyone was a natural extension of the master's property rights, and it was integral to the functioning of the slave-labor system. "The owner of slaves," reformer Edmund Ruffin noted simply, "must be free to dispose of them as future circumstances may require."[65]

Most important of all, the sale of individual family members greatly increased what economists call "labor mobility"—in this case, the ease and cheapness with which masters disposed of or acquired just the kind of human property they needed or wanted. This should have been clear to reform advocate Toombs, who in the 1850s came out in favor of "laws forbidding, under proper regulations, the separation of families."[66] Some thirty years earlier, a boy named Garland White was born to a woman named Nancy just northwest of Richmond, Virginia. When Garland was about ten years old, his owner took him from Nancy and prepared him for sale into the lower South. The man who bought the boy was Robert Toombs. The forcible dismemberment of Garland White's family enabled the up-and-coming Georgia lawyer and future politician to acquire someone who would eventually become a valued and trusted personal servant.[67]

Half a century after Appomattox, a historian sympathetic to the masters would say that in the prewar South, owning slaves was less a business than a way of life.[68] It was, in fact, both. It certainly was a business. As a Montgomery, Alabama, editor explained, "The institution of slavery is simply a branch of the great political question of capital and labor."[69] The specific economic needs of southern farmers and planters gave rise to slavery, shaped the lives of slaves, and provided a compelling argument for preserving and expanding that system of unfree labor.

But for most masters, slaveholding was not *simply* an economic necessity. It was not only the source of their own wealth and physical comfort. It was not merely one possible enterprise, one possible investment, among many. It was, instead, the unique basis of the particular outlook, assumptions, norms, habits, and relationships to which masters as a social class had become deeply and reflexively attached. It defined their privileges and shaped their culture, their religion, and even their personalities.

In 1839, Abel P. Upshur, then a judge of the General Court of Virginia and later a U.S. secretary of state, enunciated the point clearly. The "domestic slavery" that formed "the great distinguishing characteristic of the southern states," he explained, also "exerts a powerful influence in moulding and modifying both their institutions and their manners."[70] Benjamin Morgan Palmer, minister of New Orleans's First Presbyterian Church and a prominent theologian, put the matter squarely in a major sermon two decades later. "This system is interwoven with our entire social fabric," he emphasized. "It has fashioned our modes of life, and determined all our habits of thought and feeling, and moulded the very type of our civilization."[71]

Over time, more and more masters came to agree. In the immediate aftermath of the Revolution, slavery's most common justification had been one articulated by Thomas Jefferson—namely, that although it was a poor system, one beset by social, economic, and political "evils," it was still better than the alternative: emancipation. Because emancipation would impoverish the whites and unleash upon them a huge mass of uncivilized blacks. If slavery was an evil, therefore, it was a "necessary" one.

But during the following decades, growing numbers of slavery's champions adopted a more aggressive line of argument, one associated most closely with South Carolina's John C. Calhoun. Slavery was not an evil, insisted Calhoun, but "a good, a positive good."[72] To Calhoun and his colleagues, indeed, slavery came to appear to be the single, essential, irreplaceable foundation of any good society. It was "the principal cause of civilization," William Harper claimed in 1838—even "the sole cause."[73] They believed, with Abel P. Upshur, that all civilizations rested on the proposition that "one portion of mankind shall live upon the labor of another portion."[74] Every advanced society in history, they affirmed, had achieved greatness by assigning its dullest, heaviest, most exhausting, and unrewarding (but no less necessary) labors to one portion of the people. Only such an arrangement could allow the development among another portion of the kind of intellectual, cultural, and political leaders that civilization required. "In all social systems," James Henry Hammond declared, "there must be a class to do the menial duties, to perform the drudgery of life. That is, a class requiring but a low order of intellect and but little skill. Its requisites are vigor, docility, fidelity. Such a class you must have, or you would not have that other class which leads progress, civilization, and refinement."

In the land-rich and labor-scarce Americas, this could be arranged only by legally fixing the drones in place. And, since it was neither possible nor desirable to deny freedom to *white* citizens of the republic, the enslavement of some other people was necessary.[75] "Fortunately for the South," as Hammond put it in 1858, "she found a race adapted to that purpose to her hand," the children of Africa. Here was "a race inferior to her own, but eminently qualified in temper, in vigor, in docility, in capacity to stand the climate, to answer all her purposes."[76]

Slave owners like these had also convinced themselves that slavery was the only secure foundation for a republican form of government—one in which a relatively large section of the population enjoyed the rights of citizens (to vote and hold office). Since ancient Greece and Rome, republican thinkers had worried and warned about the dangers inherent in conferring full citizenship upon those who performed the republic's hardest, most disagreeable labor in return for the meanest standard of life. Wouldn't such poor and unhappy citizens use their freedoms and civic rights to cause trouble? Wouldn't they protest and act collectively to change their condition? Wouldn't they elect to public office either one of their own—or some adventurer, some demagogue, some Caesar, who appealed to the mob's resentments and frustrations in order to gain power for himself? Wouldn't any of these outcomes doom the republic, just as it had repeatedly done in the ancient world? It was clear as day to Hammond that "slavery is truly the 'corner-stone' and foundation of every well-designed and durable 'republican edifice.' "[77]

Indeed, slavery's advocates demanded, wasn't that also the experience of modern Europe and the free states of the North, where labor strikes, mass demonstrations, and other actions that challenged the prerogatives of the elite were becoming more and more frequent and where the unwashed and uneducated were acquiring an excessive say in political life? In those places, Hammond declared, the "reckless and unenlightened . . . are rapidly usurping all power." The southern states, in contrast, were spared that fate because slavery deprived the potential troublemakers of the right and opportunity to make trouble. Republican government was secure from such dangers in the South because there "the poorest and most ignorant, have no political influence whatever."[78] Laws making it a crime to teach slaves to read or write, limiting and strictly supervising their religious activity, and creating roving citizen patrols to prevent slaves from moving about the countryside at will were thus only the necessary corollaries of republican liberty.

Last but not least, these masters deemed black slavery the only tolerable and humane arrangement in a biracial society. Believing that civilization required enslaving African laborers, they were also sure that living alongside Africans was possible only if those people were kept enslaved. Blacks, Gertrude Thomas and Catherine Edmondston wrote in their diaries, were a "degraded race," "an inferior race."[79] Had whites not enslaved them, affirmed Professor Joseph Jones (Rev. Charles Colcock Jones's second son), "the African" would have "remained in the deepest degradation of ignorance, vice, and superstition."[80] Too stupid, primitive, and childish to care for themselves, Charles's wife, Mary Jones, reminded herself, they were "incapable of self-government."[81] Robert E. Lee was simply echoing conventional wisdom when he wrote that "the relation of master and slave, controlled by humane laws and influenced by Christianity and enlightened public sentiment, is the best that can exist between the white and black races."[82]

In their hearts, blacks understood the favor that slavery and slave owners did them by supervising their lives, and they were grateful for that service. Or so, at least, claimed planter spokesmen like Jefferson

Davis. "Their servile instincts rendered them contented with their lot," Davis was still affirming after the Civil War, and "a strong mutual affection" between master and slave "was the lasting effect of this life-long relation."[83]

If stripped of their shackles, however, William Harper and others warned, the Africans' innate primitiveness would reassert itself. They would then pillage, rape, and murder. And when whites fought back in self-defense, as they certainly would, the result would be a bloody race war that would inevitably end in the extermination of the inferior blacks.[84]

For all these reasons, slavery appeared an essential and irreplaceable fixture of southern society. It was inseparable from everything that masters knew and valued.

And in truth, its influence went even deeper than that. Owning other human beings outright shaped the very core of the typical planter's personality. At home, after all, they were at once employers, legislators, policemen, prosecutors, judges, juries, jailers, and executioners. They dominated those who labored for them not only economically but also legally and politically. As a Tennessee editor and Protestant minister put it, every southern plantation was a kingdom unto itself in which "the master is armed with magisterial power, by the laws alike of God and man."[85]

This system and the tremendous power it bestowed fostered personalities quite different from those of most northern businessmen, whose workforces consisted of legally free wage laborers. Visiting English journalist James Silk Buckingham was taken with the way that members of the American planter elite exercised a degree of "arbitrary power" that left them "always accustomed to command."[86] A generation later, Katherine Stone made the same point about her own family and her planter neighbors. Their domination of other human beings had made them "a race of haughty" and "waited-upon people," she noted, who expected to have their way in all things.[87]

Thomas Jefferson, who owned about two hundred slaves, had put the matter even more bluntly. Masters, he unhappily acknowledged in 1787, exercised "the most unremitting despotism" over their slaves that gave free rein to "the most boisterous passions." Having and wielding that kind of despotic power, Jefferson continued, imbued masters with a deep-seated belief in their own inherent superiority and their natural right to impose their will upon others. That belief and the personal qualities that it encouraged then passed from one generation to the next. When we dominate and abuse our slaves, he wrote, "our children see this," and they "cannot but be stamped by it." They are "nursed, educated, and daily exercised in tyranny."[88] Mary Chesnut saw the deep marks that such a life had left on her father-in-law, the great South Carolina planter James Chesnut, Sr. He was "as absolute a tyrant as the Czar of Russia, the Kahn of Tartary, or the Sultan of Turkey," she wrote. He and others like him "would brook no interference with their own sweet will by man, woman, or devil."[89]

The cast of mind here described included a quickness to react harshly to any challenge from any quarter, a casual attitude toward employing brutality generally, and an angry indignation when either neighbors or public officials tried to interfere with their prerogatives, especially concerning their human property.

This emphasis on the master's control over those around him also nourished a definition of manhood and a code of "honor" that the southern elite copied from European aristocrats. According to this code, a gentleman of publicly acknowledged authority, social standing, and reputation must be ready and able to repel all challenges to those attributes. And he defended his honor not with recourse to laws, courts, or police officials but personally, by asserting his individual martial prowess. The more promptly he responded to such confrontations, the more respect that prowess earned and the less likely he was to face challenge in the future. So it was, as James Silk Buckingham discovered, that members of the planter elite were prone to seek "instant retaliation, for any injury, real or supposed."[90]

The most obvious and dramatic expression of this code was the duel. Earlier embraced by upper-class males throughout the republic, it swiftly declined in the North during the early nineteenth century. During that same period, however, the duel became steadily more popular among members of the South's planter class.[91]

The reflection of these values in politics was the insistence that government be kept as weak as possible—at least in its ability to interfere with the masters' power. A proslavery theorist gave tongue to this attitude in the 1830s when he advised both "the imprudent philanthropist" and "the rash legislator" not to "attempt to interpose too often . . . between master and slave."[92] Frederick Porcher, a planter and professor of history and literature at the College of Charleston, later noted more delicately but also more generally that being answerable only to themselves left slave masters "little regardful" of the "claims of society."[93]

It was this great constellation of economic interests, political values, and personal characteristics that Mary Chesnut invoked when she referred to someone as "a genuine slave-owner born and bred."[94] Catherine Edmondston meant the same thing when she called herself and other masters of her acquaintance "slaveholders on principle."[95] Such people felt in the very marrow of their bones, as William Harper declared, that slavery's survival was essential to "all that is dear to us," including "human civilization" itself.[96] They were, James Henry Hammond announced, "perfectly satisfied" with their system and saw "nothing to invite" them to exchange it for any other kind. "On the contrary," they saw "everything to induce us to prefer it above all others."[97] Like him, therefore, they were "determined to continue [as] masters."[98] Professor Porcher spoke for these people when he declared in the 1850s that "the fact of slavery is here" and here "it must remain," not only in the immediate future but "until the end of time."[99] Georgia's Howell Cobb struck the same note in 1856, declaring that so far as slavery was concerned, "We do not see 'the beginning of the end,'" but instead "regard it as permanent—perpetual."[100]

Not all slave owners spoke in such categorical terms. Thomas Jefferson had earlier predicted that slavery, though necessary at present, would someday wither away. Some masters continued to repeat such phrases down through the 1850s. But the timeline that they envisioned for the system's eventual demise reduced to zero their practical differences with those who regarded slavery as permanent.

A prime example was Robert E. Lee. In 1856, he wrote a letter to his wife, Mary, in which he called bondage "a moral and political evil." But, Lee promptly added, it was "useless to expatiate on its disadvantages" because "the painful discipline" that the slaves "are undergoing, is necessary for their instruction as a race." It was just as pointless to ask when slavery might disappear. Just "how long their subjugation may be necessary is known & ordered by a wise Merciful Providence," Lee pronounced, and he expressed no impatience with the pace of that providential process. "We must leave the progress as well as the result in his hands who sees the end; who Chooses to work by slow influences; & with whom two thousand years are but a Single day."[101]

Through the workings of a wise, merciful providence or otherwise, some black southerners—about six out of every hundred, or some 262,000 people in all—had managed to leave the ranks of the slaves by 1860. Some had escaped from their masters or been freed by them during or shortly after the Revolutionary War. Others had been permitted to purchase their freedom with money acquired in one way or another. A majority of these freed blacks now lived in the countryside of the upper South, especially in Maryland, Virginia, the District of Columbia, and Delaware. Most of the rest lived in Louisiana and the Carolinas. A fraction of this already small minority had managed to acquire some significant property and a degree of legal and even social toleration from their white neighbors.

Life was best for free blacks in the areas that were more recently acquired from France and Spain (notably Louisiana, Florida, and part of Alabama), in whose empires racial barriers had long been more porous than elsewhere in North America. Aspiring above all to gain fuller legal and social acceptance, members of that free-black elite did whatever they could to distance themselves from enslaved blacks and prove their loyalty and dependability to their white neighbors.[102]

But most free blacks were poor, eking out their livings as farm tenants, farmhands, casual laborers, factory workers, peddlers, maids, and washerwomen. Whites generally treated them as social pariahs and suspected them of sympathizing with the slaves and sometimes of actively conspiring with slaves against the masters. The rights of most non-slave black southerners, therefore, were sharply circumscribed, especially in periods when the white majority felt most insecure. But whether well-to-do and eager to gain greater social acceptance or poor, vulnerable, and closely watched, the South's free blacks posed little threat to the social order before the Civil War.

As noted, the great majority of southern whites—three-quarters of them in 1860—did not belong to the dominant slave-owning class.[103]

But by the last decades of the prewar era, the adult men of this huge group had gained the right to vote, which made them a force to be reckoned with politically.

This large group was by no means uniform in either condition or outlook. Some, such as urban and rural day laborers and tenant farmers, were poor, propertyless, and had scant prospects of improving their condition significantly. But others were better-off craftsmen, small merchants, and—most numerous of all—independent ("yeoman") farmers. Slavery affected this heterogeneous white majority in various, complex, and often contradictory ways. Attitudes toward large planters and their human property were equally diverse.

Some of these so-called common whites lived in the low-country "black belt" that took its name from the rich black soil on which the largest plantations rested. Others lived in the South's "up-country" regions (the foothills, plateaus, and mountains) and had much less to do with large plantations and the market economy generally, raising crops primarily for their own consumption and buying very little from others.

Many, especially those in low-country plantation districts, looked with envy and admiration upon masters (who were sometimes also their kinfolk) and hoped someday to cross into their charmed circle. Savvy masters understood that they needed the support of these voters in order to reinforce their own domination of political life, so they encouraged these yeoman aspirations and affinities. They rented or lent slaves to yeomen and assisted them in other ways as well, employing them or their sons as overseers, lending them money, ginning their cotton, and transporting their harvested crops to market on generous terms. Whites of small means regularly served as the urban and rural patrols that sought out and summarily punished slaves found off their masters' property without written permission.[104]

Among other whites with little property, distaste for slavery and especially resentment of big slave owners was more common. When employers forced white wageworkers, urban or rural, to compete with or work beside despised blacks, whether slave or free, white employees commonly responded with outrage. Members of the elite who ostentatiously flaunted their great wealth and treated poor and middling whites high-handedly could also provoke antipathy. In a few cases, such antipathy nourished a clear opposition to slavery. William H. Younce, who was raised in the hills of North Carolina, recalled later in life that he had become "more and more convinced in my own mind" that slavery "was wrong."[105] Basil Armstrong Thomasson, a small farmer who lived just a few counties away from Younce, anticipated in the 1850s that "the time is coming when they [the slaves] will be free." And Thomasson prayed that such a time would "come quickly. Amen."[106]

But even those who found slavery repulsive usually balked at advocating (or even hoping for) its abolition, especially because of their long-inculcated and now deep-seated aversion to blacks. In 1860, nearly all whites regarded African Americans as inherently inferior, degraded, and dangerous, and found the idea of living alongside them as anything like equals simply inconceivable.

Frederick Law Olmsted discovered as much during his travels through the inland South in the mid-1850s. A number of farmers who owned no slaves spoke freely with him about the subject. One white Mississippian pronounced slaves "a great cuss to this country" and even expressed sympathy for the slaves themselves. But he would not countenance any talk of abolition: " 'Twouldn't do to free 'em; that wouldn't do no how!" Free the slaves, he was sure, "and they'd steal everything we made. Nobody couldn't live here then." Olmsted reported hearing substantially the same thing during more than a dozen conversations with "people of this class."[107]

Masters and their spokesmen worked tirelessly to reinforce those beliefs. Preserving slavery benefited all whites, they declared, including whites who owned no slaves and might never do so. In the American South, they explained, the enslavement of blacks spared poorer whites from having to perform the most degrading tasks and from the social stigma that attached to such work. It turned their white skins into guarantees—badges—of not only freedom but also social equality. It was only "by the existence of negro slavery," Jefferson Davis typically declared in 1860, that "the white man is raised to the dignity of a free-man and an equal." Such equality among all whites regardless of wealth was possible only because "your own menial who blacks your boots, drives your carriage, who wears your livery, and is your own in every sense of the word, is *not* your equal."[108]

Even the up-country contained some whites of small means who readily adapted to slavery and proved as anxious to climb the ladder of economic and/or political success in slave-based society. A prime example was Georgia's Joseph E. Brown, an ambitious young man from the Blue Ridge Mountains who set out at age nineteen to obtain an education. He soon became a teacher, an attorney, a state legislator, and ultimately the state's governor. Along the way, he purchased a few slaves and became an ardent defender of the institution.

Brown was especially adept at selling slavery to the non-slaveholding majority. His argument essentially echoed the one advanced by planter spokesmen like Jefferson Davis, but Brown's humble origins lent his words greater weight. Since "with us, every white man . . . feels and knows that he belongs to the ruling class," Brown would explain, "it is . . . the interest of the poor white laborer to sustain and perpetuate the institution of negro slavery."[109] Furthermore, he warned hill-country farmers, it was only slavery that kept most blacks *out* of their hills: "So soon as the slaves were at liberty," he predicted, "thousands of them would leave the cotton and rice fields in the lower part of our State, and make their way to the healthier climate in the mountain region. We should have them plundering and stealing, robbing and killing; in all the lovely vallies of the mountains."[110]

A majority of southern voters, most of them men without slaves, accepted this view of things, which helps to explain why they regularly gave slave owners and their advocates control of the state governments.[111] David W. Siler, who belonged to one of North Carolina's wealthiest slaveholding families, was elected and reelected to that state's legislature during the 1850s by the voters of a mountain county (Macon) that contained relatively few other masters.[112] The hill country of eastern Tennessee launched the political career of Andrew Johnson, who rose steadily from the state legislature to the U.S. House of Representatives, to the governor's mansion, and then to the U.S. Senate. Slavery, Johnson intoned, was the inevitable outgrowth of human inequality and "is in perfect harmony" with democracy.[113]

During the 1850s, this combination of economic, social, and cultural security seemed to assure slavery's survival and the slave owner's supremacy indefinitely. "Stability, progress, order, peace, content and prosperity reign throughout our borders," Robert Toombs bragged in 1856. "Not a single soldier is to be found in our widely-extended domain to overawe or protect society. The desire for organic change nowhere manifests itself."[114] The fact that the price of slaves soared during that decade seemed both to confirm and guarantee that prospect. It meant masters and would-be masters were confident enough of the system's future to bid against one another for those bound laborers. Southern editor and statistician J.D.B. DeBow felt confident in predicting in 1854 that "our domestic institutions will remain as they are," that he and his neighbors would continue to "enjoy the advantages of our labor"—indeed, that they would do so "forever."[115]

In fact, the world that DeBow enthused about would be gone in little more than ten years' time.

Chapter Two

SECURING THE MANSION:
THE SLAVEHOLDER REVOLT AND ITS ORIGINS

A fascinating quality of the human mind is its ability to hold firmly and simultaneously to contradictory ideas. Slave owners were a case in point. They regularly rhapsodized about how pleased their "people" were in slavery. In his famous 1858 speech, South Carolina planter and ideologue James Henry Hammond confidently declared that the South's slaves were "happy, content, unaspiring, and utterly incapable, from intellectual weakness, ever to give us any trouble by their aspirations."[1] Former Florida governor Richard K. Call enlarged on the subject in an 1861 letter to a northerner. The black man's "inferiority," he wrote, "physical, moral, and mental," showed he was "designed by the Creator for a slave." And because his limited brain was simply unable "to contemplate slavery as a degradation," he was typically "docile and humble," both "cheerful and contented."[2]

But even as they tirelessly repeated these stock phrases—and at one level believed them, too—slave owners also worried that their slaves secretly longed for freedom and would seize it if given the chance. "Slaves are human beings, and as such, are endowed with volition and reason," noted one Georgia newspaper editor. That fact made "property in slaves more delicate and precarious than that of any other species of property."[3] Frederick Douglass summarized the masters' problem more completely. The slaves' human intelligence combined with their equally human striving for freedom endangered the masters' power, he said. For that reason, "no property can require more strongly favorable conditions for its existence."[4] Tennessee master Oliver P. Temple confirmed that judgment retrospectively. "The supersensitiveness of slaveholders as to slavery was not unnatural," he wrote. Because of "the inherent weakness of the institution," they "had to guard it against attack, whether from without or within, with the utmost vigilance." They could therefore tolerate no open "opposition to it, without danger of the most serious consequences."[5]

Masters' concerns about controlling their human property lay squarely at the root of the escalating North-South conflict that finally erupted in war. To more firmly hold and work their slaves profitably, they strove to keep their black laborers and servants uneducated, uninformed, isolated from dangerous influences, closely watched, intimidated, and convinced that enslavement was their permanent, immutable condition. To accomplish all that required confronting slaves with overwhelming force. It also required that the white population be dependably and visibly united in support of black servitude—and ready to enforce it. To allow antislavery sentiments to spread among whites might weaken the aura of permanence with which masters tried to surround their "peculiar institution." That, in turn, would surely encourage slaves to question, test, resist, and even openly challenge the masters' power.

As the years passed, however, proslavery leaders found it harder and harder to sustain that degree of white unity in the United States as a whole. Their efforts to do so collided with the long-term pattern of economic, social, cultural, and intellectual developments in the North.

In colonial North America, slavery had existed in both the northern and southern provinces of what would eventually become the United States. But bondage had never been central to the more northerly colonies' economies, and by the time of the Revolution they had already embarked upon a course of economic and social development that differed markedly—and increasingly—from the South's. The virulent strain of anti-black racism that justified slavery still throve there and consigned African Americans to second-class status, denying them in most places not only the right to vote but also equal access to the courts, public schools, public accommodations, housing, and jobs.

But while racism remained very much alive and well in the North, enthusiasm for bound labor did not. Merchants, bankers, and manufacturers in New York, Boston, Cincinnati, and elsewhere were happy to sell goods and services and to lend money to southern slaveholders. But they did not try to run their own operations with bound labor. An economy based on a combination of small farms, lively internal commerce, and growing urban and manufacturing sectors seemed more compatible with self-employment and the hiring of legally free wage laborers than it did with slavery.

In the North just as in the South, economic development blazed a trail for culture. As middle-class northerners embraced their region's distinctive social order, they came to view personal autonomy and the ownership of one's own body as the essential pillars of a good society. As early as the 1780s, the outright ownership of one human being by another came to appear economically backward, morally repugnant, and politically poisonous. By the end of the 1850s, as one South Carolinian complained, even conservative-minded northerners were "conscientiously convinced that slavery in principle is wrong and that the institution is evil."[6] As those sentiments grew and spread, the first casualty was what remained of slavery in the northern states. Within a few decades following the Revolution, every one of them had either outlawed it outright or set legal mechanisms in motion that would do away with slavery over the course of time.

Slavery's declining support in the northern states reflected an even broader, transatlantic reality. Throughout western Europe and its colonies, popular demands for individual freedoms and self-government were undermining slavery in both thought and action. The Great French Revolution that began in 1789 opened the door to the most massive and most successful slave revolt in the western hemisphere—in France's Caribbean colony of Saint Domingue, which shortly renamed itself Haiti. Soon afterward, France abolished slavery throughout its empire. When the Bourbon monarchy returned to power in France in 1814, it relegalized slavery. But in 1848 a new republican revolution outlawed bondage once again, this time permanently.

Meanwhile, in 1833–34, Britain began abolishing bound labor in its own empire. Within a few years, it had emancipated slaves in Jamaica, Trinidad, Barbados, and the neighboring islands, as well as in Guiana, Mauritius, South Africa, and elsewhere. In much of Central and South

America colonial struggles for independence from Spain's empire had badly undermined slavery, and by 1860 it seemed to many observers to be living on borrowed time there.[7]

The slave owners of the U.S. South were keenly aware of these developments. They faced a world, one southern newspaper editor complained, in which "the social system upon which the wealth and power of the South depend" had "enemies by the thousands . . . all over Christendom."[8]

The relative ease with which slavery had declined in the northern United States and the British Empire led many critics of the institution to anticipate a similarly smooth evolution in the U.S. South. Over the course of time, they expected, the same light of reason that had illuminated northern and British minds would do the same for their southern cousins. Slavery would then disappear from the nation as a whole— gradually, peacefully, irresistibly.

But those who expected slavery to die a natural death in the United States seriously underestimated the southern masters' attachment to what they called their "way of life." Slavery had been growing steadily more profitable and ever more central to the identity and values of the elite, especially in the cotton-growing states of the lower South. Mounting challenges to slavery's legitimacy therefore spurred most slaveholders not to emancipate but to dig in.

In 1820, northern congressmen tried to give slavery's expected nationwide decline a helping hand by legally barring it from the prospective new state of Missouri. To the surprise of some, however, the South's political leaders dug in their heels, resisting slavery's restriction tooth and nail with at least as much determination as their opponents sought it. In the process, they revealed a commitment to bondage far less equivocal than were the Jeffersonian phrases they had been repeating by rote for so many decades.[9] "The discussion of this Missouri question has betrayed the secret of their souls," Massachusetts's John Quincy Adams noted in his diary. "In the abstract they admit slavery is an evil," he observed. "But when probed to the quick upon it they show at the bottom of their souls pride and vain glory in their condition of masterdom."[10] It was during this time that the "necessary evil" view of slavery began to give ground to the "positive good" ideology mentioned in the last chapter. In the end, Congress granted statehood to Missouri without requiring slavery's abolition there. (As a concession to the North, it then outlawed slavery in the *rest* of the territories purchased in 1803 that were located above Missouri's southern border.)

This stiffened proslavery stance now helped propel a relatively small but vocal group of northerners toward a more radical and more activist form of antislavery doctrine and program. They demanded immediate steps to put an end to slavery everywhere. The rise of such militant abolitionism, in turn, further irritated and alarmed slave owners. It seemed to prove that masters must assert their rights and prerogatives and exert their power more forcefully than ever. James Henry Hammond put it plainly. "In the face of discussions which aim at loosening all ties between master and slave," he lectured a British abolitionist, "we have to rely more and more on the power of fear. We must, in all our intercourse with them, assert and maintain strict mastery. . . . We have to draw the rein tighter and tighter day by day to be assured that we hold them in complete check."[11] State and local governments outlawed the teaching of slaves to read, increasingly restricted slave movement outside their owners' property, reinforced slave patrols, further reduced the rights of the small free black population, and made it ever more difficult for any master so inclined to manumit (free) a slave.

To "assert and maintain strict mastery," slave owners also deemed it essential to curb the ability of wrong-thinking whites to cause trouble. They and their allies set out to prevent or punish the open expression of antislavery views by driving dissenters out of southern pulpits, schools, editorial offices, and communities. They set out to purge abolitionist materials from the mail. They barred antislavery petitions and speeches from the U.S. House of Representatives. Their friends and sympathizers organized mob attacks on abolitionists in the North.

Meanwhile, masters sought to prevent unsympathetic northerners from using the government in Washington to challenge their interests. In the early 1830s, the planter leaders of South Carolina experimented unsuccessfully with the tactic of "nullifying" objectionable federal laws, declaring them to be null and void within the boundaries of their state. President Andrew Jackson stopped them cold, and no other slave state came to their aid. With much greater success, slave owners throughout the South strove to shore up their representation in both Congress and the electoral college by increasing the number of slave states in the

Union. Most vociferously demanded and lustily cheered first the annexation of Texas and then a war against Mexico that in 1848 transferred to the United States the huge provinces of California and New Mexico—in anticipation of opening much, if not all, of that newly acquired terrain to slavery.

But residents of the free states pushed back. The southern offensive challenged their liberties by telling them what they could say and print, what they could send through the mail, what kind of petitions they could send to Congress, and what their elected representatives could do and say there. It frustrated their practical interests by seeking to load the federal legislature with pro-southern rather than northern representatives and senators. And it affronted their sensibilities by insistently extolling the virtues and extending the life and geophysical reach of a social system that they increasingly found repulsive.

The proslavery offensive, in other words, did not end or even quash the sectional conflict; it escalated it. Northerners in growing numbers came to believe that slavery and its defense not only insulted their deeply held values but also threatened their very liberties. So it was, as Frederick Douglass later recalled, that "whatever was done or attempted with a view to the support and security of slavery only served as fuel to the fire, and heated the furnace of agitation to a higher degree than any before attained." Thus, "every effort made to put down agitation only served to impart to it new strength and vigor."[12]

In the midst of the war with Mexico, northern opposition to slavery's expansion produced the Wilmot Proviso. Pennsylvania Democrat David Wilmot asked Congress to exclude slavery from any lands taken from Mexico. Support for the proviso quickly proved overwhelming in the free states.[13] Meanwhile, the faster growth of population in the free states was gradually increasing the North's power in the federal government. In 1846–47, the U.S. House of Representatives endorsed Wilmot's measure. Only in the Senate were opponents able to block it.

Northern support for the Wilmot Proviso incensed southern leaders. State legislators in Virginia promptly and unanimously denied the federal government's right to exclude slave property from any territories. Even claiming that such a right existed, they warned, "would tend directly to subvert the Union itself." Trying to exercise such a right, they added, might well provoke civil war.[14]

The question of slavery's future in the United States had thus produced another major political crisis. Attempting to resolve it, Congress eventually enacted a series of measures that together became known as the Compromise of 1850, which President Millard Fillmore signed into law in September of that year.

These measures provided that in the newly created national territories of New Mexico and Utah, the federal government would neither guarantee nor prohibit slavery's existence; it would leave that question up to their white residents to decide. To placate the South, a new law empowered federal marshals hunting runaway slaves to compel residents of the free states to join their posses.[15] To compensate the North, another measure allowed California to bypass the territorial stage entirely and join the Union as a free state. Still another measure prohibited the further use of the District of Columbia as a regional slave market, making it illegal to bring in any additional slaves for the purpose of selling and delivering them elsewhere.

Political leaders hailed this package of measures as the final resolution of the slavery controversy. But it left many in both the North and the South deeply unhappy.

Masters welcomed the fugitive slave law, of course, but many of them also denounced Congress's failure to guarantee slavery in the new territories. And they knew that California's admission as a free state for the first time threatened the South's precious parity (and therefore its veto power) in the Senate.

Mississippi planter and senator Jefferson Davis helped lead the anti-compromise opposition.[16] This "aggression upon the people of the South," he announced, showed that "the decline of our Government has commenced" and pointed toward the Union's extinction. "The bonds which have held it together," he warned, were now being cut by a "ruthless" North, whose relentless encroachments upon the rights of the slave states threatened to continue until the South finally responded with "forcible resistance."[17]

In November 1850, delegates from seven southern states met in Nashville, denounced the compromise package, and pointedly asserted a state's right to secede from the Union. Some went further. Clement C. Clay, Sr., once Alabama's governor and then one of its senators, not only affirmed the right to leave the Union but called on all southern states to defend the first of them that departed. In the meantime, Clay advised, all slave states should cease all commercial intercourse with the North. The venerable South Carolina planter Langdon Cheves, once Speaker of the U.S. House of Representatives, called secession "the only efficient remedy for the aggravated wrongs" that the slave states had endured.[18] Amen, intoned a number of other prominent southerners.[19]

But popular support for secession was not yet broad or strong enough in 1850 to carry out such threats, and some influential lower South leaders fought energetically against leaving the Union. In the front ranks of that resistance stood Georgians from both parties, including Democrat Howell Cobb and Whigs Alexander Stephens and Robert Toombs. Toombs stumped his state to build opposition to secession. He, too, disliked some of the congressional measures, but he accepted them all for the sake of sectional peace and because, he judged, they did not yield anything essential.[20]

In December, a convention charged with defining Georgia's stand on the compromise measures sided with Toombs and his allies. While the state did "not wholly approve" the 1850 package, it declared, "she will abide by it as a permanent adjustment of this sectional controversy." Those words—known as the "Georgia Platform"—effectively summarized the position of most of the South's slave owners at that historical moment.[21]

Ten years later, on November 6, 1860, more than 1.8 million voters elected Illinois's Abraham Lincoln, the candidate of the antislavery Republican Party, president of the United States. Nearly all of those voters lived in the free states, where they composed more than half (54 percent) of the region's electorate. They felt driven to cast their ballots for Lincoln by what they saw as an aggressive campaign to increase slavery's physical reach and the slave owners' political power during the previous decade. Most northern voters were now convinced that only a party committed to halting slavery's expansion once and for all and checking the political power of slavery's champions could defend their own rights and interests.

The Compromise of 1850 had gone down hard not only with many southerners but with many northerners as well. Congress had refused to outlaw slavery in the new lands taken from Mexico. It added insult to injury by making citizens of free states liable to become active partners in the vile business of catching fugitive slaves. And just four years later, in 1854, the South had pressured Congress into making it possible for slavery to take root in federal territory (Kansas) that Congress had closed to it in 1820.

During the second half of the 1850s, things had gone from bad to worse. Northerners watched in horror as proslavery forces in Kansas employed oppressive laws and wanton extralegal violence to muzzle and intimidate antislavery settlers. On May 21, 1856, proslavery riders based in Kansas and Missouri invaded the antislavery center of Lawrence, destroyed its two newspapers, and pillaged homes and businesses. In the nation's capital the next day, South Carolina congressman Preston S. Brooks strode into the Senate chamber and with his walking stick beat Massachusetts Republican senator Charles Sumner into unconsciousness as he sat at his desk. Sumner's offense? He had denounced slavery and proslavery actions in harsh words that Brooks found personally insulting.[22]

Less than a year after that, the Supreme Court ruled (in the case of *Dred Scott v. Sandford*) that a master could carry human property into free territories and even free states and hold them there for an unspecified period of time without losing ownership of them. The court then added that neither Congress nor territorial governments had the right to outlaw slavery in *any* federal territory, a ruling that would make null and void all previous measures aimed at stopping the spread of bondage.

The Republican Party arose in the middle of the 1850s to stop this apparent proslavery crusade in its tracks. Its national convention in 1860 took a stand diametrically opposed to the Supreme Court's, flatly denying "the authority of Congress, of a territorial legislature, or of any individuals, to give legal existence to Slavery in any Territory of the United States."[23] Republicans elected to office promised to make that view government policy.

Nor was the issue of slavery's expansion hermetically sealed off from the future of slavery where it already existed. Republicans and slaveholders alike believed that the South's slave-labor society could survive only by continuing to expand. Slave-based agriculture seemed to use up the nutrients in the soil, so it required fresh lands onto which it could migrate. The existing slave states, furthermore, feared that if nearby territories and the states carved out of them outlawed slavery, that would give their own slaves sanctuaries into which to flee. New states controlled by slaveholders would add to the masters' representation in both Congress and the electoral college and thereby strengthen their control over the federal government. But new free states would weaken the masters' power in Washington. Leading Republicans therefore hoped—and said publicly—that barring slavery from the territories would eventually kill the institution even within the southern states.

Abraham Lincoln was one of the more prominent of those people. By preventing slavery's further expansion, he said in high-profile 1858 debates with Democrat Stephen A. Douglas, he expected to "put it in the course of ultimate extinction."[24] In 1860, presidential candidate Lincoln proudly reaffirmed that goal by republishing the debates' text as a piece of campaign literature. But before, during, and after his election, Lincoln solemnly promised not to directly touch slavery within the southern states. He believed that the Constitution gave him no power to do so.[25]

None of those assurances, however, could calm the winds of rebellion that were by now sweeping through the South and especially through the lower-South cotton kingdom. Robert Barnwell Rhett's *Charleston Mercury* declared that Lincoln's election did, indeed, foretell "the extinction of slavery."[26] South Carolina's James Chesnut, Jr., resigned his seat in the U.S. Senate within days of the election. His wife, Mary Chesnut, considering herself "a rebel born," by now "wanted them to fight and stop talking."[27]

On December 6, 1860, South Carolina's voters sent delegates to a special convention that unanimously declared the Palmetto State out of the Union. Charleston's church bells pealed and cannons bellowed in jubilation. Someone held the freshly signed secession ordinance aloft before three thousand residents gathered at the city's Institute Hall; the crowd's roar of approval, claimed the *Mercury*, "shook the very building, reverberating, long-continued, rose to Heaven, and ceased only with the loss of breath."[28]

That South Carolina became the first state to rebel against the verdict of the 1860 election should have surprised no one. The state's attempt to nullify federal law almost three decades earlier anticipated its later conduct. But as many now remembered, when the 1832 nullifiers had turned to sister slave states for support, they had received none; the silence had been deafening. As a result, the Palmetto State's planters had confronted President Andrew Jackson and the federal government alone—and quickly lost the duel.

What would happen in this new confrontation? Compared with nullification, secession drastically raised the stakes. The South Carolina leadership was now attempting not merely to limit federal power but to take its state entirely out of the federal Union, and it was calling upon the other slave states to do the same.

For a variety of reasons, the most stubborn southern unionists continued to resist that call. Some outside the black belt and especially in the South's up-country hill and mountain regions were frankly hostile to slavery or, at least, unsympathetic to the concerns of slave owners. But others opposed secession not out of antipathy toward masters but because they *were* masters—simply masters who assessed the risks to their beloved institution differently.[29] One of them was the planter William Preston, who—even as he opposed secession—emphatically agreed that "Slavery is our King; slavery is our Truth; slavery is our Divine Right."[30] Preston and others who thought like him still hoped to keep their precious slaves and the Union, too.[31] The fortunes of a number of prominent southern unionists depended upon the prosperity of a mixed (not only agricultural) economy and on harmonious relations with the North.[32] They viewed the Union not as an engine of the South's destruction but as the necessary framework for and promoter of a nationwide prosperity that benefited the South as much as it did the North.[33]

Southern unionists also doubted that Lincoln's election meant slavery's doom. Lincoln was "powerless to do harm to the South if he desired," the Wilmington, North Carolina, *Herald* explained, "inasmuch as he has neither judicial nor legislative power to aid him."[34] Many unionists, in fact, saw the federal government as slavery's defender of last resort. South Carolina's James Chesnut, Sr.—Mary's Chesnut's father-in-law—had long been a unionist for just that reason. "Without the aid and countenance of the whole United States," he believed, "we could not have kept slavery" as long as they had. "That was one reason why I was a Union man. I wanted all the power the United States gave me—to hold my own."[35]

As many such masters saw it, the greatest immediate threat to slavery's security came not from the Union but from attempts to break it up. Georgia's Alexander Stephens was still warning in the summer of 1860 that slavery was "much more secure in the Union than out of it."[36] William A. Graham, North Carolina's influential former governor, predicted early in 1861 that secession would certainly bring on war, which would mean betting the entire future existence of slavery on a military victory that seemed less than guaranteed.[37] In such a conflict, Mississippi planter James Lusk Alcorn foresaw, "the northern soldier would tread [through the South's] cotton fields, . . . the slave should be made *free* and the proud Southerner stricken to the dust in his presence."[38]

These were all daunting concerns and strong arguments strongly made. But by 1860–61, none of them any longer seemed compelling enough to keep the states of the lower South—those that contained the country's proportionately largest slaveholding populations—in the federal Union.[39] South Carolina's call to join it in secession now fell on mostly receptive ears. Within six weeks of the Palmetto State's departure, Mississippi, Florida, Alabama, Georgia, Louisiana, and Texas had all declared themselves out of the United States as well.

How did South Carolina's planter leadership accomplish this feat? How did it manage in 1860–61 to gain the backing that had eluded it during the nullification showdown with Andrew Jackson? Why did Georgia and the rest of the lower South now abandon the Union after refusing to do so just a decade earlier?

The answer, simply put, is that so much had happened in the intervening years to change the way that white southerners assessed slavery's security within the Union. As one major southern planter put it early in 1861, "We are differently situated" today than we were in "Jackson's time."[40] And anyone who had looked upon the pro-compromise Georgia Platform of 1850 as an immovable bulwark against disunion was not paying close attention.

In fact, the unionism for which Robert Toombs and his allies had stood in 1850 was conditional. As much as the Georgia Platform's authors valued the federal union, they had quite explicitly placed a higher value on what they called "the safety, domestic tranquility, the rights and honor of the slave-holding States." They therefore proposed to remain within the Union only so long as the North continued to abide by three conditions. First, it must accept and respect all parts of the 1850 compromise package, especially the new fugitive slave law. Second, it must abandon all attempts to outlaw slavery in Washington, D.C., *and* the federal territories. And third, northern congressmen must be prepared to admit additional slave states into the Union. Should these conditions be violated, the Georgia unionists had declared, then their state "will and ought to resist" by all necessary means, including the severing "of every tie which binds her to the Union."[41]

Considering how strong northern aversion to slavery had grown by then, these were demanding terms indeed. That fact left the Georgia Platform unable to bear much weight. And to the deep consternation of many slaveholding unionists, the 1850s had proved full of challenges to slaveholder rights. They watched in outrage as one northern state after another enacted "personal liberty laws" that were designed to block enforcement of the new fugitive slave law, one of the principal gains that the South had celebrated in 1850. Meanwhile, the Underground Railroad network grew, and a number of masters attempting to retrieve fugitives in the free states found themselves violently attacked by the fugitives and their various allies. When some northern juries simply refused to punish such attackers, southern tempers flared further.

Then, in 1854, slave owners saw the North erupt in protest against the Kansas-Nebraska Act, which nullified the 1820 congressional ban on slavery in that region. In the eyes of most southerners, that new law had given them no more than their due. They then observed the birth and breathtakingly rapid growth of the antislavery Republican Party. In that party's first national outing—the three-way presidential race of 1856—the Republican candidate (John C. Frémont) received more votes in the free states than did either of his conservative opponents. In 1859, John Brown, a New England abolitionist fresh from the guerrilla war in Kansas, led a group of white and black men in an armed assault on a federal armory in Virginia, plainly hoping to trigger a massive slave revolt that would spread first through the mountains and then down into the valleys. The attempt was a complete failure, and federal troops put it down swiftly. But the image of the slaveholders' worst nightmare coming true—northern abolitionists fomenting a slave uprising in their midst—was tremendously incendiary.

These events deeply eroded unionist sentiment in the lower South. To many they proved that the northern populace's views and aims made slavery's survival within the United States impossible. Were a Republican to be elected president, observed the unionist master Thomas Y. Simons in late 1859, it would signal how many northerners "have endorsed his principles and raised a banner on which is inscribed—death to the institutions of the South." If that occurred, Simons conceded, we could "no longer with safety remain in the same confederacy" with them.[42]

With the further passage of time, after all, the northern electorate would surely continue to grow in size relative to the South's, sooner rather than later placing the whole federal government in Republican hands. What effect would such Republican power in the nation's capital have on slaveless southern whites? Their public statements of confidence notwithstanding, some masters and their allies had long suspected that many non-slaveholders (especially in the upper South and hill country) were disloyal to the South's peculiar institution. "I mistrust our own people more than I fear all of the efforts of the Abolitionists," one prominent Charlestonian confided.[43]

Wouldn't a Republican president move swiftly to play upon and exacerbate such divisions within the South? To attract and reward supporters in southern states, a Republican president could offer lucrative printing contracts to newspaper editors and sought-after patronage jobs in both post offices and customs houses to others. Southern whites thereby recruited by the Republicans would then publish dangerous news items and editorials, run candidates for local office, deliver public speeches, and hold campaign rallies trumpeting their party's subversive antislavery message, inducing even larger numbers of disgruntled and disaffected southern whites to succumb to the Republican siren's song.

For these reasons and others, cotton states that in 1832 had stolidly abandoned rebellious South Carolina to its fate—and that in 1850 had rejected secession—were in 1860–61 unwilling to do either again. Too much had changed, and now, with Lincoln's election, too much was at stake.

Symbolizing this turnabout was the fact that Robert Toombs, one of the prime architects of the unionist Georgia Platform of 1850, emerged at the end of that decade as a leading advocate of secession. "The open and avowed object of Mr. Lincoln and the great majority of the active men of his party," Toombs warned, "is ultimately to abolish slavery in the States."[44] Even more dangerously, Toombs prophesied, Republicans would instigate "revolt and insurrection among the slaves." At the very least, they would encourage and assist slaves to slip their chains and escape in larger numbers than ever before.[45] In that case, Toombs was concluding by the end of 1859, there is "no safety for us, our property and our firesides, except in breaking up the concern." Toombs preferred to fight off the Republican revolutionaries at the North-South border than await their arrival on his plantation. In his own words, he preferred to "defend ourselves at the doorsill rather than await the attack at our hearthstone."[46]

Some of Toombs's most prominent and influential constituents reached the same conclusions. One of them was Rev. Charles Colcock Jones, Sr., who had also been a unionist in 1850. Jones's sons followed the same political trajectory. His eldest, Charles, Jr. (known as Charlie), was the mayor of Savannah. A supporter of the Georgia Platform ten years earlier, Charlie was by 1860 demanding forceful action in defense of southern rights and honor.[47] Rev. Jones's second son, Joseph, journeyed to Macon at the end of 1860 to participate in a convention of cotton planters. A noted chemistry professor, Joseph was scheduled to speak about the state's agricultural resources. But he devoted much of his platform time to furiously denouncing the newly triumphant Republican Party and insisting upon secession. For southerners to call for preserving the Union now, he declared, was to raise "the cry of submission"—submission to a party "who would degrade you to a level lower than that of the native African!"[48] The wealthy Mississippi planter Richard Thompson Archer put it more bluntly still. It was time, he declared, for all good southerners to stand "united . . . in defence of the God given right to own the African."[49]

Although Mississippi's Jefferson Davis had not supported the Georgia Platform, he had worked for many years to keep the federal union safe for slavery. But he left scant doubt how he would respond if ever forced to choose between national unity and slavery. The election of a president hostile to bondage, he told neighboring planters in 1858, would constitute "a species of revolution" transferring power "into the hands of your avowed and implacable enemies." As far as he was concerned, a federal government in such hands would have no legitimate authority, and Mississippi would have the positive "duty" to bolt from such a Union.[50] Davis repeated that opinion many times during 1860.[51]

When news of Lincoln's November victory reached Davis, he called on the cotton states to act in unison to safeguard their interests.[52] And once he determined that the Republicans would not retreat from their campaign platform, Davis joined other lower-South congressmen in declaring for secession.[53] "The argument is exhausted," they announced in mid-December; the die had been cast. Now, therefore, "the primary object of each slaveholding State ought to be its speedy and absolute separation from a Union with hostile States."[54]

The seven cotton-growing states of the lower South did just that. In early February 1861, representatives of six of them (Texas's delegates arrived somewhat later) met in the small river port city of Montgomery, Alabama, to form a new southern federation, constitute themselves as its temporary congress, adopt a provisional constitution, and elect a president. That congress's makeup testified eloquently about who was leading the secession movement and would lead the new Confederacy. Of the fifty delegates who eventually assembled in Montgomery, forty-nine owned slaves, and twenty-one were full-scale planters.[55] They chose Jefferson Davis to be their president and Alexander Stephens of Georgia as vice president. Robert Toombs became the Confederacy's first secretary of state.

Davis was at his Brierfield plantation, surrounded by his slaves, when word came of his selection as Confederate president. He accepted the office and on Monday, February 11, 1861, began the five-day journey by river and rail to Montgomery, a journey punctuated along the route by military parades, artillery salutes, and cheers from adoring crowds. Some eighty miles from his destination, a committee of dignitaries formally greeted him. Accompanied by an escort of two militia companies, his entourage reached the new national capital at ten o'clock on Friday night. Once again, artillery bade him welcome, as did large throngs. Addressing them, Davis repeated that the time for compromise had passed and that secession was a fact from which there would be no turning back. If Union officials tried to interfere, he promised, they would "smell Southern powder and feel Southern steel."[56]

The new Confederacy's leaders left little doubt about slavery's centrality to their cause and conduct. During his journey to Montgomery, Jefferson Davis assured supporters that now, in their new southern republic, "we shall have nothing to fear at home, because . . . we shall have homogeneity"—because, that is, all the member states would be slave states.[57] He repeated the point at his presidential inauguration a few weeks later.[58] And during the next few months, both Davis and Vice President Stephens repeatedly identified their new nation as a citadel of (and a sanctuary for) bondage.[59] In a major message to his Congress, Davis justified secession by citing the need to keep "the labor of African slaves." Secretary of State Toombs told his diplomats how to explain secession to European leaders: For the cotton South to remain within the United States would have "threatened not merely to disturb the peace and the security of its [the South's] people but also to destroy their social system."[60] Rather than stay in an inherently explosive "Union of two different and hostile social systems," one based on free labor and one on slave, they had opted to create a new country whose members were "bound together by the tie of a common social system and by the sympathies of identical interests."[61]

The Montgomery delegates quickly drafted and ratified a provisional constitution. In most respects it proved a carbon copy of the U.S. Constitution. That overall similarity made the few exceptions all the more telling, notably article 1, section 9, paragraph 4, of the South's version, which flatly promised that no "law denying or impairing the right of property in negro slaves" would ever be enacted by the Confederate government.[62]

For a number of months, the newborn slaveholders' republic remained based in the cotton kingdom of the lower South. Attachment to the Union remained stronger and lasted longer in the upper South, where both personal and commercial ties with the North were firmer and slavery was growing less important to the economy. The political weight of non-slaveholders was also greater there, and their ties and loyalty to large masters less firm. Because they were physically closest to the North, the states of the upper South also feared that civil war would most immediately expose them to attack and devastation. And their slaves would have the easiest time escaping to a hostile Union.[63] The special convention called in Virginia in February 1861 proved unwilling to secede. So did the one held in Arkansas. In North Carolina and Tennessee, voters rejected calls even to hold such conventions.[64]

Like unionist masters and their sympathizers everywhere, however, those in the region's more northerly tier remained firmly tied to slavery and based their political calculations upon and crafted their plans around its preservation. They intended to remain within the United States, but not if Lincoln's deeds in office proved as dangerous to slavery as some of his campaign rhetoric and literature had suggested.

Proslavery unionists planned to use their political leverage to pull the teeth of the Republican tiger. One Tennessee editor aimed to "coerce from Mr. Lincoln and from the Republican party . . . an abandonment of the unconstitutional designs of that organization."[65] Indeed, one of his colleagues wrote, the Republicans must agree to make a series of concessions, including "laws giving full protection to slave property in the Territories."[66] The wise move, agreed the slave-owning North Carolina congressman David W. Siler, was to "hold on to the Union, until every remedy has been tried" within its framework to blunt the Republican threat. Should those remedies prove wanting, he added, there "will be time enough then to get out."[67]

The most important of these remedies was a series of constitutional amendments that Kentucky senator John J. Crittenden put forward in the early months of 1861. Designed to protect and reassure southern masters and halt the Union's breakup, Crittenden's proposal would prohibit Congress from abolishing slavery itself (and not merely the slave trade) in the District of Columbia or interfering with the buying and selling of human beings across state lines. It would also compensate any master who was prevented from recovering escaped slaves in the North. But the key provision of Crittenden's plan would legalize and permanently guarantee slavery in all federal territories "now held, or hereafter acquired" south of the 36° 30' latitude line, Missouri's southern border. (The phrase "hereafter acquired" was a reminder that many masters and would-be masters hoped to annex Cuba and perhaps other parts of central America and the Caribbean and turn them first into slave territories and then into slave states.) All these Crittenden amendments, finally, were to be unrepealable, permanently in force, once ratified.

Abraham Lincoln was prepared to go to some lengths to avoid secession. In the first months of 1861, he approved a draft constitutional amendment—it would have been the thirteenth—that Ohio Republican senator Thomas Corwin sponsored. The amendment would specifically bar Congress from ever interfering with slavery within the states. Both the House and the Senate gave it the requisite two-thirds vote of approval before sending it to the states for ratification.[68]

But Lincoln refused to abandon the core of the Republican platform—the platform that defined the young party and on which it had just waged and won the 1860 campaign. To retreat on so essential an issue now, Lincoln warned party leaders in a series of letters, would mean that "all our labor is lost and sooner or later must be done over again. . . . We have just carried an election on principles fairly stated to the people. Now we are told in advance, the government shall be broken up, unless we surrender to those we have beaten." Compliance would be unacceptable in principle and futile and suicidal in practice. "If we surrender, it is the end of us," he said. "They will repeat the experiment upon us *ad libitum* [as they wish]. A year will not pass, till we shall have to take Cuba as a condition upon which they will stay in the Union."[69]

Most Republicans stood by Lincoln in this, and enough southerners still in Congress rejected the Crittenden proposal as *insufficiently* conciliatory to kill it.

In March 1861, at a special convention in Little Rock, a leader of Arkansas's (slim) unionist majority introduced his alternative to immediate secession. It called upon the nation to revive and adopt Crittenden's proposed constitutional amendments and a number of others, too. One of those would deny both the right to hold public office and the right to vote to all "persons of the African race"—not only at the federal level but at the territorial, state, and even municipal levels as well. A second would permanently enshrine the ruling in the *Dred Scott* case and reassert the right of slaveholders to "temporarily" carry their human property into non-slaveholding states. A third would radically change the way in which the American president and vice president were chosen. Those offices would henceforth be regularly passed back and forth between representatives of slaveholding and non-slaveholding states. A fourth amendment would strip Congress of any "power to legislate upon the subject of slavery, except to protect the citizen in his right of property in slaves."[70]

Unionist leaders of Tennessee and Virginia had by that time specified the conditions on which they would remain in the United States. On January 21, 1861, the Tennessee legislature's lower house also called for amending the U.S. Constitution to guarantee the property rights of masters temporarily taking slaves into free territories and free states. The essential provisions of the Crittenden compromise must be adopted as well, it declared. Should the free states reject these demands, the legislators added, all of the slave states should form a new confederation with a new constitution tailored to their own taste.[71]

Virginia's lawmakers took a similar stand on the same day. They announced with near unanimity that if compromise efforts at the national level should fail, then "every consideration of honor and interest demands that Virginia shall unite her destiny with the slave-holding states of the South."[72] A few months later the Old Dominion's special convention spelled out the kind of compromise it considered necessary. Representatives of all the states of the Union must meet to endorse either the legalization of slavery in all federal territories or the formal division of those territories into slave-labor and free-labor zones. If the North refused to go along, the delegates continued, then Virginia would "resume her old rights as an independent sovereignty."[73]

One Virginia convention delegate neatly summarized the meaning of that ultimatum. If Lincoln wished to stem the tide of secession, said William L. Goggin, he must "tell the country that, though he was elected upon the principles of the [Republican] platform," he now accepted that "these principles must be abandoned in his administration."[74] Robert E. Scott, a leader of what passed for a "moderate" faction in Virginia, endorsed that ultimatum even though he presumed that the North would reject it. So much the better, in Scott's opinion: That would stampede all the states of the upper South out of the Union and into the Confederacy.[75]

Masters in the South's two major subregions were thus taking complementary stands toward the Union. All aimed (in Frederick Douglass's succinct summary) either "to overthrow it, or so to reconstruct it as to make it the instrument of extending the slave system and enlarging its powers."[76]

By the spring of 1861, Abraham Lincoln had concluded that lower-South secession leaders were beyond either persuading or pressuring into peacefully accepting Republican rule. That fact, he believed, left him with but two choices—either to accept the Union's breakup as a perma-

nent reality or to oppose secession firmly even at the risk of war. He
chose the second course. He would risk war rather than passively accept
the Union's destruction.[77]

This decision shaped his policy in the crisis surrounding Fort Sumter, a federal installation in Charleston Harbor, where a small Union
garrison was running low on food and medical supplies. Months before
Lincoln took office, South Carolina demanded the fort's surrender. In
January 1861, it fired upon a Union-chartered commercial steamer attempting to bring supplies and reinforcements. The damaged ship
turned back.

With Lincoln's inauguration on March 4, 1861, Sumter became a
Republican problem. The new secretary of state, William H. Seward,
advised President Lincoln to let the fort fall. Doing that, he argued,
would avoid an armed showdown that would precipitate the upper
South out of the Union as well. Surrendering the fort, Seward believed,
would keep the upper South within the Union long enough for loyal
forces there to assert themselves. The new Confederacy, thereby indefinitely limited to the lower South, would recognize its isolation and
weakness and lose heart.

But Lincoln did not believe that surrendering Sumter would yield
such happy results. On the contrary, he thought, too great a delay in
reasserting federal authority would lend legitimacy and energy to the
secession movement and encourage European powers to recognize the
new Confederacy as an independent country. Surrendering the fort
without a fight would also send a terrible signal to the North. It would
confess that the Republicans, having challenged the slave owners'
domination, could not muster the courage to back up that challenge.
That, in turn, would simultaneously demoralize the Republican Party's
strongest and firmest supporters and leave it open to a charge by northern Democrats that it had provoked and then permitted the Union's
destruction. The still-young Republican Party would be destroyed.
This was not a petty, narrowly partisan, careerist concern. The Republican Party embodied the hope of wresting the nation and its government from the hands of slave owners and their allies. If that party now
succumbed and broke up, the country's future prospects would be bleak
indeed.

Lincoln therefore decided to resupply Fort Sumter with provisions
but no troops. He then conveyed that decision to South Carolina's gov-

ernor. By sending supplies, he would reassert the Union's authority and integrity. By sending *only* supplies, he gave secession's leaders a reason *not* to attack. To put it another way, he would give the Confederates no obvious *excuse* to attack. Lincoln was not going to surrender Sumter, but he was not going to allow Jefferson Davis to place upon Union shoulders the onus for starting the war. If Davis wanted that war, he would have to take responsibility for starting it.

For their part, Confederate leaders believed that their own resolve, their seriousness about forming an independent country, was on the line. Some also calculated that the outbreak of war with the Union would finally force the upper South off the fence and into their arms. The Davis regime decided to fire the first shot. Before dawn on Friday, April 12, 1861, Confederate general P.G.T. Beauregard ordered artillery on both land and sea to open up on the fort. During the next day and a half, southern cannons poured four thousand rounds into Sumter, setting much of its wooden interior afire. At last, on Saturday afternoon, April 13, U.S. major Robert Anderson and his approximately eighty men surrendered. "All honor to Carolina!" Georgian Charles Colcock Jones, Sr., crowed. "I hope our state may emulate her bravery."[78]

On April 15, 1861, Abraham Lincoln called seventy-five thousand state militiamen into federal service for ninety days to put down a rebellion against the legitimate authority of the federal government. Within two days of that call to arms, Virginia's secession convention voted to leave the Union. Arkansas and Tennessee followed suit on May 6, and North Carolina withdrew two weeks later.

Lincoln's rejection of the upper South's earlier ultimatums had already seriously eroded unionism in those states. So did the lower South's secession, by weakening the political power of slave owners as a class within the United States. The major Virginia planter Robert E. Scott, previously a unionist, was soon concluding that the cotton states' departure had "given to the non-slaveholding States such a preponderance in the Federal Government over the remaining slaveholding States as to make it incompatible with the safety of the latter." "The free States would control the Government" now, he warned, and any slave states that remained in the Union would therefore "be reduced to the condition of humble subordination."[79]

For such people, therefore, Lincoln's post-Sumter call for troops to put down the rebellion was only the last straw. They would not remain as a helpless appendage to an antislavery Union. They would not sit by idly while that Union made war upon slavery's strongest redoubt, the cotton kingdom. For they believed, as the North Carolina unionist planter John A. Gilmer had earlier warned William H. Seward, "that the whipping of a slave state, is the whipping of slavery" as a whole.[80] All four states joined the Confederacy, which now moved its capital from Montgomery to Richmond, Virginia.

By beginning an armed conflict over slavery, the cotton states had accomplished what longtime South Carolina secessionist Robert Barnwell Rhett, Sr., had told the Virginia firebrand Edmund Ruffin was necessary the previous October. The states of the upper South, Rhett stressed, "must be made to choose between the North & South." Then, he said, "they will redeem themselves but not before."[81] By precipitating war, the cotton masters had indeed forced their more cautious brethren to choose sides in a fight defined by their own most basic institutions and values.[82] The slave owners of Virginia, North Carolina, Arkansas, and Tennessee could either join one war camp, whose triumph seemed likely to kill slavery everywhere, or the other one, which was pledged to preserve it. The choice that they made in the spring of 1861 finally united the great majority of the southern master class in an armed insurrection against a federal union that most of them had once highly prized.

When secessionist masters set out to break up the Union, they transferred their struggle against the free-labor North from one arena in which they were already being defeated (that of peacetime electoral politics) to another in which they still counted themselves superior—the arena of war. The South's long-nurtured warrior image of itself made it very confident of victory.

James Henry Hammond had boasted in his Senate speech three years earlier that the South's might was above challenge. One of the weapons in its arsenal was economic. Cotton was so vital to the transatlantic economy that even "without firing a gun, without drawing a sword," he predicted, "we could bring the whole world to our feet." Slave states could accomplish that merely by refusing to sell the world their cotton, without which the textile mills of all nations would grind to a halt. "No," Hammond confidently assured the North, "you dare not make war on cotton" for the same reason that "no power on earth dares to make war upon it"—because "cotton is king."

Furthermore, said Hammond, any earthly power that *did* prove foolish enough to match arms with the South would soon regret that decision. It would find itself confronting armies of peerless fighting quality. Southern whites, after all, were "men brought up on horseback, with guns in their hands." They were natural soldiers and more than a match for any conceivable enemy. The South, moreover, would field not only better soldiers than its opponent but more of them. "At any time," Hammond boasted, "the South can raise, equip, and maintain in the field, a larger army than any Power of the earth can send against her." It could do that because of the loyalty of its slaves. Black field laborers and house servants would raise the crops and keep the home fires burning, thereby freeing all adult white males to serve as soldiers.[83]

Confederate partisans took pride in their martial skills. For many, those skills showed their descent from a breed—or, at least, a social class—distinct from the one that had sired the northern population. Planters liked to imagine themselves sprung from one or another branch of old England's warlike nobility. Surely theirs was the blood that had two centuries earlier coursed through the veins of the Cavalier party that stood by King Charles I during England's civil war. Northerners, in contrast, were the spawn of the miserable Roundhead rabble that pulled the time-honored monarchy down. Southern masters viewed themselves as tempestuous hotspurs, born to sword and lance; their foes were peasant wretches, born to grovel and serve. The men of the South came from "master races," Virginia's George Fitzhugh declared in 1861; the "masses of the North" were the brood of "a slave race," naturally "stupid, sensual, ignorant," and "depraved."[84] To others less obsessed with ancestry, northerners would make weak enemies because of their unmanly way of life. "Our army is composed mainly of gentlemen," North Carolina plantation mistress Catherine Edmondston sniffed, while "theirs is the riff raff, the off scouring of their cities!"[85] These vulgar, fanatical, cheating "counter hoppers," these selfish, money-obsessed cowards and weaklings, would flee the field at the first sign of trouble.

It naturally followed from all this that, as one Mississippi master told a slave in the spring of 1861, "I can whip a half dozen Yankees with my pocket knife."[86] So, of course, could any true "Southron." Within a few years, a southern arithmetic textbook would press these familiar axioms into instructional service. "If one Confederate soldier can whip seven Yankees," it quizzed young readers, "how many soldiers can whip 49 Yanks?"[87] Many secessionists doubted in 1860–61 that the North could long sustain a struggle against them. Virginia's R.M.T. Hunter, while still a member of the U.S. Senate, had contemptuously assured his northern colleagues that they lacked the muscle to resist secession. If you try, he sneered, you will be compelled to "abandon" the attempt within six months.[88] Initially, in fact, many Confederate congressmen questioned the need to enlist southern soldiers for terms any longer than six months. Why impose such a burden if the North would shortly back down without a fight?[89] Ideologue George Fitzhugh considered even six-month hitches to be excessive. "The confederacy should sustain a small navy," he judged in February 1861, but he questioned "whether it would need an army" at all.[90] One leading North Carolina secessionist pulled a silk handkerchief from his pocket that month and, waving it before a crowd, promised to wipe up with it "every drop of blood" that would be "shed in the war."[91]

When war *did* break out, many southerners looked forward confidently to a swift and easy victory. "Just throw three or four shells among those blue-bellied Yankees," another North Carolinian predicted, "and they'll scatter like sheep."[92] Numberless young men looked forward eagerly to the chance to prove their manhood and cover themselves with glory, all at minimal risk. Louisianan William R. Stone, Katherine's brother, fretted just a month after Sumter that "the fighting will be over" before he could even reach the front.[93]

Jefferson Davis, more experienced and sober, held a minority view, one with which (as he later recalled) "very few in the South, at that time, agreed." He told his wife, Varina, that he expected "a long and exhausting war." But when the new Confederate president shared this estimate with other southern leaders, most simply waved him off. The governor of his own state, John J. Pettus, complacently assured Davis that "you overrate the risk."[94]

Predictions of a swift and easy southern triumph partook of some other assumptions as well. One was that the outbreak of war had finally healed whatever divisions previously plagued southern society. Now whites of all political backgrounds and economic circumstances thought with a single mind and would march to the same drummer. As Katherine Stone enthused, the Confederacy boasted not only "wise rulers" and "brave and successful generals" but also "a united people."[95] The "whole South is now United," agreed Mississippi planter Edward Fontaine.[96] There "never was known," Catherine Edmondston felt sure, "such unanimity of action amongst all classes."[97]

The acceptance by Georgia ex-unionist Alexander Stephens of the Confederate vice presidency symbolized the closing of the once-divided planters' ranks. Throughout the South, wealthy masters now volunteered for both political and military service. They organized the Richmond government and assumed its leadership. Every man in Jefferson Davis's cabinet owned or had once owned slaves. Slave owners occupied nine out of every ten seats in the Confederate Congress over the course of the war as a whole. And in four out of every ten of those seats sat fully fledged planters.[98] The wealthiest planter families—those with at least 250 slaves each—contributed an outsized number of senior officers to the Confederate army.[99]

As fighting began, these political and military leaders received the willing cooperation of other masters, major and minor alike. The wealthy paid substantial taxes, bought war bonds, volunteered to outfit whole companies and even regiments, and helped to support the families of poorer soldiers. Formerly unionist planters such as North Carolina's Thomas P. Devereux gave as generously as longtime secessionists.[100]

Many southern white women took special pride in their southern patriotism. A handful disguised themselves as men and marched off to war. Thousands more acted within the bounds of gender conventions. They joined ladies' aid associations that fashioned uniforms, tents, blankets, battle flags, and cartridges. They provided Bibles, bandages, and foodstuffs for the soldiers. They held fairs and concerts and staged dramatic *tableaux vivants* (in which suitably costumed individuals posed like statues to depict scenes purportedly taken from history) to raise funds with which to purchase items they could not make, donate, or collect by themselves.[101]

The Confederate government, press, and clergy encouraged women of the planter class to bring their personal habits in line with the spirit of self-sacrifice. They must put aside extravagance, fashionable attire, and frivolous ways generally. "Fold away your bright tinted dresses," one poem of the day urged. "No more delicate gloves, no more laces." A popular new song called on wealthy females to "take their diamonds from their breast / and their rubies from the finger."[102] Those who took these injunctions to heart would help foster the idea that all southerners shared a common lot as well as a common purpose—and thereby also help, perhaps, to mute class envy and resentment.

Slaveholding families made their slaves available to labor for the Confederate army. Other slaves were assigned to grow and prepare much of the army's food; mine iron ore, coal, salt, and saltpeter; fashion horseshoes and nails, harnesses and bridles, collars and saddles, guns and ammunition. Slaves transported essential cargoes for southern armies. They emplaced artillery and built fortifications; they drove wagons and tended horses; they carried stretchers, drove ambulance wagons, nursed the sick and wounded, and buried the dead.[103]

Meanwhile, small farmers and non-elite urban dwellers flocked to the Confederacy's new Stars and Bars banner. Raw numbers told the tale. About two-thirds of all white families in the seceding states owned no slaves. The Confederate force later dubbed the Army of Northern Virginia drew approximately the same proportion of its early volunteers from just such non-slave-owning families.[104]

Towns and villages in up-country districts, too, provided volunteers to the Confederate cause, some units carrying flags emblazoned with mottoes such as "Come, boys, let's meet them" and "Don't tread on us." In May 1861, the president of Alabama's secession convention, Judge William M. Brooks, pointed proudly to three volunteer companies raised in just two weeks that were "composed almost entirely of men from 'the hills'—poor laboring men, who own no slaves."[105] Within six months of Fort Sumter's fall, thirteen hill counties in western North Carolina sent at least 4,400 men into Confederate service. "The mountains," cheered a Raleigh newspaper, "are pouring forth their brave sons in great numbers, and still they come." During the war's first years, perhaps 20,000 soldiers volunteered from the hills of eastern Tennessee.[106]

One of the South's leading journalists and most consistent secessionists, Louisianan J.D.B. DeBow, thought he knew why yeomen signed on with the Confederacy. They did so, he said, to shore up the South's peculiar institution, because they knew that even slaveless whites had an economic stake in the system. They recognized, DeBow wrote at the start of 1861, that "the interest of the poorest non-slaveholder among us is to make common cause with, and die in the last trenches, in defence of the slave property of his more favored neighbor."[107]

Leading Texas secessionist W. S. Oldham later attributed southern white unity to something else: a dedication to white supremacy and to keeping the black population down and under strict control. "The great mass of non-slaveholders in the South, and especially in the cotton States," he judged, shared with masters "an interest in social order and domestic peace, which were threatened to be destroyed by the emancipation of the slaves, and allowing them to riot without restraint."[108] And Judge Brooks of Alabama credited a third factor with filling out the ranks of southern armies: a more general devotion to the southern homeland, an ardent southern patriotism, "a desire to take up arms in defense of their country."[109]

In fact, all three of these motives were in play. One sector of the slaveless white population did have (or, at least, felt) a strong if indirect economic stake in slavery's survival. This was especially marked in the low-country plantation districts. And as South Carolina's last wartime governor, A. G. Magrath, noted, at least some of "the men who did not own a negro" fought for slavery in "the expectation or hope of having" some one day.[110]

Secession advocates also mobilized sections of the white South's slaveless majority by presenting their cause less as a defense of slavery than as a defense of the South's prerogatives, honor, mores, and right to govern itself. And Republican rule, they stressed, would impair the lives of the non-slaveholding southern white majority in myriad ways. Confederate leaders stoked the provincial small farmers' notorious suspicion of outsiders, especially those trying to encroach upon local autonomy.

With the actual outbreak of war, these chronic suspicions took on flesh and blood as Union troops marched into the South. At that point, slaveless whites holding various views about slavery's merits felt duty-bound to protect their states, their local communities, their neighbors, and their families from those perceived as armed intruders. An Alabama corporal thought of himself as defending "the same principles which fired the hearts of our ancestors in the revolutionary struggle" against the British Empire.[111] A Virginia private, taken prisoner early in the war, reportedly put it more tersely when his Union captors asked him why he had taken up arms. "I'm fighting," the man replied, "because you're down here."[112]

Directly or indirectly, however, many appeals to the yeomen touched upon matters of slavery and race. For, in truth, few who thought of themselves primarily as defenders of the South could imagine that beloved South without slavery at its center. Typically, therefore, Joseph D. Stapp of the First Alabama Infantry regiment automatically linked the two things together, declaring his readiness "to bear any hardship" if he and his comrades could "only whip the Yanks . . . and live independent of old Abe and his negro Sympathizers."[113]

It was the nearly universal determination of southern whites to keep blacks subordinate that ultimately proved to be the secessionists' strongest card. Only slavery, they believed, could guarantee white supremacy. And here southern race and gender mores tightly intertwined. Confederate leaders repeatedly invoked one of the stock-in-trade gambits of antebellum proslavery ideologues by conjuring up lurid nightmare visions of emancipated black males imposing themselves upon helpless white females. In North Carolina, for example, circulars warned that continued statehood in the Union would bring emancipation, which would mean "having three hundred thousand idle, vagabond free negroes turned loose upon you with all the privileges of white men—voting with you; sitting on juries with you; going to school with your children, and intermarrying with the white race."[114] An Alabaman predicted that Lincoln would "free the negroes and force amalgamation between them and the children of the poor men of the South." A group of South Carolina secessionists, led by Baptist minister James C. Furman, warned that "abolition preachers will be on hand to consummate the marriages of your daughters to black husbands."[115]

North Carolina governor Zebulon Vance received a message in November 1862 that both summed up the general point and seemed to confirm it. The writer was the slave owner and now Confederate congressman David Siler, who represented one of North Carolina's hill counties. It was true, Siler wrote, that his neighbors had "but little interest in the value of slaves." But there was nonetheless "one matter in this connection about which we feel a very deep interest. We are opposed to negro equality." "To prevent this," he declared, and to avoid being "equalized with an inferior race," he as well as his constituents were prepared to die fighting. "Every thing even life itself stands pledged to the cause," he affirmed.[116]

The new Confederacy's champions counted for achieving military victory over the Union not only on the unity of the white population, master and yeoman alike; they also expected the enslaved population to do its duty. "Our slaves will be found loyal to their masters," a Tennessee editor assured his readers, "and if necessary, we will arm such of them as we can spare from our fields to resist our foes." If we do, the North will then find themselves facing "the ugliest customers they will have to encounter."[117]

Proofs of slave allegiance seemed everywhere, in high places and in low, in great things and in small ones. Charles Colcock Jones, Sr., needed only to think of Cato, his plantation driver. Cato had assured Jones of his "love and gratitude" for being "so kind a master" and of his determination to "try and be a better Servant than ever." As a token of his devotion, Cato had even informed on Phoebe, his own sister-in-law, for being insufficiently docile and obedient.[118] Catherine Edmondston found reassurance in the conduct of a domestic servant named Gatty. One day in December 1860, Edmondston looked on approvingly as Gatty fed some black children. Gatty told them to thank their mistress for dinner and then "drew a harrowing picture" for the little ones "as to what they would [be] if they didnt have no Master & Missus to give it to them." To Edmondston, that small scene was big with meaning. It showed clearly that Gatty had no confidence that her own people had "the power of self government." Obviously, Edmondston concluded, Gatty knew that "their manifest destiny is to wait upon white folks."[119]

When Union forces assaulted Roanoke Island in the winter of 1862, Catherine Edmondston's husband, Patrick, left his plantation to help repel them. Before departing, he called together his slaves and instructed them to obey his wife during his absence. The slaves, Catherine believed, "were much affected" by that tableau; "they entreated me not to leave them" as well.[120] Similar scenes took place on the plantations of Katherine Stone and Gertrude Thomas.[121] The Confederate president stood at the center of another. Before Jefferson Davis set out from Brierfield for Montgomery on February 11, 1861 (so Varina recorded), he "assembled his negroes and made them an affectionate farewell speech, to which they responded with expressions of devotion."[122]

Masters found still clearer proof of slave loyalty on the battlefield. In the early months of war, many took their personal servants with them to camp. Once there, those servants tended to the needs not only of their own masters but of other soldiers as well. Some servants even fired their masters' weapons at Union soldiers, much to the approval and merriment of the Confederate troops around them.[123] A Mississippi body servant named Ike accompanied his owner, Kit Gilmer, to war. When Gilmer was later wounded in battle, Ike loaded his master onto a horse and carried him off to safety.[124] Because of such conduct, George Fitzhugh affirmed, southern women did not fear for their men bound for the front. They could be "confident, that when their sons and husbands are called to the field, they will have a faithful body-guard in their domestic servants."[125]

Black people in the Confederacy who were not enslaved often asserted their loyalty to the cause as well. In April, a Lynchburg, Virginia, paper reported that some seventy "of the most respectable free negroes in this city" had volunteered to perform whatever tasks "in defence of the state" the governor might assign them.[126] Similar scenes occurred elsewhere in that state. A west Tennessee newspaper told readers at the end of 1861 that free blacks there were happily working in a military hospital, and "most of them express their satisfaction that they are able there to contribute to the cause of the country."[127]

A group of light-skinned colored residents of Charleston assured city officials that "our attachments are with you, our hopes and safety and protection from you, . . . our allegiance is due to South Carolina and in her defense, we will offer up our lives, and all that is dear to us."[128] The *Charleston Mercury* announced in January 1861 that 150 of that city's free black residents had volunteered to help build redoubts along the coast.[129] Other free black men served Confederate military units as musicians, cooks, and in other support roles.

In late April 1861, some 1,500 *hommes de couleur libre* staged a rally in New Orleans to declare their support for the Confederacy. Shortly afterward, the same population formed a regiment of free blacks, called the Native Guards, which Louisiana's Confederate governor, Thomas O. Moore, promptly inducted into the state militia.[130] A year later, Governor Moore commended "the loyalty of the free native colored population" of the Crescent City.[131] Eight months after that, the Alabama legislature authorized Mobile's mayor to enroll free black males into militia companies. One company of such men, dubbed the Creole Guards, stood watch over Mobile warehouses holding government supplies.[132]

So it was evidently true: The Confederacy could count on active support not merely from a particular party or class . . . or even from just one race. "The cry, to arms, to arms! is heard from every lip," one southern volunteer enthused.[133] "Throughout the length and breadth of the land the trumpet of war is sounding," cheered Katherine Stone, "and from every hamlet and village, from city and country, men are hurrying by thousands, eager to be led to battle against Lincoln's hordes."[134]

And if all that were not enough, there was also the aid of heaven. The vast majority of southern clergymen had long ago committed their churches to slavery's defense. As one of their most prominent members, the Protestant Episcopal bishop Stephen Elliott, typically put it, "slavery, as we hold it here" was not only "essential to the welfare of the world"; it was also "a sacred trust from God."[135] Surely God would safeguard the new nation being created to observe that trust. As Charles Colcock Jones, Jr., exclaimed, "Surely the Lord of Hosts is with us."[136]

Could victory, therefore, be far off? "A short time of conflict & the day is ours," Catherine Edmondston predicted.[137] "On to Washington!" cheered many, including the Confederacy's new secretary of war, the Alabama master Leroy Pope Walker.[138] "The flag which now flaunts the breeze here will float over the dome of the old Capitol at Washington before the first of May," Walker predicted. "Let them try southern chivalry and test the extent of southern resources," he added, "and it may float eventually over Faneuil Hall in Boston."[139]

If Walker and his colleagues proved right, little would change in the southern states. There would be no second American revolution, and the Union born of the first revolution would not long survive. The first year and a half of war would put such optimistic predictions to the test.

Chapter Three
_____

EARLY PORTENTS:
THE FIRST PHASES OF WAR

April 1861 through December 1862

The initial phase of the Civil War confirmed some of the sunny expectations of the new slaveholder republic's champions. The conflict's first major battle occurred on July 21, 1861, pitting two armies of about thirty thousand soldiers apiece against each other some twenty-five miles southwest of Washington. (Confederates named the battle "Manassas" after a nearby railroad junction; the Union called it "Bull Run," after a stream that ran through the battlefield.) At one point, Union forces seemed on the verge of victory as they pressed against both flanks of the Confederate line; southern soldiers began to retreat in panic. But reinforcements soon arrived, calming those already on the field, enabling them to regroup, and then turning the tide against the Union. With their own right flank now crumbling, federal troops began to fall back—a retreat that turned into a rout as Union soldiers fled from the field in disarray. Pro-Union civilians who had come to watch an easy and entertaining victory now joined the headlong flight back toward the capital's defenses, adding to the atmosphere of chaos, disaster, and shame.[1]

Usually sober-minded and cautious, an exhilarated Jefferson Davis told triumphant Confederate soldiers at Manassas that theirs was a "victory great, glorious and complete." And, he promised, it was "but the beginning" of the successes that the Confederacy would shortly achieve. When he returned to Richmond two days later, an exultant crowd greeted him at the railroad station. The still-elated Davis told his listeners that "we had whipped them this time and we could whip them again as often as they offered us the opportunity."[2] In the late summer of 1862, blue-clad soldiers fared no better in a second battle at Manassas than they had in the first. And those two southern triumphs bookended a dazzling, textbook-brilliant campaign in Virginia's Shenandoah Valley, where General Thomas J. "Stonewall" Jackson led a small but fleet force of seventeen thousand men that outmarched, outthought, and outfought three Union armies whose combined size was nearly twice as large as his own.

In March 1862, General George B. McClellan loaded the Union's Army of the Potomac—by far the largest of the various Union armies in the field—onto a fleet of troop-carrying vessels and sent it on a massive strategic flanking maneuver designed to bypass Confederate general Joseph Johnston's forces and then drive northwest toward Richmond. At first, McClellan made considerable, if painfully slow, progress, at last bringing his army to within six miles of the Confederate capital. It seemed to many at that point, North as well as South, that the war was about to end in Union victory.

But McClellan's peninsula campaign fell victim to a duo of factors. One was a fortuitous change of leadership on the Confederate side, as a wounded Johnston handed over command to the far more aggressive Robert E. Lee in late May of 1862. The other was McClellan's signature mix of sluggishness and timidity. Lee's newly named Army of Northern Virginia launched a series of ferocious assaults during the Seven Days' battles outside Richmond between June 25 and July 1. Those assaults convinced the jittery McClellan that the enemy army he confronted—though in fact smaller than his own—was, instead, twice as big. He panicked and ordered a hasty retreat from Richmond's outskirts—a retreat that soon became (in one Union officer's words) "a regular stampede" toward the protection afforded by the guns of Union ships anchored on the James River.[3]

Then, in August 1862, two Confederate forces invaded Union-held Kentucky. The southern commanders, Generals Braxton Bragg and E. Kirby Smith, entertained high hopes for that campaign.[4] "It is a bold move, offering brilliant results," they assured Jefferson Davis. "Everything is ripe for success."[5] Just a month later, in September, Robert E.

Lee launched a raid across the Potomac into Union-held Maryland for which he had even greater expectations. He would enable the slave state of Maryland to throw off "this foreign yoke" and once again "enjoy the inalienable rights of freemen." And his presence on Union soil would allow Davis to dictate terms to Lincoln.[6]

These events produced great consternation and dejection in the North, while strongly buoying Confederate morale. "The spirit of the army is high," exclaimed the *Richmond Dispatch,* and its soldiers "exult in a sense of their superiority not only to the Yankees, but to any army that treads the earth."[7] In light of "our many recent triumphs," Louisi-anan Katherine Stone anticipated, Confederate victory in the war as a whole "may be near."[8]

But other developments during the war's opening stages portended a much more protracted struggle. Some of them, perhaps even more om-inously, revealed the opening of cracks in the House of Dixie's façade. Confident assurances about solid white unity and enthusiastic black loyalty began to ring somewhat hollow.

A key factor was the strength of the Union war effort. Predictions that the North would simply roll over and play dead badly underesti-mated popular devotion to the Union there. By firing upon and seizing Fort Sumter, the Confederacy had galvanized the people of the free states into outraged action. That bridged differences in occupation, class, region, and even political outlook and party loyalty. Many who had only recently clamored loudly for compromise with the slave own-ers in order to preserve the Union now pledged mortal enmity toward a slave-owner regime making war upon that Union.

In New York City, long a stronghold of pro-southern sentiment, thousands of residents thronged Union Square in April 1861 and filled the windows and roofs surrounding it to cheer speeches cursing seces-sionist traitors and promising to put them down promptly and force-fully. On the day that Sumter surrendered, an alarmed transplanted Georgia banker and Confederate supporter named Gazaway B. Lamar reported to fellow Georgian Howell Cobb that "the people of this city who have professed to sympathise with the South" in the past "have recently changed their expressions to hostility," including "even many influential Democrats." The consequences for the South were dire, he thought: "You may calculate that you may have to fight out and fight long too."[9] The *New York Times* was glad to see that even "the thick insulation which the commercial spirit puts between the conscience and duty" in the city had been unable "to withstand the electric fire of loyal indignation" and the "intense, inspiring sentiment of patriotism."[10]

Hundreds of similar meetings took place in Boston, Chicago, Philadelphia, Cincinnati, and smaller population centers across the North.[11] By the end of the year, more than 640,000 northern men had volunteered for Union service.[12]

Some economic considerations influenced this fierce northern response to secession. Manufacturers and their employees worried that an adjacent but hostile Confederacy would become an enormous conduit through which cheap British goods would be smuggled into the United States, circumventing U.S. ports and tariffs, and stealing away domestic markets. Northern merchants and shippers feared that Confederates would cut them out of the lucrative transatlantic shipping trade between Europe and the cotton states and turn it over instead to European carriers. Northern creditors feared that southern planters would repudiate their quite substantial debts to them or pay them off in Confederate banknotes of doubtful value. Midwestern farmers trembled especially at having the mouth and lower half of this water link to the oceans—the Mississippi River—fall into the hands of a hostile nation.[13]

But most northerners resisted secession for other, less economic, more political reasons.

A minority, identifying the coming war as a struggle between the forces of freedom and slavery, hoped to train their muskets on the latter. Andrew Walker, an Illinois schoolteacher, volunteered for action in hopes that his country, finding itself in a life-or-death struggle with slave owners' armies, would decide to abolish slavery everywhere within its borders.[14] "Slavery must die," vowed Vermont-born corporal Rufus Kinsley, "and if the South insists on being buried in the same grave I shall see in it nothing but the retributive hand of God."[15] For Walker, Kinsley, and others like them, the approaching war already meant the onset of a new (and welcome) revolution.

A much larger number of northern volunteers reacted furiously to secession because it seemed to endanger their own rights, welfare, and security. Disunion would shatter a country and government that most residents of the free states still prized as liberty's last best hope on an earth dominated by monarchs and aristocrats. That could not be permitted; the stakes were simply too great. As a Columbus, Ohio, newspaper put it a few days after Sumter's surrender, this conflict would decide "not only . . . whether we have a government or not, here" but also the fate "of constitutional liberty the world over." The war would determine "whether a free government shall again spring up in any quarter of the globe."[16]

Lincoln himself emphasized this general issue in his July 4, 1861, message to Congress. This conflict, he said, "embraces more than the fate of these United States. It presents to the whole family of man, the question, whether a constitutional republic, or a democracy—a government of the people, by the people—can, or cannot, maintain its territorial integrity, against its own domestic foes."[17] Many who volunteered to put down the rebellion appraised the war's stakes in the same way. Captain Alphonso Barto of the Fifty-Second Illinois regiment explained to his father that in fighting to preserve the Union he was also fighting to prove that "man is capable of self government."[18] "Admit the right of the seceding states to break up the Union at pleasure," an Ohio private mused, "and how long will it be before the new confederacies created by the first disruption shall be resolved into smaller fragments and the continent become a vast theater of civil war, military license, anarchy, and despotism? Better settle it at whatever cost and settle it forever."[19] These men would fight not to launch a new revolution but to safeguard the gains of the last one.

Roughly a quarter of all those who served in Union armies were born in some other country, especially Ireland and Germany, and had come to the United States in search of greater individual freedom and economic opportunity. Many felt that they had just as big, if not bigger, a stake in the Union's survival than did the native born. Before the war, most had come to identify with the Democratic Party. Thomas Francis Meagher, a leader of the Irish struggle against English rule, had fled from his homeland in 1852 to resettle in the United States. Nine years later, that staunch Democrat stepped forward to defend the one country that seemed able and willing "to redress and right the wrongs dealt upon disgraced and depressed humanity." The American republic had offered Irish emigrants opportunities available to them nowhere else. If they did not now fight to sustain that republic, Meagher wrote, "then, any one who speaks to me of Irish liberty is a dreamer and a driveler."[20]

Friedrich Kapp was an exiled German revolutionary who headed the New York Republican Party's German-language unit. He insisted in 1861 that "the American people" were "fighting the same battle in which the European nations are engaged. . . . The conflict now on the eve of decision in the United States is neither more nor less than one of the manifold phases of the struggle between aristocracy and democracy."[21] Peter Klein, a German-born miner living and working in America, explained the Union cause in similar terms to his father. "The war or rather the rebellion was started by the slave owners," Klein wrote. Those slave owners were "great lords who have a hundred and more black serfs." To maintain their grip on those serfs, the American lords now sought "to overthrow the free constitution of the country and set up a government by the nobility." But, Klein continued, "we, free men and honest workers, we don't want to put up with that."[22]

But while most northern soldiers joined up to preserve the Union and the freedoms it stood for, many—and more and more over time— also recognized that it was slavery and the slaveholders who had endangered the republic that was so dear to them. Philip Smith of the Union's Eighth Missouri regiment, for example, believed that "the best and noblest government on earth" needed defending in the first place only because "a band of contemptible traitors" was trying to destroy it "merely for the purpose of benefiting themselves on the slave question."[23] In the eyes of northerners like Smith, the so-called Slave Power had struck its most dangerous blow at liberty by trying to break up the national Union.

Jefferson Davis knew better than to take such sentiments lightly. Despite his public predictions of an early victory, he had never shared his associates' low estimate of the Union's martial capabilities. Yes, he acknowledged, southern white men were quicker to anger than northerners, readier in everyday life to take offense and respond with violence. But during the Mexican War and then as U.S. secretary of defense, Davis had fought beside, commanded, supervised, and generally taken the measure of both northern and southern soldiers. He now expected that in the coming war, Yankees and Southrons would prove to be evenly matched.[24]

The first year of the war proved just that, though few Confederate stalwarts were yet willing to face it. One who did was Captain B. E. Stiles, who in April 1862 scoffed at the familiar claim that "the Yankees are cowards." Nor was that the experience of Captain Shepherd Green Pryor. On the contrary, he told his wife, northern soldiers "fought as boldly as men ever fought and they fight well every time I've been in front of them."[25]

The unexpected upsurge of war spirit in the free states was only one early intimation of trouble for the slaveholders' new republic. Major problems also arose within U.S. states where slavery was legal—problems created by the fact that the South's white population was by no means as united politically as some secessionists had claimed. While four slave states of the upper South had joined the Confederacy, another four (Missouri, Kentucky, Maryland, and Delaware, which together became known as the "loyal border states") remained in the Union.

Of these, Delaware mattered least. For one thing, slavery had all but dissolved there by now. For another, it was too small in both size and resources to count for much militarily. But the Union's retention of the other three states delivered a heavy blow to the Confederacy, both morally and practically.

Slavery was alive and well in Missouri, Maryland, and especially Kentucky. Almost one in every ten Missouri residents was enslaved, one in every eight in Maryland, and one in every five in Kentucky. Those who owned slaves were correspondingly numerous. About one in every eight Marylanders and Missourians boasted at least some human property—as did almost one in every four Kentuckians. In parts of each of those states, moreover—in southern Kentucky, in Maryland's most southerly counties and on its eastern shore, and in southeastern Missouri as well as the counties lining the Missouri River, which runs across the middle of the state from east to west—slavery's specific gravity was considerably higher than any of these statewide averages suggested. Not a few of these border-state masters and their friends sympathized with the Confederacy. One of these was John C. Breckinridge, vice president of the United States in the late 1850s and later a Confederate general.[26]

But many other border-state masters rejected secession for economic or political reasons or both. Some had business interests that tied them to the North more strongly than to neighboring slave states. And many considered any attempt to leave the Union not only illegitimate constitutionally but foredoomed militarily.

The arguments that upper South unionists had advanced before the fall of Fort Sumter therefore continued to carry weight even afterward with these border-state masters. They did not abandon slavery; they simply set out to safeguard it by different means. Rather than do so by joining the Confederacy, they would do so from within the Union, fighting to keep Union war policy free of antislavery aims or consequences. Meanwhile, they would strive to pull their hotheaded brethren farther south back into the Union fold.[27]

The Richmond government publicly insisted that only military force had kept these slaveholding border states in the Union and that their residents' real loyalties lay with the Confederacy. Symbolizing that claim, the Confederate flag included two stars for Missouri and Kentucky. But that assertion failed the test of events. In February 1861, Missouri's voters elected a pro-unionist constitutional convention that five months later removed pro-secession state officials.[28] In June, Maryland voters sent three unionist representatives to the U.S. Congress.[29] And in legislative elections held in June and August, Kentuckians cast their ballots overwhelmingly for unionist, not secessionist, candidates. Most residents of these border states had consciously refused to stand with the rest of the South. Southern masters such as the Edmondstons of North Carolina and the Stones of Louisiana understood this and concluded that those states had betrayed them, their institutions, and their values.[30]

Hopes for a surge in pro-Confederate sentiment in Kentucky rose when Confederate general Braxton Bragg's army invaded in the summer of 1862. Bragg, Davis, and many others predicted that Kentuckians would now flock to the Stars and Bars. "I cannot doubt that Kentucky will prove worthy of our love and her own proud traditions," Davis assured Bragg. In fact, he added, "without the aid of Kentuckians, we could not long occupy the state and should have no sufficient motive for doing so."[31] But the aid that Davis awaited never arrived.[32] In October, Bragg left Kentucky unaccompanied by any substantial number of new recruits. "Kentucky's heart," Catherine Edmondston sighed, "does not seem to be with us!"[33]

Disappointment was as great when Robert E. Lee led his massive raid into Maryland in September 1862. On September 5, he congratulated himself for "affording the people of that State an opportunity of liberating themselves." But just a few days spent there made clear to him that there would be no "general rising of the people on our behalf."[34] Indeed, as Katherine Stone learned, Marylanders showed Lee "but little enthusiasm and few recruits."[35]

By standing with the Union, these border states not only dampened the Confederacy's morale; they also dealt it a weighty military blow. The failure to attract them cost the Confederacy—and simultaneously gave to the Union—great numbers of horses and mules, foodstuffs, manufactured goods, and soldiers. Most white Kentuckians who fought in the war did so under the Stars and Stripes. Among white Marylanders, the proportion was two-thirds; among white Missourians, three-fourths.[36]

Military geography told a similar story. Union control of Maryland protected—where it could have menaced—the federal government in Washington, D.C., just as it did Pennsylvania. Union control of Kentucky pushed the border between the United States and the Confederacy significantly southward and gave the Union much quicker and easier access to the rivers through which its ships and troops would soon surge into Tennessee and then into Jefferson Davis's home state of Mississippi.

In early February 1862, combined forces of Union navy and infantry used Kentucky as a staging ground for thrusts farther southward along the river systems that pierced the Confederacy's northern frontier. One force, jointly commanded by General Ulysses S. Grant and Flag Officer Andrew H. Foote, took the recently erected Fort Henry (on the Tennessee River) and a week later Fort Donelson (on the Cumberland) and captured some twelve thousand troops there.[37]

The loss of these two installations and the destruction of a nearby railroad bridge threatened the rest of Confederate forces in the state with encirclement. Recognizing the danger, General Albert Sidney Johnston ordered a hasty retreat far southward. Nashville fell to Union forces on February 25, 1862, and Tennessee governor Isham Harris and the entire state legislature had to flee, reestablishing itself in Memphis.[38]

In early April 1862, Confederate forces then massed and counterattacked Grant, by then encamped at Shiloh, Tennessee. The assault got off to a promising start, catching Grant's men, who were not entrenched and were poorly served by pickets, by surprise. But once the Union soldiers managed to rally and regroup, the Confederate offensive sputtered, stalled, and then failed.

When the smoke of this battle cleared, Union forces controlled Kentucky, slivers of northern Alabama and Mississippi, and much of central and western Tennessee—key sources of gunpowder and other war materials—as well as the city of Memphis. Once again driven out of its quarters, the pro-Confederate state legislature now sought refuge in Mississippi, while the governor became an itinerant, attaching himself to General Bragg's army.

To the west, meanwhile, Union general Samuel R. Curtis scored a victory at the battle of Pea Ridge in northwest Arkansas in early March 1862 over a more numerous Confederate force led by General Earl Van Dorn. Curtis then crossed the state and in July seized the black-belt city of Helena.[39]

But perhaps the biggest Union prize that season, certainly in symbolic terms, was the seizure in April of New Orleans, by far the Confederacy's largest city and its principal Gulf port. That achievement reflected the wisdom of a method that Abraham Lincoln would repeatedly urge upon his generals—simultaneous advances on multiple fronts that forced Confederates to stretch their smaller resources to the limit and beyond.[40] In this case, Grant's penetration of Tennessee had led the Confederate high command to transfer northward many soldiers and ships originally based in Louisiana.

That left a flotilla of warships, rams, and assorted support vessels plus two seemingly formidable forts (Jackson and St. Philip) to guard the seaward approach to the Crescent City. Some 1,400 soldiers manned those forts. Home guard units filled with members of the city's financial and governmental elites garrisoned New Orleans itself.[41]

After pounding the forts from schooners for nearly a week, Union flag officer David Farragut ordered ships from a navy blockading squadron to run the gauntlet of enemy artillery fire under cover of night on April 24, 1862. The next day saw the ships approach the city itself. As they came into view, members of the home guard turned tail.[42] Farragut's marines hoisted the Stars and Stripes over government offices on the twenty-ninth.

Meanwhile, Forts Jackson and St. Philip, once passed, found themselves surrounded, cut off from their base of supply, and battered by naval artillery barrages front and rear.[43] On the night of the twenty-ninth, much of the Fort Jackson garrison—made up largely of foreign-born residents of the city who, as a Confederate officer later put it, were "without any great interests at stake in the ultimate success" of secession—rose in mutiny against their officers. They refused to continue what they considered a fruitless, hopeless resistance. The Confederate commander, seeing no alternative, "let those men go who wished to leave the fort," at which point (as one of the officers reported) "about one-half of the garrison left immediately." Of those who remained, "it was soon evident that there was no further fight in the men . . . that they were completely demoralized and that no faith or reliance could be placed" in them.[44] The forts' surrender and their investment by Union forces permitted the bigger, heavier, and slower troop carriers to ferry the bulk of the eighteen thousand U.S. infantry troops present (commanded by General Benjamin Butler) to the city proper, which they occupied on May 1, 1862.

The fall of the biggest city in the Confederacy shocked Confederate partisans near and far. A stunned Katherine Stone feared that now her "fair Louisiana" lay "powerless at the feet of the enemy."[45] The War Department heard from Tuscaloosa, Alabama, that New Orleans's surrender had "produced fear and alarm" there, too—although it was almost three hundred miles distant.[46] The same news left North Carolina planter Catherine Edmondston "deeply dejected, nay humiliated."[47] During the next few months, Union land and naval forces extended their control over the river and its valley from the Gulf of Mexico up to a point just below Vicksburg—in the process demanding and obtaining the surrender of both Baton Rouge and Natchez.

Coldness toward secession was not confined to the loyal border states; it cropped up within some states that had joined the Confederacy as well. Anti-secession sentiment before the war had been most vocal and visible in the southern hill country, and it remained so in the war's first period.

A resident of Georgia's up-country thus warned governor Joseph E. Brown in February 1861 that neither he nor his neighbors intended "to Submit to . . . Secession." He hoped the Confederacy would leave him and his "in peace." But "if not we will try what venture there is in flint and steel."[48] Was it "right that the poor man should be taxed for the support of the war," another up-country Georgian demanded to know that fall, "when the war was brought about on the slave question"? Was it right that "the poor man's farm [should be] left uncultivated, and a chance for his wife to be a widow, and his children orphans" while "the slave [was] at home accumulating for the benefit of his master"?[49] In the hill country of northern Alabama, farmer James Bell cautioned his son Henry in April 1861 not to be seduced by the rhetoric of the South's large "Negroholders." "All they want," the elder Bell advised, "is to git you pupt up and go fight for there infurnal negroes and after you do there fighting you may kiss there hine parts for o they care."[50]

These three men were by no means alone in harboring such sentiments. The jurist and major planter William M. Brooks presided over Alabama's secession convention. In May 1861 he noted that while some of the non-slaveholding public were showing "a desire to take up arms in defense of their country," others were displaying "improper and unfounded jealousies" and declaring "that they will 'fight for no rich man's slaves.' " Some enlistment patterns, Brooks believed, reflected the baleful result. The two volunteer infantry companies raised in his own Perry County "include in their ranks but few of the non-slave-holding working class."[51] A year's experience led another north Alabama master, Joshua Moore, to similar conclusions. Non-slaveholders "are not going to fight through a long war" to save slavery, he predicted. "They will tire of it and quit."[52]

In North Carolina, state legislator Kenneth Rayner saw signs of trouble even in some low-country districts. There, he reported in December 1860, "people who did not own slaves were swearing that they 'would not lift a finger to protect rich men's negroes.' "[53] Confirmation came from another prominent low-country figure, Thomas Goode Tucker. The son of a coastal planter, by 1861 Tucker owned slaves and land in three states. With the outbreak of war, Tucker organized a home guard unit in his home district in the Tar Heel State. But he was soon advising his governor of trouble with "a most desperate and lawless group of white men" who had become "too formidable to be punished by the ordinary forms of law & too strong to be expelled by our Home Guard without a most terrible affray."[54]

But in North Carolina, too, the strongest resistance to Confederate power came from outside the low country. Basil Armstrong Thomasson lived, farmed, and taught school in the foothills of western North Carolina. Opposed to both bondage and secession, he looked forward to seeing those twin evils die in tandem. By precipitating war, he told his brother with evident satisfaction in April 1861, the South would soon be "killing off her darling institution" as quickly as any abolitionist or Republican "could wish her to."[55]

Anti-secession views were no more unusual in North Carolina's up-country than in Alabama's. The Tar Heel state's secessionist governor, John W. Ellis, was reminded of that fact in late May 1861 with a warning from Balis Edney, a rich landowner and attorney in the western hill country's Henderson County. A captain in a North Carolina infantry regiment, Edney reported not only that enlistment in newly formed companies was lagging but that recruitment attempts were sparking widespread anger. Much of the local population, he reported, was "as deadly hostile to our raiseing volunteers" and, in fact, to "the whole defence of the south" as was "any portion of Pennsylvania." Edney added that "some of the most respectable of these traitors said in my presence they should take no part" in that defense, that "the south was wrong & corrupt & *ought* to be subdued." In fact, Edney claimed, local unionists had already set fire to "houses, & other buildings" of pro-secession residents.[56]

The level of violence had risen even higher some forty miles north of Edney's home. In Madison County longtime neighbors faced one another in the streets and exchanged angry cries of "Hurrah for Jeff Davis and the Southern Confederacy!" and "George Washington and the Union!" The pro-secession sheriff then shot the son of a local unionist, whereupon the boy's father returned fire and killed the sheriff.[57]

Hostility to the Confederacy also flourished in central North Carolina, especially in eight counties of the piedmont region whose population included a much smaller proportion of slaves (24 percent of the total population) and slaveholders (24 percent of free families) than did the eastern low country (which was 44 percent slave and where 36 percent of free families owned slaves).[58] Independent small farmers predominated in the central counties, and they were strongly influenced by Quaker, Moravian, and Wesleyan religious traditions, in all of which antislavery sentiment had long been strong.[59]

In June 1861, three pro-Confederate residents of the region warned Governor Ellis that "we have Abolitionists and Lincolnites among us" who "say they have as many armed men as we can raise."[60] Ellis's informants were referring to about five hundred people who came together secretly to form a group known variously as the Heroes of America, or the "Red Strings." (The second name came from the biblical story of Rahab, a Canaanite woman who aided Israelite spies planning the conquest of her people's land. In return for her assistance, the Israelites promised to spare Rahab and her family once the fighting began. The invaders would identify her dwelling by the red cords she would place in its window.) The Heroes' leaders included prominent professionals of various kinds, but rural and urban whites with little or no property evidently supplied most of its support.[61]

In September 1862, cooling enthusiasm for a war already lasting longer than expected and unhappiness with some of the Richmond government's policies sent a political "outsider," Zebulon Vance, to the North Carolina governor's mansion. A mountain slave owner who had opposed secession until the last minute in 1861, Vance defeated the candidate of the more consistent secessionists by a margin of nearly three to one. Vance and his Conservative Party nonetheless promised full support to the war effort. But non-slaveholding small farmers such as Martha Coltrane looked to him "not to let the confederate congress have the full sway over your State" and to protect the interests of common white cultivators "as strictly as cngress has to the slaveholders."[62] Like Georgia's up-country-born governor, Joseph E. Brown, Vance would maintain his political position with a delicate balancing act, trying to satisfy disgruntled constituents like Coltrane while also striving to keep his state in the war.

The strongest early blow dealt to the Confederacy from within its claimed borders came in the spring of 1861 from the northwestern counties of Virginia, beyond the Allegheny Mountains. With a population of some 350,000, this region held great strategic value to both sides. In Confederate hands it would expose western Pennsylvania, eastern Ohio, and the Ohio River to attack. It would also cut the Baltimore and Ohio Railroad and thereby hinder the movement of Union troops along that major east-west conduit.[63]

There were slaves and slave owners in this up-country region—and even full-fledged planters—though proportionately far fewer of them than in the eastern low country. But a number of the masters in the area abjured secession, feeling themselves too exposed militarily to an invasion from the north that, moreover, seemed likely to strip them of their slaves.

Most who lived in the western counties were merchants, professionals, and especially small farmers. Some of these people—and, in the most southerly districts, many—cherished values and harbored interests that linked them to the plantation South. But they were decidedly in the minority. Many of the region's small cultivators had little interest in commerce; those who did more typically traded with people in neighboring free states. Contempt for the haughty planter elite of eastern Virginia was common.

The Old Dominion held a referendum on secession on May 23, 1861, that made clear the political sympathies of the up-country. Statewide, Virginians voted to leave the Union by more than three and a half to one. But in the thirty-five northwestern counties, voters opposed secession by almost as lopsided a margin.[64] And they took that stand with strong feelings. "The Union men of Northwestern Virginia are becoming more firm every day," one of their leaders reported to Lincoln's secretary of war in May. "They want to see secession put down and the leaders hung."[65] And, he added, they were ready to back up those wishes with action. "We are now enrolling men and drilling every day, collecting such arms as may be had, and manufacturing cartridges, &c."[66]

But for all intents and purposes, Virginia had by then already joined the Confederacy—had effectively done so, in fact, as early as April 17, 1861, with the pro-secession vote of the state's special convention. On May 3, the pro-Confederate governor, John Letcher, ordered local units of the state militia to converge on the key railroad center of Grafton, some twenty-five miles south of the Pennsylvania border. A secessionist native of the up-country, General Thomas J. Jackson (who would acquire the nickname "Stonewall" in the first battle of Bull Run), led a force into Harpers Ferry on the Maryland border and seized a number of coal trains. To the west, former governor Henry A. Wise, one of the state's most aggressive secessionists, led a force that occupied the town of Charleston, in the strongly unionist Kanawha River valley. Wise's troops hailed from the state's distant eastern low country, with members of the western counties' secessionist minority providing additional support. In many parts of the up-country, the arrival of pro-Confederate militia triggered an exodus of unionists into adjoining parts of Ohio and Pennsylvania.

Confederate forces operating in Virginia's western counties confronted a number of obstacles. The concentration of secessionist troops in and around Richmond, soon to become the independent South's national capital, drained forces away from the rest of the state. But the political complexion of the western population was a big military problem, too. A militia major there warned early in May 1861 that "the feeling in nearly all of our counties is very bitter" toward the Confederacy.[67] "These people," General Robert S. Garnett exclaimed, "are thoroughly imbued with an ignorant and bigoted Union sentiment."[68] And General Wise put it most graphically. "The grass of the soil we are defending," he complained, "is full of . . . traitors," and there was nothing passive about their treason. "They invite the enemy, feed him, and he arms and drills them. . . . A spy is on every hill top, at every cabin."[69]

Local militia units that Richmond attempted to mobilize in the western part of the state often proved unreliable. Two regiments around Martinsburg were full of "strong Union men" who were "so obstinate" in asserting their views that state officials soon decided not to arm them.[70] In Morgantown, efforts to mobilize a regiment collapsed when the militiamen reportedly "drove the colonel and brigadier-general (secessionists) from the field."[71] General Robert E. Lee, then in command of all pro-Confederate forces in Virginia, learned that secessionists at Harpers Ferry, outnumbered and intimidated by the well-organized unionist population there, were afraid to volunteer for Confederate service—or even to openly avow themselves loyal to Governor Letcher and his government.[72] General Wise summarized the situation for Lee: "The militia are [good for] nothing for warlike uses here," and those who were true to the South were "worthless," and—worse—"there is no telling who *is* true."[73]

At the end of May 1861, General George B. McClellan, then commanding Ohio's militia forces, sent three thousand troops across the

Ohio River to occupy the western Virginia town of Grafton. There his troops found a reception as warm as his enemies had found theirs cold. "The feeling of the people here is most excellent," McClellan happily reported. "We are welcomed wherever our men go."[74] Rendezvousing with another Union force, McClellan's troops then proceeded ten to fifteen miles south to Philippi in order to confront eight hundred secessionist recruits raised in that anomalously pro-Confederate town. The Union forces took Philippi with little trouble on June 3, 1861. Other Union troops moved against Charleston, from which Wise withdrew on July 24.[75] And as Wise's force retreated southeastward, between three hundred and five hundred soldiers deserted its ranks.[76]

Union troops continued their successful advances during the rest of the summer until they had driven Confederate troops out of the trans-Appalachian counties.[77] Robert E. Lee directed a series of attempts to retake the region, all of which came to nothing. Most of western Virginia remained in Union hands for the rest of the war. Contrary to some secessionists' sunny predictions, most of the white population there had proved deaf to the eastern slaveholders' exhortations and had spurned calls to abandon the Union for their sake. And as pro-federal units consolidated their hold, it became the Confederate sympathizers' turn to flee or be driven out and to have their property confiscated.[78]

In the up-country districts of eastern Tennessee, many well-to-do individuals who had been unionists before the war began became committed secessionists afterward. But, as Oliver P. Temple later recalled, "the majority of the people had not gone with them."[79] Temple was one of the few local masters who continued to oppose secession even after Lincoln's call to arms. "I was a slave-owner, as my father and grandfather had been," he wrote later. "I believed that secession would destroy slavery," that "secession was only a short cut to emancipation." Like others of his kind, therefore, he opposed secession not *despite* being a master but *because* of it.[80] His political allies included entrepreneurs of various kinds who enjoyed strong economic and social ties to the North and believed that a planter-dominated Confederacy would prove hostile to the tariffs and governmental support for economic development and diversification that their particular interests required.[81]

But as in western Virginia, the great majority of the unionists in eastern Tennessee were slaveless white farmers who held both large planters and their black slaves in contempt. Most of them refused to take orders from a new would-be national government that planters would surely dominate even more thoroughly than they had once controlled governments in Washington. They were certainly not ready to risk their meager possessions, much less their lives, in a war fought on such a new government's behalf.

For most of these people, Lincoln's April 1861 call to suppress secession did nothing to increase the Confederacy's charms. And in June of that year, a referendum revealed a pattern strikingly similar to Virginia's. In the state as a whole, voters opted to leave the Union by a margin of about two to one. But in the state's eastern third, about the same proportion was opposed,[82] and within a few days unionists there began preparing to secede from secessionist Tennessee and to create a new state of their own.[83]

That summer and fall, pro-Union and pro-Confederate militia bodies formed and clashed in one locale after another.[84] Alarmed, the Confederate Congress declared the property of its internal enemies forfeit and liable to be sold at public auction. But east Tennessee unionists refused to back down.[85] They contacted federal troops based in Kentucky and laid plans to coordinate a Union infantry advance with a unionist uprising.

In early November, perhaps two thousand local guerrillas set out to cut eastern Tennessee off from Confederate forces by burning bridges, disrupting railroad traffic, and cutting telegraph lines.[86] "The whole country is now in a state of rebellion," a Confederate colonel on the scene reported. Indeed, a local secessionist editor informed Richmond, "civil war has broken out at length in east Tennessee."[87]

But the regular Union infantry units that might have crowned this uprising with success never arrived. General William Tecumseh Sherman, plagued by doubts and fears about the security of his command in Kentucky, had canceled the original invasion plans. That default allowed seven Confederate regiments to converge without challenge on eastern Tennessee and crush the insurrection.[88] Vengeful secessionists then executed four of the unionists, jailed another thousand, and banished others from the region. Thousands went into hiding in nearby hills and mountains or fled northward into Union-held Kentucky.[89]

The Confederacy retained control of eastern Tennessee until the second half of 1863. But most of the inhabitants remained obviously hostile. When General E. Kirby Smith assumed command of the Confederate military district of East Tennessee in March 1862, he found it "more difficult to operate in than the country of an acknowledged enemy."[90] Confederate major general John P. McGowan, himself an east Tennessean, seemed to confirm Smith's evaluation when he turned his back on his command in the summer of 1862 and denounced the Confederacy as "a *damned* stinking cotton oligarchy."[91]

So, despite continuing repression of unionists and suspected unionists there, "apprehensions of internal revolt" (as one local secessionist foresaw) continued to haunt Confederate civilian and military officials alike.[92] Those apprehensions probably pinned down five to six thousand more Confederate soldiers in the region than would otherwise have been needed.[93]

Like the border states' decision to remain in the Union, the revolts against secession in western Virginia and eastern Tennessee gave early notice that the image of a solidly united white South concealed a more complicated reality.

To be sure, western Virginia and eastern Tennessee were not typical. A majority of the citizens of the seceding states remained Confederate patriots throughout the war. A combination of perceived self-interest and regional, religious, and cultural loyalties—including a deep devotion to white supremacy—served as a powerful glue binding them to the slaveholders' republic. But it is also true that the burdens of conducting and sustaining the Confederate war effort deeply angered and severely tested the commitment even of people who counted themselves staunch supporters of both slavery and secession.

Proslavery writers and politicians had long dismissed as inconsequential their states' relative lack of financial and industrial power. But the necessity of waging a war, on southern terrain, against a foe with far greater material resources and a much larger population began taking its toll. To conduct, much less to win, that war, the Davis government had to take steps that trod upon the notoriously sensitive toes of outspoken and politically influential slave owners. Some of those measures infringed upon jealously guarded personal prerogatives. Others required members of the southern elite to sacrifice their property and risk their lives.

Many of the regime's policies also violated political, social, and cultural imperatives and taboos that over the decades had become central to southern white identity. Those entrenched beliefs included the necessity of keeping government small and weak, exalting local and state sovereignty over that of a national government, and keeping black people firmly subordinated and strictly excluded from many spheres of life. Ironically, some of those doctrines, which had long served to safeguard slave society, now impeded its defense.

By the late spring of 1861, the existence, words, and actions of Abraham Lincoln's government had finally arrayed the great majority of slave owners behind the Confederate cause. But as initial expectations of a short, glorious, and inexpensive war faded and the government's demands upon them increased, some members of the planter elite began to reassess, recalculate what they were prepared to risk, and rethink earlier pledges of all-out sacrifice.

In the spring of 1862, officials in Richmond began calling upon planters to cut back on the cultivation of cotton in favor of corn and other grains. Many states were soon imposing acreage restrictions on the production of cotton (and tobacco). The purpose was twofold: to increase southern food supplies (endangered especially by the loss of Kentucky and large parts of Tennessee), and to strengthen the Confederate government's campaign for diplomatic recognition and even active assistance from European governments. The Richmond regime believed that starving the big textile industries of England and France of cotton would force London and Paris to do whatever was necessary to appease the South and bring this troublesome war in the Americas to an end on the Confederacy's terms.[94]

Many masters cooperated with calls to curtail cotton production. But some dismissed those calls as gross impertinence and unconstitutional. And in those ranks stood quite a few who counted themselves ardent secessionists. One of them was Georgia's Robert Toombs, who had served as the Confederacy's first secretary of state between February and July 1861, when he left office to become a brigadier general.[95]

Toombs was prepared to grow less cotton and more foodstuffs that season, provided he did that on his own initiative. But, as a zealous defender of the absolute sovereignty of masters over their own land and slave laborers, he bridled at attempts by anyone to tell him "what I may choose to plant on my own estate," no matter what the reason. In such matters, he would bend the knee neither "to newspapers nor to public meetings nor to legislatures."[96]

As Union forces began to penetrate the Mississippi valley in 1862, Confederate leaders called on area masters to burn whatever cotton their slaves had already harvested, lest it fall into Yankee hands and enrich them. In early May, Katherine Stone described her fellow planters' response. All, she said, were saddened by that call, "but all realize its stern necessity and we have not heard of anyone trying to evade it." As a result, she wrote proudly, "from every plantation rises the smoke of burning cotton. . . . All the cotton of the Mississippi Valley from Memphis to New Orleans is going up in smoke."[97]

Not quite all, as it turned out. General P.G.T. Beauregard noted in late April 1862 that some "planters along the Mississippi" were "hesitat[ing] to burn cotton." He therefore ordered the deployment of soldiers on small steamboats along the river who would take into their own hands the job of destroying all cotton "within their reach."[98] Planter James Lusk Alcorn evaded the order to burn his bales, concealing some from both neighbors and Confederate officials in order to secretly sell them to northern buyers. Others in the valley did likewise.[99] Even the Confederate president's brother, Joseph Davis, reportedly hid two hundred cotton bales in a nearby swamp . . . until his neighbors informed on him and exposed the evasion.[100]

This kind of conduct, indeed, became sufficiently widespread in the Mississippi valley to reach the ears of Richmonders, prompting the capital's arch-secessionist *Examiner* to report on and hotly denounce it. "When it is remembered that the secession movement was inaugurated by the cotton population of the South," snapped its editor, and "that the Confederate Government is conducted almost exclusively under the auspices of cotton states men . . . these shameful transactions of mercenary cotton planters on the flats of the Mississippi appear still more strange and reprehensible."[101] Isaac Applewhite, who did not own slaves, complained to the governor of Mississippi of such behavior in July 1862. Here were rich planters complacently ordering their slaves to grow cotton while the soldiers fighting for them and their families went hungry, and the "poor soldiers' wives are plowing with *their own* hands to make a subsistence for themselves and children—while their husbands are suffering bleeding and dying for their country" and to "protect the property of these rich misers."[102]

A related source of friction stemmed from the army's need for slave laborers to emplace artillery, build and maintain fortifications and river obstructions, and perform similar tasks. During the war's first year, most masters seemed not only willing but even eager to lend or rent their slaves to local, state, and national authorities for such purposes. But then their enthusiasm began to wane, more quickly in some places than in others. They increasingly resented the disruption of their production schedules and the loss of their valuable slaves through injury, death, or escape. They also noticed that slaves sent to work for the army often returned with too much dangerous information and were, in general, "demoralized" (a word that, in this context, meant unwilling to follow orders).

Menaced in the fall of 1861 by Union general Benjamin Butler's force at Fort Monroe on the Virginia peninsula, General John B. Magruder repeatedly begged local slaveholders to send him laborers to strengthen his fortifications. When masters turned a deaf ear to him, the general resorted to force. "Some wealthy men" had "refused to send their slaves," he informed Richmond, so he had "ordered detachments of Dragoons to bring them." That, however, only infuriated the masters, who left no stone unturned in their search for some authority that would countermand Magruder's orders.[103]

In January 1862, Magruder protested to Richmond once more. "I cannot hire slaves, as I was informed I would be enabled to do," he reported, and as a result "absolutely necessary" but unfinished fortifications remained "all in a dangerous state."[104] In March, as George B. McClellan prepared his army's massive seaborne transfer to the peninsula, Magruder encountered the problem yet again. Despite "all my efforts to procure negroes" from nearby masters, he complained, "I have recd but eleven from the Counties in my district."[105] The consequence was to leave a key defensive position (this time around Yorktown) "incomplete in its preparation."[106]

So it went, too, in the western war theater, the region between the Appalachian Mountains and the Mississippi River. When General

Albert Sidney Johnston called for laborers to strengthen the works at Forts Donelson and Henry and around Nashville, masters sent him less than a tenth the number he requested.[107] Later, as Johnston prepared for the battle of Shiloh, his emissaries asked masters to rent him slaves to work as cooks and teamsters. They ruefully reported back to him, however, that while "those people have given their sons freely enough," it was "folly to talk to them about [giving] a negro or a mule." They "do not seem to be aware," Johnston concluded, "how valueless would be their negroes were we beaten."[108]

On this subject, too, General Robert Toombs displayed similar short-sightedness. In mid-June 1862, a county citizens' meeting instructed Toombs and some of his neighbors to furnish laborers to reinforce defenses on the Chattahoochee River.[109] Outraged, Toombs shot off a defiant telegram. He would "refuse a single hand," he declared, adding that "my property, as long as I live, shall never be subject to the orders" of such "miscreants."[110] In July, South Carolina planter and politician James Henry Hammond heatedly denounced a requisition from the state government for sixteen of his slaves to bolster fortifications around Charleston. Hammond denounced this attempt to impinge upon his prerogatives as a master as "wrong every way and odious."[111] In coastal North Carolina the following month, Catherine Edmondston labeled as "oppressive" a requisition of five hundred slaves "to work on some defences or other."[112] Five months later, her father flatly refused, on the same grounds, to send slaves to work on fortifications at nearby Weldon.[113]

The *Richmond Examiner* found such conduct inexplicable. After all, "the war originated and is carried on in great part for the defence of the slaveholder in his property rights, and the perpetuation of the institution." Wasn't that reason enough to expect the master "to be first and foremost in aiding and assisting, by every means in his power, the triumph and success of our arms"?[114] Instead, masters increasingly focused on their own short-term interests as property owners, even if that weakened the government and armies created precisely to protect their property. The same grim determination to hold on to their slaves that had fueled secession from the Union was now hobbling the proslavery war effort.

A quick and easy war like the one most staunch secessionists had predicted might have required few soldiers to fight it. But as the actual war grew in length and scale, it demanded more and more of them. The need to increase the size of Confederate armies generated its own antagonisms, between masters and their government and among different social classes. Here, too, the enthusiasm and bravado of the war's early months increasingly gave way to hesitation, reticence, and the discovery that one's presence was urgently required someplace other than on the battlefield.

Cold numbers reveal that slaveholders shirked their military duties no more often than any other group of white southerners; they made up at least as large a proportion of the Confederate soldiery as they did of the population at large. But the failure of an individual planter to serve could provoke severe recrimination that exposed among some plebeians a deep-seated, long-brewing resentment of planter wealth, privilege, arrogance, and political power.

Louisianan Katherine Stone of Louisiana observed the results at close quarters. A growing number of non-masters, she recorded, were beginning to complain about being called upon to fight a "rich man's war." In early 1862, when one local planter's son failed to volunteer for the army, "the overseers and that class of men" began "abusing him roundly" for being "a rich man's son too good to fight the battles of the rich." The Confederate government, they said, should send "the rich men" to war, since they were the ones "most interested" in it, and allow the rest of the male population to "stay at home." But many local non-masters *were* staying at home. Or so, at least, it seemed to Katherine Stone, who specified acidly that in her neighborhood "so few overseers have gone."[115]

The Confederate war effort always suffered from a shortage of military manpower. The Union contained more than three times as many military-age white males as did the new slaveholder republic.[116] Concerned about the weariness of troops in the field and Grant's dramatic successes in the western war theater, Jefferson Davis decided in the spring of 1862 that the Confederacy's survival required a national conscription system. In April, the Confederate Congress adopted a draft law that made all able-bodied white men between eighteen and thirty-five years of age liable to service in Confederate armies. Subsequent emendations to the law would further extend the age limits.

Some Confederate notables promptly objected. Starke Hunter, a planter's son, denounced the law as the work of "military despots." While "there is no man who is more willing to do his duty than I am," he assured his wife in May, "I think I am worth more to my family and their interest at home than I would be in the Army."[117] National conscription, Vice President Alexander Stephens objected, violated the most basic principles that had underlain secession and the Confederacy's creation, including state sovereignty and individual autonomy.[118] Georgia governor Joseph E. Brown had turned against the old Union, he declared, "to sustain the rights of the states and prevent the consolidation" of the national government. He was not now willing to see a new national government assert the same kind of unacceptable power over him and his. Indeed, he asserted, "no act of the Government of the United States prior to the secession of Georgia struck a blow at constitutional liberty" as damaging as the new conscription law.[119] Brown did more than protest; he also threatened to block implementation of the draft in his state.[120] If Jefferson Davis needed troops, Brown (and Stephens and their friends) held, it should solicit "voluntary enlistment." If he could not obtain enough soldiers that way, he could *ask* the individual states to come up with more.

But the conscription law of 1862 contained some provisions that seemed designed to anger those of little property even more. The law allowed drafted men to avoid serving if they could find (that is, pay) someone else to muster in their stead, a provision that remained in force until the end of 1863.[121] Few beside the wealthy could afford to take that way out. And six months after Congress passed the first draft law, it also voted to exempt one able-bodied male on every plantation containing twenty or more slaves, on the grounds that either planters or supervisors needed to remain in place in order to discipline and control the slave population. In May 1863, it tightened the terms of that exemption, but in February 1864 it extended it to cover farms containing only fifteen slaves.[122]

Many viewed what they called the "twenty nigger law" as flagrant discrimination against the great non-slaveholding majority. James Phelan, one of Mississippi's Confederate senators, confidentially advised his friend Jefferson Davis at the end of 1862 that "never did a law meet with more universal odium than the exemption of slave-owners. . . . Its influence upon the poor is most calamitous, and has awakened a spirit and elicited a discussion" that would surely produce "the most unfortunate results."[123] Another Mississippian protested to his governor in November that "the law now makes the rich man superiour to the poor, forcing the poor [to] the [battle]fields, . . . showing to the world that the rich is to[o] good to become food for bullets."[124] South Carolina farmer William McNeely wondered what "the poor soldier," the man who was "trudging suffering and fighting through this war," was saying about it all. What did that common soldier think, with his "family at home suffering" while his "rich neighbor with his thirty or forty negroes and fine plantations [was] faring sumptuously every day"?[125]

According to Robert E. Lee's aide, Colonel Charles Marshall, this measure's effect was "very injurious" and "severely commented upon in the army."[126] Private Ollin Goddin of the Fifty-First North Carolina regiment poured out his resentment in a letter to Governor Vance. Goddin had "*volunteered . . . to* go to fight for his country," he explained, and to do so had "left a wife with four children" back home. He had done this in part out of reverence for a society in which all whites, rich and poor, partook equally of its rights and benefits. But now, growled Goddin, "the Govt. has made a distinction between the rich man (who had something to fight for) and the poor man who fights for that he never will have." Goddin had now concluded that in this war "poor soldiers" were "fighting for the 'rich mans negro.' " Ollin Goddin didn't threaten to leave the ranks. But he and others like him, he warned Vance, were getting "tired of the rich mans war & poor mans fight."[127]

Vance himself later acknowledged that Goddin's claim to speak not only for himself but for many others, too, was well founded. The Confederate draft's planter exemption, Vance recalled, "produced a decided effect on public sentiment" and was, indeed, "perhaps the severest blow the Confederacy ever received." It gave potent ammunition to anti-Confederate agitators seeking "to appeal to the non-slaveholding class, and make them believe that the only issue was the protection of slavery, in which they were to be sacrificed for the sole benefit of the masters."[128] Even more fundamentally, it helped undermine a claim critical to widespread support for slavery—the claim that black slavery's mere existence automatically assured all whites equal rights and privileges.

The class frictions surfacing here became visible around this time to a Union cavalry commander campaigning in northern Virginia. "I find there are two classes of white people in this country—the poor class and the wealthy or aristocratic class," General Alfred Pleasonton reported in November 1862. "The poor ones are very bitter against the others; charge them with bringing on the war, and are always willing to show where the rich ones have hid their grain, fodder, horses, etc. Many of them tell me it is a great satisfaction to them to see us help ourselves from the rich stores of their neighbors."[129]

The Confederate government could in theory have sought to relieve its manpower deficiency in another way. It could have resorted to a measure that other slaveholding regimes had tried when facing a military challenge. It might have armed its own slaves, who represented almost 40 percent of its population.[130]

The idea was in the air at the outbreak of the war and was not alien to the American tradition. Black soldiers had participated in the American Revolution on both sides. In 1775, the British governor of Virginia, Lord Dunmore, had promised freedom to slaves who would abandon rebellious masters and join the royal army. To counter that move, many patriot state militias, as well as the Continental army itself, also decided to enlist free blacks and slaves into their ranks. Of the slaves who served, most did eventually become free.[131]

But in 1861–62, most masters—indeed, most southern whites generally—considered the notion of black soldiers absolutely unacceptable. When his overseer raised the idea during the war's first year, for example, South Carolinian James Chesnut, Sr., had brusquely waved it away. "You can't trust them—not on our side," he said.[132]

The Confederate government early, firmly, and consistently rebuffed all such suggestions. When General Richard S. Ewell urged the Confederate president to enlist slaves right after the first battle of Bull Run, an appalled Jefferson Davis dismissed the idea out of hand. It was "stark madness," he reportedly exclaimed, that "would revolt and disgust the whole South."[133] Indeed, the Confederacy wanted no black soldiers at all, either slave or free. And it held rigidly to that position until the last few months of the war.

Confederates did that in part, as Secretary of War James A. Seddon explained, because they were fighting to preserve African American

slavery and the categorical doctrine of white supremacy and black inferiority that justified it. The innately inferior black male, it held, had
little of true manhood about him. He was uniquely suited to dull but
arduous labor but utterly unfit for the responsibilities of a free man,
citizen, or soldier. Having taken this stance both before "the North and
before the world," the Confederacy could "not allow the employment as
armed soldiers of negroes."[134]

That racial ideology, moreover, had long ago penetrated deeply into
the psyches of southern whites generally. They would therefore look
upon the suggestion that they serve alongside black soldiers as demean-
ing in the extreme. Wholesale desertion by southern whites would
surely follow.

Finally, how could a Confederacy founded on such a code of racial
inequality and domination ever fully trust the loyalty of any black men
in *this* conflict? What would they do with weapons if given them? At
the very least, Confederate leaders feared that any blacks placed in the
ranks would (in the words of cabinet member Judah P. Benjamin) desert to the enemy "in mass."[135]

These considerations led to banning not only slaves but also free
blacks from the soldiery. Any light-skinned free black man who somehow managed to enter the ranks was to be booted back out again if his
racial identity was discovered.[136] The local, irregular free-black militia
units that did exist in New Orleans and Mobile were kept out of regular
Confederate service, usually restricted to their own immediate neigh-
borhoods, and permitted to see little if any action. The demands of racial ideology and race control trumped the call even of military necessity.

This consistent refusal even to consider employing black men as soldiers reflected a more general insecurity about the aspirations and loyalties of slaves and the security and stability of the whole "peculiar
institution" during the war. During the first half of the century southern masters had constantly assured themselves and others of their slaves'
fundamental contentment. But beneath that confident façade there had
always lain profound doubts and fears. The same "Africans" who normally appeared to be as mild and docile as household pets, they believed, could under certain circumstances reveal a savage and violent
side. Georgia plantation mistress Gertrude Thomas could thus con-

gratulate herself one day on her slaves' devotion to her and worry on another day "that we are like the inhabitants at the foot of Vesuvius, remaining perfectly contented" while actually living "among so many dangers."[137]

As the prewar political conflict between the North and South sharpened, so did anxieties about the slave loyalty. Masters had long worried that open divisions within the white population about slavery's rights and wrongs could weaken their control over their unfree laborers, encouraging them both to wish for and to act to obtain their freedom. It was partly to remove slaves from those influences that the South left the Union in 1860–61. But now that political debate among whites had given way to actual warfare among them, and warfare waged on southern soil, those influences seemed closer and more dangerous than ever.

In public, Rev. Charles Colcock Jones dismissed such concerns. After all, he assured a gathering of fellow leaders of the Presbyterian Church's southern branch (by then known as the Presbyterian Church in the Confederate States) in December 1861, "no laboring class in any country has remained throughout its existence more quiet, obedient, and peacefully associated with their superiors than our negro population."[138] As the Confederacy mobilized for war, however, those familiar homilies grew less reassuring, even to Jones. In the days before delivering this soothing message, he and his neighbors strove to retain nearby "such a military force . . . as will be sufficient to keep our colored population under supervision and control"—more specifically, to discourage attempts "to abandon the plantations and escape to the enemy."[139]

Like Jones, Jefferson Davis's public messages continued to express full confidence in slaves' loyalty to masters. In private, however, and from the very outset, he confided very different opinions to his wife, Varina. For an independent South simply to keep its slaves in bondage, he worried, it would need to raise and maintain an "immense" standing army, one so big that it would "deplete the resources of the country."[140]

Others shared such concerns. Beginning with the lead-up to the 1860 election, southern masters and state and local officials worked to strengthen restrictions on southern blacks, free as well as slave. This escalation of vigilance and discipline continued into the months of secession and the onset of war.[141] Officials tightened state and local laws barring slaves from trading with whites or simply traveling alone, by night, across plantation boundaries, or without passes. They also reinforced home guard units and slave patrols. Masters and their neighbors petitioned state and national officials for draft exemptions for men who owned good "Negro dogs" trained to catch runaways and generally keep blacks "in order."[142] The Irish-born journalist William Howard Russell, visiting the newly formed Confederacy in the spring of 1861, detected "something suspicious in the constant never ending statement that 'we are not afraid of our slaves.' " Surely, he noted in his diary, "the curfew and the night patrol in the streets, the prisons and watch-houses, and the police regulations prove that strict supervision, at all events, is needed and necessary."[143]

The worries that Russell detected helped shape Jefferson Davis's hopeless and ultimately self-defeating early attempt to defend the Confederacy's entire perimeter—"all of the frontier, sea-board and inland"—against Yankee incursion.[144] Robert E. Lee's aide-de-camp, Colonel Charles Marshall, remembered that in his memoirs. Planters like Rev. Jones and his neighbors made very clear to the Confederate government their morbid "fear of the consequences that might result from the influence of Northern troops on the slaves," including "the horrors of servile insurrection," wrote Marshall. To guard against those dangers, they insisted, required keeping "a sufficient force" throughout the Confederacy to assure "local protection."[145] Trying to do that, however, spread those forces so thin as to make them incapable of countering large-scale attacks by Union armies almost anywhere—such as at Forts Henry and Donelson on the Confederacy's northern frontier and at a multitude of points along both the Atlantic and Gulf coasts.

This anxiety about keeping slaves under control also strengthened the determination of state officials such as Joseph E. Brown and Zebulon Vance to keep local troops close to home in order to guarantee and enforce local security. As early as May 1861, Brown began resisting Richmond's attempts to centralize control over the Confederate armed forces—specifically objecting to the transfer of state troops to Confederate authority. When Brown finally relented, he did so only on condition that those troops be used for the defense of Georgia alone. Meanwhile, he announced that weapons supplied to Georgia troops could be carried out of that state only with the express permission of the governor.[146]

About a year later, as the enlistments of many Confederate troops mustered in Georgia were due to expire, Brown called on Richmond to return the soldiers' arms to him, since they were "the property of the State." The Davis government refused. So when a ship carrying a different cache of arms, this one bound for Virginia, docked en route at the port of Savannah, Brown ordered the arms seized and used thereafter solely for the defense of Georgia. The Confederate secretary of war complained that if such acts continued "it would be better to abandon at once all attempts to conduct the defense of the country on an organized system." Brown ignored those words and resolved to repeat the tactic at the next opportunity.[147]

Southern masters' conflicted views about what their slaves thought, felt, and intended stemmed from a number of causes. One was uncertainty about just what kind of creatures their slaves really were. Were they a distinct and inferior branch of the human race (and perhaps even a separate subhuman species, as some claimed)? Or were they fully human beings with the same kinds of feelings and aspirations that masters saw within themselves? If the latter, then how could blacks be any more satisfied in chains than their masters would be in their place?

Many masters also came to recognize that the face that slaves turned toward them differed from their true, inmost selves. Georgia planter and minister Charles Colcock Jones had made that point almost twenty years before the war. "Persons live and die in the midst of Negroes," he admitted, "and know comparatively little of their real character" because blacks "are one thing before the whites, and another before their own color. Deception towards the former is characteristic of them. . . . It is a habit—a long established custom that descends from generation to generation."[148]

Enslaved people had developed that habit, of course, and passed it on to their children, as a basic form of self-defense. Experience had taught them that too much candor, even with the most apparently kindly of masters and during the most seemingly peaceful of times, could result in severe punishment.

As slaves watched whites' nerves fray and tempers flare in 1860–61, most grew still more cautious and outwardly impassive than ever. South Carolinian Mary Chesnut marveled in April 1861 that "not by one word or look can we detect any change in the demeanor of these negro servants." Even as cannons thundered in nearby Charleston Harbor, "dinning in their ears night and day," and even though whites discussed the war and its meaning in front of them "as if they were chairs and tables," her servants made "no sign." Her husband's valet, Laurence, "sits at our door, as sleepy and as respectful and as profoundly indifferent" as ever. All the others appeared similarly uninterested. But Chesnut found that appearance hard to accept at face value. She suspected it was a performance for her benefit—one the less credible because "they carry it too far." What, she wondered, if they were not as "stolidly stupid" as their manner suggested but were actually "wiser than we are, silent and strong, biding their time?"[149]

Seventy-five years ago, the great black historian W.E.B. Du Bois challenged two then-common views of how slaves had responded to the outbreak of the Civil War. The old South's nostalgic apologists propounded one view, "that the Negro did nothing but faithfully serve his master until emancipation was thrust upon him." Some of the slaves' overly romantic latter-day admirers enunciated the other, claiming that the typical slave had "immediately" turned against his or her master and "took his stand with the army of freedom."

Both views, Du Bois explained, were wide of the mark. Those who talked only of slave "faithfulness" were simply ignoring the voluminous evidence to the contrary. Those who imagined an immediate and united slave rebellion underestimated the obstacles that prevented that from occurring.[150] The four million slaves of the American South were not homogeneous in either condition or outlook. They lived in different places and different *kinds* of places. Most worked in the fields and performed the most arduous of labors. Others were domestic servants. Most lived in rural isolation. Some worked in towns and cities, often with considerably greater skills and freedom of movement. Some lived far from early scenes of combat or sources of fresh information. Others, differently located, more quickly grasped the drift of events. Masters and their governments had kept nearly all slaves illiterate. But a small minority, perhaps one in twenty or twenty-five, had somehow learned to read. And, of course, like any section of humanity, the enslaved population displayed a wide range of personal qualities. Some were quick;

others were not. Some were audacious; some were not. Some were physically courageous; others were more cautious. Such varied circumstances and traits produced diverse experiences, outlooks, and actions.

Told incessantly from childhood that they belonged to a distinct race incapable of living in freedom and destined by their god for hard labor and poverty, some came to believe it. Didn't the evidence of their lives, after all, prove it was true? Weren't they, in fact, less blessed than whites? Weren't they radically poorer, uneducated, and less informed than whites? Mustn't that be the will of God?[151]

In the minds and hearts of some, furthermore, seemingly contradictory thoughts and feelings uneasily coexisted. Especially privileged slaves and those with comparatively lenient masters could feel gratitude for being spared worse treatment. Personal servants could develop an emotional bond to masters with whom they had grown up.

But that was not the same thing as being reconciled to slavery. An enslaved servant named Martin Jackson struggled with conflicting feelings while accompanying his master with the First Texas Cavalry regiment. "I knew the Yanks were going to win, from the beginning," he later recalled. And, wishing devoutly to be free, "I wanted them to win and lick us Southerners." At the same time, though, "I hoped they was going to do it without wiping out our company."[152] Many such men took the first opportunity to seek refuge with Union forces. One was the Mississippi slave named Ike (mentioned in chapter 2) who followed his master, Kit Gilmer, into the Confederate army. When Gilmer was shot in the leg in the fall of 1862, Ike picked him up, put him on a horse, and carried him to safety. But Ike then rode on to find and remain with the nearest Union infantry company.[153] James S. Clarke, an Alabama legislator, complained about a servant he had known since childhood. The man had accompanied him into the Confederate army but had then "seized the first opportunity which presented of deserting" him and "joining the Yankees."[154] The number of servants who did the same eventually discouraged masters from bringing body servants with them into the army.[155]

Other slaves simply accepted that their lot, whatever its rights and wrongs, was fixed and unchangeable. "We didn't know nothing else but slavery, never thought of nothing else," a man named Chapman later recalled of his youth in Tennessee. "I just know I belonged to the man who provided for me, and I had to take whatever he give me."[156] If the only alternative was severe physical punishment, then pragmatic ac-commodation to the reality of slavery made sense. Frederick Douglass remembered thinking that as unhappy as he had been in bondage, he had long assumed that "there was no getting away, and naught re-mained for me but to make the best of it."[157]

Some slaves had long been attending as closely as possible to political news. In 1856, the Republican Party ran its first national campaign, with John C. Frémont as its presidential candidate. As masters snarled about abolitionists seeking control of the federal government, slaves pricked up their ears.

Four years later, during the Lincoln campaign, the level of excite-ment and boldness in the quarters rose still higher. At "every political speech," a Georgia editor complained, a "large number of negroes" would gather outside the hall and "managed to linger around and hear what the orators" said.[158] In the weeks before the balloting, a vigilance committee in Spartanburg, South Carolina, accused two slaves of "talking about being set free" and accused one of saying that "he would fight if he was obliged to."[159] In Mississippi, a group of eleven slaves tried to escape as a group, furiously fighting off pursuers as they did so; half of them successfully eluded capture. Another band of fugitives in that state reportedly cheered Lincoln's name as they fled. Officials in Leake County, Mississippi, jailed a group of forty slaves and five whites for allegedly planning an uprising. Meanwhile, suspicious incidents of arson multiplied throughout the South.[160]

Black southerners watched and listened closely during the secession crisis, trying to ascertain exactly what it all meant for them and how best to make use of the novel and rapidly evolving situation. George E. Stephens observed that process firsthand. A free black northerner, he worked as a cook for the Twenty-Sixth Pennsylvania regiment while sending news dispatches back to the *Anglo-African,* the most important newspaper of the day published by and for blacks. As that regiment moved through the Chesapeake region in December 1861, Stephens discovered that "the slaves, to a man, are on the alert. They are watch-ing the events of the hour, and . . . hope lights up their hearts; bright and all-absorbing visions of liberty and freedom crowd upon their mind."[161]

Masters did what they could to mislead their slaves about the events unfolding around them. The most common tactic was to paint terrifying word pictures of how northerners would deal with black people. Some bondspeople believed these warnings; most, it seems, did not. Many simply concluded that, whatever the Yankee did or thought, their enemy's enemy must still be their friend. Young Susie King Taylor's grandmother instructed her simply to shut her ears to the master's dishonest stories.[162] Harry, a slave foreman on one plantation, remembered his master telling him "dat de Yankees would shoot we, when dey come." But Harry "knowed he wasn't tellin' de truth all de time." He and most others had heard that "de Yankees was our friends, an' dat we'd be free when dey come, an' 'pears like we believe *dat*."[163]

Many slaves had learned to dismiss what their masters told them about the war and its meaning. "On that subject," Mary Chesnut discovered, "they do not believe a word you say."[164] For one thing, they had for years heard the whites loudly equating Republicans and abolitionists and depicting Republican rule as the overture to general and complete emancipation.[165] And it was hard to misrepresent, much less conceal, big events from servants whose duties placed them everywhere. Candid opinions and hard news related over dinner in the big house could quickly find their way into the slave quarters. A young Tennessee slave named Thomas Rutling was just six or seven years old when the war began. His principal duty was to wait on his master's table. Older slaves on the plantation regularly told Thomas to "listen sharp up at the house" and then relay what he heard there to them. His mistress, fearing as much, regularly turned to the boy and instructed, "Now Tom, you mustn't repeat a word of this." And the boy, in turn, "would look mighty obedient,—but—well—in less than half an hour, some way, every slave on the plantation would know what had been said up at massa's house."[166]

This communication network, known as the "grapevine telegraph," could spread quite widely and helped to keep some slaves almost as well informed about the war as were their masters—and sometimes more so. One Mississippi planter fretted in the spring of 1861 that blacks in his vicinity "all knew of the war and what it was for," and they believed that "Lincolns troops would be here for the purpose of freeing them all."[167] John J. Cheatham likewise alerted Richmond that "numbers of them" around Athens, Georgia, "believe that Lincoln's intention is to set them all free."[168]

Emboldened by such hopes, Louisiana's Katherine Stone complained, slaves were becoming slow, or flatly unwilling, to obey orders.[169] And some began to reappropriate the fruits of their own labors. Stone learned that the storeroom of her Brokenburn plantation had been robbed, and such thefts continued through the summer of 1861.[170] North Carolina plantation mistress Catherine Edmondston sympathized with an acquaintance whose servants "have plundered her shamefully—old servants, too, in whom she had every confidence."[171] In Adams County, Mississippi, whites claimed that some thirty slaves, including some of the more privileged, had been caught planning to massacre local masters and seize their land.[172]

In the spring of 1861, slaves in both Georgia and South Carolina unnerved their masters by singing versions of a spiritual that promised,

We'll soon be free,
We'll soon be free,
We'll soon be free,
When the Lord will call us home.

My brother, how long,
My brother, how long,
My brother, how long,
Before we done suffering here?
It won't be long
It won't be long
It won't be long
Before the Lord will call us home.

And this verse was surely the most shocking of all:

We'll soon be free
We'll soon be free
We'll soon be free
When Jesus sets me free
We'll fight for liberty
We'll fight for liberty
We'll fight for liberty
When the Lord will call us home.[173]

Most slaves initially conducted themselves with greater caution. They well understood that the white population was better armed and organized than ever before—that Confederate cavalry and infantry as well as home guards and other irregular forces were everywhere mobilized, on the alert, and on the move. They understood, in other words, what a northern magazine explained to its readers—namely, that "the very fact of the war, and of the wholesale military organization of the Southern people, have rendered insurrection much less likely to be successful than it ever was."[174]

The outbreak of war raised hopes for change, but caution remained essential. As Tennessean Isaac Lane remembered, he and others talked it out and concluded that "the best thing to do was to be friendly & loyal & obedient to massas till freedom come."[175] Littleton Barber, owned by a master in the Natchez region, was "determined to get away the first chance that I got." But until that chance came, Barber "took good care that no white persons heard me say anything" about such plans. The penalty of doing otherwise was plainly visible: The Confederate provost marshal in that county, Alexander K. Farrar, had "hung too many men who just said that they were for the Union."[176] In eastern Virginia, an elderly woman preparing Sunday dinner for her masters in July 1861 could hear the artillery fire on the Manassas battlefield. To each cannon roar she responded quietly, under her breath, "ride on Massa Jesus."[177]

Some early professions of Confederate allegiance by southern free blacks also arose from a complicated reality. A few had atypically managed to acquire substantial property and a degree of toleration from their white neighbors. That was far easier for those with light complexions, such as the free black residents of Charleston who had boasted that in their "veins flows the blood of the white race, in some half, in others much more than half white blood." For them and others like them, declarations of Confederate loyalty expressed an ardent, long-time wish to distinguish and distance themselves from slaves in particular and from those regarded as Africans in general.[178]

Other free blacks simply assumed that the Confederacy would win the war and hoped that public professions and displays of fidelity would help allay white suspicion and maybe even buy them some personal relief from the heavy legal and practical burdens that most non-white southerners carried. Charles Sauvenet, a captain in Confederate New

Orleans's black militia, later explained himself in just such terms. "If we had not volunteered" to fight for the Confederacy, he said, "they would have forced us into the ranks" anyway, but as distrusted Union sympathizers.[179]

The approach of war and the proximity of Union troops changed the relationship of forces on the ground and offered some black southerners the chance to discard masks of docile contentment. On March 12, 1861, eight Florida slaves escaped from their masters and appeared at the gates of Fort Pickens, a federal installation off the Florida coast. A similar scene unfolded some two months later at Fort Monroe, perched at the far eastern end of the Virginia peninsula. A token U.S. force had occupied the fort for many years, but the Union garrison grew after Fort Sumter fell, and it began flexing its muscles with forays into the surrounding area. Most local slave owners fled, managing to take with them much of their movable property, including many domestic servants.

Three of the slaves who stayed behind belonged to a local Confederate colonel named Mallory. Colonel Mallory had planned to take them to South Carolina and set them to work in support of the southern war effort. But as secessionist masters began to evacuate the Fort Monroe vicinity, these three bondsmen took advantage of the confusion to elude the colonel, make their way to the fort, and present themselves before its sentries.[180] The fort's new commander, General Benjamin Butler, allowed them to remain and assigned them to a construction crew inside the fort.

When other escapees realized that the Union soldiers had not turned the first three away, they began a general exodus toward what they were soon calling "Freedom Fort." One morning, sentries found some 60 men, women, and children standing before them. Over the next few days and weeks, additional groups of 20, 30, or 40 appeared. Within a couple of months, they numbered about 900; by the end of 1862, some 3,000.[181]

At first, such fugitives behaved with hard-learned caution around the blue-coated soldiers, some addressing them as "massa" and becoming alarmed when the soldiers asked the names of their legal owners. At another Union camp, one fugitive, asked whether he desired freedom, replied, "The white man can do what he pleases with us; we are yours now, massa."[182] But as they began to feel more secure, these black men and women made it clear to their hosts both that they wished to be free and that they considered freedom to be theirs by right.

On April 19, 1861, Abraham Lincoln declared a blockade of the Confederacy. Within days Union vessels were capturing enemy ships off the Virginia coast. But to extend the blockade much farther southward, Union squadrons would need fueling and provisioning stations close to the Confederacy's principal ocean ports.

In August, therefore, Union naval and land forces began to seize key southern harbors and coves and establish beachheads elsewhere along the Atlantic and the Gulf of Mexico. In late August, they captured Cape Hatteras, North Carolina, which opened up the enormous Pamlico Sound to the Union navy. In September, they took Ship Island, Mississippi, on the Gulf. In November, Port Royal, South Carolina (the principal deepwater port between Cape Hatteras and Florida), fell, as did a number of the offshore "sea islands." During the following months Union forces extended their grasp farther up and down the Atlantic coast. They took North Carolina's Roanoke Island and other ports in that state in February 1862. Union troops captured the important North Carolina town of New Berne in March along with Fernandina, St. Augustine, and Jacksonville, Florida. In April, the Union navy closed the port of Savannah, Georgia.

Each of these successes opened wider the doors to freedom.

At the start of September 1861, residents of the Virginia coast informed the Confederate War Department about "frequent escapes" by their slaves to the enemy, including to enemy vessels along the coast and on the nearby rivers. And the successful flight of some left those slaves who remained behind "restless and discontented," creating "a great danger of losing a very large number" of the rest.[183]

So it was, too, along the coast of North Carolina. There Confederate general T. L. Clingman estimated in August 1862 that "Negroes [were] escaping rapidly, probably a million of dollars' worth weekly in all."[184] Catherine Edmondston heard in October that during the preceding six months at least ten thousand slaves had made their way to the Yankees from the eastern counties of North Carolina. "All our acquaintances have lost their men," she complained, "many of them their negro women also." And one man had "lost 97 negroes in one night!"[185]

During the first week of November 1861, a fleet of almost fifty Union warships and troop-transport steamers commanded by Commodore Samuel F. du Pont carried an infantry force led by General Thomas W. Sherman down to Port Royal Sound, a coastal inlet across from the sea islands. The islands contained some of the richest soil in the South and some of its oldest and wealthiest plantations. Members of the local elite had lustily cheered on South Carolina's nullification campaign in the early 1830s, and almost thirty years later they and their offspring were giving equally enthusiastic support to secession.[186]

On the morning of November 7, 1861, as the Union ships neared the sound's entrance, Confederate batteries on the islands opened fire. The fleet returned fire, pouring artillery shells into the three forts guarding the sound until they lowered their flags in surrender. Sherman's troops then landed and occupied the forts. Despite Sherman's public promise not to "harm your citizens, destroy your property, or interfere with any of your lawful rights or your social and local institutions," many planters promptly beat a retreat to the mainland.[187] But they left too hastily to force most of their slaves to go with them. One major planter, John Chaplin, ordered Moses Mitchell, an enslaved carpenter, to get to the Chaplin family's large flatboat and help man the oars. Hearing this, Moses's wife, Tyra, told her husband, "You ain't gonna row no boat to Charleston, you go out dat back door and keep a-going." And so he did. As Chaplin and his family rowed off to Charleston, Moses, Tyra, and their young son Sam watched them leave. Sam thought the roar of the big guns he heard was thunder. "Son," his mother told him, "dat ain't no t'under, dat Yankee come to gib you Freedom."[188]

As ships of the Union navy's blockading fleet probed other inlets along the South Carolina coast, they found that "the whole surrounding country was seized with a perfect panic." Masters had pulled inland, so that "all the plantations up the river seemed to be deserted except by the negroes, who were seen in great numbers." When federal vessels neared, they "came down to the shore with bundles in their hands," evidently "expecting to be taken off" in the ships.[189] In the months and years ahead, thousands more risked a dash across the water from the mainland to Union vessels or the sea islands, which became havens for such refugees.[190]

At the end of October 1862, the wealthy South Carolina rice planter Francis Weston discovered (as a neighbor, Adele Petigru Allston, recorded) that Weston's "head carpenter and 18 others of his finest, most intelligent and trusted men had taken his family boat . . . at an early hour after dark and made their escape to the enemy." In doing that, Allston recognized, the slaves had acted on longings that were "widespread . . . through the neighborhood."[191]

Charles Colcock Jones eventually had to face the same truth. Some of his slaves had begun planning their escape as soon as Union ships appeared off the coast in the spring of 1862. By July, those plans were maturing. Jones at first comforted himself by noting that as yet "not many" had gone. But he could not silence his inmost misgivings. "The temptation of change, the promise of freedom and of pay for labor," he suspected, "is more than most can stand; and no reliance can be placed *certainly* upon any."[192] Sure enough, within five days, eight more people owned by Jones's relatives had escaped, and in the county at large more than fifty had done the same.[193]

Louis Manigault was managing his father's rice plantation when Union vessels and soldiers captured Port Royal in November 1861. "Then at once was a change discerned amongst all the Negroes," Manigault recorded. Along the coast "great numbers" of slaves whose masters had fled inland now began to gather up the belongings of those masters and make their way to the Yankees.

Manigault noted with special bitterness that those who had previously seemed the most loyal and dependable now were among "the first to desert us." Those included house servants, who "from their constant contact with the family [had] become more conversant with passing events" and were "often the first to have their minds polluted with evil thoughts." Another of the Manigaults' "prime hands," a man named Charles Lucas, had been in charge of the livestock. He escaped in September 1862. It was, Manigault thought, so unfair. "This war," he resentfully concluded, "has taught us the perfect impossibility of placing the least confidence in any Negro." It had proved, at least to Manigault's satisfaction, that "ingratitude" was ingrained in "the African character." He now anticipated that "sooner or later *every negro* will leave, or those who remain [will] become so insolent as to force us to shoot them."[194] Virginia planter Colin Clarke predicted in August 1862, "There is not *one negro in all the South* who will remain faithfull from *attachment to their master & mistress*—not one."[195]

And, indeed, wherever U.S. troops penetrated Confederate territory, the result was much the same. Those who entered western Virginia in the spring of 1861 got active aid from slaves who struck the northerners as not only friendly and helpful but also remarkably well informed about both military and political developments. George L. Wood, a major in the Seventh Ohio regiment, was "deeply impressed with the profound interest the slaves were taking in passing events. That down-trodden race, who had for years suffered every injustice at the hands of their white oppressors, were now the first to assist the Federal commanders. Through darkness and storm, they carried information, and acted as scouts and guides on occasions when it would try the heart and nerve of their white companions."[196]

Although it accomplished little militarily, George McClellan's campaign on the Virginia peninsula in the spring of 1862 profoundly shook plantation society there. In April, Union general Irvin McDowell led an army of thirty thousand men to Fredericksburg, Virginia, in anticipation of linking up with McClellan's army. When those troops reached her plantation and others, Betty Herndon Maury noted anxiously that "the negroes . . . are leaving their owners by the hundreds," and others who remained began to demand payment for their labor.[197]

The much larger Army of the Potomac wreaked even greater havoc as it moved through eastern Virginia. Almost as soon as the army arrived on the peninsula, slaves began streaming toward it, some of them fresh from work on Confederate fortifications.[198] Union soldiers passing by three of the Ruffin family's properties (Marlbourne, Beechwood, and Evelynton) told slaves that they were now free and no longer needed to work for their masters. To Edmund Ruffin's surprise, "the slaves almost universally readily received these instructions, & availed themselves of the offered privileges." In early 1862, more than two hundred slaves had worked those fields. By summer's end, seven out of every ten had fled, including virtually "every able man & every boy above 12."[199] At Marlbourne, where there had previously been "not an indication of disobedience or discontent," twelve young men and boys suddenly "went off to the enemy." And the next day, *all* the remaining slaves refused to labor.

All of this shocked Ruffin, who confessed that "the number, & general spreading of such absconding of slaves" was "far beyond any previous conceptions." The entire plantation labor force, Ruffin fumed, was "in a state of open & avowed rebellion."[200]

Things went no better for Virginia planter John A. Selden, master of the imposing Westover plantation near Williamsburg. From his property, as he noted in early April, one "could hear the cannon very distinctly" as they roared in the fighting around Yorktown, Virginia. Selden's young slave Robert, apparently encouraged by the proximity of blue-clad soldiers, "gave me insults and ran away," though not before Selden managed to shoot him in the leg. A month later, as Union troops approached, Selden himself fled, taking with him cattle, two daughters, and seventeen of his approximately sixty slaves. He proudly informed his diary that the slaves who watched him leave the plantation "wept bitterly" as he departed. But he learned later that most of them had before long "gone away with the Yankees." Nor did those people whom Selden took with him prove immune to freedom's lure. Within a month, three of them, too, managed to escape his control.[201]

In the western war theater, between the Appalachian Mountains and the Mississippi River, the advance of Union forces began to erode slavery's bonds slowly and unevenly, but before long dramatically and on an even larger scale than in the East. Caught off guard by the speed of the Union advance, some masters took flight here, too. And as in the East, many slaves refused to accompany them.

Fugitives began entering General Grant's lines as soon as his forces moved into western Kentucky in September 1861.[202] As his army continued southward, the refugees' number grew. Ebenezer Hannaford, an Ohio soldier, saw "unmistakable delight" in the eyes of field laborers who watched him and his comrades march past.[203] "At every plantation," recorded Ohio officer John Beatty, "negroes came flocking to the roadside to see us." The laborers clapped their hands and stamped their feet in time with the music of the army's marching band and shouted "hurrah 'fur de ole flag and de Union.'" Some of them accompanied Grant's army for miles.[204] A Wisconsin soldier found it "astonishing how soon the blacks have learned" that "where the army of the Union goes, *there slavery ceases forever.*"[205]

Union army chaplain John Eaton, Jr., of the Twenty-Seventh Ohio Infantry Volunteers, marched with Grant's troops as they pushed southward into Mississippi after their April 1862 victory at Shiloh. As cotton planters fled, he wrote, their laborers "flocked in vast numbers—

an army in themselves—to the camps of the Yankees." It was an arresting sight. "With feet shod or bleeding, individually or in families," this virtual "army of slaves and fugitives" was "pushing its way irresistibly" forward, in numbers so large it seemed to Eaton "like the oncoming of cities."[206] When Union forces occupied Memphis in June, slaves from the surrounding countryside flocked to the city.[207]

Robert H. Cartmell was one of those masters who remained on his land when the Yankees marched in. He must sometimes have wished he had not. "To one born and raised in the South & accustomed to keeping the Sons of Ham in their proper place," he grumbled, the "impudence of these negroes is hard to endure."[208] Jefferson Davis now discovered that his family's reputation as comparatively mild masters gained them no immunity from slavery's disintegration. As Union naval forces commanded by David Farragut approached the Davis brothers' plantations, Joseph Davis fled.[209] He tried, but failed, to induce his laborers to accompany him. Most of them melted into the surrounding countryside instead, taking with them articles of the masters' furniture and clothing.[210]

Meanwhile, after their conquest of New Orleans in April 1862, Union forces moved out into the southern Louisiana countryside. As they did so, plantation discipline began to collapse there as well. On Woodland plantation in Plaquemines Parish, Louisiana, one morning, slaves told the overseer (as the latter reported) that "they would not work eny moore unless they got pay for their work." Most planters in the area soon acceded to the same demand.[211] In October 1862, slaves on the Magnolia plantation, about sixty miles southwest of New Orleans, sent their owner a wordless message by erecting a gallows.[212] They announced in December (as the overseer informed his employer) "that never having had a chance to keep [Christmas] before, they would avail themselves of the privilege now, they thought." And with that, they quit work for the day.[213] Slaves on another plantation, brandishing firearms, demanded that their owner free them. When he refused, they fired upon him and drove him into his house, where he remained trapped for days.[214] One Union commander wrote in alarm to his superiors that "symptoms of servile insurrection are becoming apparent."[215]

As masters below New Orleans cowered, Union ships farther north on the Mississippi menaced the area around the Stone family's plantation, Brokenburn. In June 1862, Amanda Stone, Katherine's mother, assembled all the male slaves and told them that if federal troops appeared they must "run away and hide."[216] But as Union soldiers moved toward nearby Vicksburg that month, Katherine noted that "the Negroes [were] generally going most willingly" with them, "being promised their freedom by the vandals."[217] In late July 1862, Katherine admitted that neither she nor her relatives would "be surprised to hear that all of ours have left in a body any day."[218]

In 1860, Virginia planter and political theorist Edmund Ruffin had published a little book designed to spur the slave states to leave the Union. Entitled *Anticipations of the Future, to Serve as Lessons for the Present Time,* it was a work of political fantasy couched in the form of imagined newspaper dispatches reporting the progress of a successful southern bid for national independence taking place between 1864 and 1870. In Ruffin's political daydream, all of the independent South's efforts bore glorious fruit; those of the Union yielded only weeds. Crucial to his triumphalist vision were ties of solidarity binding together all residents of the South. The border states of Kentucky, Missouri, and Maryland all promptly joined the secession movement. The slaveless whites of western Virginia likewise proved themselves "sound and true southerners." Finally, Ruffin offered readers a loving account of "the zealous feelings of patriotism evinced by negro slaves" toward secessionist slaveholders. Although the Union's leaders in his tale tried to induce southern slaves "to desert their masters and seek freedom in the camp or country of the invaders," that attempt went badly awry. In his version of events, southern blacks proved "in general, and with few exceptions" to be "more alarmed at, and more fearful of the invading forces than were the masters." They therefore labored in great numbers and in myriad ways to support the southern war effort. They "enjoy it greatly, and soon become as zealous partizans, and as hostile in feeling to the northern enemy, as any citizens."[219]

By the end of the actual war's second calendar year, the difference between these expectations and the unfolding reality were already marked, as Ruffin himself recognized. Secession had provoked a far stronger reaction in the free states and a much more effective military response than most secessionists had predicted. In the face (and under the pressure) of the resulting war, southern white unity was proving considerably less complete than in Edmund Ruffin's novel. Four slave states stood by the Union, and their terrain, material resources, and soldiers were now enhancing Washington's war against the Confederacy. In the western counties of Virginia, most whites had firmly and actively rejected secession, too, and eastern Tennessee had been pulled out of the Union only by forcibly repressing the majority of its white residents.

The great majority of whites in the secessionist states, it is true, had endorsed disunion in 1860–61 and remained staunchly committed to that cause, energetically and effectively backing it up by force of arms. But even here, signs of trouble had appeared. Several policies of the Davis government were generating class resentment among some sectors of the Confederacy's slaveless white majority. And members of the planter elite were denouncing and resisting Richmond's infringements on their accustomed rights and privileges. (England and France, meanwhile, had yet to make any significant move on the Confederacy's behalf.)

But the House of Dixie's greatest and most severe structural weakness was beginning to show in its foundation—the enslaved third of the Confederate population whose labor drove its economy and undergirded its war effort. Southern masters had bolted from the Union precisely to strengthen their grip on those black workers. Instead, however, secession and the war that it initiated were now enabling thousands of slaves to bolt toward freedom. Their actions, in turn, challenged the Union, its supporters, and its leaders to decide how to respond.

The first eighteen months of war took a toll on chattel slavery but by no means killed it. The great majority of slaves were at this stage still physically distant from Union armies; so long as that remained true, freedom remained for them only a hope.

Even bondspeople close enough to Union lines to seek sanctuary behind them, moreover, confronted daunting obstacles. They would have to part from friends and immediate family without knowing when or if they would ever see them again. And they had good reason to fear that those left behind would feel the wrath of vengeful masters. Those opting for flight, meanwhile, had to evade not only their own masters and overseers but also mounted slave patrols and southern troop detachments and pickets. Nor could people who reached and were accepted into Union-occupied regions ever feel assured of their safety.

Rebel counterattacks could and often did recapture individuals, groups, and even whole communities.

When two of Rev. Charles Colcock Jones's escaped slaves were recaptured, Jones determined to deal with them firmly. He sent them to the hill country to be rented out for hard labor.[220] "Some example must be made of this matter," Jones explained. "If the absconding does not stop, the Negro property of this county will be of little value." Even worse than their "absconding" was the service too many of them performed for the Yankees. "They know every road and swamp and creek and plantation in the county, and are the worst of spies. . . . They are traitors who may pilot an enemy into your *bedchamber!*"[221] Edmund Ruffin's son punished male slaves who had escaped his property and control during the Peninsula campaign by selling off nearly thirty members of their families.[222]

Many recaptured fugitives would have envied those people their fate. More severe punishments were common, including torture and immediate execution.[223] "Within the last 12 months," a Mississippi provost marshal reported in July 1862, "we have had to hang some 40 [slaves] for plotting an insurrection, and there has been about that number put in irons."[224] When, in the fall of 1862, three South Carolina men who had recently escaped to freedom returned to the Georgetown district to free their wives, Confederate troops recaptured, tried, and hanged them. The execution was staged as a public spectacle to drive home to others the price of such conduct.[225]

Masters punished lesser acts of insubordination with similar brutality. In the summer of 1862, Patrick Edmondston discovered that some of his slaves had tried to break into his storehouse. He called all the male slaves together and demanded that they produce the one responsible within an hour. When they failed to do so he made them draw straws. The two who drew the shortest straws were promptly whipped. This, he explained to his wife, "makes it the duty of the whole plantation to detect offenders."[226]

These deliberate attempts to terrorize had their intended effect. In the minds of many slaves, they reinforced the need for extreme caution and the recognition that the masters, their government, and their army were still very much alive and determined to retain or reassert control. "We was afraid to talk of the war," as one man later explained, " 'cose they hung three men for talkin' of it, jest below here."[227]

Chapter Four

RECOGNIZING THE "LOGIC OF EVENTS": UNION WAR POLICY EVOLVES, 1861–63

In December 1861, the African American newspaper correspondent George E. Stephens was circulating among Union troops on duty in the slave South. As he did so, images of revolutions past filled his mind.

The units around him had been raised in New England. That reminded him of the Puritans—and of the Puritan army that Oliver Cromwell had led against the English king and nobility during the civil war of the 1640s. Cromwell's soldiers, the journalist reflected, had fought "for equal rights and . . . civil and religious liberty," while their foes had fought "for the prerogative, for titles, and for the dignities" of aristocratic privilege.

To Stephens, that earlier historical era seemed in many ways to parallel his own. Some 220 years later, in North America, the forces of liberty, equality, and progress were once again arrayed against those of "barbarism, ignorance, and moral imbecility." But one key element prominent in that past seemed completely missing in the present. The modern-day revolution, alas, seemed to have no resolute revolutionary leader. "We have," Stephens lamented, "no Cromwell!"[1]

Abraham Lincoln's party did not incline toward revolution. Yes, it was committed to altering American (or, specifically, southern) society. But very few of its leaders relished the prospect of imposing change through radical measures. Most instead preferred the kind of transformation that was measured and gradual. And if such slow and careful change required an assisting push, the methods of normal peacetime politics could apply it.

The Republicans had accepted war in early 1861 because the alternative—watching both their cause and their cherished republic disintegrate—was unacceptable. But they did not view the war as an *instrument* of progress, much less of radical revolution. Most initially expected—or, at least, hoped—that the war needed to restore the Union would be brief in duration and limited in scope. Washington had no choice but to respond firmly to attacks. But it must also avoid doing anything that unnecessarily antagonized the South's white population and therefore made reunification more difficult.

The Republican Party, the federal government, and the Union army and navy altered that policy only in response to the pressure of events—and even then they did so at first only hesitantly, incrementally, step by step. They turned their guns on slavery in a deliberate, determined manner only once they concluded that doing so offered the sole means of winning the war. Only, that is, when the foe eventually proved more determined, united, powerful, and able than anticipated and the war became more difficult, costly, and protracted than expected. And only after the slaves themselves had demonstrated in action that their emancipation could empower the Union war effort.

From the start of the secession crisis through the war's first stages, Abraham Lincoln stated and reiterated his promise not to interfere with slavery within the southern states. More than two months before he took office, the president-elect sent a letter to his former political associate, Georgia's Alexander Stephens, who in December 1860 was still committed to the Union. Lincoln promised Stephens and his constituents that the incoming administration would do nothing to endanger slavery in Georgia or any other state. Southerners had no cause to fear that the new president "would, directly, or indirectly, interfere with their slaves, or with them, about their slaves." In fact, he added, "the South would be in no more danger in this respect, than it was in the days of [George] Washington."[2]

When the lower South announced its departure nonetheless, Lincoln continued to utter similar phrases, first in hopes of avoiding war and later in hopes of bringing the war to an early end. He stood by that commitment even after Fort Sumter's bombardment. In calling for volunteers to put down the rebellion, Lincoln enjoined prospective Union soldiers to exercise "the utmost care" to avoid "any destruction of, or interference with, property" in the South.[3]

None of these promises and cautions signified any decrease in Lincoln's abhorrence of slavery. He was no abolitionist, he believed in the inherent inequality of blacks and whites, and he doubted that free blacks and free whites could live together in peace and harmony. He therefore held that those slaves who did obtain their freedom should be invited and assisted to leave the country. But Lincoln had also felt since boyhood that slavery was grounded in "injustice" and that (as he would later say) if slavery was not wrong, nothing was.[4] Most important, he shared the view central to mainstream Republicanism that slavery was retarding the nation economically and corroding its democratic principles and spirit politically. It was a cancer that needed removing from the body of the republic.

But in 1861 Lincoln did not view the war that the slaveholders had forced upon him as the proper scalpel with which to perform the needed surgery. He would use whatever force was necessary to keep the South in (or bring it back into) the Union. There would be plenty of opportunity afterward to resume the political struggle to stop slavery's expansion and encourage gradual, voluntary, and compensated emancipation accompanied by the voluntary emigration of freed blacks abroad.

Lincoln reaffirmed his commitment to that limited war program in December 1861, in his first annual message to Congress. "In considering the policy to be adopted in suppressing the insurrection," he said, "I have been anxious and careful" that the "conflict . . . shall not descend into a violent and remorseless revolutionary struggle. . . . The Union must be preserved. . . . [But] we should not be in haste to determine that radical and extreme measures . . . are indispensable" to preserving it.[5]

Lincoln's attachment to this policy of limited war reflected his views on two subjects—the nature of the United States' federal system of government and the practical demands of winning the war.

Lincoln and his party subscribed to an interpretation of the U.S. Constitution shared by nearly all of the country's political establishment. In that view, the government in Washington had no right to act directly against slavery within already existing states. The power to do that rested solely with the states themselves.

At least as important for Lincoln as this legal doctrine were the practical requirements of military victory as he understood them. Lincoln presumed, as did other Republicans, that most residents of the seceded states, including many of the largest slave owners, were unionists at heart. They had, he believed, simply been outmaneuvered, stampeded, or bullied by southern political extremists into allowing their states to leave the Union. From this premise Lincoln deduced the need to defend the Union without giving any unnecessary offense to the implicitly loyal southern white majority. Only such a policy, he believed, would allow that Union-loving majority to regain the political initiative and bring the rebellion to a swift end. A grand strategy for winning the war that General Winfield Scott proposed in May 1861—the so-called Anaconda Plan—stood on the same premise and aimed at the same objective.[6]

In the meantime, Lincoln also felt sure, only the circumspect policy that he advocated could keep the people of the Union solidly behind him and his armies. Even in the country's free states, nearly half of the voters in 1860 had supported one of his three more conservative opponents—northern Democrat Stephen A. Douglas, southern Democrat John C. Breckinridge, or John Bell of the newly formed compromise-above-all Constitutional Union Party. Fifty-four percent of the voters of the free states had proved enough to send Lincoln to the White House. But he would need the active support of a much larger proportion of the Union's populace in order to prosecute and win the war.

Lincoln knew, too, that his party's political support was almost nil in the four slave states that remained within the Union. And he considered the loyalty of those states absolutely crucial. "I think to lose Kentucky is nearly the same as to lose the whole game," he confided to a fellow Illinois Republican in September 1861. "Kentucky gone, we can not hold Missouri, nor, as I think, Maryland. These all against us, and the job on our hands is too large for us. We would as well consent to separation at once, including the surrender of this capitol."[7]

That belief on Lincoln's part gave the political representatives of Kentucky and the other border states outsized influence on the federal government's policy. That leverage became apparent within a few days following the first battle of Bull Run. On July 25, 1861, more than three months into the war, the U.S. Congress passed a resolution flatly denying any intention "of overthrowing or interfering with the rights of established institutions of those States" then in rebellion. Federal forces would fight solely "to defend and maintain the supremacy of the Constitution and to preserve the Union with all the dignity, equality, and rights of the several States unimpaired."[8]

Both authors of this resolution came from slaveholding states—John J. Crittenden from Kentucky and Andrew Johnson from Tennessee. Both men had rejected secession, but they sharply distinguished between the issues of slavery and Union. They would strive to uphold the latter; they would not fight to dissolve the former.[9]

Republicans held a considerably more negative view of slavery than did these two upper South politicians. But they nonetheless voted overwhelmingly in support of the Crittenden-Johnson resolution. The Senate approved the resolution by a vote of thirty to five; the House voiced its agreement with even greater unity. One hundred nineteen of its members voted for it; only two voted no.[10]

Abolitionists, black and white, condemned the refusal to touch slavery as both morally and practically bankrupt. They brushed aside hopes that it would placate Confederate slaveholders or even seriously divide their ranks. Lincoln underestimated southern masters' support for the Confederacy, Frederick Douglass warned. "The ties that bind slaveholders together are stronger than all other ties," he insisted. Counting on any significant fraction of them to help save the Union was therefore hopeless. "The safety of the Government can be attained only in one way," and that was "by rendering the slaveholders powerless."

To do that, Douglass and others argued, the Union must strike directly and forcefully at the *source* of their power, both economic and military—slavery. "The Negro is the key of the situation—the pivot upon which the whole rebellion turns," he said.[11] Anyone who doubted that should simply listen to the rebels themselves. Listen to them boast of the way that slaves kept them fed, clothed, and sheltered while their soldiers went off to war. Listen to them boast of how slaves performed all variety of labor directly in support of their war machine—building and maintaining fortifications, emplacing cannons, hauling supplies, obstructing rivers, and so on. Black labor would continue to empower the Confederate cause, Douglass argued, so long as "the National Government refuses to turn this mighty element of strength into one of weakness." The abolitionist *Anti-Slavery Standard* summed up this message: "Success in the War, without Emancipation, is a Military Impossibility."[12] It all seemed so obviously true to Douglass that he felt sure that the mainstream Republican leadership would eventually come to accept it. "The American people and the Government at Washington may refuse to recognize" this reality "for a time," he wrote, but surely, in the end, "the 'inexorable logic of events' will force it upon them."[13]

In the meantime, the era's closest approximations to Oliver Cromwell would be found in the Republican Party's more radical wing. The radicals shared much with the abolitionists, strongly condemning slavery on moral grounds and openly sympathizing with the plight of the slaves. One of them was the Illinois congressman Owen Lovejoy, whose abolitionist brother had died at the hands of a mob twenty-five years earlier. Slavery, Representative Lovejoy declared, was quite simply "the sum of all villainy." "Put every crime perpetuated among men into a moral crucible," he said in 1860, "and dissolve and combine them all, and the resulting amalgam is slaveholding."[14]

One of the radical Republicans' wartime leaders in the House of Representatives was the flinty Pennsylvania ironmaster Thaddeus Stevens. More than one observer would eventually compare him to both Cromwell and the eighteenth-century French revolutionary leader Maximilien Robespierre. Stevens did not support the Crittenden-Johnson resolution promising not to interfere with slavery during the war. Like Frederick Douglass, he was sure that war and the requirements of victory would drive the Union to lay hands upon bondage. To balk on constitutional grounds at taking slaves away from armed insurrectionists he considered simply absurd. The treasonous masters had already declared themselves beyond that constitution and had, in effect, fired upon it. They therefore "had no right to the benefits" of it.

As 1861 wore on, congressional radicals including Stevens, Lovejoy, Michigan's Zachariah Chandler, Ohio's Benjamin Wade and Joshua Giddings, Indiana's George Julian, and Massachusetts's Charles Sumner advanced the same argument that abolitionists did—that military success required an assault upon bondage.[15] These, they believed, were the firmest grounds on which to urge policies rooted in their fundamental convictions.

Emancipation, Sumner counseled his allies, should "be presented strictly as a measure of military necessity . . . rather than on grounds of philanthropy."[16] The wartime "logic of events" made such arguments steadily more compelling. Every Confederate victory pointed up the need to reinforce Union power and reduce the resources of the enemy—even as it stoked northern rage at the South's planter leaders. Every Union advance carried northern troops deeper into slavery's heartland and closer to Confederate-owned slaves—and thereby into an ever more direct confrontation with the value of slavery to the enemy's war effort. Each Union advance also lengthened Union supply lines and consequently increased its need for rear-echelon labor—labor that slaves could provide if taken from their owners.

As the war drove home these facts, abolitionists and Republican radicals found themselves receiving an increasingly positive public reception. At the start of 1861, Frederick Douglass's attempt to speak publicly in Syracuse, New York, had provoked a riot. By the end of the year, that same city was welcoming him warmly. Wendell Phillips addressed a huge friendly crowd in New York City, and he, William Lloyd Garrison, and other prominent abolitionists found the same kind of reception at the nation's capital and nearly everywhere else in the North.[17]

Meanwhile, thousands in the free states began to call upon the government to take a harder line on slavery. The U.S. Senate received ten petitions to that effect on a single day in January 1862.[18] By the summer, the *New York Tribune* found itself inundated with letters criticizing the administration for its timidity toward slavery and the slaveholders.[19] In August 1862, Ohio's moderate Republican senator John Sherman advised his more conservative brother, General William Tecumseh Sherman, that "the change of opinion here as to the Negro Question" was more dramatic than the latter could imagine. This groundswell of antislavery sentiment had probably helped nudge Senator Sherman toward "meet[ing] the broad issue of universal emancipation."[20]

Others also began to see the logic of—and recognize the mounting support for—laying hands on slavery. One of those people was Benjamin Butler, a Massachusetts politician commissioned as a general in order to help raise troops and sustain support for the war in his state. By chance, it was Butler who commanded the Union-held Fort Monroe, on the Virginia peninsula, to which the three Virginia slaves had escaped from their owner on the night of Thursday, May 23, 1861 (as described in chapter 3).

Benjamin Butler was a political opportunist, a chameleon. Far from being an abolitionist before the war, he had built his career in Massachusetts as a pro-South Democrat. In mid-1860, in fact, he had urged his party to nominate Jefferson Davis for the U.S. presidency. But Butler firmly and sharply condemned secession, and troops that he led from his state had been among the first to reach Washington after the president's call to arms in April 1861.

Butler's transformation into a militant enemy of secession did not automatically make him a friend of the slave. While commanding Union troops in Maryland during the first week of the war, he had made a point of promising not only to respect slave property but also of ordering his men forcibly to put down any slave revolt that might break out. (Other Union officers, including Generals George B. McClellan, Fitz John Porter, and Robert Patterson, made the same promise.)[21]

But when a Confederate officer approached Fort Monroe under a flag of truce in May and demanded that Butler return the three fugitives to their owners, the general refused. He refused not because of any newfound antislavery principles, but because he recognized the pointlessness of fighting a foe while helping that foe to retrieve valuable war-making materials. More specifically, Butler realized the absurdity of returning slave laborers to masters who had taken up arms against the U.S. government, especially when those slaves had just been working on enemy fortifications and were about to be set to similar tasks elsewhere.

As for the legal issues involved, Butler judged that a nation at war could seize the property of its enemies, especially property used by those enemies against the nation. The general, a lawyer by profession, referred to such property as "contraband of war." Human property, he held, was as subject to seizure as any other kind of property.

Butler was not, thus, declaring the three fugitives to be legally free. He simply transferred them from the control of their former owners to the control of the federal government. More specifically, he put them to work under the direction of his own quartermaster—and under his protection. When the indignant Confederate slave owner and colonel reminded Butler of the Fugitive Slave Act and its dictates, the general smoothly responded that the rights granted by the U.S. Constitution and its amendments did not govern the United States' relations with "a foreign country, which Virginia claimed to be."

General in Chief Winfield Scott, Secretary of War Simon Cameron, and President Lincoln all endorsed Butler's decision. Cameron directed Butler "to refrain from surrendering to alleged masters any persons who may come within your lines." Cameron emphasized the makeshift, unfinished nature of this policy by adding that the "final disposition" of those persons "will be reserved for future determination."[22]

News of what Butler was doing and the administration's endorsement spread through the country. The public response in the North was overwhelmingly positive, and some other commanders hastened to follow Butler's lead. They, too, saw the value of placing slaves' labor at the disposal of their own forces. If nothing else, appropriating black laborers would free up white Union civilians and soldiers for frontline action.

At the urging of Congressman Owen Lovejoy, the House of Representatives also put its stamp of approval on providing refuge to escaped slaves. It resolved on July 9, 1861, that it was "no part of the duty of the soldiers of the United States to capture and return fugitive slaves." (Congress put sharper teeth into that statement of opinion early the next year, passing a new article of war formally prohibiting Union soldiers from returning fugitive slaves who had entered their lines.)

In August, Congress took another, bigger, step toward interfering with slavery by passing the Confiscation Act of 1861. The new law provided that any master using slaves (or permitting slaves to be used) in aid of the Confederate war effort "shall forfeit all right" to those slaves. But it did not formally emancipate any of the slaves that it affected. Following Butler, it simply placed them in the hands of the Union army.

But a chasm soon opened between such legal niceties and the practical reality, a chasm obvious to Butler. At Fort Monroe he had originally taken in and granted sanctuary to male fugitives and employed them in the service of the Union army. But by the end of July the refugees' numbers had far outgrown his needs, and they now included large numbers of women and children he deemed unsuited for military support work.

Exactly what *was* the status of these people, he wondered. If they were still property, it seemed to him, surely they were now *his* property, as the representative of the U.S. Army and government. But did the free states or the Union government wish to own that kind of property? If not, had, therefore, "all proprietary relation ceased?" Had they not become, in fact, simply "men, women, and children"? In other words, hadn't they reverted to "the condition, which we hold to be the normal one, of those made in God's image"? Butler confessed himself driven to that conclusion, to look upon and treat these people in practice as free— "if not free born, yet free, manumitted," and "never to be reclaimed" as slaves.[23]

In the meantime, two Union commanders tried to accelerate further the evolution of Union policy. In late July 1861, John C. Frémont, a famous explorer and in 1856 the Republican Party's first candidate for the presidency, took command of the Union's Department of the West (which covered all states and territories between the Mississippi River and the Rocky Mountains). In response to the particularly vicious pro-Confederate irregular warfare in Missouri, he proclaimed martial law throughout the state at the end of August and ordered the execution of all captured enemy guerrillas and the emancipation of all slaves of Confederate sympathizers there.

Seven months later, in March 1862, General David Hunter assumed command of the Union's Department of the South, which nominally included all of South Carolina, Georgia, and northern Florida but was effectively limited to the sea islands captured the previous year. Unusually for a West Point graduate, David Hunter was not politically conservative. He was, on the contrary, a confirmed abolitionist. In early May, he declared all slaves throughout his department to be free.

Free blacks and white abolitionists in the Union hailed the actions of Frémont and Hunter as gains for human freedom and brilliant strokes of military strategy. So did many of the Union's substantial contingent of German-born troops. For them the American Civil War was an extension of a larger, international struggle against oppressive social and political institutions, a war that some of them had already fought (and lost) in Europe during the failed democratic revolutions of 1848. In their eyes, Frémont's militant policy represented the right way to pursue the fight for freedom.[24] Kindred sentiments were common among Union soldiers recruited in Kansas. Many of them were veterans of the already years-long guerrilla war there. Now serving in Tennessee, they continued to advise slaves to flee from their masters, and they welcomed into their camps those who did.[25]

But Abraham Lincoln was less pleased with what Frémont and Hunter had done. It was one thing for a commander such as Benjamin Butler to seize rebels' property on a pragmatic and case-by-case basis. It was another thing for a commander to issue a sweeping manifesto of emancipation that covered all slaves in an entire region. That amounted to a major change in policy; Frémont and Hunter had overstepped their authority. If the power to make this kind of change belonged to anyone, Lincoln told Hunter, it belonged to the president, not to one of his subordinates.[26]

More important than Lincoln's procedural objection was his substantive one. He feared the reaction in the border states. Kentucky politicians, including some of Lincoln's personal friends, warned him in 1861 that Frémont's policy would destroy unionism in their state. Robert Anderson, the southern-born hero of Fort Sumter, was now commander of the Union Department of Kentucky. He telegraphed Lincoln that a company of Union volunteers from the Bluegrass State, upon hearing of Frémont's words, had thrown down its arms and disbanded.[27] The president concluded that any sweeping declaration of emancipation would "alarm our Southern Union friends, and turn them against us—perhaps ruin our rather fair prospect for Kentucky."[28] He countermanded the orders of both generals.[29]

Some conservative Union officers strove more energetically to protect the South's "peculiar institution," and Lincoln allowed them to do so. General Henry W. Halleck, replacing Frémont as commander in Missouri, decreed that no fugitive slaves would in the future be "permitted to enter the lines of any camp, or of any forces on the march; and that any now within such lines [would] be immediately excluded therefrom." He repeated that order three months later, and he directed his subordinates to follow the policy not only in the loyal border states of Missouri and Kentucky but also as they moved into Confederate Tennessee. General John A. Dix followed suit in Virginia.[30]

This conduct, of course, confused and antagonized many slaves. In Maryland, reporter George E. Stephens discovered in November 1861 that with "so many fugitives having been returned" to Confederate masters by Union troops, "the slaves are almost their enemies." They "look upon Union men as little better than secessionists."[31] And when neither the White House nor the War Department countermanded these exclusionary orders, the actual nature of federal policy toward slaves of Confederate masters became hopelessly ambiguous.[32]

In the war's first phase, President Lincoln often seemed more firmly wedded than the Congress to a war policy that was both militarily and socially conservative. But, as Frederick Douglass and others argued, it was far easier to talk about winning the war while sparing slavery than to do that. Lincoln had begun implicitly to acknowledge as much when he accepted Benjamin Butler's "contraband" decision and then signed the Confiscation Act of 1861.[33] And although he refused to allow Frémont and Hunter to proclaim broad-based emancipation throughout their departments, the president was well aware that the more limited policies he had already approved (particularly the Confiscation Act) were inevitably taking their toll on bondage. He recognized that, as he would later put it, the war to restore the Union was already grinding slavery down, wearing it away "by mere friction and abrasion."[34] According to the Democratic historian George Bancroft, Lincoln confided in him at the end of 1861 that "slavery has received a mortal wound," that "the harpoon has struck the whale to the heart."[35]

But if so—if Union military policy and practice was even then starting to kill slavery in its heartland—how could Lincoln hope to retain the loyalty of the slaveholding border states? Lincoln seems never to have addressed this problem in words, but then he notoriously played his cards very close to his chest. It seems possible, however, that a policy initiative that he pursued zealously and tenaciously from the end of 1861 onward represented an attempt to resolve that problem practically. Between November 1861 and July 1862, he repeatedly urged border-state legislators to enact programs of gradual, compensated emancipation within their own borders. And he urged the U.S. Congress to appropriate sufficient moneys to fund those programs.

Lincoln urged this course in the name of military necessity. It would, he said, appreciably shorten the war. "Let the states which are in rebellion see, definitely and certainly, that in no event, will the states you represent ever join their proposed Confederacy," he assured border-state congressmen in July 1862, and they will then understand that "they can not, much longer maintain the contest." But to prove to the Confederates that they would never pull the border states toward them, those states would have to give up their own slaves. "You can not divest them of their hope to ultimately have you," Lincoln insisted, "so long as you show a determination to perpetuate the institution within your own states."[36]

Lincoln argued, in other words, that the Confederacy grounded its hopes for victory principally in the expectation of eventually attracting the loyal border states to its side. Deprive Davis and company of that hope and that confidence, he insisted, and they would give up the fight.

Lincoln made no attempt to substantiate this claim, and most border-state politicians found it unconvincing. It has perplexed many historians, too.[37] Davis and his supporters were certainly disappointed when Maryland and Kentucky failed to rally to the Confederate armies that crossed onto their soil in 1862. But where was the proof, or even any serious suggestion, that this disappointment was remotely strong enough to bring the seceding states back into the Union?

Both the policy and Lincoln's depiction of it as militarily urgent make much more sense if viewed from another angle. Perhaps Lincoln's real purpose in urging voluntary, compensated emancipation on border-state masters was less to dishearten the secessionists than to smooth the political way *within the Union* for an attack on slavery in the Confederacy. Union troops, as he well knew, were already helping to undercut slavery in enemy territory. He acknowledged in a March 1862 conversation that that process necessarily (even if unintentionally) weakened slavery in the border states as well. By the very nature of the war, Union armies "must, of necessity, be brought into contact" with the slaves of border-state masters, who consequently "complained that their rights were interfered with, their slaves induced to abscond." These complaints, Lincoln noted, "were numerous, loud, and deep; were a serious annoyance to him and embarrassing to the progress of the war." They "kept alive a spirit hostile to the Government" in those states.[38] Perhaps Lincoln hoped that if he could induce such border-state masters to cede their chattels voluntarily and with compensation, they might cease to feel any stake in what happened to that same kind of property in the Confederacy. Then Lincoln could cease worrying that the Union war effort might yet propel Kentucky, Missouri, and Maryland into Confederate arms.

If this was Lincoln's hope, he was soon disappointed. The political leaders of the border states rejected his appeal. Their objections included a fundamental one: Although standing by the Union politically and militarily, they firmly resisted the "radical change of our social system" that Lincoln was politely asking them to make. It would mean surrendering "the right to hold slaves." But "our States are in the enjoyment of that right," and "no one is authorized to question the right or limit the enjoyment" of it. They "did not see why" they "should now be expected to yield it."[39]

In thus disappointing Lincoln, border-state slave owners resembled their once-unionist counterparts in the Confederacy. The latter, upon whom Lincoln had once so strongly counted, were in the middle of 1862 still proving very hard to find and—even when found—harder still to mobilize. After a full year of war, and despite Lincoln's efforts to spare their property and sensibilities, precious few masters in the Confederacy were displaying any active sympathy with the Union or Union forces. Most southern whites whom federal troops encountered were obviously and aggressively hostile and apparently unappeased by the Lincoln government's deference toward them and their property concerns.

The *New York Times* was the principal journalistic voice of mainstream Republicanism and often served as the unofficial voice of Lincoln's White House. In May 1862 the paper took note—"with feelings of surprise and disappointment"—"of the nonappearance" in recently occupied parts of the South "of that Union sentiment, upon the existence of which the nation has counted with confidence."[40] The Ohio soldier John Beatty summed up the Union army's experience in the Confederacy (or at least its low country, where most fighting had occurred) when he noted that the "negroes" were "the only friends we find" here.[41]

The lack of support from supposedly unionist masters was all the more worrisome in the light of bad news coming from Virginia battlefields in mid-1862. The ignominious end of McClellan's peninsula campaign, followed by the Union's second defeat at Manassas that summer, demonstrated that the Confederate military was not going to be defeated easily or soon.

The conciliationist war policy's evident inadequacy was therefore compelling the Republican government and its commanders to revise it in practice. Both Ulysses S. Grant and William Tecumseh Sherman, for example, had initially been strong advocates of an accommodating stance toward southern whites. But by the summer of 1862, their bitter experiences in western Tennessee were driving them to adopt ever sterner measures toward white civilians there.[42]

As the implications of such experience sank in, more and more Republican leaders concluded that the abolitionists and radicals had been right after all, that attempting to fight the war without offending the enemy population was impossible—that, on the contrary, the Union's armies must become more aggressive and ruthless toward the Confederate leadership and its supporters. It was time, moderate Republican leaders such as William Pitt Fessenden of Maine agreed, to abandon "kid-glove warfare." Even the Virginia-born Winfield Scott, earlier hoping to win the war without such measures, now reluctantly reached the same conclusions.[43] And a bolder policy, it was also becoming clear, must include a firmer and more resolute stance toward slavery. Union armies must free slaves more systematically and in larger numbers than in the past. They must also make more deliberate and extensive use of the people whom they freed.

A measure of changing congressional attitudes on this subject came as early as December 1861, when a Democratic congressman from Indiana tried to have the House of Representatives "solemnly reaffirm" the conciliationist Crittenden-Johnson resolution it had passed almost unanimously just five months before. Thaddeus Stevens immediately moved to table the Democratic motion and thereby kill it, and a majority of the House backed him up.[44]

More affirmative steps came in April 1862, which marked the end of the war's first full year. First, the United States signed on to a multilateral treaty intended to more effectively suppress the international slave trade. Second, a bill to begin the immediate, minimally compensated abolition of bondage in the District of Columbia passed into law.[45] And third, Congress authorized diplomatic recognition of the black governments of Liberia (born of the expatriation of manumitted American slaves) as well as Haiti (born of a fierce rebellion against slavery). Two months later, in mid-June, Congress enacted the central plank of the Republican Party's 1860 electoral platform. It decreed that "there shall be neither slavery nor involuntary servitude" in any of the federal territories "now existing, or which may at any time hereafter be formed or acquired."[46]

Then, on July 17, 1862, Congress approved the Second Confiscation Act, which held that whenever Union armies encountered slaves of rebel owners, those slaves "shall be deemed captives of war, and shall be forever free of their servitude, and not again held as slaves." The act both clarified and emphasized the free status of contrabands while also expanding dramatically the number of people to whom it applied. It freed not only slaves who had been used directly in support of the rebellion but all slaves belonging to any individual "engaged in rebellion against the government of the United States, or who shall in any way give aid or comfort thereto."[47] As one Union politician aptly noted, the new law marked "the transition from military suppression to *revolutionary* suppression" of the rebellion.[48]

By now Lincoln himself was growing frustrated with conservative military officers such as George B. McClellan and the advocates of supposedly pro-Union slave owners in both the border states and the Confederacy. The president vented his impatience in correspondence with two southern unionists.

The first was Reverdy Johnson, a Maryland politician and lawyer who had represented the slave owner in the explosive Dred Scott case of 1857. Five years later, in mid-July 1862, Johnson wrote to President Lincoln to complain about the antislavery conduct of Union general John W. Phelps.

Phelps had participated in the conquest and seizure of New Orleans in April 1862. Afterward he obtained command of nearby Camp Parapet. A Vermonter who shared General David Hunter's strong antislavery convictions, Phelps not only admitted black fugitives into Parapet but energetically sought to attract them to it. He also sent his troops on punitive raids against nearby masters notorious for being especially brutal toward their slaves. As word of Phelps's actions spread, some laborers on surrounding plantations took heart and grew bolder in defying their owners' orders.[49]

Supposedly unionist Louisiana masters were displeased. Phelps's conduct, Reverdy Johnson warned Lincoln, was creating the "impression" that Washington meant "to force the Emancipation of the slaves." If that impression persisted, previously loyal slave masters in the South would surely turn against the Union. "Depend upon it, my Dear Sir,"

Johnson lectured Lincoln, "that unless this is at once corrected, this State cannot be, for years, if ever, reinstated in the Union."[50]

Lincoln had in the past heard—and had himself employed—this reasoning. But he had now had his fill of it. He replied to Johnson with a bluntness and curtness unusual for him. "I distrust the wisdom if not the sincerity of friends," he snapped, "who would hold my hands while my enemies stab me," the more so because this type of "appeal of professed friends has paralyzed me more in this struggle than any other one thing."

You warn me, Lincoln continued, that "the Union feeling in Louisiana is being crushed out by the course of General Phelps. Please pardon me for believing that is a false pretense." The people of that state, he said, had displayed precious little Union feeling at any stage in the national crisis. If they were now "annoyed by the presence of General Phelps," they knew quite well what the remedy was. They could rid themselves of Phelps simply by abandoning the rebellion and returning to their proper place within the Union. That remedy had been available to them for the past fifteen months. All their present difficulties sprang from their refusal to make use of it, Lincoln argued. Having remained in rebellion against the country's lawful government all this time, why should they now be surprised to "receive harder blows rather than lighter ones?" As a matter of fact, Lincoln heatedly continued, "if they can conceive of anything worse than General Phelps" that is "within my power" to impose upon them, they should now "be looking out for it."[51]

The president's note must have stunned Reverdy Johnson. Perhaps that gentleman dismissed it as the product of a passing mood, as a merely momentary outburst of frustration. But if so, he was sorely mistaken. Lincoln sent a very similar letter to a Louisiana unionist named Cuthbert Bullitt two days later.[52]

These letters marked a critical turning point in Lincoln's thinking about the war and what was necessary to win it. Still uncomfortable and unhappy with confiscation policies, Lincoln could no longer see an alternative to them.

The Union president had shared this conclusion with two cabinet members on July 13, 1862, three days before Reverdy Johnson penned his letter. Lincoln had come to realize, he explained, that "we must free the slaves or be ourselves subdued." The need to weaken the enemy and to add a crucial labor resource to the U.S. war effort had made a declaration of emancipation "a military necessity essential for the salvation of the Union."[53] On July 22, on the authority of Congress's newly passed Second Confiscation Act, Lincoln ordered U.S. commanders in rebel territory to "seize and use any property, real or personal, which may be necessary or convenient for their several commands as supplies, or for other military purposes" and to "employ as laborers, within and from said states, so many persons of African descent as can be advantageously used for military and naval purposes, giving them reasonable wages for their labor."[54]

On the same morning that he issued that order, Lincoln informed his cabinet that he intended to go considerably further. The way to encourage slave owners to rejoin the United States, he had decided, was not to appease them but to show them the grim alternative to obeying the law. If they did not return to the Union, they would forfeit all their slaves. Lincoln then read the cabinet a first draft of his proclamation.[55]

At the suggestion of some of those present, the president agreed to postpone public announcement until some signal Union victory could cast the measure as an expression of strength rather than weakness. That opportunity arose a couple of months later, with the September 17, 1862, battle of Antietam. Union commander George B. McClellan did not win an impressive victory there, but he did appear to stop Lee's army in its tracks and put an end to its dangerous raid into unionist Maryland. That achievement also helped discourage the British government from attempting to interfere diplomatically in the war.

On September 22, 1862, Lincoln declared that on the first day of the coming year, all slaves found in any part of the United States still controlled by Confederate forces (not merely those slaves owned by open partisans of the rebellion) would become, in the eyes of the U.S. government, "then, thenceforward, and forever free," a status that the U.S. government and its armies would "recognize and maintain." Early in the war, as noted, a number of Union commanders had offered to help put down any possible revolt on the part of even disloyal masters. No longer. Now, Lincoln warned, federal forces would refuse "to repress such persons, or any of them, in any efforts they may make for their actual freedom."[56]

On January 1, 1863—by which time no Confederate state had responded to the September warning—Lincoln finalized the Emancipation Proclamation, declaring that "all persons held as slaves within said designated States are, and henceforward shall be, free." That document more clearly and effectively encouraged slaves to assist and flee toward Union troops than had any previous measure of the Union government. Union regiments soon received thousands of copies of the proclamation to distribute as they penetrated farther into the Confederacy.

Much of the Union's population responded to Lincoln's change of policy with relief and enthusiasm. None, of course, expressed stronger approval than black men and women, those long free in the North as well as those in the South whose chains had fallen only since the war began. New Year's Eve and New Year's Day of 1863 saw monster crowds gather to celebrate in churches, in meeting halls, and in the streets in one place after another—including such Union-occupied parts of the Confederacy as Corinth, Mississippi. Norfolk, Virginia, saw two thousand black people march in joy through its streets and five times that number line those streets and shout their exultation.[57]

White abolitionists were nearly as thrilled. William Lloyd Garrison called it "a great historic event, sublime in its magnitude, momentous and beneficient in its far-reaching consequences."[58] Emphatic approval came from many northerners who would have considered emancipation a fantasy and even a crime before the war began. They had come to recognize and accept a change in policy as the only way to save the Union.

But others remained adamant in their opposition and furiously denounced this revolutionary turn in Lincoln's policy. A Democratic editor in Illinois sneered that Republicans were preoccupied with "the grand object of hugging niggers to their bosoms. Hoop de-dooden-do! The niggers are free!"[59] Democratic politicians and newspapers shrilly prophesied that freedom for southern slaves would bring ruin to northern plebeians. Emancipated southern blacks would stream northward to steal the jobs, the women, and the dignity of white men there. In New York, party leader Horatio Seymour claimed that "scenes bloodier than the world has yet witnessed" were about to "be enacted in the name of philanthropy." The new proclamation would lead to "the butchery of women and children," to "scenes of lust and rapine, of arson and murder unparalleled in the history of the world."[60] A northern newspaper warned, "Workingmen! Be Careful! Organize yourselves against this element which threatens your impoverishment and annihilation."[61]

Many in the loyal border states were more furious still. A Kentucky newspaper branded the proclamation "a flagrant outrage of all constitutional law, all human justice, all Christian feeling."[62] Hundreds of Union soldiers mustered in Kentucky tried to resign from the army; their officers were particularly incensed. And in that state as well as in Missouri, the emancipation policy fueled the growth of pro-Confederate guerrilla bands.[63] In North Carolina, it led the man whom Lincoln had appointed as war governor of Union-occupied districts to resign his office.[64]

Another, potentially even more dangerous, center of anti-emancipation backlash was the mostly conservative officer corps of the U.S. Army as a whole—but especially those officers in the headquarters of General McClellan. In early July 1862, McClellan had handed Lincoln a document pompously instructing the president on proper policy. The Union war effort, McClellan stressed, must not under any circumstances aim at "the subjugation of the people of any state." The general was willing to confiscate particular slaves when federal armies found it necessary—so long as they honored "the right of the owner to compensation." But as a rule, McClellan insisted, the "military power should not be allowed to interfere with the relations of servitude." As for the "forcible abolition of slavery" as a whole, that must not even "be contemplated," not even "for a moment." McClellan warned his commander in chief darkly that any "declaration of radical views, especially on slavery, will rapidly disintegrate our present Armies."[65]

When Lincoln issued his preliminary proclamation a few months later, McClellan found it "almost impossible . . . to retain my commission & self respect at the same time." He was soon sounding out wealthy Democratic merchants to gauge whether and to what degree they would second his outrage.[66] Washington hummed with rumors that the general, whom admiring journalists had already dubbed "the young Napoleon," was now flirting with the idea not only of opposing Lincoln's policy publicly, but of flatly refusing to implement it—and perhaps even of threatening the government with his army.[67] McClellan surrounded himself with officers who knew their commander's contempt for Lincoln and the Republicans, and who felt free, and perhaps even encouraged, to express the same views more loudly still.

In fact, McClellan told his wife in July 1862 that he was even then hearing from northern Democrats "urging me to march on Washington & assume the Govt!!"[68] That suggestion evidently appealed to him at some level; within a few weeks he was indeed muttering about "taking my rather large military family to Washn to seek an explanation of their [the government's] course." One of his aides later confided to a reporter "that a plan to countermarch to Washington and intimidate the President had been seriously discussed" shortly before Antietam "by the members of McClellan's staff."[69] In fact, such talk began to float freely through McClellan's circle, as Lincoln soon heard.[70]

A number of factors long limited Lincoln's ability to deal with McClellan as he might have wished to. The man commanding the Union's largest army was enormously popular with many northern voters as well as with his own troops, who followed the general in blaming others for his many military failings and blunders. Lincoln ruefully acknowledged his wariness about antagonizing those troops during a visit to McClellan's camp. At one point Lincoln asked a traveling companion what they were looking at. "Why, Mr. Lincoln," the man replied, "this is the Army of the Potomac." "No," Lincoln corrected him. "This is General McClellan's body-guard."[71]

As soon as the 1862 fall elections were past, however, Lincoln did relieve that inept, obstructionist, insubordinate general of his army. The president had by then already removed the like-minded Don Carlos Buell from command of the Army of the Ohio.[72] "The Government seems determined to apply the guillotine to all unsuccessful generals," General Halleck had earlier noted, adding with some historical insight that "perhaps with us now, as in the French Revolution, some harsh measures are required."[73]

During the autumn 1862 elections across the Union for state and congressional offices, Democrats placed opposition to emancipation at the forefront of their campaigns. And when all the ballots were counted, they had picked up thirty-five seats in the House of Representatives, governors' mansions in both New Jersey and New York, and legislative majorities in both Indiana and in Lincoln's home state of Illinois. Indiana and Illinois voters also strongly backed new restrictions on the right of blacks to vote and even live in those states. These results, Democrats insisted, proved that the Union population supported their party's repudiation of Lincoln's radicalizing war policy.[74]

But although many northerners did indeed balk at the prospect of so extensive and immediate an abolition of slavery, opposition to the Republicans was by no means as widespread as it first appeared in the fall of 1862. As Civil War historian James McPherson has pointed out, Lincoln's party that season actually suffered the smallest net loss of congressional seats by a dominant party in an off-year election in a full generation. And despite those losses, the Republicans retained a majority in the House of Representatives and even netted six new seats in the Senate. Just as important, these election results failed to reflect the political opinions of the hundreds of thousands of Union soldiers whom state laws barred from voting while away from home. Those disfranchised troops included many of the administration's most fervent supporters.[75]

Most sweeping statements about what "the soldiers" thought overlook the fact that the Union army's rank and file was anything but uniform in its views. The soldiers were, after all, recruited from the same population that at home had grown sharply divided over war policy. Abolitionists made up only a tiny minority of the ranks, of course. But a far larger proportion identified with the Republican Party and shared its contempt for slavery. A New York private spoke for such soldiers when he exulted that, as a result of the Emancipation Proclamation, "the contest is now between Slavery & freedom, & every honest man knows what he is fighting for." The day Lincoln issued his proclamation, judged a Minnesota corporal, would become "a day hallowed in the hearts of millions of the people of these United States and the *world* over."[76]

About half of all Union soldiers, however, were probably Democrats or residents of border slave states, and in that group the emancipation decrees of the fall and winter of 1862–63 aroused strong hostility. "I came out to fight for the restoration of the Union and to keep slavery as it is without going into the territories," one soldier wrote his family members, "& not to free the niggers."[77] An Indiana private announced that "if emancipation is to be the policy of this war ... I do not care how quick the country goes to pot."[78] But this sentiment was growing weaker.

Virginia's Edmund Ruffin was sure that when northern soldiers got a closer look at "slavery & the slaves at home, & both in something like their true colors, instead of through the false medium of ignorant prejudice," hostility to the slaves themselves would grow swiftly in the Union armies.[79] In the event, however, Union soldiers' firsthand contact with slavery usually had the opposite effect.

For those who already despised slavery, close encounters with it usually produced the kind of reaction that one private in a Pennsylvania regiment expressed: "I thought I hated slavery as much as possible before I came here, but here, where I can see some of its workings, I am more than ever convinced of the cruelty and inhumanity of the system."[80] And many northern soldiers who started the war unmoved by the slaves' plight experienced a change of heart. One Ohio soldier, initially a firm anti-abolitionist, explained that while serving in the South he had "learned and seen more of what the horrors of Slavery was than I ever knew [of] before."[81] An Illinoisan later confessed to his brother that he had previously had no more regard for a black person than for a dog and that he had "respected slavery." But now that he had "seen its practical workings" he had been "*forced* to change my opinion."[82] "There is a mighty revolution a going on in the minds of the men on the nigger question," Illinois soldier John Russell informed his sister in July 1862.[83]

Some soldiers had begun to conceal fugitive slaves and frustrate the attempts of owners to recapture them months before the Emancipation Proclamation was issued.[84] That occurred even in the loyal border state of Maryland. "There is quite an audible murmur here about the return of fugitives," George Stephens reported in February 1862. "One group of New York soldiers, observing the whipping of recently returned [black] fugitives, freed the slaves and flogged the masters," he recorded. And "an officer of high rank" advised another master demanding the return of an escaped slave "that in a very short time he would not guarantee his life five minutes in the lines [while] on a slave hunt."[85] Similar scenes played out on other fronts.[86]

Far more influential in changing the minds of Union soldiers than empathy for the slaves was a growing recognition of the military role that slavery played in the war. In January 1863, Chauncey B. Welton of the 103rd Ohio Volunteer Infantry growled that "we did not enlist to

fight for the negro and I can tell you that *we never shall.*" By June, however, he had reconsidered and was now admonishing his still-opposed
father that emancipation had proved itself "a means of hastening the
speedy restoration of the union and the termination of this war."[87] An
Illinois soldier bluntly voiced a widespread view when he confessed to
"lik[ing] the Negro no better now than" he did before the war, "but we
hate his master worse and I tell you when Old Abe carries out his Proclamation he kills this Rebellion and not before. I am henceforth an
Abolitionist and I intend to practice what I preach."[88] The need to attack
slavery in order to save the Union—what Frederick Douglass had called
"the inexorable logic of events"—pushed these and many other Union
soldiers to embrace a revolutionary policy.

This dynamic became clear in elections for state office held across
the Union in the spring and fall of 1863. Having lost ground in the fall
of 1862, the Republicans (sometimes in a fusion with pro-war Democrats) now swept to victory everywhere.[89] Republican confidence in
Lincoln's emancipation policy swelled. Ohio congressman James A.
Garfield gave voice to that spirit in a speech on the House floor in
January 1864. Democrats, he noted, complain "that this is an Abolition
war." Well, he told them, "if you please to say so, I grant it. The rapid
current of events has made the army of the republic an Abolition
army."[90]

To abolitionists and radical Republicans, freeing slaves was the crucial
first step in an appropriate military policy. It was also necessary, they
believed, to arm those made free. "If this war is continued long, and is
bloody," Thaddeus Stevens predicted in the summer of 1861, "I do not
believe that the free people of the North will stand by and see their sons
and brothers and neighbors slaughtered by thousands and tens of thousands by rebels," without asking those rebels' "enemies to be our friends,
and to help us in subduing" the common foe.[91]

Nothing would more radically subvert the Confederacy's slave-based
economy and society than sending black soldiers into slave country.
"Let the slaves and free colored people be called into service, and forged
into a liberating army," Frederick Douglass urged in May 1861. Let
them "march into the South and raise the banner of Emancipation
among the slaves. . . . One black regiment alone would be, in such a

war, the full equal to two white ones," he explained, because from its mere appearance "the slaves would learn more as to the nature of the conflict" than they could from the lips "of a thousand preachers."[92] Their mere presence would recruit thousands more into their ranks.

Plenty of black residents of the Union eagerly sought to join in that work. Three hundred free African American residents of Washington offered to take up arms to defend their city from Confederate attack. A group in Pittsburgh named itself the Hannibal Guards, after the African general of old, and offered its services to the Union. Black men in Cleveland announced themselves ready "as in the times of '76, and the days of 1812 . . . to go forth and do battle in the common cause of the country." In Boston and New York City, more would-be soldiers began to drill in preparation for combat.[93]

News of the war and the change in Union policy reached Canada, where the fugitive slave Garland White, formerly the property of Georgia's Robert Toombs, had settled after escaping in 1860. In Ontario, White had pursued his religious calling, becoming an ordained Methodist minister by October 1861. But he also followed the progress of the American Civil War in the newspapers and wrote to U.S. secretary of state William Seward offering to serve the Union cause "to the best of my humble ability." In May 1862, White volunteered to form a Union regiment composed of "my people" in hopes that a Union victory would lead to the "eternal overthrow of the institution of slavery."[94]

During the first phase of the war, however, the Union had categorically—often crudely and brutally—rebuffed such offers and initiatives. "This Department," Lincoln's first secretary of war, Simon Cameron, announced at the end of April 1861, "has no intention to call into the service of the Government any colored soldiers." In various locales, political authorities went further, outlawing public meetings in support of black recruitment as "disorderly gatherings." Racist mobs assaulted some who tried to organize such rallies. The Cincinnati police warned would-be black soldiers there that "we want you damned niggers to keep out of this; this is a white man's war!"[95]

Washington's refusal to accept black volunteers into the U.S. Army grew in part out of the common early belief (shared, as we have seen, with many Confederates) that this would be a brief, limited war. If the South was about to be subdued easily, why inflame the well-known racial hatreds of most northern whites by asking them to serve in uniform beside blacks? Especially if, as was widely assumed, black men had neither the courage nor the intelligence to make good soldiers?

But within six months of the war's outbreak, stunning military setbacks in the East were prompting second thoughts even in the Union's conservative secretary of war. On a number of occasions, Simon Cameron now proposed revising the government's policy. In late December 1861, he did so formally. The national government has the right, he argued in a preliminary draft of his annual report, "to use the voluntary service of slaves liberated by war from their rebel masters, like any other property of the rebels, in whatever mode may be most efficient for the defence of the Government, the prosecution of the war, and the suppression of rebellion." And it was "clearly" as much "a right of the Government to arm slaves when it may become necessary as it is to take gunpowder from the enemy."

Lincoln objected to those words, however, and forced Cameron to delete them from the report's final version.[96] Even after his own short-war illusions evaporated, the president continued to fear that enlisting blacks would prove to northern Democrats and the border states that Republicans aimed to overturn white supremacy. And that, he remained convinced, would doom the Union war effort.

But congressional Republicans had by now come to disagree with Lincoln's policy here, too. The Confiscation Act of 1862 authorized the president to "employ as many persons of African descent as he may deem necessary and proper for the suppression of this rebellion, and . . . in such manner as he may judge best." So did the Militia Act, passed the same day, adding a promise of freedom for all men so employed. Lincoln declined to exercise that authority. When a group of Indianans offered to form two black Union regiments in early August, Lincoln turned them down.[97]

The first practical challenge to this policy came from the field, from individual commanders who thought it folly to spurn so large a potential source of military manpower. During the spring and summer of 1862, a number of Union officers sorely in need of additional forces began on their own initiative to use "contrabands" to guard Union-occupied plantations against Confederate raids.[98] On St. Simons Island off the Atlantic coast, black men guarded a camp of some four hundred refugees. When a Confederate unit landed there, apparently intending to recapture those people, the black guardsmen "vigorously attacked" them. Two guards were killed and one was wounded in the fighting, but the defenders drove the raiders from the island.[99]

In April 1862, General David Hunter sought to transform makeshift, informal arrangements like that one into official policy. He asked Edwin M. Stanton (who replaced Simon Cameron in the War Department in January 1862) for permission to arm contrabands in the Department of the South. Receiving no reply, the abolitionist general set about implementing that plan on his own, beginning to recruit, equip, and drill a full-scale infantry regiment. By the end of June, he was already declaring his "experiment" to be "a complete and even marvelous success." His new black troops, he informed the War Department, were "sober, docile, attentive, and enthusiastic, displaying great natural capacities for acquiring the duties of the soldier." They were also "eager, beyond all things, to take the field and be led into action." Hunter looked forward to organizing "from 48,000 to 50,000 of these hardy and devoted soldiers" by the fall of 1863.[100]

But this initiative ran headlong into a barrage of criticism. Democrats denounced it, and the government refused to endorse it. Having already rejected Hunter's May 1862 emancipationist edict, Lincoln was not now ready to muster blacks into his armies. A frustrated and angry Hunter therefore dissolved his regiment shortly before resigning his command and leaving the Department of the South altogether.[101]

A similar story played out that summer above New Orleans, at Camp Parapet, where General John W. Phelps began forming three hundred fugitives into five companies of Union infantry to help defend his position and police the vicinity. When ordered instead to confine fugitives in his district to manual labor, Phelps submitted his resignation.[102]

But while the Lincoln government moved toward accepting black troops more slowly than it did toward emancipation, it did begin that journey in the summer of 1862. At a July 21 cabinet meeting, Lincoln opposed arming blacks. But a day later he gave Treasury secretary Salmon P. Chase the impression that while he still thought "that the organization, equipment, and arming of negroes . . . would be productive of more evil than good," the president now seemed readier to allow individual field commanders to "arm, for purely defensive purposes, slaves coming within their lines." And within a few more days Lincoln was considering how, once Union troops took Vicksburg, they could retain control of the Mississippi River with the active aid of "the black population on its bank." By early August he was wondering whether to send black soldiers on combat missions against some of the Confederacy's Indian allies.[103]

This advancing transformation of the government's thinking allowed a brigadier general named Rufus Saxton to pick up where David Hunter had left off. A graduate of West Point, Saxton had been an abolitionist since his Massachusetts boyhood, considering slavery "the foulest wrong which has disgraced humanity in the nineteenth century."[104] Now serving as military governor of the sea islands, General Saxton faced the same debilitating shortage of soldiers that had plagued Hunter, a shortage recently aggravated by the transfer of troops from the sea islands to the Virginia theater.[105] Saxton responded to this problem by urgently requesting the right to uniform and arm contrabands, who would act as auxiliaries to the white Union soldiers on the islands.[106] On August 25, 1862, Stanton authorized him "to arm, uniform, equip, and receive into the service of the United States" as many as five thousand "volunteers of African descent" and to "detail officers to instruct them in military drill, discipline, and duty, and to command them."[107]

Here were the origins of the First South Carolina Volunteers. A few months later, Colonel Thomas Wentworth Higginson, a prominent Massachusetts abolitionist who had been both a friend and ally of John Brown, took command of the new black regiment.[108] He found it composed overwhelmingly of men only recently emancipated. In bondage, most had toiled in the fields, but some had been carpenters, barrel makers, masons, shoemakers, and house servants. All had now volunteered for Union duty.[109] As the forty-year-old Sergeant Prince Rivers of Company A put it, "This is our time. If our fathers had had such a chance as this, we should not have been slaves now." And if he and his comrades did not make the most of this chance, "another one will not come, and our children will be slaves always."[110]

The federal government formally assigned Higginson's regiment a limited role. It was "to guard the plantations and settlements occupied by the United States from invasion and protect the inhabitants thereof from captivity and murder by the enemy."[111] But Higginson and his superiors on the scene chose to interpret defense actively, mounting attacks on enemy forces along the South Carolina coast and later in northern Florida.

Meanwhile, General Benjamin Butler—formerly of Fort Monroe, Virginia, and now in command of Union troops occupying New Orleans—was again pioneering new federal policy. This time, he did so with regard to free black residents of the South.

New Orleans contained a large and in many ways unique population of free blacks. Many were of very light complexion, some eight out of every ten being of mixed African and European descent. They enjoyed considerably greater legal rights than most counterparts elsewhere in the South, a result of the terms on which the United States had acquired this part of the continent half a century earlier. These two facts gave rise to a third: Many of the city's free black residents owned a considerable amount of property.

The relatively privileged position of these people helps to account for the April 1861 rally in the Crescent City (mentioned in chapter 2) by some 1,500 *hommes de couleur libre* in support of the Confederate cause. And for the formation shortly afterward of a regiment of free blacks, called the Native Guards, which Confederate governor Thomas O. Moore formally inducted into the state militia.

State and city officials, however, proved quite ambivalent about the regiment. After Farragut's and Sherman's Union forces managed to pass the two forts defending the city in April 1862, the governor called upon the Native Guards "to maintain their organization, and to hold themselves prepared for such orders as may be transmitted to them." But, armed only at the last minute and then only with antiquated muskets, they remained on the periphery of the action as Union troops took control of the city.[112]

After New Orleans's surrender, four of the Native Guards' line officers called on General Butler to offer him their services.[113] They explained that they had previously sought to prove themselves loyal to suspicious Confederate authorities in order to safeguard their lives and property. But they would rather fight against the slaveholders' republic than for it.[114]

Butler accepted their offer. Two developments evidently influenced his decision. The first was Butler's apprehension in early August that a Confederate force was about to attack the city. The second was word from Treasury secretary Chase that both the northern public and the Lincoln administration were rethinking the subject of black soldiers.[115] Nothing if not politically shrewd and agile, Butler was soon exhorting all former members of the Native Guards to volunteer for Union service.[116] The United States' First Regiment of Louisiana Native Guards officially began its life on September 27, 1862. By Thanksgiving, two additional black regiments stood beside it.[117]

On paper Butler's overture extended only to already-free members of the city's black population. But as a Union official noted concerning the enlistment process, "nobody inquires whether the recruit is (or has been) a slave." As a result, the new Union regiments admitted not only members of the original Native Guards and other free blacks, but "the boldest and finest fugitives" from slavery as well. In fact, nearly nine out of ten of Butler's First Regiment of Louisiana Native Guards had never served in the Confederate militia, and at least half were probably contrabands. Nearly all of those who joined the Second and Third regiments had recently been slaves, too.[118]

These freedmen brought to their new duties a fervor that those who had never lived in bondage could hardly match. One such man found his unit marching down Canal Street one Saturday morning. As he passed his former master's place of business, this soldier shook his musket toward the place and exclaimed, " 'Dat's de man *I* wants to meet on de field oh battle!' "[119]

Events were moving still more rapidly in Kansas. There James H. Lane, James Montgomery, and Charles Jennison, all veterans of the fierce prewar conflict over slavery in that territory, began in August 1862 to recruit black refugees from Missouri and Arkansas into irregular combat units. That the War Department explicitly denied them permission to do so seems not to have slowed them down at all. They had formed as many as seven companies by the end of September, and in October they engaged pro-Confederate guerrillas in Missouri. The black soldiers "fought like tigers, each and every one of them," a Kansas journalist reported, "and the main difficulty was to hold them well in hand."[120]

The final Emancipation Proclamation announced Lincoln's intention to formalize and generalize these experiments. By January 1863, he had decided to bring black men "into the armed service of the United States to garrison forts, positions, stations, and other places, and to man vessels of all sorts."

One of the first fruits of the new policy was the formal mustering into federal service in late January 1863 of James Lane's First Regiment, Kansas Colored Volunteers. And on January 26, the War Department authorized the strongly antislavery governor of Massachusetts, John A. Andrew, to raise as many black troops as he deemed suitable, thereby initiating the formation of what would become the Fifty-Fourth Massachusetts Infantry regiment. Abolitionists energetically set about recruiting to its ranks, and because Massachusetts contained only a small population of free black men of military age, they were permitted to seek recruits far beyond the borders of the Bay State. Frederick Douglass's sons Charles and Lewis joined the regiment, and their father crisscrossed the free states urging black men to follow suit. Four companies were ready for service by late March, and the continuing influx of recruits prompted the formation that May of the Fifty-Fifth Massachusetts Infantry regiment.[121]

These developments contained strong implications for other aspects of federal policy. Those now being asked to take up arms and risk their lives in Union uniforms could hardly be urged simultaneously to prepare to leave the country. Lincoln's turn toward the recruitment of black soldiers therefore required an end to his public calls for colonizing free black people abroad.

The Lincoln government's decision to free and arm black men infuriated the Confederacy's leaders and supporters. It was, announced the *Richmond Examiner*, "the most startling political crime . . . yet known in American History."[122] General Lee denounced Lincoln's "savage and brutal policy" for consigning "our social system" to "destruction," subjecting "the honor of our families" to "pollution," and in general condemning the South to a "degradation worse than death."[123] Gertrude Thomas scorned this base "attempt to arouse the vindictive passions of an inferior race."[124] The *Mobile Register and Advertiser* was horrified by the thought that "our sons" might now "meet their own slaves on the field." It was therefore time, said the paper's editor, to have "the black flag . . . raised, and war to the knife proclaimed."[125]

In July 1863, Confederate general P.G.T. Beauregard, the son of Louisiana sugar planters, sent a note across the lines to a Union counterpart, lecturing him about the evils of emancipating and arming people like the slaves of North America. "The employment of a merciless, servile race as soldiers," Beauregard admonished, always invited "atrocious consequences." That was so obvious, he continued, that when Napoléon invaded Russia in 1812, he "refused to receive or employ against the Russian Government and army the Russian serfs," even though those serfs "were ready on all sides to flock to his standard" if he would only liberate them.[126]

Beauregard knew his Napoléon—or at least, knew Napoléon's version of those events. What Beauregard didn't seem to grasp was the crucial difference between Napoléon and Lincoln: the very different roles that they played in the course of their two nations' great national revolutions.

Napoléon Bonaparte was a parvenu who gained fame by military service for the French Revolution's cause. But when he seized political power in 1799, destroyed the young republic, and then anointed himself as emperor five years later, he was dragging that revolution backward, far away from its earlier radically democratic impulse. The man who invaded Russia in 1812 did so to aggrandize and enrich himself and the new imperial aristocracy he had created. Emperor Napoléon I certainly had no desire to emancipate Russian serfs.[127]

Abraham Lincoln showed in 1862–63 that he was made of very different stuff and stood at the head of very different forces. He did not, as we have seen, think of himself as a revolutionary. Indeed he initially set his face determinedly against revolutionary measures. He certainly did not regard himself as the representative of America's enslaved population. But he was fighting a war to defend a democratic republic against its foes, a war born of his party's determination to place chattel slavery on the road to extinction for the sake of that republic's economic, political, and moral health.

Lincoln first tried to achieve his aims with relatively conservative methods. The failure of those methods confronted him with three alternatives. He could give up the whole attempt, as some northern ("Peace") Democrats wanted to do. That is, he could concede defeat and allow slave states to withdraw from the nation. Or, he could continue trying to prosecute the war while clinging to the now demonstrably inadequate, halfway methods of the past, as McClellan and other ("War") Democrats wished to do. Or, finally, he could stand by his initial determination to fight and win the war while making the changes necessary to do that. He could, that is, recognize and accept the "inexorable logic of events"—the need for a more aggressive military strategy and a revolutionary, emancipationist war policy.

Lincoln chose the third course. Confronted with the impossibility of winning the war in the old way, he would not abandon the goal. "We must disenthrall ourselves," he said, of "the dogmas of the quiet past" and recognize the imperatives of "the stormy present." We know "how to save the Union," he said: By "giving freedom to the slave, we assure freedom to the free."[128]

In choosing that path, Lincoln proved himself capable of revolutionary leadership and a figure less like Napoléon Bonaparte than like Cromwell, Robespierre, or South America's Simon Bolívar. Half a century before the U.S. Civil War began, Bolívar—the would-be liberator of most of South America from Spanish rule—discovered that he could not accomplish that goal without doing still more. In order to triumph, he would also have to mobilize, arm, and promise freedom to the continent's black slaves.[129]

In the spring and summer of 1862, Abraham Lincoln confronted a problem similar to Bolívar's, and he, too, resolved upon a revolutionary solution. As he did so, the popular base and constituency of the Union war effort changed, shifted. Initially preoccupied with maintaining the support of northern conservatives and border-state masters, Lincoln now turned away from those sectors and toward the enslaved population and their champions in the North. He would henceforth depend upon them, far more than on northern conservatives or union masters, to bring the struggle against the rebellious slave states to a successful conclusion.

These decisions confirmed an appraisal of Lincoln's character and place in history that a prominent revolutionary across the ocean made of him. European socialists Karl Marx and Friedrich Engels watched events in the U.S. Civil War closely from afar by studying northern newspapers and letters they received from friends and supporters in America. The Union's conduct by the spring of 1862 left Engels disgusted. "Where, amongst the people, is there any sign of revolutionary vigour?" he demanded. "Where, throughout the North, is there the slightest indication that people are in real earnest about anything?"

But Marx had formed a more positive view. "President Lincoln never ventures a step forward before the tide of circumstances and the general call of public opinion *forbid* further delay," he wrote. "But once 'Old Abe' realizes that such a turning point has been reached, he surprises friend and foe alike by a sudden operation executed as noiselessly as possible." And Lincoln's emancipation proclamation, Marx judged, was "the most important document in American history since the establishment of the Union."[130]

Katherine Stone's family owned a 1,200-acre Louisiana plantation called Brokenburn and more than 150 slaves. *The Louisiana State Universities Library.*

Catherine Ann Devereux Edmondston and her husband owned two plantations in northeastern North Carolina. *Courtesy of the North Carolina Office of Archives and History, Raleigh, NC.*

Mary Boykin Chesnut of South Carolina in 1856. The Chesnut family owned almost 450 slaves in 1860.

Ella Gertrude Clanton Thomas and her husband, Jefferson Thomas, owned a plantation in Georgia and ninety slaves. *Permission from Ed Jackson.*

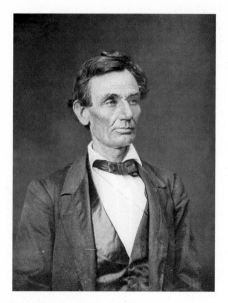

Abraham Lincoln in 1860.

Robert Toombs of Georgia owned more than two thousand acres and 176 slaves. He became the Confederacy's first secretary of state. *The Library of Congress.*

Jefferson Davis, president of the Confederacy, owned a 1,400-acre Mississippi cotton plantation named Brierfield. *The Library of Congress.*

Robert E. Lee of Virginia. He and his wife, Mary Anna Custis Lee, owned sixty slaves and the 1,100-acre Arlington plantation. *The Library of Congress.*

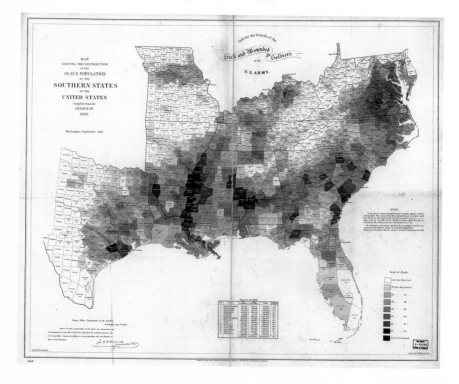

An advertisement offering slaves for sale. *The Library of Congress.*

A map based on the 1860 census showing the location of slaves by county. The darkest shadings represent the heaviest concentrations of enslaved people. The census bureau produced copies of this map in 1861 and sold them to raise money for sick and wounded Union soldiers. *The Library of Congress, Geography and Map Division.*

A planter and his family on the South Carolina sea islands attend a sanctioned prayer meeting for their slaves. *From* The Illustrated London News, *courtesy of the American Social History Project, CUNY.*

Impressed slaves working on fortifications at Savannah, Georgia, 1863. *From* The Illustrated London News, *courtesy of the American Social History Project, CUNY.*

A mass meeting in
New York City calls for
suppressing secession,
April 20, 1861. *The
Library of Congress.*

Born a slave, Frederick
Douglass escaped to the
North and became a
leading abolitionist.
*Collections of the New-York
Historical Society.*

Zebulon Vance in 1862. Initially opposed to secession, as North Carolina governor Vance supported the Confederate cause while opposing Jefferson Davis's policies in the name of state rights and white families of little property. *Courtesy of the North Carolina Office of Archives and History, Raleigh, NC.*

William G. Brownlow, a newspaper editor in eastern Tennessee who steadfastly opposed secession. *The Library of Congress.*

Harper's Weekly depicted unionists in eastern Tennessee meeting secretly to plan an uprising. *The Library of Congress.*

Virginia slaves seek refuge at Union-held Fort Monroe in the spring of 1861. *From* Frank Leslie's Illustrated Newspaper, *courtesy of the American Social History Project, CUNY.*

"Contrabands" crossing the Rappahannock River to reach Union lines in 1862. *The Library of Congress.*

Lincoln reads the Emancipation Proclamation to his cabinet in 1862. *The Library of Congress.*

A Union army recruiting poster aimed at black men. *The Library Company of Philadelphia.*

MEN OF COLOR
To Arms! To Arms!
NOW OR NEVER
THREE YEARS' SERVICE!

AND JOIN IN FIGHTING THE

BATTLES OF LIBERTY AND THE UNION

FAIL NOW, & OUR RACE IS DOOMED

SILENCE THE TONGUE OF CALUMNY

VALOR AND HEROISM

OUR BROTHERS DISPLAYED AT

PORT HUDSON AND MILLIKEN'S BEND,

ARE FREEMEN LESS BRAVE THAN SLAVES

OUR LAST OPPORTUNITY HAS COME

MEN OF COLOR, BROTHERS AND FATHERS!

WE APPEAL TO YOU!

STRIKE NOW!

Sgt. J. L. Balldwin of the Fifty-sixth U.S. Colored Infantry with a book in his hand. *The Chicago History Museum (ICHi-22172).*

Like many other black women, this unidentified "washerwoman" worked for the Union army in Virginia. *Photographic History Collection, Division of Information Technology and Communications, National Museum of American History, Smithsonian Institution.*

At age fourteen or fifteen, the former slave Susie King Taylor organized and taught in a school in the Union-occupied Georgia sea islands for other freedpeople.

Black Union troops in General Edward A. Wild's command freeing slaves in North Carolina in 1863. *From* Harper's Weekly.

Sketch of a Confederate cavalry officer impressing slave laborers from a South Carolina plantation. *Collections of the New-York Historical Society.*

This *Harper's Weekly* engraving depicts Unionists welcoming General Burnside's troops to Knoxville, in eastern Tennessee, September 1863. *The Library of Congress.*

Frank Leslie's Illustrated Newspaper carried this depiction of the April 1863 riot in Richmond that demanded bread at lower prices. *The Library of Congress.*

North Carolina "peace" editor William Woods Holden. *Courtesy of the North Carolina Office of Archives and History, Raleigh, NC.*

Newton Knight, leader of anti-Confederate guerrilla forces in Jones County, Mississippi. *Courtesy Victoria Bynum.*

In April 1864 at Fort Pillow, Tennessee, Confederate soldiers led by General Nathan B. Forrest slaughtered surrendering Union soldiers, white and especially black. *From* Harper's Weekly.

Members of the Fifty-fifth Massachusetts regiment singing John Brown's song as they enter Charleston, February 12, 1865. *From* Harpers Weekly, *courtesy of the American Social History Project, CUNY.*

Members of Company E of the Fourth Regiment, United States Colored Troops (USCT), 1865. That regiment took part in the campaign at Richmond and Petersburg and the capture of Wilmington, North Carolina. *The Library of Congress.*

The fall of Richmond. Currier & Ives; *The Library of Congress.*

' MARRIAGE OF A COLORED SOLDIER AT VICKSBURG BY CHAPLAIN WARREN OF THE FREEDMEN'S BUREAU.

This engraving of a black Union soldier's wedding in Vicksburg, 1866, appeared in *Harper's Weekly. Courtesy of the American Social History Project, CUNY.*

Charleston's "Zion" School for Colored Children at the end of 1865. *From* Harper's Weekly, *courtesy of the American Social History Project, CUNY.*

Freedpeople discussing politics after the war. *From* Harper's Weekly, *courtesy of the American Social History Project, CUNY.*

Chapter Five

_____

"THE CLOUDS ARE DARK OVER US": THE CONVULSIONS OF 1863

January 1863 through April 1864

Even as conservative northerners and Confederates denounced Lincoln's Emancipation Proclamation as a crime against civilization, they also derided it as hypocritical and toothless. It was hypocritical, they said, because the supposedly antislavery president who issued it had carefully denied its benefits to slaves within the Union. Nor did the proclamation free any slaves in those parts of the Confederacy that Union troops had by then already reoccupied (including Tennessee, parts of both Virginia and Louisiana, and points along the Atlantic coast). "While the Proclamation leaves slavery untouched where his decree can be enforced," the anti-Republican *New York Herald* jeered, it "emancipates slaves where his decree cannot be enforced."[1] Many later commentators have repeated that dismissal.

But among those who said this at the time, the accusation of hypocrisy revealed either ignorance or dishonesty. The proclamation covered and excluded those it did because of its very nature as an extraordinary war measure, which Lincoln had issued in his capacity as commander in chief of national armies fighting to suppress violent rebellion. Lincoln believed that this circumstance, and it alone, allowed him to go beyond the powers that the federal Constitution assigned to a peacetime president. And such a war measure would be legitimate only in the war's theaters, not behind the lines, in secure sections of the Union.

As for its being an empty threat, Republicans pointed out that the proclamation was no less potent than the Declaration of Independence had been on the day that *it* was issued. As Massachusetts Republican William Robinson noted, "that old Declaration of July 4, 1776" seemed an empty boast for more than seven years following its promulgation— until, that is, the Continental army finally defeated the British and thereby made good on the declaration's promise. Until then, Robinson added, "many a mad wag among the Tories of that day had his jeer at it" with as much glee as the Confederacy now did at Lincoln's procla- mation.[2]

Robinson's comparison was telling. Like the Declaration of 1776, the Proclamation of 1863 immediately became a revolutionary banner borne—and the revolutionary policy enforced—by the army as it ad- vanced into enemy territory. And precisely because it came from the army's commander in chief, it significantly clarified federal policy and materially influenced the army's conduct. Abolition-minded Union of- ficers now felt vindicated, took heart, and pressed with greater confi- dence to implement the emancipation policy on the ground. And more recalcitrant, conservative-minded officers found it far more difficult to act on their proslavery inclinations.[3]

But Confederate loyalists ridiculed the proclamation on other grounds as well. It was no threat to either the Confederacy or slavery, they insisted. For one thing, the slaves would not respond to Lincoln's offer of freedom. They would not leave their masters, much less aid Union soldiers, because they did not *want* freedom, the loyalists main- tained. The slaves knew they needed those masters, and that knowl- edge left them satisfied with their lot. Therefore, a Virginia editor claimed, "the people of the South never felt the institution of slavery was ever safer than at the present time."[4] The *Richmond Dispatch* crossed the t's and dotted the i's. "No proclamation which the Yankees have issued or may issue will have the slightest effect upon the slave popula- tion of the South," its editor declared serenely, and "slavery will con- tinue intact and impregnable as the rock of Gibraltar."[5]

This was not a stance taken only in public. Masters wrote the same words in private—to one another as well as to themselves. Even as Katherine Stone cursed Lincoln's measure as a "diabolical move," she doubted in her diary that it would have much effect on her or her world.[6] John B. Jones, a popular novelist and journalist who had become a War

Department clerk, noted in his private journal in early January 1863 that, proclamation or no, slaves were continuing to work on fortifications around the Confederate capital. Surely that proved that southern blacks "have no faith in the efficacy of Lincoln's Emancipation." To be sure, Jones also knew that to Richmond's southeast, in Union-held Norfolk, thousands of black Virginians had just celebrated their newly gained freedom with an ecstatic parade. But Jones assured himself that before long those freedmen "will bewail their error."[7]

Confederate confidence in the first months of 1863 also drew upon belief that the coming year was full of promise for the slaveholders and their republic. Jefferson Davis was soon suggesting that it "will be the closing year of the war," and there seemed reason to think so.[8] On January 1, the same day that Lincoln issued his final Emancipation Proclamation, a combined Confederate naval and land force recaptured the Texas port city of Galveston, lost to the Union only a few months earlier. At the end of 1862's fighting season and again at the beginning of 1863's, Robert E. Lee's Army of Northern Virginia twice soundly and bloodily defeated the largest Union army in the field.

The first of those encounters took place at Fredericksburg, a small city of about five thousand souls on the Rappahannock River in northern Virginia. Ambrose Burnside, who had replaced George B. McClellan as commander of the Army of the Potomac, led his 114,000 troops to Fredericksburg as a first step in an intended advance against Richmond, some sixty miles due south. On the Union right, Burnside repeatedly hurled troops across open ground against an enemy that, though smaller (with about 74,000 men), was well positioned, well entrenched, and fully expecting the assaults. The result was a bloody catastrophe for the Union cause. George Washburn, a member of the 108th New York Volunteers, recalled that as his comrades advanced, "from houses, rifle-pits, barricades across the roads, and other shelter, the rebel sharpshooters . . . opened with fearful effect." The bloodied Union line staggered forward, but now "the vigor of the rebel artillery also steadily increased" until "a perfect storm of shot fell upon it . . . and in a short time acres of ground were covered with killed and wounded boys in blue." In short, "it was a great slaughter-pen." Some of Washburn's comrades cursed that "they might as well have tried to take Hell."[9]

Within six weeks of that debacle, command of the Union's luckless

Army of the Potomac changed hands again, with General Joseph Hooker now replacing Burnside. But neither the change in leadership nor the fact that the northern army enjoyed an even greater numerical advantage over Lee's than it had at Fredericksburg materially changed the outcome. In their next clash, in early May 1863, Lee achieved a brilliant and devastating victory on nearly the same ground, just ten miles to the west in a battle named after the crossroads village of Chancellorsville.

A northern reporter was present when Abraham Lincoln received the news about Chancellorsville, and he recorded the Union president's reaction to this sanguinary setback. With ashen face and wet eyes, Lincoln burst out, "My God! my God! what will the country say? What will the country say?"[10] Robert E. Lee's star rose higher than ever while Hooker's brief tenure as army commander soon ended.

For the Union war effort, prospects seemed little brighter on the other side of the Appalachians. There Ulysses S. Grant's critically important campaign against Vicksburg, Mississippi, was apparently bogging down.

Vicksburg's strategic location made it a major prize. It sat astride the Southern Mississippi Railroad that linked the big river to the Atlantic coast. The state capital of Jackson, just to Vicksburg's east, was a key rail connection between northern and southern sectors of the western war theater. Most important, continued Confederate control of the river ports of Vicksburg and Port Hudson, Louisiana (some 150 miles to the south), blocked the Union's freedom to freely navigate the Mississippi River for either military or commercial purposes.

Conversely, if Grant could take those two strongholds, then Arkansas, Texas, much of Louisiana, and the southern troops stationed there would find themselves cut off from the rest of the Confederacy and effectively sidelined for the rest of the war. General in Chief Henry W. Halleck quite rightly advised Grant that "the opening of the Mississippi River will be to us of more advantage than the capture of forty Richmonds." Both the Union and the Confederate publics understood Vicksburg's significance, which added morale, both military and civilian, to the Vicksburg campaign's stakes. As Halleck emphasized to Grant, "The eyes and hopes of the whole country are now directed to your army."[11]

In November, Grant divided that army in two, leading forty thousand troops from Tennessee down through western Mississippi while William Tecumseh Sherman led the remaining thirty thousand southward by way of the Mississippi River. But when Confederate cavalry forces under Earl Van Dorn and Nathan Bedford Forrest successfully broke Grant's supply and communication lines, that Union commander fell back toward his base. Sherman's forces, unaware of Grant's retreat, attacked the Confederates at Chickasaw Bayou, just north of the city, on their own. As he wrote afterward, Sherman "reached Vicksburg at the time appointed, landed, assaulted and failed."[12]

Grant and Sherman then reunited at Milliken's Bend, some fifteen miles northwest of Vicksburg, and tried to approach the city by water. But the terrain posed major problems of its own, and multiple, futile attempts to solve them with engineering schemes absorbed more than two more months. Much of the northern press loudly ground its teeth, and even Lincoln—who had placed great confidence in Grant—let it be known that he was growing quite "impatient." "If the rebels can blockade us on the Mississippi, which is a mile wide," he told a New York Tribune reporter, "they can certainly stop us on the little streams."[13] And in that case, how much more progress could the Union war effort, which had thus far depended so heavily on naval power, expect to make? After two bloody, devastating defeats in Virginia and with Grant's army now seemingly stalemated on the Mississippi, Union morale sank.

A sense that lives were being lost in a hopeless cause fed the rage that eventually erupted in bloody draft rioting in New York City.

The U.S. Congress passed a conscription act in March 1863, about a year after the Confederacy took the same step. The Union law provided for selecting draftees with an impartial lottery. But, similar to the Confederate version, it also permitted any man who could afford to do so the right to hire a substitute—or to pay a $300 commutation fee— instead of serving. In Chicago, a Union soldier's German-born father protested that "the patricians . . . need not think that only the sons of plebeians are fit and worthy to be slaughtered and that the wealthy can sidestep their obligations."[14]

Serious economic grievances stoked such class resentments. The demands of the war sharply cut into the supply of consumer goods while the paper currency printed to help pay for the war drove prices high. Poorly paid urban workers, who were disproportionately foreign born, suffered the worst.[15]

When the new draft law actually went into effect that summer, protests, often violent, erupted in cities across the North. By far the biggest and most destructive exploded in New York City. On Monday morning, July 13, 1863, a mass march against the law proceeded, generally peacefully, through the streets. But soon and during the days that followed, the city witnessed the bloodiest rioting the country had ever seen. Before it ended, an estimated one hundred people had died. Protestant missionaries, wealthy businessmen, draft officials, and Republican newspaper offices all felt the rioters' wrath. Class, ethnic, and racial passions combined to focus the rage of many against members of the city's defenseless black population, whom rioters blamed for the war. Mobs burned an orphanage for black children and attacked and lynched black men in the streets. It all suggested to Catherine Edmondston and doubtless many other white southerners that henceforth "Seward and Lincoln will . . . have their hands full in recruiting their army."[16]

During the month after Robert E. Lee's convincing May 1863 victory at Chancellorsville, Confederate anticipations of further triumphs mounted. After reinforcing, resting, and restructuring his Army of Northern Virginia, Lee led it in early June on its boldest raid yet into Union territory, this time not into a loyal slave state (like Maryland in 1862) but into a major free state—Pennsylvania.

Lee entertained great expectations for his Pennsylvania campaign. He hoped to draw Union troops away from both Richmond and the West, encourage France and England to assist the Confederate cause (at the very least by recognizing it diplomatically as an independent state), and demoralize and weaken the resolve of the Union populace.

The Army of the Potomac confronted Lee at the town of Gettysburg. The battle's first day ended in signal Confederate achievements; Union troops were driven from the town itself into defensive positions south of it. On the second day, however, dogged attempts to dislodge the federal troops from their entrenchments failed. On the third day, Lee—evidently convinced by earlier victories that his army could do nearly anything—launched some twelve thousand of his men across a mile of open field in the teeth of devastating musket and artillery fire. Within less than an hour, more than half of those men were dead, wounded, or missing. The next day, July 4, 1863, Lee's mangled army limped back across the Potomac.

Although it took a while to sink in, Gettysburg had been a disaster for the South. "It was a second Fredericksburg," a member of the Twenty-Sixth North Carolina regiment observed. "Only the wrong way."[17] Over the course of three days, the Army of Northern Virginia had suffered perhaps twenty-eight thousand casualties, depriving Lee of about a third of his force, including the same proportion of his generals. The army never fully recovered from this blow, which eventually compelled Lee to curb his preference for the offensive. And instead of demoralizing the Union, as Lee had expected, the battle's outcome energized it and deepened its hostility toward the South. Accurate reports that Lee's army had systematically hunted down black residents of Pennsylvania and then sent them southward into slavery did little to burnish Lee's reputation in the North.[18]

Meanwhile, in the western war theater, Ulysses S. Grant had at last hit upon a successful way to assault Vicksburg. In April 1863 he led his force south along the western shore of the Mississippi and crossed it below the city on transport ships. After a victory on May 1 at Port Gibson, Grant struck to the northeast, won a skirmish at the town of Raymond, and invested the state capital of Jackson on May 14. In the process, he cut Vicksburg's supply lines from the East. Then, pivoting westward, Grant defeated General John C. Pemberton's army in a series of encounters, driving it back into the city proper. In late May, after unsuccessfully attempting to storm its defenses, Grant laid siege to Vicksburg.

During the next seven weeks, both northerners and southerners kept their eyes fixed on the struggle for that city. Hopeful Confederates snatched at rumors repeatedly claiming that Grant's forces had been routed.[19] But on July 4, 1863, the same day that the Army of Northern Virginia retreated from Pennsylvania, Pemberton surrendered Vicksburg and his entire army, about thirty thousand strong. Four days later, Port Hudson fell as well, and Union troops occupied Natchez on July 13.[20] The Mississippi River and both of its banks were now firmly in Union hands.

The reports that Richmond received from elsewhere in the western theater were just as gloomy. In the summer and fall of 1863, Union forces completed a campaign that pushed Confederates across the face of Tennessee and then drove them out of the state entirely. At the beginning of August, Union general Ambrose Burnside led two corps through the Cumberland Mountains toward Knoxville in the overwhelmingly unionist eastern part of the state.

Confederate leaders had hoped that the Emancipation Proclamation would propel unionist east Tennessee masters into the Confederacy's arms. It did have that effect on slave owner Thomas A. R. Nelson, who now declared that "of all the acts of despotism" committed by either side during the war, "there is not one which in the slightest degree equals the atrocity and barbarism of Mr. Lincolns proclamation," which claims the right "to abolish slavery without our consent." Nelson had therefore decided "to join that side which at present affords the only earthly hope of successful resistance"—the Confederacy.[21] But few others followed his lead, least of all among the unionists' less wealthy rank and file.[22]

On September 2, 1863, Confederate forces evacuated Knoxville. That afternoon, Union cavalry colonel John W. Foster rode into the eastern Tennessee city with a small escort. "Men, women, and children rushed to the streets," Foster reported, the women "shouting, 'Glory! Glory!' 'The Lord be praised!' 'Our Savior's come!'" As for the men, the colonel continued, they "huzzahed and yelled like madmen, and in their profusion of greetings I was almost pulled from my horse." Throughout that afternoon and into the night "the streets resounded with yells, and cheers for the 'Union' and 'Lincoln.'" Banners bearing the Stars and Stripes, hidden away during the two years of Confederate occupation, reappeared.[23]

During the following days and weeks, many more east Tennesseans who had fled the region when the unionist uprising of November 1861 was put down returned to reclaim their lives and homes and rejoin families and friends. Now it was the turn of Confederate supporters to flee the region, seeking refuge in North Carolina, Virginia, and especially Georgia. Local whites who refused to swear an oath of allegiance to the Union often found themselves banished or sent far behind Union lines. Leading rebels in the region could find themselves jailed or made to work on Union fortifications.[24]

As Burnside was driving toward Knoxville, General William Rosecrans led another Union army that forced General Braxton Bragg's Army of Tennessee to retreat almost seventy miles from the middle of the state all the way to Chattanooga in the East. Along the way, Rosecrans's force, too, encountered unionists throwing off the Confederate yoke. Moving through up-country districts in February, Union general Joseph J. Reynolds ran across a band of men who had withdrawn into the hills to evade the Confederate draft. Spying Reynolds and his troops, the men now ran toward them. They "joined our column, expressing the greatest delight at our coming, and at beholding again what they emphatically called 'our flag.'"

It seemed to General Reynolds that these "generally illiterate" people did not "understand much about the present troubles." What exactly he found lacking in their view of the war is unclear. According to the general's own summary of their words, these Tennesseans resented the fact "that their more wealthy and better-informed neighbors insisted upon the poor people taking up arms to oppose the [federal] Government that they had been taught to love, and which had never oppressed them," in support of "a so-called Government which they knew only by the fact that they had been oppressed by it from its very beginning" and for the sake of people "whom they only knew by name and sight, as wealthy and overbearing, and for the defense . . . of a species of property with the possession of which they had never been burdened, and were not likely to be."[25]

Rosecrans's army drove Bragg's troops out of Chattanooga in September 1863 and then resumed the pursuit. At that point, however, the Union commander stumbled badly. In the battle of Chickamauga, some fifteen miles to the south, the South's Army of Tennessee, reinforced by divisions sent by two other Confederate forces, broke through a gap in Union lines and then routed the bluecoats, driving them back behind the Chattanooga defenses. Bragg's army then threw up siege lines around the city anchored in high ground to the east (Missionary Ridge) and southwest (Lookout Mountain).[26]

On November 26, 1863, Confederate secretary of war James A. Seddon crowed that Chickamauga, "one of the grandest victories of the war," had "relieve[d] all the more southern States from the dread of invasion and ravage" while reducing "the dismayed and shattered remnants of the enemy's grand army" to a state of "privation and suffer-ing."[27]

Unbeknownst to Seddon, however, the fruits of the Chickamauga triumph had already spoiled by the time he wrote these words. The Army of Tennessee was too small to fully surround Chattanooga and seal it off from reinforcements. Before long, General Grant relieved the siege with the aid of his own army plus two additional corps borrowed from the Army of the Potomac.

On November 25, 1863, the resulting Union force of some seventy-five thousand troops smashed through Confederate positions on the high ground outside the city. One Union division stormed up Lookout Mountain and hurled Confederate troops from its crest. Meanwhile, veterans of the Union defeat at Chickamauga, determined to reclaim their honor, charged straight up the steep north face of Missionary Ridge. They drove enemy soldiers they encountered on that charge up and over the top of the ridge so fast that they nearly trampled other Confederate troops dug in at the crest. Most of those gray-clad soldiers then scrambled in panic down the southern slope and into the Chicka-mauga valley, followed soon afterward by the remainder.[28]

This battle cost the Confederate Army of Tennessee six thousand casualties and drove it out of the trans-Appalachian war theater and into the chilly hills of northwestern Georgia.[29] Only a determined rear-guard defense, directed by Confederate general Patrick Cleburne, pre-vented the retreat from dissolving into an utter rout.

A chagrined southern journalist on the scene nonetheless thought it certainly the South's "most ignominious defeat" to date and found it hard to explain "how a defeat so complete could have occurred on ground so favorable."[30] One Confederate general had confidently de-clared during the battle that if his men couldn't fight at Missionary Ridge, they couldn't fight anywhere.[31] In the aftermath, W. A. Ste-phens of the Forty-Sixth Alabama drew the logical conclusion. "If we canot hold as good a place as the Misherary ridge," he wrote glumly, "we had as well quit."[32]

The major defeats at Gettysburg and Vicksburg in mid-1863 alarmed and depressed Confederate leaders and supporters alike. The secretary of war acknowledged to Jefferson Davis that "the campaign in Missis-

sippi was certainly disastrous" and had filled the public mind with a
"shock of despondency and foreboding of the consequences."[33] The soldiers of the Army of Northern Virginia were acutely aware of what they
had suffered in Pennsylvania, and Robert E. Lee offered to resign his
command.[34] Davis refused the offer, but rumors had Lee advising his
president that unless additional troops could be found, the South would
have "to make peace on the best terms we can."[35]

"The clouds are dark over us," Davis told associates, and he himself
felt "shrouded" in "the depths of . . . gloom."[36] Word of his depression
circulated through the capital.[37] The well-connected general Richard
Taylor (his father was former U.S. president Zachary Taylor; one of his
sisters had been Jefferson Davis's first wife) later recalled that it was at
this point that he and a number of other Confederate commanders first
perceived signs of eventual defeat.[38] Vice President Stephens had the
same premonition.[39] Coming only a few months after the debacles of
July, the humiliating defeat outside Chattanooga seemed almost gratuitous. Confederate ordnance chief Josiah Gorgas judged it "the worst
defeat we have had during the war."[40] It forced General Bragg to resign
his command. (Davis replaced him with Joseph Johnston.)[41]

Not long afterward, Mary Chesnut attended an elite ball in the
Confederate capital and there had a "long talk" with Secretary of State
Judah Benjamin and senators James L. Orr of South Carolina and
R.M.T. Hunter of Virginia. Their frank, pessimistic words and mood
shocked her. "These men speak out their thoughts plainly enough," she
recorded. "What they say means 'we are rattling down hill' " with " 'nobody to put on the brakes.' "[42]

The chill that Chesnut felt that night in Richmond was spreading
through the Confederacy.[43] Morale in the South's Army of Tennessee,
by then encamped in northern Georgia, plunged to new depths.[44]
Georgia governor Joseph E. Brown watched a "feeling of despondency"
take hold of his state's white population.[45] A prominent Alabama
planter thought public anxiety "unequaled since the Formation of our
Government."[46]

The Confederacy began the war convinced that God was on its side,
and since 1862 southern soldiers had found comfort and reassurance in
camp prayer meetings.[47] But especially during the second half of 1863
the worshipful voices raised there were increasingly infused with
alarm.[48] "I went into the last battle feeling that victory must be ours—

that such an army could not be foiled," dispirited Confederate soldier Randolph McKim wrote after Gettysburg. "Now I feel that unless He sees fit to bless our arms, our valor will not avail."[49] An ominous event seemed to capture those dangers and anxieties. One evening some Confederate Tennessee troops were praying near a tall hickory. Unbeknownst to them, the tree had earlier been ignited accidentally during the preparation of the campgrounds. It remained standing, but its trunk smoldered internally. As the troops conducted their service, the big tree suddenly burst into flames and collapsed, crushing ten soldiers beneath its weight.[50]

A growing number, both within and outside the army, began to wonder whether these martial blows and dark portents spoke of some deeper truths about the war and God's intentions therein. Georgia soldier William Stillwell soberly informed his wife in August 1863 that "unless the great God help us we are gone"—but "how can we expect Him to bless such a people as we"? Stillwell had "once believed in the justice of our cause," but the greed and selfishness that by now seemed everywhere left him regarding that cause as "a curse & not a blessing."[51] The doubts of Tennessee master Henry Craft went deeper. "If we adopt the theory that God intended the war to free the slaves," he reflected early in 1864, then "all the phenomena of the war harmonize and fall in with it most wonderfully."[52]

Craft's words point to the impact that Union military victories in 1863 had on slavery, especially in Tennessee and Mississippi. There and elsewhere, word of Lincoln's Emancipation Proclamation was spreading rapidly among the bondspeople. Union soldiers distributed about a million printed copies of the proclamation as they marched through the South. Mississippi planter James H. Maury found it "amazing with what intuitive familiarity the negroes recognized the moment of deliverance."[53] When Protestant minister James Freeman Clarke inspected a refugee camp in the nation's capital, he asked a black woman he met there whether news of Lincoln's recently issued proclamation had reached slaves in the Old Dominion. "We-all knows about it," the woman replied, "only we darsen't let on" around the masters. "We pretends not to know. I said to my ole massa, 'What's this Marse Lincoln is going to do to the poor nigger? I hear he is going to cut 'em up awful bad. How is it, massa?' I just pretended foolish, sort of."[54]

A federal provost marshal asked a group of captured Confederate officers what effect the proclamation was having. One replied ruefully that it "had played hell" with them. A number said they had first heard about it from their slaves. How could that be, asked the puzzled Union man, since so few slaves could read the proclamation's text?[55] The words of a black refugee in South Carolina spoke to the apparent mystery: "We'se can't read, but we'se can listen."[56]

The news reached illiterate slaves through many conduits. Some heard it from the lips of a Union soldier, or from the unusual slave who had managed to learn to read despite official prohibitions, or from a literate free black man or woman, or from the curses uttered by a Confederate master. And once the news reached a region, the slaves' "grapevine telegraph" could pass it along widely and quickly. In one district in Mississippi, the young George Washington Albright, then fifteen years old, moved from one plantation to another carrying word of the proclamation's existence. In each locale, as he later remembered, he "got together small meetings in the cabins to tell the slaves the great news. Some of these slaves in turn would find their way to still other plantations—and so the story spread."[57]

However it traveled, notice of Lincoln's proclamation helped transform the trickle of fugitives of 1861 and 1862 into a flood. Some three thousand contrabands had reached Fort Monroe by the end of 1862. During the first five months of 1863, that number more than tripled, to ten thousand.[58] Even the Confederate White House was affected. Jefferson Davis's wife, Varina, acknowledged that after the Emancipation Proclamation "the condition of our servants" became "unsettled."[59] That was putting it mildly. Jefferson Davis's personal servant and Varina Davis's maid together "decamped" toward the Yankees in January 1864. Another servant tried to torch the presidential mansion.[60]

As Union armies pressed forward, they began to put Lincoln's revolutionary policy into action, and nowhere with more dramatic effect than in the plantation-rich Mississippi valley. In January 1863, Ulysses S. Grant and William Tecumseh Sherman united their forces at Milliken's Bend and Young's Point, about twenty miles north of Vicksburg in Louisiana's Madison Parish. In search of food and other material, Union foraging parties now began to comb through the environs of Katherine Stone's Brokenburn plantation. And as they moved, they spread the word of freedom.[61] From one plantation after another, black laborers made their way to the Union camp. In some cases, they returned shortly to the plantations—but now as guides for Union soldiers looking for food and other supplies.[62] "The country seems possessed by demons, black and white," Stone exclaimed indignantly.[63] Months before Vicksburg's fall, its Confederate commander, John C. Pemberton, learned by telegram that in northern Mississippi "the negroes on divers plantations [have] taken possession and driven owners away."[64] In March 1863, Union ships and troops crisscrossed the area as they prepared to move against Vicksburg itself. Wherever they went, black people took heart.

The same was true on the Louisiana side of the river. Katherine's mother, Amanda Stone, got a close look at this change in temperament one day when she summoned a troublesome servant named Jane, intending to reprimand her. Jane duly appeared, but "with a big carving knife in her hand and fire in her eyes" and displaying "a very surly, aggressive temper." That night, Jane, her two children, and a man owned by a neighboring planter slipped away and headed for a Union encampment.[65]

Then, during the third week in March, two Union soldiers presented themselves at Brokenburn itself. After the visit, Katherine initially recorded with satisfaction that "the Negroes all behaved very well," including Webster, "our most trusted servant." Some of them remained out of sight, as they had been instructed, and the rest showed not "the slightest disposition to go with them, though the Yankees asked them to go."[66]

Nevertheless, the Stone family, judging that "the sword of Damocles in a hundred forms is suspended over us," decided to leave Louisiana and head west to calmer Texas.[67] As they prepared to depart, Jane's defiant independence began to manifest itself among the rest of Brokenburn's labor force. Servants and laborers alike now hardly bothered to conceal their excitement and impatience. So while most of them still "behaved well enough," Katherine Stone now noted, "you could see it was only because they knew we would soon be gone. We were only on sufferance. Two days longer and we think they would all have gone to the Yankees, most probably robbing and insulting us before we left."[68]

Moving at night by horse and wagon, the Stone party reached a railroad station where the family encountered other masters in the same situation.[69] Katherine found the scene heart-wrenching. Here were her illustrious neighbors, accustomed to comfort, ease, and deference. They had only yesterday owned "princely estates and hundreds of Negroes."

Now they were driven from their finery and mansions with nothing but "the clothes they have on"—along, perhaps, with only "ten or twenty of their hands."[70]

As Union troops moved into a region, many masters tried to send or bring their slaves into the Confederate interior, a practice that became known as "refugeeing." By late 1862, some 150,000 slaves had been refugeed into Texas alone.[71] The Stones, too, had taken enslaved servants with them, including the dependable Webster. But on the road Webster discarded his mask of docile devotion. Managing to separate himself momentarily from the rest of the party, he found a horse and rode back to Brokenburn, where he rejoined the community of servants and laborers who now claimed the plantation as their own.[72]

As it did in Louisiana, Grant's army carried emancipation with it wherever it went. The Mississippi planter James H. Maury felt the effects when Grant's forces captured Port Gibson, Mississippi, on May 1, 1863. Upon the arrival of Union troops, Maury fumed, most of his slaves departed "at once."[73] When federal soldiers took Jackson a few weeks later, so planter and diarist Edmund Ruffin heard, three thousand slaves promptly abandoned masters in the surrounding county.[74] And when Grant's army finally marched into Vicksburg at the start of July, black people poured into the streets to cheer.[75]

The capitulation of Vicksburg and then of Port Hudson finally removed Confederate military power from the Mississippi River and its valley. And, as Robert Toombs had foreseen, that Union achievement cost the Confederacy not only its link to Texas, Arkansas, and western Louisiana but also a "vast number of slaves on both sides" of the river.[76] In the days and weeks that followed the seizure of Vicksburg, tens of thousands of slaves from the countryside sought sanctuary in this new center of Union power. The Union commander in Natchez, too, watched refugees stream into that city "by thousands."

Plantation mistress Fanny E. Connor wailed that whole stretches of the Mississippi River valley quickly became "almost depopulated of negroes."[77] On plantations where rebel masters stayed in place, many black workers now refused to either follow orders or leave the premises. Remaining on the land, they subsisted on whatever produce and cattle Union soldiers did not seize.[78] When planter A. M. Paxton ordered his former slave Israel to perform a previously routine task, the man looked him in the eye and replied, "Mr. Paxton, I want to tell you that that thing is played out."[79] Elsewhere, black people did what servants and laborers on Brokenburn had already done—appropriated and farmed lands that fleeing masters had abandoned. Those estates then became places of succor for other freedpeople.[80]

William J. Minor, one of the wealthiest planters in the Natchez region, found the laborers on one of his plantations "completely demoralised—They are practically free—going, coming, and working when they please." Moreover, he noted in amazement, "the most of them think, or pretend to think that the plantation and every thing on it belongs to them."[81] Things were no better on Minor's other estates, where most of the workforce was refusing to follow orders by February 1863. Minor confronted one of them, Isaac Simpson, and demanded that he do as he was told. In response, Simpson took out a knife and began sharpening it on a brick. Minor followed him and asked Simpson what he was doing. Simpson coolly replied that "he was sharpening his knife to *cut his nails*." (The ironic emphasis was Minor's.)[82] A few months later another bondsman broke into Minor's house on that plantation, took money, and threatened two white men.[83]

In the spring of 1864, Union general Nathaniel Banks undertook a campaign along the Red River in northwestern Louisiana. Like McClellan's march across the Virginia peninsula two years earlier, this campaign proved a dismal failure militarily. But as Banks's troops moved through the river counties, they left slavery in tatters. Once again, blacks cheered their appearance. An Illinois soldier recorded that "one group of col'd girls welcomed us with waving of handkerchiefs, bonnets and aprons and a song and a hurra for Lincoln too."[84] Federal troops stripped plantations of movable property, including many male slaves of military age. Those who remained on the land, one planter griped, became "insolent & refractory, and . . . are more trouble & vexation than they are of use."[85]

As noted, the Emancipation Proclamation did not formally apply to either Tennessee or parts of southern Louisiana that were already in federal hands before the start of 1863. But slavery was steadily collapsing there nonetheless. Catherine Edmondston learned as much in August 1863 from her sister, Honoria Cannon, who lived in a part of western Tennessee that the Union had by then controlled for a year.

"All of our negroes have left," Cannon complained, and those who still nominally owned slaves found that their "negro property is worse than useless for they do no work unless they choose & the owners dare not correct them," for "they keep the Federals informed of everything."[86]

As Union soldiers swept through middle and eastern Tennessee in the summer and fall of 1863, slavery began to break down all along the route. Here, too, slaves seemed well informed of military events. A Chattanooga editor noted that "the spirits of the colored citizens rise and fall with the ebb and flow of this tide of blue devils," and when "the whites are depressed and go about the streets like mourners," the blacks appear "glad as larks."[87]

When northern armies reached Knoxville and Chattanooga, slaves from the countryside began making their way toward them.[88] Although the Emancipation Proclamation excluded Tennessee, slavery no longer enjoyed the active, enthusiastic support of and enforcement by those who now wielded political power. It had lost, in other words, precisely the monopoly of violence that its champions always knew was essential to its survival. In January 1864, William Tecumseh Sherman judged that "slavery is already dead in Tennessee." Where "a negro . . . can run off without danger of recapture," he observed, "the question is settled."[89] The same might have been said of other parts of the Confederacy in the hands of Union armies, including counties in eastern Arkansas, western Mississippi, eastern and southern Louisiana, northeastern Virginia, and coastal North Carolina.

Jeers about the supposed impotence of Union emancipationist policies rang all the more hollow as slavery began to buckle not only where Union troops went but even in parts of the Confederacy they had not yet reached. Hearing that northern soldiers were even in the vicinity increased the boldness of black laborers while simultaneously weakening the self-confidence of their masters. Laborers began working more slowly, less intensively, and sometimes for fewer hours—or began to spend more and more of their time tending food crops for their own consumption. Hungry slaves were now also more likely to seize foodstuffs from their masters' storehouses or kitchens.

As their ability to intimidate shrank, especially where flight to Union lines became a real option for slaves, some masters found it advisable to make concessions to their laborers.[90] This had first become apparent when Union forces seized Port Royal, South Carolina, in 1861. Con-

federate authorities on the still-secure mainland, fearing slave flight to
the enemy offshore, counseled rice planters on the nearby Savannah
River to avoid "extreme coercive measures with the negroes except in
cases of dire necessity" so as to "quell the uneasy feeling at present
among that class of our population."[91]

But reports of Confederate setbacks and Union emancipation policy
spread among the slaves even in regions far from the front lines via
slaves from farms and plantations closer to the fighting whose masters
had transported ("refugeed") them inland. Masters in the interior
began to object to the practice. As one Virginia legislator put it, "refugeeing" exposed their own slaves to the influence of men and women
who had seen and perhaps had even spoken with Union soldiers—men
and women who thereby "had become imbued by the enemy with ideas
and habits" that were not "consistent with the obedience and subordination proper to their condition and necessary to the peace and safety
of the whites."[92]

Here, too, some masters began grudgingly to bid for their slaves'
work. Mississippi slaveholder George Gorman had to offer his laborers
half of whatever cotton they would raise on his land. Other masters felt
driven to offer cash rewards, shorter work hours, or greater freedom of
movement. In some cases, they promised to free their slaves outright at
a later date. Even some Confederate army officers found themselves
having to bargain with enslaved military laborers to keep them from
"absconding."[93]

Most slave owners greeted their sudden loss of accustomed mastery
with outrage and vituperation. This was not merely an economic blow;
it was a challenge to and rejection of their most basic views, values, and
identities. Their "people" had betrayed them—had repaid their masters' many kindnesses with treason. They had proved themselves to be,
indeed, immoral wretches without loyalty or conscience. "As to the idea
of a *faithful servant, it is all a fiction,*" wrote Honoria Cannon, Catherine
Edmondston's sister, in the late summer of 1863. "I have seen the fa-
vourite and most petted negroes the first to leave in every instance." She
was "so disgusted" with "the whole race," in fact, "that I often wish I
had never seen *one.*"[94]

Cannon now wished "sometimes" that "there was not a negro left in the country." The whites would certainly be better off without them, "tho the learning to do our own work," she admitted, "would be hard."[95] Few other former masters found that prospect inviting, either, including the Tennessee mistress who could not "see how we are to get through the winter for I do *hate* to work."[96] The same was true of the Louisiana planter family that Katherine Stone heard about in March 1863. Discovering one morning that almost all of their seventy-five slaves had fled, they realized unhappily that they now "actually had to get up and get breakfast" for themselves.[97]

More and more whites, Confederate as well as Union, now came to wonder how slavery could possibly survive the war. Too many black southerners had won their freedom. Too many others, previously resigned to their servitude, had formed hopes, expectations, and determinations that were incompatible with slavery. Too many of them were pulling hard at their chains.

Some Union generals recognized the implications. Within two months of occupying Vicksburg, Ulysses S. Grant mused that trying to reimpose slavery throughout the South would prove a daunting task even if the Confederate states were to reenter a Union based on the "constitution as it was." "Slavery is dead and cannot be resurrected," he wrote. "It would take a standing Army to maintain slavery in the South if we were to make peace to-day guaranteeing to the South all their former constitutional privileges."[98]

The more perceptive, less blinkered slave owners and their politicians began grudgingly to recognize such truths. North Carolina senator William A. Graham supposed in September 1863 "that two years more of war will (whatever be its event) destroy the institution of slavery."[99] Georgia's Margaret Daily would have found that estimate optimistic. She already considered slavery "well nigh done for."[100] A Georgia editor reported in August 1863 that "thousands of men in Georgia, Alabama, and Mississippi look upon slavery as doomed" whether the Confederacy survived or not.[101] The Confederate vice president's brother Linton Stephens agreed with them. "I believe that the institution of slavery is already so undermined and demoralized," he wrote a confidant in October 1863, that it would never again "be of much use to us, even if we had independence to day."[102]

Developments along the Atlantic coast could only reinforce such views. While Grant was mounting his campaign against Vicksburg during the first half of 1863, black soldiers based on the South Carolina sea islands tried to bring emancipation to the Confederate seaboard. Aiming to establish a sanctuary on the mainland for fugitives from nearby farms and plantations, black soldiers from the First and Second regiments of the South Carolina Volunteers landed on northern Florida's coast in February and March, capturing the town of Jacksonville. Their success helped to demonstrate to Lincoln and his cabinet that blacks could indeed make able soldiers and to spur large-scale black recruitment at the end of March.[103] In May, the Union's War Department created a Bureau of Colored Troops to supervise that work.

Black men responded to the new Union policy in various ways. Some, having accepted the idea that this was a white man's war, declined to participate. Attempts by Union officers to recruit them by brute force alienated others.[104] So did the initial refusal to commission black men as officers and especially the insulting policy of paying black soldiers less than white ones—a policy abandoned only in June 1864.

But black abolitionists threw themselves into the recruitment work. "By every consideration which binds you to your enslaved fellow countrymen, and the peace and welfare of your country," Frederick Douglass exhorted an audience in Rochester, New York, "by every aspiration which you cherish for the freedom and equality of yourselves and your children; by all the ties of blood and identity which make us one with the brave black men now fighting our battles in Louisiana and in South Carolina, I urge you to fly to arms, and smite with death the power that would bury the government and your liberty in the same hopeless grave."[105] Adjutant General Lorenzo Thomas went to Mississippi to encourage and direct the process there, recruiting many future soldiers straight out of the refugee camps. By December 1863, more than twenty thousand black men had filled thirty new regiments. An additional fifteen to seventeen thousand black soldiers enlisted in southern Louisiana with General Benjamin Butler and his successor in command, General Nathaniel P. Banks. Still more former slaves were joining up in Tennessee and Missouri.[106] General Edward A. Wild, another Massachusetts abolitionist, began in the spring of 1863 to form an "African Brigade" made up of freedmen in Virginia and North Carolina.[107]

The U.S. Congress's decision in the spring of 1862 to cease enforcing the fugitive slave law allowed Garland White to return to the United States. In 1863, White became the pastor of a black Methodist congregation in Toledo. After the Lincoln administration initiated the organization of black regiments, White began recruiting to them in Ohio as well as Indiana, New York, and Massachusetts. He played a particularly active role in building the Twenty-Eighth Regiment of the U.S. Colored Infantry. Later that year White joined that regiment as a private and was soon serving as its acting chaplain.

By then the African American newspaper reporter George H. Stephens had joined in the work of forming the Fifty-Fourth Massachusetts regiment. Black churches hosted mass meetings early that spring where Stephens exhorted male listeners to sign up. After all, he said, "we have more to gain, if victorious, or more to lose, if defeated, than any other class of men." So if we do not place "our interests, our arms, and our lives" in "the balance against oppression, treason, and tyranny," he told a Philadelphia crowd in April, "we do not deserve the name of freeman."[108] Stephens led by example, joining the Fifty-Fourth as a private, before long being promoted to sergeant in the regiment's Company B. The words he uttered resonated with his audiences. A black Pennsylvanian who remembered the whipping of both his mother and sister at the hands of southern masters was ready "to go down and whip them."[109]

Most Confederates continued to shrug it all off. "It would astonish our 'Northern brethren,'" Catherine Edmondston thought, were they to "know how little" she and others feared black soldiers.[110] Edmondston *knew* that "Cuffee wont fight. He is afraid of cold iron & shot terrifies him."[111] The Confederate War Department clerk John B. Jones was equally unperturbed. If the North enlisted black soldiers, he predicted confidently, "we shall get their arms."[112] Surely, a New Orleans editor presumed, "the unfitness of the negro for military service" must be "known to everybody." After all, "the inferiority of the negro, his natural dullness and cowardice, his great indolence, and his awe of the white man" was common knowledge. And if all that wasn't enough to make the South rest easy, he went on, there was the fact that "the vast majority of negroes are contented with their situation in life."[113] Such stalwarts waved away mounting evidence to the contrary; asked to choose between those reports and beliefs deeply held and central to their entire worldview, they chose the latter.[114]

Quite a few northerners seemed almost as slow to grasp the emerg-
ing truth. Even after black troops proved themselves at Jacksonville,
Florida, the Lincoln government continued to restrict most of them to
support labor and other rear-echelon tasks, such as manning Union
installations and base camps, in order to release more white troops for
frontline fighting. But even such duty could plunge black soldiers directly into murderous combat.

That is what happened on June 7, 1863, about a month before Vicksburg's fall. About three weeks into the siege of the city, a brigade of
some fifteen hundred Texas infantrymen assaulted the thirteen hundred federal troops—including members of one white regiment (the
Twenty-Third Iowa) and three black ones (the Ninth and Eleventh
Louisiana and the First Mississippi)—who defended Grant's base
camp at Milliken's Bend, Louisiana. The defenders had dug in on the
levee some 150 yards west of the Mississippi's bank. Most of the men
in the black units had been laboring in cotton fields shortly before and
were as yet barely trained. They had received arms only days earlier.

When the Confederate troops attacked, ferocious hand-to-hand
fighting ensued, waged with bayonet blades and muskets wielded like
clubs. At last the Texans managed to break through the left side of the
Union line and, flanking the rest, drove the defenders back to the river.
But there, using the river's bank for cover, Union soldiers held off their
enemies until northern gunboats arrived to help persuade the Texans to
retreat.

The black soldiers' performance under fire at Milliken's Bend impressed white observers, northerners and southerners alike. During the
rebels' initial assault, a white Union officer marveled as one especially
large black soldier "passed me like a rocket" and "with the fury of a
tiger . . . sprang into that gang and smashed everything before him."
Having broken his musket stock in the process, the man then laid into
the enemy with the barrel alone and with it continued "smashing in
every head he could reach." At last the Texans surrounded him, yelling
"Shoot that big nigger, shoot that big nigger," until one of them finally
managed to do so.

Union colonel Hermann Lieb later remembered that "not until they
were overpowered and forced from their position" by fierce enfilading
fire "were the blacks driven back" from the levee. In his own subsequent report, the Texas infantry commander, General Henry E. McCul-

loch, claimed that the white Union troops "ran like whipped curs almost as soon as the charge was ordered." But "the negro portion of the enemy's force" resisted "with considerable obstinacy."[115]

Katherine Stone received news of the clash at Milliken's Bend from Confederate troops wounded in the fighting there. But she found it hard to believe "that Southern soldiers—and Texans at that—have been whipped by a mongrel crew of white and black Yankees." Surely her informants were wrong. Told that "the Negro regiments fought there like mad demons," she simply refused to believe it. "We know from long experience they are cowards. . . . There must," she insisted, "be some mistake."[116]

The only mistake was the one made by Stone and others like her, who clung stubbornly to their long-cherished certainty that black people would not—and could not—fight to gain their freedom. Growing numbers of white soldiers, both Union and Confederate, had the testimony of their own eyes to prove the contrary.

Black Union soldiers serving in the Vicksburg campaign had fought their first major battle a couple of weeks before Milliken's Bend, at the end of May 1863. Regiments of free blacks and freedmen formed in New Orleans mounted three assaults in one day on Port Hudson, which then still anchored the southern end of the last Confederate-held stretch of the Mississippi River. Those attacks failed, but there, too, the courage that the black troops showed left a deep impress upon whites who saw them in action.[117] "No troops," General Nathaniel Banks reported, could have been "more determined or more daring."[118] Another white officer agreed. "You have no idea how my prejudices with regard to negro troops have been dispelled by the battle the other day," he wrote. "The brigade of negroes behaved magnificently and fought splendidly; could not have done better. They are far superior in discipline to the white troops, and just as brave."[119]

Some 750 miles to the east, a Union force too small for the task was struggling to capture Charleston harbor. The Fifty-Fourth Massachusetts regiment joined the effort in July. Three of the regiment's companies seized a position on one of the sea islands south of the harbor and tenaciously defended it against a surprise counterattack. That defense saved a white Union regiment from encirclement and destruction. As at Milliken's Bend, the black soldiers fended off their attackers long enough for Union naval forces to arrive and turn the battle's tide.[120]

Three days later, on July 18, 1863, the Fifty-Fourth Massachusetts spearheaded an assault on Battery Wagner, a formidable earthen fortification that formed an important part of the harbor's defenses.[121] At dusk the black soldiers surged forward through a narrow approach. Sergeant George Stephens recalled that the enemy "withheld their fire until we reached within fifty yards of the work." Then, suddenly, "jets of flame darted forth from every corner of the embrasure." But the fusillades did not stop the charge. As the advanced ranks fell, the soldiers massed behind rushed forward, even over the bodies of their fallen comrades.

This desperate but hopeless charge was ultimately driven back, and the fighting that day took a terrible toll on the black regiment.[122] Almost half of its men were killed, taken prisoner, or wounded—and the Fifty-Fourth's wounded suffered grievously. After most Civil War engagements, opposing armies allowed each other to retrieve and minister to injured soldiers. Confederate officers at Battery Wagner refused the same minimal consideration to black Union troops, whose bodies therefore remained torn and bleeding on the field through the whole night after the fighting.[123] The Confederate commander, General Johnson Hagood, ordered the Fifty-Fourth's fallen white colonel, Robert Gould Shaw, to be buried in a mass grave with dead black troops. Hagood considered this a fitting way to shame the dead officer. But Shaw's father, a longtime abolitionist, saw things differently. "We can imagine no holier place than that in which he is, among his brave and devoted followers, nor wish for him better company. . . . What a body-guard he has!"[124]

Three months earlier, in April 1863, Union troops mustered in Kansas captured and held Fort Gibson, on the Arkansas River, thereby menacing Confederate power in the so-called Indian Territory (today's Oklahoma). In July, nine thousand Confederate troops, white Texans and Indians, massed at nearby Honey Springs to prepare an assault on the fort. A second Union force of about three thousand white, Indian, and black troops launched a preemptive attack against the Confederate encampment on July 17. The Union commander, General James G. Blunt, placed the First Kansas Colored Infantry regiment at the center of his line, giving it the job of leading the line forward. After more than two hours of fierce combat, the Confederate soldiers fled the field, thereby leaving the Indian Territory north of the Arkansas River in

Union hands.[125] "The question that negroes will fight is settled," General Blunt declared. Indeed, he added, "they make better soldiers in every respect than any troops I have ever had under my command."[126]

Despite his deepening disenchantment with border-state slave owners, Abraham Lincoln at first hesitated to authorize full-scale recruitment of black soldiers in the loyal border states of Maryland and Missouri or in Tennessee (which, like them, had been exempted from the Emancipation Proclamation's provisions).[127]

But the tide of events and ideas soon washed away this self-limiting policy, too. In October 1863, an order from the federal Adjutant General's Office welcomed free blacks from Missouri, Maryland, and Tennessee into the army's ranks. It also initiated the enlistment and emancipation of slaves owned by both disloyal masters and those loyal ones who gave their consent. Slaves owned even by recalcitrant loyal masters would be permitted to join if the rest of these measures failed to yield a "sufficient" number of black troops within a month's time.[128]

Lincoln remained chary enough about alienating Kentucky masters to keep slave recruitment off limits there even after it began in Missouri and Maryland. To evade those restrictions, many black Kentuckians made their way into northern states, where they joined regiments formed by free blacks. Others moved *southward* from the Bluegrass State into Union-occupied parts of Tennessee and, claiming to be owned by Confederate masters in that state, joined black regiments mustering there. By early 1864, the steady erosion of slavery throughout the loyal border states was as difficult to miss as it was in Union-occupied portions of the Confederacy.

That spring saw Washington at last begin formally recruiting both free and enslaved African Americans throughout Kentucky as well.[129] Black Kentuckians responded so readily—between one and two hundred enlisting every day—that they at first overwhelmed the recruiters' ability to process them. By mid-September 1864, the Union had enrolled fourteen thousand black soldiers there with another six thousand expected by the end of October. When William Tecumseh Sherman, a consistent opponent of black recruitment, questioned the quality of those recruits, General Lorenzo Thomas snapped that the new black regiments were filling up with "the very best class of men." Given "a month's drill," he added, he would "put the two regiments of cavalry in competition with any white cavalry in this whole country."[130]

Black soldiers understood their cause. "We are fighting for liberty and right," one sergeant explained, "and we intend to follow the old flag while there is a man left to hold it up to the breeze of heaven. Slavery must and shall pass away."[131] " 'Fore I would be a slave 'gain, I would fight till de last drop of blood was gone," a middle-aged black sergeant named Spencer told his comrades in Mississippi in the summer of 1863.[132] The words of a poem by Oliver Wendell Holmes, published in a Boston paper in August 1862, became an especially popular song among black troops:

Where are you going, soldiers,
With banner, gun and sword?
We're marching south to Canaan
To battle for the Lord.
What Captain leads your armies
Along the rebel coasts?
The mighty One of Israel,
His name is Lord of Hosts.

To Canaan, to Canaan,
The Lord has led us forth,
To blow before the heathen walls
The trumpets of the North.[133]

With the erosion of slavery in and near Union-held regions and the success of black regiments in 1863 and 1864, some Confederate partisans began to face squarely the toll that the war had taken on slavery and the successes that their enemy's emancipationist policy was registering. One of these partisans was General Patrick Cleburne of the Army of Tennessee.

Having been driven out of Chattanooga at the end of 1863, that army licked its wounds in winter quarters at Dalton, in northwest Georgia. After protecting the retreat, Cleburne and his division camped at nearby Tunnel Hill, where the general spent much of December pondering what the Confederacy could do to stave off the defeat and destruction that the future now appeared to hold.

An attorney in civilian life, Cleburne produced a lengthy, carefully reasoned memorandum stressing the South's inadequate supply of soldiers, as a result of which "our soldiers can see no end . . . except in our own exhaustion; hence, instead of rising to the occasion, they are sinking into a fatal apathy, growing weary of hardships and slaughters which promise no results." The only way to supply the Confederacy with the combat forces so sorely required, Cleburne concluded, was to "immediately commence training a large reserve of the most courageous of our slaves, and . . . guarantee freedom within a reasonable time to every slave in the South who shall remain true to the Confederacy in this war."

To justify his iconoclastic proposal, Cleburne went on to coldly review the condition to which the war had reduced slavery by the end of 1863. Slavery, he wrote, has become "our most vulnerable point, a continued embarrassment, and in some respects an insidious weakness" as well as "a source of great strength to the enemy." "All along the lines," Cleburne specified, "slavery is comparatively valueless to us for labor, but of great and increasing worth to the enemy for information," an "omnipresent spy system, pointing out our valuable men to the enemy, revealing our positions, purposes, and resources."

The slave population, the general frankly acknowledged, had proven hostile to the Confederate cause and firm in its support for the Union. Nor, he added, was there anything mysterious about those loyalties. "For many years, ever since the agitation of the subject of slavery commenced, the negro has been dreaming of freedom, and his vivid imagination has surrounded that condition with so many gratifications that it has become the paradise of his hopes." The Union had won the slaves' loyalty precisely by promising them that freedom.

The black population's increasingly obvious pro-Union sentiments, meanwhile, were undermining morale in the white South. They stirred "fear of insurrection in the rear" and filled Confederate soldiers with "anxieties for the fate of loved ones when our armies [have] moved forward." And when Union forces entered plantation districts, they found "recruits awaiting the enemy with open arms." There was no point denigrating their military record, either. After donning Union blue, black men had proved able "to face and fight bravely against their former masters."[134]

Cleburne circulated his memo among the officers in his command, at which point four brigade commanders, ten regimental commanders, and one cavalry division commander added their signatures to it. The general then requested and received the chance to present his views to the rest of the army's leadership. On the evening of January 2, 1864, Cleburne rode into its main encampment, where he read his memo at a meeting of corps and division commanders.[135]

A few of those present seconded Cleburne's arguments. But most angrily rejected and repudiated both the diagnosis and prescription. In the eyes of Cleburne's opponents, suggesting that they emancipate and mobilize black men was blasphemous and treasonous. It insulted almost everything that they fervently believed about race, law, God, custom, and their economy's most basic demands. Cleburne's "propositions contravene principles upon which I have heretofore acted," General William B. Bate portentously proclaimed. The memo proposes "to discard our recieved theory of government [and] destroy our legal institutions and social relations."[136] Jefferson Davis and his cabinet rejected Cleburne's proposal shortly afterward.

The slaveholding republic, compelled to address its developing crisis, had made a decision. It would not respond to slavery's disintegration by bidding for black southerners' loyalty and service. It would count instead on force, as it had always done. Davis decreed that "all negro slaves captured in arms" would be turned over to officials, who would then return them to slavery. Their officers would be treated as criminals attempting to incite slave insurrection, a crime punishable by death.[137]

Over time, the Confederate army took on much of the policing work previously assigned to civilian slave patrols.[138] Some soldiers took to disguising themselves as Union troops in order to ferret out "disloyal" black people, slave and free. In the summer of 1863, for example, southern cavalry scouts impersonating Union soldiers approached a middle-aged free black man named Samuel Hargrave and asked him to point out the location of southern troops. When Hargrave offered to do so, the Confederate soldiers whipped him and threw him in jail. Confederate troops employed the same ruse in Georgia, and a South Carolina slave caught in a similar trap was immediately hanged.[139]

The South's soldiers took their most brutal revenge on blacks in—or after—battle. A young Confederate officer named John W. Graham told his father that as his troops had marched through North Carolina, white women had called out, urging them to "kill the negroes." But, Graham added, his brigade "did not need" that encouragement in order "to make them give 'no quarter.'" It was already "understood amongst us that we take no negro prisoners."[140]

Southern soldiers put that understanding into practice in April 1864 at Fort Pillow in western Tennessee, some forty miles north of Memphis. There General Nathan Bedford Forrest led between 1,500 and 2,000 Confederate cavalrymen in an assault that overwhelmed a Union force about half as large. The fort's garrison was made up in about equal parts of white Tennessee unionists and black recruits from the ranks of former slaves in Tennessee and Mississippi.

Many of Forrest's men refused to allow Union soldiers to capitulate, massacring them after they had thrown down their weapons or raised their arms in surrender. The carnage was twice as bad among black troops as among white. "God damn you," one southern soldier raged. "You are fighting against your master."

"The slaughter was awful," Confederate sergeant Achilles V. Clark subsequently recalled. "Words cannot describe the scene. The poor, deluded, negroes would run up to our men[,] fall upon their knees, and with uplifted hands scream for mercy but they were ordered to their feet and then shot down. . . . Their fort turned out to be a great slaughter pen."[141] Some of the black soldiers were lined up and executed, firing-squad style. Others were gored repeatedly with bayonets or hacked to death with sabers. Wounded men discovered in the fort's hospital beds were murdered where they lay.

Soldier James Madison Brannock was one of many who celebrated the massacre. He was "glad that Forrest had it in his power to execute such swift & summary vengeance upon the negroes."[142] Forrest himself subsequently denied any wrongdoing and had his adjutant charge "dastardly Yankee reporters" with fabricating the massacre's accounts out of whole cloth.[143] But Forrest also boasted that after the battle the Mississippi River was "dyed with the blood of the slaughtered for 200 yards." Perhaps, he suggested, what had occurred there "will demonstrate to the northern people that negro soldiers cannot cope with Southerners."[144]

In the days following the Fort Pillow bloodbath, Confederate troops executed black Union captives at Plymouth, North Carolina, and at Poison Springs, Arkansas, where they reportedly drove wagons back and forth across the bodies of wounded black troops. "Repeat Fort Pillow," the *Richmond Examiner* urged the troops. "Repeat Plymouth a few more times and we shall bring the Yankees to their senses."[145]

Widespread agreement with that idea explains the aftermath of a fierce battle fought a few months earlier at Olustee, in northern Florida.[146] Before that February 1864 clash began, Confederate colonel Abner McCormick told his men that the force opposing them was "made up largely of negroes from Georgia and South Carolina, who have come to steal, pillage, run over the state, and murder, kill, and rape our wives, daughters and sweethearts." "Let's teach them a lesson," he proposed. He, for one, would "not take any negro prisoners in this fight." When the day's fighting had ended, the main Union force was in retreat. But a white Georgia cavalryman passing over the battlefield could still hear "firing going on in every direction." A junior officer explained the mysterious sounds to him; his men were killing black Union prisoners. Or, in the officer's own words, they were "shooting niggers Sir."[147]

Chapter Six

BOUND FOR "A LAND THEY KNEW NOT": AFTER SLAVERY, WHAT?

1862 through 1864

As the war raged, the erosion of bondage confronted both camps with a host of problems, practical as well as ideological. The Confederacy's enemies soon faced a particularly pressing question: What would become of the men, women, and children who had already ceased to be slaves? To put this another way: If the Union had now embarked upon a revolutionary road, where exactly did that road lead? Full and final answers would come only once the war ended. But the press of circumstances demanded at least a provisional reply immediately.

In the spring of 1863, black refugees aboard a Mississippi riverboat sang the words of a recent poem by John Greenleaf Whittier:

Oh, praise an' tanks De Lord he come
To set de people free;
An' massa tink it day ob doom,
An' we ob jubilee.
De Lord dat heap de Red Sea waves,
He jes' as strong as den;
He say de word: we las' night slaves,
To-day de Lord's free men.

. . . .

Ole massa on his trabbles gone
He lebe de land behind;
De Lord's breff blow him furder on,
Like corn-shuck in de wind.
We own de hoe, we own de plow,
We own de hands dat hold;
We sell de pig, we sell de cow,
But neber chile be sold.[1]

That same season, Union nurse Mary Livermore observed three to four hundred black people on another riverboat. "Mothers carried their piquant-faced babies on one arm," Livermore observed, "and led little woolly-headed toddlers by the other. Old men and women, gray, nearly blind, some of them bent almost double, bore on their heads and backs the small 'plunder' they had 'toted' from their homes, on the plantation." They were "subdued, impassive, solemn" but with "hope and courage now and then lighting up their sable faces." To Livermore, they seemed to be "going forth, like the Israelites, 'from the land of bondage.'" And while, like those biblical Hebrews, they were now going "to a land they knew not . . . they trusted implicitly in God to guide them."[2]

Just where were they headed?

In one sense, that was a simple question. These were freedpeople who were unable or unwilling to remain on the lands where they had lived in servitude. They were now likely bound for "contraband camps" that Union officers and government officials set up in Memphis, La Grange, and Bolivar, Tennessee; Helena, Arkansas; Corinth, Mississippi; Craney Island, North Carolina; Camp Barker, in the national capital district; and elsewhere.[3]

In a more general sense, though, the future—the destination—of these and other freedpeople was anything but clear. What would become of them now? What would their lives look like under freedom? What would happen to the plantation lands? Or to the plantations' immensely valuable staple crops? To the former masters themselves? Slavery's progressive breakdown raised all these questions and others more and more insistently.

Every mass-based revolution is a school of political education and clarification for people caught up in it. This is strikingly true of the Civil War era, where so many had been kept not only disfranchised but enslaved.

Although they had been maintained in a state of near-total illiteracy and had been forbidden to meet and discuss their views freely, black people did not take long to formulate at least preliminary answers to the questions that the new reality was posing.

Those who had already been free before 1861—nationwide, they numbered approximately half a million—discussed the subject most amply and openly, not only in one-on-one conversations but also in newspapers of their own and "Colored People's Conventions" held before, during, and just after the war.[4] But slaves, too, had been discussing these subjects for many years—indirectly in the form of religious words and practice, more explicitly among themselves as the Civil War progressed and the prospect of emancipation brightened, and then openly and in a great outpouring of talk and planning once liberation began. They wanted personal freedom—ownership of their own bodies—but also other rights that freedom entailed. They wanted freedom from physical coercion and abuse. They wanted to learn. They wanted to worship their god freely and in their own way. Not least of all, they needed a new way of earning their daily bread. And they wanted legal recognition of and protection for their families.

Slaves regularly married, but no laws recognized or protected those unions. Masters imposed themselves sexually on black women, married and unmarried alike, and broke up black families at will. At the top of freedpeople's post-emancipation agenda was the legal consecration of existing marriages and the work of finding and reclaiming family members who had been separated from them.

For those fortunate enough *not* to have been separated from loved ones under slavery, emancipation meant being able to breathe more easily when contemplating the future. They no longer need fear that some master would tear them away from spouses, parents, or children. Charlie Barbour, enslaved as a child in North Carolina, decades later remembered his first reaction to emancipation. "I wuz glad ter git free," he recalled, "cause I knows den dat I won't wake up some mornin' ter fin' dat my mammy or some ob de rest of my family am done sold."[5]

In wartime South Carolina, the wife of a black Union soldier in the Thirty-Fourth Regiment, U.S. Colored Troops, gave birth to a son. She named the boy James, after her husband. But because neither she nor her husband had a last name, the mother created one for little James; she dubbed him James Freeman. The boy's father warmly approved the choice. "That just suits me," he told her, for "he is born free—free as the birds, free as the wind, and free as the sun." "Thank God!" he exclaimed; young James "shall always be a free man."[6]

The less fortunate—those who *had* been forcibly parted from their parents, or children, or both—had always hoped and prayed that they might at least see their loved ones in heaven. Freedom meant that they might yet reunite with them here on earth. Northern missionaries who came to the Union-occupied sea islands spent much of their spare time writing letters for freedpeople seeking word about distant family members.[7] Of the thousands of black couples formally wed in Union-occupied Vicksburg during one eight-month period, one in every six had been forcibly separated from each other under slavery and had been able to find and rejoin each other only after liberation.[8]

Some reunions required armed force to achieve. Near Lynchburg, Virginia, at the end of 1864, a detachment of federal cavalry rode up to the farm of slave owner B. E. Harrison. Among the troopers was a man who had been Harrison's slave until he managed to escape; his name, like so many, was not recorded. He had been forced to leave his wife and child behind in order to reach Union lines. But that day, with a cavalry saber in his hand, he demanded that Harrison return his family members to him. B. E. Harrison nervously replied that he could not do that; he had already refugeed the woman and child farther away from Union soldiers in order to make their escape more difficult. Hearing this, the husband and father promised Harrison that unless he retrieved and produced his family by the new year, Union soldiers would return and torch every building on the place.[9]

To sanctify de facto marriages before the law, thousands of freedpeople now turned to military chaplains and northern missionaries. Chaplain John Fisk, who supervised contrabands in west Tennessee, conducted one mass wedding ceremony that legally united 119 couples.[10] On the sea islands, northern teacher Elizabeth Hyde Botume was deeply affected by "the eager, expectant look on the faces of the old couples" as they anticipated a "higher and better" form of union than slave masters had permitted them.[11]

The ceremonies that reconsecrated these unions formed only one part of the revolution in religious life that accompanied emancipation. Before the war, slave owners had controlled organized Christianity and bent it to their own purposes; they used it to endow the bonds of slavery with a divine origin and divine approval. Southern missionary societies had distributed booklets designed, as one pamphlet put it, to prove "from the Scriptures of the Old and New Testament, that slavery is not forbidden by the Divine Law."[12] White preachers and approved black prayer leaders working under white supervision endlessly spun variations on their favorite passage from Saint Paul's Epistle to the Ephesians: "Servants, be obedient to them that are your masters according to the flesh, with fear and trembling, in singleness of your heart, as unto Christ."[13]

For decades, enslaved Christians had been forced to listen to such injunctions. In Tuskegee, Alabama, Sarah Fitzpatrick remembered, whites would hold their own church service on Sunday morning and conduct a separate one afterward for slaves who lived in the vicinity. Addressing those black Christians, the white minister would "tell 'em to mind deir Marster an b'have deyself an dey'll go to Hebben when dey die."[14] Rev. Charles Colcock Jones prepared special catechisms for use among slaves. An 1844 version enjoined them to ask, "What did God make you for?" The approved response was, "To make a crop."[15]

These efforts to convince black people that their servitude was God's work and God's will largely failed. The fact that those who were hammering away on that key were often the same people who profited from their listeners' captivity did little to affirm their credentials as disinterested messengers of Christ. "Dey come 'round an' tell us to pray, git 'ligion," Sarah Fitzpatrick noted, but "dat wuz on Sun'dy, but dey'ed beat de life out'cha de next day ef ya didn't walk de chalk line."[16]

Little more success crowned attempts to contain slaves' religious practice within the narrow confines prescribed by official Christianity. "Most of the verses of the plantation songs had some reference to freedom," Booker T. Washington later observed, although the singers were "careful to explain that the 'freedom' in these songs referred to the next world."[17] And people who obediently attended and participated in the religious services that whites had staged for them on Sunday morning might later that day or well into the night come together in their quarters or deep in the woods for what they considered the "real meeting." There, black Christians spoke and sang of their misery in bondage and their desperate hope to one day leave their chains behind.[18]

The outbreak of war lent new hope to the slaves and new optimism to their prayers. They held secret meetings throughout the war entreating God for their freedom.[19] And as prospects of emancipation improved, black people began raising a version of Christianity very different from the sanctioned one up from underground. Booker T. Washington recalled that as freedom peeked above the horizon, "there was more singing in the slave quarters than usual. It was bolder, had more ring, and lasted later into the night." And as the confidence of bondspeople grew, "they gradually threw off their masks and were not afraid to let it be known that the freedom in their songs meant freedom of the body in this world."[20] Later still, blacks were heard more openly intoning the words,

Oh! Fader Abraham
Go down into Dixie's Land
Tell Jeff Davis
To let my people go.[21]

When freedom actually arrived, it sparked a still fuller, broader, full-throated eruption of religious reawakening. On the offshore Atlantic sea islands freedpeople held Sunday "praise meetings" at dawn and additional services before midday.[22] In New Orleans in April 1864 they gathered to "praise God for this day of liberty to worship God!" An older man there exulted, "Bless God, my son, we don't have to keep watch at that door to tell us the patrollers are coming" to punish us "for prayin' and talkin' of the love of Jesus."[23]

Freedpeople now sought access to portions of the Christian message beyond the passages their masters had deemed safe enough to share with them. An older woman named Tamar wanted to learn to read "because I want to read de Word of de Lord."[24] "Now we is free," said another, "dar's heaps o' tings in dat ole book, we is jes' sufferin' tu larn."[25]

As their words suggested, the determination to openly organize religious life in a new way added to the urgency of another priority—to learn to read, write, and through the written word gain access to a wide world of knowledge and communication. As one northerner recounted, "They had seen the magic of a scrap of writing sent from a master to an overseer, and they were eager to share such power."[26] Tennessee freedman Charles Whiteside long remembered the words with which his master grudgingly informed him that Union decrees had made him free. "Charles, you is a free man they say but Ah tells you now, *you is still a slave* and if you lives to be a hundred, you'll STILL be a slave, cause you got no education, and education is what makes a man free!"[27] One Louisiana freedman made the same point a few years later: "Leaving learning to your children was better than leaving them a fortune; because if you left them even five hundred dollars, some man having more education than they had would come along and cheat them out of it all."[28]

Black parents went to great lengths to found schools and find teachers for their sons and daughters. They recruited some teachers from among the scores of northerners—mostly youthful, well-to-do members of abolitionist and benevolent societies based in Boston, New York, and Philadelphia—who now came south to join in the work of social transformation. Some Union soldiers were pressed into duty as well. Missionary societies and free black pastors set up schools in Union-occupied cities and in the surrounding countryside.[29]

Many of the well-meaning teachers expressed surprise at the alacrity with which their charges took to their letters. "*All* engaged in teaching the Negros" discovered that black children "can learn to read and write as readily as white children," a Union captain reported from Norfolk, Virginia.[30] Another officer agreed that the children "are smart, bright and quick to learn, and one can scarcely observe any difference in the rate of progress, between them, and so many white children."[31] Visiting one of the schools, a Union general asked a class what to tell his friends in the North about the students there. A young boy piped up, "Massa, tell 'em we is rising."[32] Children like him (as the former slave William Davis recalled) "thought it was so much like the way master's children used to be treated, that they believed they were getting white."[33]

Adults proved as eager to learn as children—eager, in their cases, to make up for lost time. Teaching on an island near Portsmouth, Virginia, Lucy Chase found her students "all very anxious to learn and full of ambition." In fact, she never before "saw such greedy people for study."[34] A freedwoman told teacher Elizabeth Hyde Botume, "Us ain't had no school, but us'll do anything ef you'll come over an' larn we."[35]

Adult students commonly went to class during the evenings, after their workdays were through.[36] But sometimes they attended alongside their children. Botume witnessed one such scene that especially touched her heart. "A man and his wife stood together in a class to read," she recounted. "Their three children were in the class above them, having conquered words of one syllable. As soon as the parents began to read, the children simultaneously darted to their sides to prompt them."[37]

Black Union soldiers commonly spent as much time as they could mastering the basics of literacy. As one chaplain put it, their "cartridge box and spelling book [were] attached to the same belt."[38] Rev. Joseph Warren supervised contraband schools in the Mississippi valley. One day he watched a unit of black infantrymen that found itself stationed near a family of Protestant missionaries. "The soldiers had not been there an hour," Warren recalled, "when those not on sentry duty had, of their own motion, procured spelling-books, and begged one of the ladies to aid them occasionally; they soon were busily at work on the alphabet."[39] Men like these used their newly acquired skills to write to family members in Union-occupied regions of the South. And "each letter," Botume noted with satisfaction, "was an improvement upon the one before."[40]

As important as religious liberty, literacy, and basic personal (including family) rights were, they did not by themselves provide the foundation for a new way of life for former slaves. They did not provide the means for surviving from day to day.

The towns, cities, and makeshift camps to which many freedpeople had initially journeyed offered no long-term solutions, either. The refugees' numbers soon exceeded supplies of food, clothing, and housing. Hungry, malnourished, and exposed to the elements, people began to succumb to disease. In Vicksburg, Mississippi, Colonel John Eaton saw "refugees . . . crowded together, sickly, disheartened, dying on the streets, not a family of them all either well sheltered, clad, or fed; no physicians, no medicines, no hospitals."[41]

In an overwhelmingly rural and agricultural country, the great majority of freedpeople would have to build their new lives in the country-side, on the land. But in what capacity would they now till that land? As forcibly driven laborers? As legally free wage earners? As tenants? As owners? Freedpeople would offer their own answers to these questions, but they would not be alone in doing so. Landowning former masters, Union army officers and civilian officials, and even northern businessmen would also have their say. Agreement among them all proved exceedingly rare.

One of the most widespread aspirations among freedpeople was to own the land that they and their ancestors had so long cultivated. They wished to see great plantations divided into small farms for themselves and their neighbors. As early as November 1861, the North's leading free black newspaper, the New York *Anglo-African*, asked,

> What course could be clearer, what course more politic, what course will so immediately restore the equilibrium of commerce, what course will be so just, so humane, so thoroughly conducive to the public and the national advancement, as that government should immediately bestow these lands upon those freed men who know best how to cultivate them, and will joyfully bring their brawny arms, their willing hearts, and their skilled hands to the glorious labor of cultivating as their own, the lands which they have bought and paid for by their sweat and blood.[42]

It became abundantly clear that black southerners shared this belief. A federal official reported from the sea islands that "the anxiety of these people to obtain a home in their own right, and feel safe in its possession, is intense."[43] The secretary of war created the American Freedmen's Inquiry Commission in March 1863 to investigate the condition of those whom the Emancipation Proclamation had freed.[44] It delivered its preliminary report that June: "To own property, especially to possess land, if it be only a few acres, in their own State" was "the chief object of ambition" among the freedpeople.[45]

They did not expect to receive those lands as charity, out of sympathy for their neediness. They believed, as one northerner found, "that they have a sort of *right* to live upon their own plantations."[46] It seemed a matter of simple justice—of long overdue compensation. "My master has had me ever since I was seven years old and never gave me nothing," one young man told a visiting northern writer. "I worked for him twelve years, and I think something is due me."[47]

Some, then and later, and in the North as well as the South, reacted with horror to such suggestions. The very idea, they objected, threatened the onset of "a war on property."[48]

Of course, calls for breaking up and dividing the plantations looked not to the abolition of property as such but to its more equal distribution—to make it available to a larger number of people. Landless white farmers and even urban workers had similarly been urging this kind of thing for decades under the heading of "land reform."[49]

In proposing their own version of the time-honored goal of land redistribution, some freedpeople invoked another idea with a long history. It held that only those who were not economically dependent upon others for a livelihood—who could feed, clothe, and shelter themselves and their families with the use of their own property—could be considered truly free and safely granted all the rights of citizens. Many of the country's founding fathers—including Alexander Hamilton, John Adams, and James Madison—subscribed to such a view.[50] Thomas Jefferson famously called independent farmers "the chosen people of God, if ever he had a chosen people," precisely because they were free of the "dependence" that "begets subservience."[51]

Almost four score years later, freedpeople and their advocates warned that even the fullest formal legal freedom for black southerners would be meaningless if they were denied the economic independence and security that owning land promised. Without soil of their own, they would be forced to work for the white landowners, often their former masters, who would turn control over their subsistence into a whip with which to compel freedpeople to do their bidding. "Gib us our own land," freedmen told a Union naval officer later, "and we take care of ourselves; but widout land de ole massas can hire us or starve us, as dey please."[52]

An extension of this argument warned of the dangers to the American republic as a whole of leaving the most fertile soil of the South in the hands of disloyal great landowners. Dividing those lands among the freedpeople was the only sure way to secure the Union's victory and establish a truly democratic republican society in the South. Break the economic power of the old slaveholding aristocracy and plant in its place a loyal, small-holding peasantry, urged the *New Orleans Tribune*, which was now published by free blacks there. "Let us create a new class of landholders who shall be interested in the permanent establishment of a new and truly republican system—the prize for which we are now fighting."[53]

Some black laborers went beyond such words to action. Even as war raged around them, they began farming the land of rebel slave masters who had fled when Union armies approached, generally raising food crops, especially corn and potatoes, for their own subsistence. They did so in Virginia (including on the Arlington estate of Robert E. Lee), along the coast of North Carolina, on the sea islands,[54] as well as along Georgia's Savannah River,[55] in southern Louisiana, and in various parts of the Mississippi valley.[56]

Some departing masters, attempting to make the best of their situation, tried to enlist slaves who stayed behind as their trustees, promising them all or part of whatever crops they raised if they would safeguard the masters' interests. When Joseph Davis abandoned the Hurricane and Brierfield plantations in Davis Bend, Mississippi, most of the black servants and laborers began to cultivate the lands, nominally on behalf of the Confederate president and his brother, but in practice for themselves and their families.[57]

More often, black people took possession of the land in open defiance of the masters. So it was on Katherine Stone's Brokenburn plantation, where servants and laborers established control as soon as the whites left.[58] In southeast Louisiana's Plaquemines Parish, one group of slaves reportedly drove the overseer off the plantation and swore "they will not allow any white man to put his foot on it." On another plantation, the laborers made themselves "masters of the place," and the overseer found himself "entirely at their mercy."[59] A few parishes to the west, sugar planters complained in January 1863 that "negroes led astray by designing persons" were now insisting that "the plantations & everything on them belong to them."[60]

The "designing persons" complained of included Union soldiers, both black and white.[61] During the Vicksburg campaign, federal troops who raided the countryside around Jackson informed slaves that they were free and gave them guns to protect that freedom. Black men and women promptly laid claim to the farm implements and began marking off the land with a plow line, the better to divide it among themselves.[62] After a battle in southern Virginia that induced most local masters to evacuate, a Union soldier approached West Turner and asked the young man whether his master whipped him. Turner replied, "Yessir, boss, gimme thirty and nine any ole time." The soldier then advised Turner to take for himself one acre for every stroke suffered and an extra acre as a bonus. "So," Turner later explained, "I measure off best I could forty acres of dat corn field an' staked it out."[63]

Some abolitionists, Union officers, Republican officials, and reform-minded northern civilians who went south during the war to work with the contrabands also raised hopes that the plantation lands would soon be divided among the former slaves. "If we want a lasting peace," argued the radical Ohio congressman James A. Garfield, "if we want to put down this rebellion so that it shall stay forever put down . . . we must take away the platform on which slavery stands—the great landed estates of the armed rebels of the South."[64] James McKaye, who chaired the American Freedman's Inquiry Commission, emphasized the political importance of breaking up the plantations. "You can never have in any country a democratic society . . . where the land all belongs to a few people," McKaye warned. He pointed to France as a positive example of a revolution that had destroyed an aristocracy and given land to the toilers.[65] The commission as a whole called on the federal government to help freedpeople buy lands by using moneys received from selling cotton and other property confiscated from Confederate masters.[66] The American Anti-Slavery Society endorsed that view in mid-1863.[67] "All that is needed to establish a loyal and prosperous community," agreed radical Massachusetts Republican Francis W. Bird, "is that the men and women who have watered the soil with their tears and blood, should be allowed to own it."[68]

In Washington, Congress enacted a series of laws that seemed to point in the same direction. The Second Confiscation Act of 1862 gave Abraham Lincoln the formal right not only to appropriate the slaves of disloyal owners but also to seize their other property and then use or sell it "for the support of the army of the United States." But at Lincoln's insistence, Congress specified that upon the death of such expropriated rebels, all property (other than slaves) that had been seized from them would be returned to their heirs.[69] For that reason, and because of the very cumbersome judicial process that the law specified, it ultimately affected very little land at all.[70]

Another set of laws proved more potent. In August 1861, Congress had levied a tax upon all states to help support the war effort. In June 1862, Congress followed up with the Direct Tax Act to facilitate collecting the impost in the secessionist states. As subsequently amended, this second law imposed tax liabilities on individual landowners and empowered the federal government to seize and sell the property of those who failed to pay them. Prospective buyers (specified as "loyal citizens" and soldiers) could purchase seized lands by putting down a quarter of the sale price and then paying the rest over three years. By late 1862, the machinery necessary to implement the law was in place in South Carolina and Florida.

But if the freedpeople had their hearts set on owning plantation lands, the government seemed more interested in using those lands to cultivate cotton that could then be sold to help pay the costs of the war. To that end, Union officials on the sea islands initially ran abandoned plantations as government-owned enterprises, employing some sixteen thousand former slaves as paid laborers, permitting them to raise provision crops for their families on designated parts of the plantations.[71]

Direct government administration of those lands was always intended as a temporary arrangement; they were eventually to be transferred into the hands of private owners. Some influential figures on the scene, civilian as well as military, thought that those owners should include the people who had previously tilled the land as slaves. One of them was abolitionist-minded General Rufus Saxton, the military governor of the sea islands. He believed that "simple justice" demanded that the Union "parcel out the fertile lands of these islands among the different families in lots large enough for their subsistence" and "with their rights of property secure."[72]

Many of the teachers, social reformers, and religious missionaries who appeared on the islands in the army's wake agreed with him.[73] A Methodist minister named Mansfield French arrived on the sea islands as a representative of the New York–based American Missionary Society. Enslaved laborers, Rev. French held, "had made [the land] what it was," so "it belonged to them, and them only."[74]

But few of those who made policy in Washington took such opinions very seriously. William Tecumseh Sherman enunciated the more common view: "The negro on his becoming free, has no right to the property of his former owner."[75] Freedpeople would obtain land only if they could pay for it.

In early March 1863, the federal government set about selling off some 16,500 acres of confiscated land on the sea islands.[76] A small group of freedpeople managed to scrape together and pool enough money to buy a fraction of that soil—perhaps one in every eight acres sold.[77] But their acquisitions were dwarfed by the large-scale purchases of major northern investors, such as the New England businessman Edward S. Philbrick.

Philbrick had arrived in the sea islands in 1862 and initially served as a superintendent of government plantations.[78] He looked forward to bringing plantation lands "within the reach of private Enterprise" and to proving thereby that even without whips and shackles "blacks are capable of becoming a useful laboring class"—to prove, in fact, as Philbrick's general agent put it, that such "paid labor is *more* profitable to the Landowner than slave labor."[79]

The freedpeople's advocates, dismayed at the money men's initial success, pressed the federal government to help black families obtain a larger share of the land. Abraham Lincoln and his associates responded with ambivalence.

The Union president's first impulse was sympathetic. He directed Treasury officials on the sea islands in September 1863 to set aside about a quarter of the next levy of land earmarked for sale. Those acres would be divided into smaller tracts and sold to selected black household heads, those who, "by their good conduct, meritorious services or exemplary character, will be examples of moral propriety and industry to those of the same race."[80] Additional prodding induced Lincoln to go still further in December, granting to "any loyal person" who physically occupied or had occupied any of the lands in question the right to "pre-empt" (that is, to claim a priority right to purchase) between twenty and forty acres of the land at a price lower than would be charged for other sections.[81]

News of this directive elated the islands' freedpeople. With General Saxton's encouragement, they eagerly set about staking claims to the land they expected would soon be theirs.[82]

But even as they did that, northern investors and allied federal tax agents worked to derail the preemption option—blocking its implementation on the ground while they vigorously lobbied against it in Washington.[83] While claiming to fear that speculators would somehow use preemption to *deprive* freedpeople of land, they also complained that the policy "out radicals all the radicalism . . . ever heard of in agrarian history."[84]

Opponents of the preemption policy enjoyed a number of advantages. One was the government's need for revenues to help finance the war—revenues that would prove smaller if confiscated land were given or sold cheaply to freedmen rather than sold at auction at whatever price they could fetch. Another factor was the New England textile industry's hunger for cotton. Many freedpeople now seemed unwilling to plant that crop, identifying it too strongly with slavery. If the lands were given to them, where would owners of northern textile factories obtain the raw material they depended upon to produce their goods?

Opponents of special consideration for the freedpeople also had deeper, ideological sources of support. Only a handful of Republican leaders seemed anxious to revolutionize the South's agrarian system by confiscating and dividing plantation lands.[85] Lincoln himself had earlier expressed strong qualms about such an enterprise. The broad powers granted him by the Second Confiscation Act had left him plainly uneasy. He doubted that such powers could be exercised fairly; still hoping to avoid antagonizing white southerners any more than was necessary, he also cautioned that "the severest justice may not always be the best policy."[86] He did sign the Direct Tax Act, but he displayed little enthusiasm for or urgency in implementing it.[87]

By February 1864, opponents of preemption had persuaded Treasury secretary Salmon P. Chase to kill that provision.[88] As a result, while some black families did manage to purchase homesteads that year, investors such as Philbrick were able to snap up more than two-thirds of the sixty thousand acres put up for sale.[89]

Some freedpeople initially thought Philbrick was purchasing land as their custodian and that he intended to eventually resell it to them at the same below-market price per acre that he himself had paid.[90] But he soon disabused them of those expectations. If and when he were to resell, Philbrick declared, he would do so only at "full price."[91] Moreover, he pontificated, "No race of men on God's earth ever acquired the right to the soil on which they stand without more vigorous exertions than these people have made." To allow them to receive land so easily would only encourage them in their "idleness and unthrifty habits."[92] For their own good, they had to learn that they must pay for whatever they got.

Freedpeople showed little appreciation for such paternal concern for their welfare and reeducation. Watching lands they had worked so long, so arduously, and in return for so little pass into the hands of strangers filled them, as Rev. French noted, with an "almost unbearable" sadness and bitterness.[93] "Why did Government sell all our Masters Land's to Mr Philbrick for so trifling a sume?" asked a petition from St. Helena Island.[94] Another freedman beseeched a white teacher (in the Gullah dialect of the islands) to "speak to Linkum" and "tell him for we po' folks" that they were thankful to him and to God for their freedom, but also that "we wants land—dis bery land dat is rich wid de sweat ob we face and de blood ob we back."[95] Some freedpeople protested against government policy more angrily, in one case reportedly threatening to shoot one of the new landowners.[96]

A second experiment in restarting plantation agriculture took place at Davis Bend, Mississippi, the home of Jefferson and Joseph Davis's plantations and others. When federal forces arrived there during the Vicksburg campaign, they found about a thousand black residents already in possession of and farming those lands.[97] Ulysses S. Grant and Admiral David Dixon Porter allowed them to continue doing so. Grant promised that the area would "become a Negro paradise."[98]

It soon developed, however, that his vision of paradise had no room for independent black farmers. Grant claimed the Bend's estates for the U.S. government; associations formed by former slaves would be permitted only to lease the land.[99] In 1864, northern investors and professedly unionist local planters succeeded in obtaining or regaining title to some of those properties and hired freedpeople to work on them in return for subsistence wages.[100] Colonel John Eaton, superintendent of freedpeople in the valley, resisted this trend, persuading the Union army's district commander to decree that after January 1, 1865, the whole of Davis Bend would be "exclusively devoted to the colonization, residence, and support of the Freedmen."[101] In practice, this meant that black people would occupy the great bulk of the land (about five thousand acres in all). But they would do so, once again, not as owners but as renters.[102]

The great majority of slaves liberated by the last months of 1864 lived in other parts of the Mississippi valley, where their prospects of acquiring land of their own grew steadily dimmer. In southern Louisiana—in the cotton and sugar parishes that the U.S. War Department designated as the Department of the Gulf—General Benjamin Butler had in 1862 pioneered the system that would eventually prevail throughout the valley.

The Union army began confiscating some of the South's biggest plantations after the conquest of New Orleans and the flight of some secessionist masters in April 1862. On other estates, a large group of planters stayed in place when U.S. troops arrived. Some of those planters professed to be unionists; others did not.

Though slaves there were not technically free—since this part of the valley had come under Union control before the Emancipation Proclamation went into effect—they were *effectively* free as a result of the severe toll that the war had taken on bondage. Resident planters called on the federal government for aid in controlling their workers. "We are ready to give up the name of 'slavery,' we care nothing about the name," one planter reportedly explained. "But we must have certain control over these men."[103]

Wanting to satisfy elite white unionists and to reconcile even conquered secessionists to restored U.S. rule, General Butler agreed to compel black laborers to work the planters' fields in return for low wages, food, and some assistance for the sick and aged.

When General Nathaniel P. Banks replaced Butler in command at the end of 1862, he inherited and continued the basic elements of his predecessor's labor program. And as Union power spread through more of Louisiana, so did that system.[104]

In fact, Banks proved even more eager to please the planters than his predecessor. In early 1863, he ordered freedpeople to perform "continuous and faithful service" and to do so with "respectful deportment, correct discipline and perfect subordination." The army would consign any workers who left their employers to compulsory labor on the public works.[105] Banks imposed pay rates that were extremely low—even lower than Butler's. Enterprising planters found ways to recoup even those paltry wages, setting up forerunners of company stores that charged physically isolated laborers exorbitant prices for the goods they needed. Meanwhile, more than a few Union army provost marshals averted their eyes when planters used corporal punishment to enforce their will on laborers.[106]

The harsh conditions of black life under Banks's system appalled many northerners in and out of government, who condemned the general for his unseemly devotion to the ex-masters' interests. Stung, Banks retreated somewhat in early 1864, easing the terms of freedpeople's employment, notably by raising wages and reducing the length of the workday. While freedpeople were still required to remain on the plantations for the duration of year-long contracts, Banks increased their liberty to choose the employers with whom they contracted. When planters protested even these changes, Louisiana's new military governor courted their compliance by promising them a large say in naming the local officials who would enforce discipline upon the field workers.[107]

As the Union army brought more and more of the Mississippi valley under its control in 1863, the Butler-Banks system was extended northward into western Tennessee, northeastern Louisiana, and Mississippi, in the process covering some of the South's biggest cotton plantations and adding more than seventy thousand freedpeople to the fifty thousand it already controlled.[108]

Only a small fraction of those people were permitted to lease any of the confiscated land—notably around Helena, Arkansas; Vicksburg, Mississippi; northeastern Louisiana's Lake Providence; and Norfolk, Virginia.[109] And of those few who managed to do that, most could afford to rent only small parcels.[110] As a result, of all valley properties in the hands of pro-Union individuals in 1864, only about 7 percent were occupied by black people.[111]

The great bulk of the acreage had gone instead to northern whites, such as New York lawyer George B. Field, who leased it in large tracts in order to grow cotton by employing recently emancipated slaves.[112] Field—much like Edward Philbrick on the South Carolina sea islands—was eager to demonstrate that "free negro labor under good management can be made a *source* of *profit* to the *employer*."[113] In the spring of 1863, U.S. adjutant general Lorenzo Thomas assisted the entrepreneurial Field by appointing him to the commission empowered to award plantation leases in the Mississippi valley.[114]

The motives of these northern leaseholders, as Colonel Eaton later noted, were "primarily commercial and involved patriotism or humanity only as secondary and incidental considerations." They were determined "to make money, whether the Union cause—not to mention the Negro—suffered by their operations or not." Afflicted with this "money-making fever," the lessees cut wages or withheld them entirely, ignored contractual obligations to provide employees with housing and food, and often hired overseers from the slavery era to supervise the freedpeople's labor.[115]

Indiana-born general John P. Hawkins, then commanding the Union's military district of northeastern Louisiana, complained in October 1863 that most of the lessees "cared nothing how much flesh they worked off of the negro provided it was converted into good cotton." As a result of their growing power, he said, "the Adventurer, the Gambler and the Projector have control over the interests of thousands of helpless human beings."[116]

Hopes that freedpeople might yet possess the land suffered an even stronger blow when Abraham Lincoln unveiled his plans for reintegrating conquered sections of the Confederacy into the United States. To bring the war swiftly to an end, he sought to make rejoining the Union as palatable as possible to members of the southern elite.

This goal helped shape Lincoln's "Proclamation of Amnesty and Reconstruction" of December 1863, which aimed to encourage the creation in occupied portions of the Confederacy of new state governments that would resume their place within the Union. To hasten the creation of such governments, Lincoln required them only to recognize the end of slavery and grant freedpeople access to public education. If individual Confederate masters went along with this plan and promised their future loyalty to the United States, most would receive "a full pardon . . . with restoration of all rights of property, except as to slaves." Only those land parcels already sold to others would be excluded from this promise of restitution.[117] In February 1864, Lincoln's acting attorney general, Titian J. Coffey, reaffirmed that promise.[118]

Sales, leases, and the return of lands to recently secessionist owners left the vast majority of blacks in Union-occupied parts of the Confederacy working the soil not as property owners or even as renters but as poorly paid employees of wealthy whites.[119]

Some freedpeople refused to go along—refused any longer to labor for others on lands they considered rightfully their own. Others made it clear that if circumstances compelled them to do that, they intended at least to influence the terms of that labor. They would not submit docilely and in all things to their employers' will.[120] On the sea islands, for example, some who worked on Edward Philbrick's plantation stubbornly raised corn for their own consumption where they were told instead to grow cotton for their employer. One man, upbraided for misusing Philbrick's land, angrily retorted, "Man! Don't talk about Mr. Philbrick lan'. Mr. Philbrick no right to the lan.'"[121]

White employers complained endlessly of the bold spirit of self-assertion that seemed to have gripped their employees. The upheavals of the war had broken the life-and-death power that Mississippi valley landowners had previously exercised over black labor and awakened the laborers to new possibilities. When the northern teacher Elizabeth Hyde Botume talked with black refugees in Savannah at the end of 1863, she found them confident "that *emancipation had lifted* them out of old conditions into new relations with their fellow beings." They were "no longer chattels," but had "rights and privileges like their neighbors."[122] Their experiences had also given them a new sense of their own potential collective power. Union provost marshal John W. Ela reported in mid-1863 that former slaves would "not endure the same treatment, the same customs, and rules—the same language—that they have heretofore quietly submitted to." They had gained "a spirit of independence," he wrote.[123]

At first their demands were mostly defensive ones. They would not tolerate whipping or any other physical punishment from the landowners. They would not permit employers to harm family members or intervene in their family lives.[124] But over time, freedpeople became bolder and readier to act in concert to advance their common interests. Now, Ela noted, "the negroes band together, and lay down their own rules, as to when, and how long they will work etc. etc. and the Overseer loses all control over them."[125] They refused to work under such overseers in gangs as so many had been forced to do in the old South.[126] In general, they refused to work as intensively as they had under slavery. They wanted the same right to move about freely that white people enjoyed, and they began to insist on a shorter workweek and a shorter working day than had previously been imposed upon them. They wanted better food, shelter, and clothing. Families, furthermore, should have the right to withdraw women from the fields so they might work in their homes and care for their children.[127] Children, too, must be relieved of field duty so that they could help their mothers or attend school.[128]

Planters generally found this situation intolerable. No "people on the

face of the earth of their rank in civilization," the transplanted northerner Edward Philbrick grumbled, were "so independent as they are."[129]
Louisianan William J. Minor wrote in November 1863 that "a man had
as well be in pergatory as attempt to work a Sugar plantation under
existing circumstances."[130]

To planters who had so recently owned their laborers outright, even
low wages were an unjust imposition.[131] Having to negotiate with blacks
about such things was agony. Stephen Duncan, who had boasted fifteen plantations in Louisiana and Mississippi and some two thousand
slaves, certainly saw it that way. That he was a genuine unionist—had
always considered secession a major mistake—made it no easier for this
ex-master to stomach the new relations. He had "at last paid off all the
Negroes," he wrote in January 1864, "& a more unpleasant, disgusting
business I never have attended to."[132]

Being denied the use of whips and other instruments of labor discipline added insult to injury. One Louisiana planter typically dismissed
as ridiculous the idea that black workers could be made to labor "without coercion, & without that fear of punishment which is essential to
stimulate the idle and correct the vicious."[133]

Fundamentally disbelieving in any labor system where workers were
fully free—and deeply frustrated with their first attempts to bend
freedpeople to their will—former masters strove hard to reimpose some
form of legal controls over former slaves. Louisiana sugar planters urged
General Banks to give them "such power & authority as will enable us
to preserve order & compel the negroes to work." To do that, they
added, "some *coercion* is absolutely necessary."[134] The War Department's
special inspector reported at the end of 1863 that "no small portion" of
the Mississippi valley masters "entertained a lingering hope that they
would be able to restore the old system"—that is, outright slavery—"if
not in form, in substance."[135]

Lincoln's December 1863 amnesty proclamation nodded toward and
encouraged such hopes, promising that "as a temporary arrangement"
Washington would allow new, loyal southern state governments to pass
special laws governing this "laboring, landless, and homeless class"—
laws that would presumably deprive members of that class of many
rights that white workers took for granted.[136]

The inclusion of that language was not accidental. Lincoln had used
similar words a month earlier when instructing General Banks about

how to reconstruct state government in Louisiana.[137] Secretary Chase had counseled dropping words like those. The government's reconstruction plans, Chase emphasized, should include "*no suggestion . . . of any apprenticeship* of the freedpeople or other special legislation for them" and contain "no, even apparent sanction of legislation which may be easily perverted into virtual re-enslavement."[138]

Lincoln either ignored or rejected Chase's plea. As he made plain in a letter written soon afterward, he would personally prefer to see black workers treated "precisely as I would treat the same number of free white people in the same relation and condition." But he hoped that his "acquiescence" in what southern landholders considered such a "vital matter" would leave "the deeply afflicted [white] people in those States . . . more ready" to renounce secession and rejoin the Union.[139] General Lorenzo Thomas observed with approval that "history does not exhibit" a clemency policy more lenient than the one that the Union was offering the secessionist planter "at a moment when, by his own acts, the very soil was washed from beneath his feet."[140]

In response to the generous terms offered, a number of rebel planters in the Mississippi valley did begin in 1864 to make their peace with the reality of restored Union rule. They requested and received pardons and (sometimes in alliance with northern investors) regained title to their estates.[141] Plantation-leasing commissioner George B. Field was soon congratulating himself on bringing together "*loyal Northern men* upon harmonious terms with the *owners* of the soil," thereby forming the perfect partnerships "by which negro labor may be *at once* applied to the peaceful pursuit of agriculture."[142] Before the year had fairly begun, in fact, the federal government had already returned to their original owners two of every three of the Mississippi valley plantations that it had previously seized and leased out.[143]

Abraham Lincoln thus displayed little interest in fundamentally changing the pattern of land ownership in the rebellious slave states. But he remained committed to uprooting slavery, and before long he would further broaden and deepen that commitment.

Chapter Seven

CRACKS IN THE WALLS WIDEN

Autumn 1862 through Spring 1864

While planters in the Mississippi valley strove to shape the terms of reunion, Jefferson Davis's government and armies still fought for a new republic in which ownership of human beings would remain secure. In that effort, they retained the support of most white residents of the Confederacy. Despite all that they had endured, William Tecumseh Sherman reported to his wife in March 1864, "I see no sign of let up." Instead, he wrote, "the masses" seemed "determined to fight it out." The *Richmond Dispatch* crowed the next month that the Yankees had thrown everything at the Confederacy "without producing the slightest disposition to succumb, or in the remotest degree shaking the firm and confident faith" of its population.[1]

There was considerable truth in both assessments. During the first three years of war, a potent combination of ideas and causes sustained most whites in their commitment to the slaveholders' new republic and its armies. Bolstering that commitment were local and sectional loyalty and pride; feelings of insulted honor (both individual and regional); outrage at the death and destruction wrought by Union armies and determination to spare family members and friends from further losses; and certainty that the Confederate cause was also God's and that He expected all, men and women alike, to do their duty. Not least important was unwavering belief in the sacrosanctity of white supremacy and slavery, certainty that preserving the former required perpetuating the latter, and a visceral revulsion at the prospect of living in a society without either. For many, these motives only grew in power as the war lengthened, more loved ones suffered and died, and the hated enemy's commitment to abolition and employment of black troops increased.[2]

But Sherman's depiction of a seamlessly united and confident white South was an exaggeration. The cracks evident in the House of Dixie's structure even at the start of the war widened over time. Military defeats, including those at Gettysburg, Vicksburg, and Chattanooga, were wearing down the optimism of many, and the multiple privations imposed by the war gradually sapped their will. Governments in Richmond and the state capitals took steps to address these problems, but a number of those steps also angered their constituents. The opposing pressures of war-spawned problems and controversial government solutions formed a vise that would squeeze popular support for the Davis regime. As the conflict continued and grew fiercer between the fall of 1862 and the spring of 1864, the jaws of that vise tightened.

To sustain themselves, Confederate armies had early on begun to seize temporarily, or "impress," the property of the Confederacy's citizens— foodstuffs, wagons, and livestock as well as slaves. During the war's first two years, Confederate officers and officials did that at their own discretion and then under the authority of state laws passed in the fall of 1862. The results were arbitrary and insufficient, angering citizens without fully meeting the armies' needs.[3]

In late March 1863, the Confederate congress for the first time wrote impressment into national law. The new legislation aimed partly to mollify citizens incensed at the way impressment had been carried out previously, and partly to suppress attempts to evade or resist it. The law promised to pay property owners for whatever the army took from them, but the prices set were far below market value. Still worse, payment would be made in Confederate currency, which was plummeting in value as the number of notes in circulation increased.[4]

By autumn of 1863, many people had heard of "planters . . . who have declared that they will allow their fodder to rot in the field" rather than sell it to the army at the low prices they were offered.[5] "When this war commenced," an Alabaman observed in November 1863, "every man was ready & willing, nay, anxious, to make every sacrifice for the good of the cause." But "now, how changed the scene! Selfishness & greed of gain has taken possession of a large portion of our people."[6]

One evening in July 1864, a Confederate officer named Hamilton arrived at James Henry Hammond's Redcliffe plantation in South Carolina. Bearing a requisition calling on Hammond to provide the army with a share of his corn, Hamilton left it on the planter's desk. When Hamilton returned the next day, Hammond claimed in his diary, the planter tore the order up and threw it out the window. Hammond justified himself on two grounds. The first was financial; impressment would give him less money for his corn than he could obtain on the open market. The second was social and cultural. For proud plantation autocrats like him, submitting to impressment meant "branding on my forehead 'Slave.' "[7]

The physical location of real slaves and the steps required to keep them out of Union hands became another bone of contention between masters and their government. "Refugeeing" bondspeople away from approaching Union armies was an expensive undertaking—one that wealthier masters could afford but smaller-scale slave owners could not. That difference aggravated envy and resentment within the slaveholders' ranks. In December 1863, Alabaman Sarah Espy visited a more prosperous and better-connected neighbor who was preparing to evacuate the area along with her human property. Espy also owned slaves but was not wealthy enough to follow suit. Surely this demonstrated, she thought, that "there is a great wrong somewhere, and if our confederacy should fall, it will be no wonder to me for the brunt is thrown upon the working classes while the rich live at home in ease and pleasure."[8]

While some masters resented their inability to refugee slaves, others stubbornly refused to move theirs. Union occupation of the Carolina sea islands led a master named Warren to abandon his plantation on the nearby mainland. But when he departed, Warren left a handful of slaves behind, and a Confederate commander heard subsequently that those slaves were in regular contact with Union soldiers. That, the officer explained, endangered the safety of his pickets on the mainland. He and his subordinates therefore asked Warren to remove his slaves from that location. Warren refused.[9]

In the face of such noncooperation, Secretary of War James A. Seddon declared it "a clear obligation" of Confederate officers to take matters into their own hands—"to remove from any district exposed to . . . or overrun by the enemy the effective male slaves."[10] To do otherwise meant, at the very least, leaving in place a likely source of intelligence about Confederate troop positions and movements. At worst, it meant allowing those slaves to become Union laborers or soldiers.

But Richmond and its officials repeatedly backed away from confrontations over this subject. A case in point was Seddon's own Virginia. In December 1863, Confederate general George E. Pickett wrote from Petersburg, just south of Richmond, that large numbers of slaves were passing into enemy hands. The only way to prevent the upper South as a whole from being "entirely denuded of slaves," Pickett believed, was to remove such slaves, forcibly if necessary, to places more distant from Union armies.

But Old Dominion state legislators loudly objected to that suggestion. It would tread upon the masters' right to keep and use their human property wherever they saw fit. Wyndham Robertson, a major planter and influential state legislator (he had once been governor of Virginia), presented these objections to the War Department in January 1864. This was, he emphasized, an issue of "much delicacy," a matter "vitally affecting our citizens." Richmond would do well to keep that in mind, Robertson admonished, and "refrain . . . from exercising a power which any state might deem seriously objectionable and prejudicial to her most important interests." Seddon responded quickly. "In deference to the wishes and judgment entertained by the owners," he promised, Confederate officials would forcibly relocate slaves only with "great reluctance" and only as a last resort.[11]

The retreat was more complete in Jefferson Davis's Mississippi. Following the fall of Vicksburg, the Confederate president ordered all adult male slaves removed from the vicinity of Union troops. But both the governor and state legislature of Mississippi promptly branded the decree "illegal" and disruptive of some of the biggest and richest plantations in the South. Rather than force the issue Davis simply backed down.[12]

The army's attempt to borrow, rent, or impress not only food and other goods but also slave laborers provoked still louder and more widespread resistance. Before Congress placed impressment in Confederate

law, General Thomas Jordan requested the loan of 2,500 South Carolina slaves to help strengthen the defenses at Charleston. Less than a
fifth of that number arrived.[13]

The same obstructionism plagued Confederate general Gideon Pillow in Alabama. In early March, he called upon masters around Huntsville to rent him slaves for use as army teamsters. He reminded them
again of their special stake in the war effort. Help me, he urged, and
you will not only be "performing a patriotic duty." You will also be "advancing your own interest by preserving your property and aiding the
army to protect the homes and property of the owner." But if you short-
sightedly resist my call for assistance, he said, you will thereby help the
enemy to conquer us, and you will then be robbed of your "negro property."[14]

If the logic seems inescapable, many masters nonetheless ignored it.
In a balance sheet drawn up later that year, Seddon reported that attempts to obtain the labor of slaves for the war effort through the voluntary cooperation of masters had "been generally found to be
unavailing."[15]

The government hoped that the national impressment law of March
1863 would solve the problem by regularizing the process and equal-
izing the burdens. But at least some masters remained unappeased, including North Carolina plantation mistress Catherine Edmondston.
Confederate policy, she complained a year later, had so impinged upon
the rights and wealth of the masters that "it almost amounts to an abolition of Slavery entirely so far as the profits are concerned."[16] One
Texan swore in January 1864 that a recent requisition of slave laborers
"would not be obeyed except at the point of the bayonet."[17] For such
people, preoccupation with immediate, individual interests trumped
the needs of the slave-labor system as a whole. Willing to lend Jefferson
Davis their slaves when the war promised to be a brief one, they resented the continuing and growing government requests that the
lengthening and deepening war made necessary.

Some highly placed officials gave such obstructionists aid and comfort. This was particularly true of Confederate governors Zebulon
Vance of North Carolina and Joseph E. Brown of Georgia. Both men
were practiced political tightrope walkers. Both staunchly defended
slavery and swore fealty to the Confederate war effort. At the same
time, both presented themselves as ardent protectors of local and state

rights, opponents of the national draft, and champions of white families with little property.

This Janus-faced pose served them well overall. But it frequently brought them into collision with Richmond. In the spring of 1863, General H. W. Mercer requested that Governor Brown and the Georgia state legislature assist him to impress laborers for work on the Savannah defenses. They refused, claiming that the new national law freed the states from any responsibility for impressment. Brown then suggested that if Mercer found himself in need of labor, he should offer his own soldiers some extra pay to perform it.[18] A South Carolina legislative committee offered similar advice to General P.G.T. Beauregard, adding helpfully that an offer of additional pay would hold special appeal for white troops from the state's up-country districts, presumably because they were poor.[19]

John A. Campbell, the assistant secretary of war, would sum up the general problem in restrained language in 1863. "The sacrosanctity of slave property in this war," he concluded, "has operated most injuriously to the Confederacy."[20] The Georgia congressman Warren Akin acidly inquired of a correspondent, "Have you ever noticed the strange conduct of our people during this war? They give up their sons, husbands, brothers & friends, and often without murmuring, to the army; but let one of their negroes be taken, and what a houl you will hear."[21] Nearly identical accusations could be heard throughout the South.[22] John Forsyth, Jr., who edited the *Mobile Register and Advertiser,* put it less delicately. Too many "wretches," he wrote, had allowed themselves to be blinded to "their peculiar interest in this struggle" and the "tremendous stake they have in it."[23]

Recalcitrant planters and their political representatives rejected these accusations. No, they insisted, the government's difficulty in obtaining the soldiers, laborers, and other things that it needed was not their fault. The responsibility lay with the regime in Richmond. According to the *Memphis Appeal*'s zealously secessionist editor, masters understood the war's importance to their own interests perfectly well; there was no need to lecture them on the subject. They knew that "the material issues" at the crux of the Civil War were indeed "the interests of the planters" and that therefore this was "eminently their war." That was why throughout the war's first year "the lofty & uncalculating spirit of this class" had been on display for all to see. If that selfless spirit had later flagged, the

Appeal claimed, it was not because the masters were selfish but because the Confederate government had treated them unfairly—had imposed unjust laws and insupportable burdens upon them. Let Richmond simply repeal those unwarranted and harmful edicts and planters would "do their full duty by the country and army."[24]

Prominent politicians such as Robert Toombs echoed those sentiments: Government arm-twisting had created all Confederate supply problems, they said, and the solution lay not in making greater demands on masters but in making fewer. Richmond, Toombs wrote, must "let the production and distribution of wealth alone." Imposing all these rules upon whites was no way to run or defend a slaveholders' republic. "The road to liberty for the white man does not lie through [his own] slavery."[25] For Toombs's old friend Alexander Stephens, the principle involved was a constitutional one—one even more important than the success of the Confederate war effort. "Independence without constitutional liberty," he declared repeatedly, "is not worth the sacrifices we are making."[26] All would be well, and the people would spontaneously and voluntarily offer up whatever the war effort required, if only government would remove its heavy hand from their necks.

Despite these objections, in the spring of 1863 Richmond enacted a series of measures to finance the war effort and cope with war-spawned privation. In May the southern Congress passed new taxes on incomes, bank deposits, "commercial paper," and agricultural goods as well as on profits gleaned from the sale of food, clothing, and iron. Another provision required those engaged in virtually all occupations to purchase government licenses in order to conduct business. The law also included a tax in kind. In the future, a tenth of all agricultural products in excess of a quantity of goods deemed adequate for a farm family's subsistence was to be handed directly over to the government.[27]

Measures like these provoked considerable resentment. The tax in kind became a particular focus of popular anger, weighing most heavily not upon major planters but middling and small commercial cultivators ("the hard-laborers of the Confederacy," as one group of protesters dubbed themselves) who were already struggling to make do with meager harvests. Even the Confederacy's tax commissioner recognized that flat-rate taxes necessarily "operate harshly and oppressively on the poor." Already, he warned in November 1863, the tax had produced "discontent and murmurings against the government."[28] Private James Zimmerman complained that "the tax collector and produce gathere[r] are pushing for the little mights of garden and trash patches . . . that the poor women have labored hard and made." He instructed his wife to refuse to pay and tell them that "you thought your husband was fighting for our rights and you had a notion that you had a right to what little you had luck to make."[29] Private Marcus Hefner told his wife the same thing.[30] In the summer of 1863, public meetings denounced the tax in kind as "unjust and tyrannical," "anti-republican and oppressive." North Carolinians gathered at such meetings "pledge[d] ourselves to each other to resist, to the bitter end."[31]

When farmers refused to pay the tax, they exacerbated a food shortage that was already sharpening in the spring and summer of 1863. Union forces by then occupied key southern grain and livestock centers in Kentucky and Tennessee. Warfare was destroying acreage elsewhere. The steadily tightening blockade of the southern coast was restricting the movement of those foodstuffs that existed, and the South's road and railroad network, always weak, buckled under the weight of the war. Confederate armies aggravated shortages among the civilian population by diverting food to themselves.[32] The steady fall in the value of Confederate currency drove all prices ever higher—severely higher in 1862, astronomically higher in 1863.[33] The cost of food multiplied from seven to ten times just between 1860 and 1863.[34]

The shortage of food and its soaring price brought hunger to broad layers especially in towns and cities, but it drove many among the white poor to despair. On April 2, 1863—only a few months after one great Confederate victory (at Fredericksburg) and on the eve of another (at Chancellorsville)—a peddler named Mary Jackson led hundreds of working-class women and children on a march through Richmond's streets demanding food for themselves and their families. A bemused well-to-do onlooker inquired of one marcher if this was a parade in celebration of something. Yes, the young woman replied sharply, they were celebrating their "right to live." "We are starving," she said, and "as soon as enough of us get together we are going to the bakeries and each of us will take a loaf of bread." She saw nothing immoral in doing that. "This is little enough for the government to give us after it has taken all our men."[35]

As it moved, the angry crowd swelled to perhaps a thousand, including handfuls of men. When it reached the city's business district, marchers began taking bread and other goods from stores on Cary and Main streets.

Both the governor and the mayor rushed to the scene. The mayor ordered the crowd to disperse; the protesters ignored him. Then the Confederate president himself appeared, followed shortly afterward by a company of infantry reserves. To shield themselves from attack, protesters commandeered a wagon and turned it into a barricade.

As he later recorded, Jefferson Davis felt contempt for the protesters. They were, he was sure, "bent on nothing but plunder and wholesale robbery." Climbing atop the wagon, he shouted, "You say you are hungry and have no money," he shouted. "Here is all I have. It is not much, but take it." And with that Davis emptied his pockets and threw the contents "among the mob." He then pulled out his pocket watch and gave the still mostly female crowd five minutes in which to disperse. The soldiers would open fire if they did not. When the infantry captain ordered his men to load their muskets, the protesters dispersed. By their actions, Davis had apparently decided, these women had forfeited their claims to the courtesy normally paid to southern ladies.

The next day, groups of hungry people returned to Richmond's street corners; once again stores were broken into. Officials reportedly distributed some food. But the government also ordered troops back into the downtown to scatter the hungry, and the city fathers sent some members of the previous day's crowd to jail.[36]

Davis's government instructed the local press and telegraphers to quash news of what had occurred. But the underlying food crisis could not be so easily contained. It sparked riots in at least six towns and cities in Georgia and North Carolina that spring.[37] Catherine Edmondston sniffed that these were merely Yankee-incited "mobs for plunder" composed of transplanted northerners, Germans, Irish, and "low foreigners" generally.[38] But in Salisbury, in her own state, women who openly confiscated food from public stores included many wives of Confederate soldiers.[39]

And food prices continued to rise. Richmonders were still "in a half starving condition," clerk John B. Jones noted in mid-July, and he said so again three months later. That fall, Richmond workingmen called public meetings to demand that government impose price ceilings on

202 The FALL of the HOUSE of DIXIE

necessities. The state legislature turned them down. Meanwhile, groups of women in search of flour, corn, yarn, cloth, and other staples took to attacking wagons, mills, and merchants' stores in the countryside. Arson struck Lynchburg enterprises suspected of profiting from the food crisis.[40] Protesters in Mobile hoisted placards calling for "bread or blood."[41] In Alabama's hilly northeast, the small-scale slave owner Sarah Espy recorded an example of the friction that war-spawned privation was exacerbating between social classes. As one of Espy's neighbors was threshing her harvested wheat, some poor white women "came and impressed 70 bush[els] of it."[42]

Something had to be done. Confederate authorities at the local, state, and national levels implemented a series of measures that sought to alleviate the worst effects of the food crisis. In Richmond, Lynchburg, Charleston, and elsewhere, special stores were created to make foodstuffs available to the needy at lower prices. Some members of the elite who supported such steps were motivated by a long-standing code of paternalistic noblesse oblige. Behind that code was a concern voiced by one Richmond editor now—"that important reforms" were necessary in order "to prevent serious disturbances of the social order."[43]

Such measures achieved some success, staving off at least outright starvation among the white poor—and especially among families of serving soldiers. But drastic inflation and corresponding hikes in food prices continued to plague the Confederacy (and especially urban dwellers) for the duration of the war.[44]

These multiple grievances combined with horror at battlefield bloodshed and fears raised by battlefield setbacks in the second half of 1863 produced anguished calls for peace. In July and August, public meetings protested various policies of the Davis administration and called for initiating peace talks with the Union. About a hundred such meetings took place in North Carolina, whose units in the Army of Northern Virginia suffered tremendous losses.[45] Another thirty or so meetings occurred the following year.[46] William Woods Holden's newspaper, the *North Carolina Standard*, became the peace movement's principal journalistic champion in that state.[47]

Those who called for an end to the war did so for different reasons and with a range of goals in mind. Most, hoping that northern Peace

Democrats would add to the gains they had registered in 1862 Union elections, were optimistic that negotiations with the United States would leave the Confederacy independent.[48]

Others, however, were prepared to rejoin the old Union. Governor Vance heard in early June 1863 from a longtime supporter in the hills of North Carolina that "thousands believe in their hearts that there was no use breaking up the old Government." And that "the whole people" (or at least those "who are not in high office") were by now "tired of this unfortunate war, and want it stopped in some way."[49] William Woods Holden made it clear that while he would prefer peace based on Confederate independence, even peace achieved through reunion (so long as it left slavery intact) was preferable to a prolonged war.[50] A number of public meetings in his state endorsed the same view.[51]

For some of those who sought peace even if it meant returning to the Union, war on behalf of the South's "peculiar institution" had by now lost much of its appeal. Such people, as the *Fayetteville Observer* acknowledged, accepted "that peace and reconstruction would only result in the abolition of slavery," but since "many . . . owned no slaves, they need not care."[52] Alexander Pearce, a farmer in central North Carolina, believed that slavery was "an evil thing"; he stood, he said, for "freedom to all man kind."[53] His was evidently an extreme case. Many more Tar Heel State residents were less opposed to slavery on principle than they were unwilling to make any further sacrifices on its behalf.

But others joined the peace campaign because they believed that only an early end to the war, either with or without reunion, could now *prevent* slavery's complete destruction. As Union troops spread through the Mississippi valley following the July 1863 fall of Vicksburg, a Raleigh newspaper editor argued that "peace now would save slavery" while a continued war would "obliterate the last vestige of it."[54] Those words, according to North Carolina's sympathetic state treasurer and planter Jonathan Worth, echoed the sentiments of "many who are largely interested in slave property."[55] In the Union, Democrats encouraged the idea that this was possible by insisting that any state that sought reentry into the Union be spared the effects of the Emancipation Proclamation—be allowed, that is, to resume its former place with slavery fully intact.[56]

Nonetheless, talk of reunion (or "reconstruction," as it was then commonly called) in 1863 infuriated the great mass of Confederate whites. Soldier Lancelot Blackford reported that summer that "the chief source of depression, when any exists among the troops, is the intelligence of faint-heartedness, and in some sections base 'caving-in' that reaches them from home." "Any man who advocates reconstruction," another soldier exclaimed, "should be hung to the nearest tree."[57] A soldier from Florida longed to "go home and whip every body there that in the least is opposed to us."[58] In August, state militia men shut down a peace meeting in North Carolina.[59] In September, Confederate (possibly Georgian) troops passing through Raleigh ransacked the office of Holden's newspaper, the *North Carolina Standard*.

But this attempt to silence the dissidents backfired. Two hundred of Holden's supporters avenged the attack on his paper by laying waste to the office of the pro–Jefferson Davis Raleigh *State Journal*.[60] And Zebulon Vance cautioned Davis that the attack on the *Standard* had aroused indignation far beyond the circle of Holden's close supporters.[61] The governor therefore begged the Confederate president to prevent any similar incidents or prepare himself to see "the North Carolina troops [rush] home to the defense of their own State and her institutions."[62]

Vance also hoped that this explosion would make Davis finally realize "what a mine [he had] been standing on and what a delicate and embarrassing situation" he was in.[63] The governor had advised Davis in July 1863 that there was "a bad state of feeling [in North Carolina] toward the Confederate Government."[64] In early November Vance traveled into the mountains in order to gauge personally the extent and depth of the dissatisfaction. To his evident surprise, he found not only widespread discontent but also "an astonishing amount of disloyalty."[65]

At the end of the year, sharp differences over the peace issue broke the already strained political alliance joining Vance to editor William Woods Holden. Vance feared that Holden's call to bypass the Davis government in order to sue for peace would dishonor North Carolina, precipitate civil war *within* the Confederacy, and end in the disintegration of order and civil government generally.[66] But Vance also knew that the peace movement expressed a broad-based feeling of "discontent" in his state, especially strong among "the humblest of our citizens." Davis's government should do something to appease that powerful longing for the war's end and redirect popular anger away from the Confederacy. In December 1863, Vance urged Richmond to publicly request peace talks with the Union, and thereby prove to disaffected people in the Confederacy "that the Government is tender of their lives & happiness & would not prolong their sufferings unnecessarily one moment."[67]

Jefferson Davis rejected that advice. The North Carolina governor judged that a serious tactical mistake, but he soon voiced an even deeper anxiety about the future. As he confessed only to his closest confidants, Vance no longer believed that the Confederate population was willing to make the sacrifices necessary to defeat the Union armies. To achieve a military victory, he said in January 1864, would cost the South a great deal more "blood and misery." But he had now become "satisfied" that "our people will not pay this price."[68]

The peace movement seems to have been strongest in North Carolina, where firm unionist traditions and a large population of non-slaveholders—some of whom had always disliked slavery—made the war's now swiftly mounting costs in both blood and treasure especially hard to take. But peace sentiments were mounting elsewhere in the Confederacy and among slave owners as well. A Union major traveling through Mississippi's Natchez region in July 1863 found the people "hopeless of the rebellion and ready to do almost anything to keep their negroes in the fields."[69] A planter in Jackson, Mississippi, who claimed to have been a "zealous secessionist" at the war's inception, now urged Jefferson Davis "to lose no time in making the best terms possible" with the U.S. government.[70]

Abraham Lincoln's Proclamation of Amnesty and Reconstruction—including its apparent promise to allow post-reunion southerners to impose special restrictions upon the former slave population—probably strengthened pro-peace views. That much seemed evident in March 1864 at a convention in the Union-occupied city of Huntsville called to seek reentry into the United States. One of the delegates was Judge D. C. Humphreys, a once-secessionist Madison County planter.[71] "Alabama should at once rescind the ordinance of secession," Humphreys told the attendees. "I believe the institution of Slavery is gone as a permanent thing—overthrown by the action of the Southern States." But all was not lost, for "in case of a return to the Union, we would receive political cooperation so as to secure the management of that labor by those who were slaves." "Of course," Humphreys conceded, "we prefer the old method"—full-blown slavery. But while that option had now disappeared, others yet remained. After all, he believed, "There is really no difference . . . whether we hold them as absolute slaves, or obtain their labor by some other method."[72]

Similar plans were being hatched simultaneously in parts of Alabama still in Confederate hands. On March 1, 1863, a Confederate major came across two Confederate colonels named Holly and Seibels conversing in hushed tones on the veranda of a Montgomery hotel. Suspicious, the major later asked Holly what the discussion had been about. Holly told him that Seibels (who had been the governor's military adjutant when the war began) was planning an overture to Lincoln, offering to return Alabama to the Union in return for allowing the survival of at least the vestiges of slavery until the end of the nineteenth century.[73]

Peace advocates of whatever variety remained a minority in the Confederacy in this period. But state-level Confederate elections between May and November 1863 did reveal a widespread if largely unfocused mood of disappointment and dissatisfaction. Voters turned many incumbent congressmen out of office, including strong supporters of the Davis government and its most unpopular policies. That outcome did not reflect a rejection by the electorate as a whole of the Confederacy, the war, or slavery; most of the winners still pledged themselves to southern independence.[74] But it did signify a growing popular sense that the government was being mismanaged, that the war was not going well, and that too many citizens of the southern republic were being treated unfairly.

And in some cases, the shift in mood looked more ominous than that. In Texas's gubernatorial contest, the principal contenders were Thomas J. Chambers and Pendleton Murrah. While Chambers reviled Murrah as a pro-Union coward, Murrah denounced Chambers for being a rich planter. The accused coward beat the rich planter with ease.[75] Five newly elected "peace" candidates joined North Carolina's ten-member delegation to the Confederate House of Representatives. All five were slave owners, three of them closely allied with the pro-peace editor William W. Holden.[76]

In Georgia, Governor Joseph E. Brown ran for reelection in 1863 against two opponents—one, Timothy Furlow, a staunch Jefferson Davis supporter, and the other, Joshua Hill, a peace candidate. Like

Zebulon Vance, Brown was a skillful political tightrope walker. While striving to promote the Confederate war effort, he cast himself as the paladin of states' rights and of the interests of Georgians with little property. He opposed the tax in kind as well as the Confederate conscription system,[77] a stance that won him sharp criticism from some for being "an oily flatterer of the masses" and for "attempting to get up a war of classes."[78] But Brown's adroit self-presentation served him well overall. In the final balloting, a large majority of the state's voters kept him in office.

Brown's act played less well in the state's northern hills and mountains, where resentment of the war and the Richmond government was broader and deeper than elsewhere. There peace candidate Joshua Hill demonstrated significant strength. Hill had opposed secession in 1861, and Brown's supporters now flayed him as a submissionist and reunionist. Statewide, those labels (and Brown's own popularity) were enough to limit Hill's share of the vote to 27 percent. Even that share, however, was larger than the one garnered by Furlow, the Davis loyalist. And in the northern up-country generally, Joshua Hill's vote share jumped above 42 percent. In eight up-country counties, Hill beat Brown outright.[79]

The situation seemed little better in the heart of Dixie. Alabama planter Benjamin H. Micou alerted his old friend Judah P. Benjamin that "some of our best men" had been defeated at the polls by candidates with weak secessionist credentials. And everywhere, he fretted, one heard more and more calls for peace, including for peace through reunion if necessary.[80]

Micou's intelligence was accurate. In Alabama's gubernatorial election, the pro–Jefferson Davis incumbent, John G. Shorter, lost in a landslide to Thomas H. Watts. Shorter later reflected that his assistance to Confederate armies in impressing slaves had been "the strongest element which carried the state so largely against me."[81] More broadly, he believed, he had come to symbolize the burdens and sacrifices that the war had imposed on the state's white population.[82] He had been "stricken down," as he put it, "for holding up the state to its high resolves and crowding the people to the performance of their duty." Perhaps the triumph of his opponent, Watts, also owed something to the campaign that the Shorter camp waged against him. Shorter's supporters accused Watts of being a reunionist. The accusation was false;

Watts was foursquare for the Confederacy. But he chose not to deny the unionism charge publicly until the election was over. His well-timed silence may have swung a segment of the electorate toward him.[83]

The souring political atmosphere also transformed Alabama's representation in the Confederate Senate. The outgoing state legislature, growing sensitive to its constituents' disaffection, relieved Davis ally Clement C. Clay of his seat and replaced him with Richard W. Walker, who was less closely identified with the Richmond regime. Even more tellingly: After the state's fire-eating senator William L. Yancey died that July, the legislature gave his seat to Robert Jemison, who had voted against the state's secession ordinance in January 1861. (If the state legislators thought these gestures toward war weariness would keep them in office, they were mistaken. Alabama voters sent many of them packing anyway, electing in their place men who were even less enthusiastic about the war than the defeated incumbents.)[84]

The picture was still clearer in that state's popular vote for the Confederate House of Representatives, in which Alabamans occupied nine seats. Incumbent J.L.M. Curry, a firm and prominent Davis supporter, was defeated overwhelmingly. According to his ally Texas senator W. S. Oldham, what swept Curry out of office was "his defence of the Government and efforts to sustain it in the public confidence."[85] A Confederate conscription officer in the state seconded that evaluation. Curry had gone down, the man reported to Richmond, "chiefly . . . on account of his identification with the Government, and with what we have been accustomed to consider the established principles of the Confederacy."[86]

The man who beat Curry, Marcus Henderson Cruikshank, was a peace candidate rumored to favor reunion.[87] And five other new Alabama congressmen seemed similarly inclined. One of them was Williamson R. W. Cobb, a prewar unionist later derided for being "singularly popular with the humble and unlearned." After his election, Cobb declined to take his congressional seat. Reports reached Richmond that Union armies were allowing Cobb free passage through their lines, presumably because they counted him a friend. The Confederate Congress eventually voted unanimously to expel him from its ranks.[88]

These election results, Alabaman Benjamin H. Micou warned the

Confederate secretary of state, revealed a strong "feeling of doubt &
distrust" and a "dissatisfaction of the people with their lawmakers."
Strengthening that sentiment was the belief among "some poor men"
that "the war is killing up their sons & brothers for the protection of the
slaveholder." That sentiment, Micou said, was "gradually bringing into
antagonism the rich & the poor."[89]

The 1863 election results did not threaten Jefferson Davis's grip on
government. The Confederate president retained a strong core of congressional allies, including many who hailed from districts imminently
threatened or already occupied by Union forces. These men spoke and
voted in far greater practical independence of their actual constituents,
who had by then lost contact with and political control over their representatives. (In the words of the head of the Confederate War Bureau,
they represented "imaginary constituencies.") Over the course of the
war, Davis relied more and more upon them to support his most controversial measures—an arrangement that gave his government considerable effective freedom from popular control while retaining the
appearance of governing with popular consent.[90]

But Davis's parliamentary security could not spare his regime from
the practical impact of popular disaffection and indiscipline of various
kinds. Increasingly, the Confederacy found it hard to keep its soldiers
in the ranks over extended periods of time. The War Department in
Richmond estimated in July 1863 that between forty and fifty thousand men were absent without leave from its armies. By the end of the
year, it was calculating that deserters, absentees, and stragglers combined constituted between one-third and one-half of its soldiers.[91]

By no means were these all men who lacked or had lost a belief in the
Confederacy. Many left the ranks to return home to assist family members who were suffering without a breadwinner or who were alarmed by
the approach of Union troops or their inability to control black laborers.
In April 1863, Nancy Mangum had warned North Carolina governor
Zebulon Vance that "we wiimen will write our husbans to come . . . home
and help us we cant stand it." And so they did. By the time Mangum
wrote those words, growing numbers of southern soldiers were receiving letters from parents and wives beseeching them to return home and

attend to the welfare of their relatives. "I hope . . . you will [now] think," one woman wrote her son, that "the time past has sufficed for public service, & that your own family may require yr protection and help—as others are [already] deciding." "What do I care for patriotism," another woman demanded. "My husband is my country. What is country to me if he be killed?"[92]

Army officers, editors, and political leaders pleaded with "southern women" to cease trying "to keep husband, son or brother from the Confederate army."[93] Savvy officers turned a blind eye toward the absence of soldiers responding to such calls, and most soldiers away without leave eventually rejoined their units.[94]

But while deserters of this kind could leave the ranks without abandoning their commitment to the Confederacy, others—more and more as the war wore on—left because they had given up hope of victory.[95] Another potent influence was mounting resentment of the social elite, its privileges, and its treatment of those of lesser means. Many soldiers and civilians blamed rich landowners and merchants for the soaring price of food and other necessities, accusing them of "extortion." Alabama's governor heard from a semiliterate citizen named J. A. Sullivan that "the cruellty of the [rich] to the Soldiers famileys is the caus of thear deserting."[96] It was surely no coincidence that deserters disproportionately hailed from parts of the South where support for the Confederate war effort was notoriously the weakest.[97] Those who looked askance at the men who had led them into war also tended to blame them for the privations, suffering, and deaths that the war created.

Compounding the problem of absent soldiers was a rise in draft resistance. A Mississippian reported to his governor in October 1862 that the draft's planter-exemption law had produced "a ginerl Bacckought [general back out]" from army service in that state's southern districts.[98] And in the summer of 1863, Virginia senator Allen T. Caperton reported growing resentment of the substitute system, which allowed a wealthy conscript to avoid military service by paying someone else to replace him. "The idea is expanding that the rich, for whose benefit the war is waged, have procured substitutes to fight for them, while the poor, who have no slaves to lose, have not been able to procure substitutes."[99] By the end of 1862 and the beginning of 1863, substitutes in Virginia were demanding compensation of $1,500 to $2,000 apiece, a price far beyond the reach of most non-slaveholders.[100]

In 1863, deserters and draft resisters began to form organized groups for mutual protection. That September, Assistant Secretary of War John A. Campbell warned that "the condition of things in the mountain districts of North Carolina, South Carolina, Georgia, and Alabama menaces the existence of the Confederacy as fatally as either of the armies of the United States."[101] To that list of regions beset by internal conflict Campbell could have added northern Arkansas, parts of southern Mississippi and Alabama, and some coastal and piedmont districts of North Carolina, in all of which slaveholders made up a relatively small percentage of the total white population.

In late 1862, a group of deserters and unionists took refuge in the hills and mountains of northeastern Georgia. In January 1863, the state's adjutant and inspector general, Brigadier General Henry C. Wayne, noted that resisters and deserters were "inciting rebellion" and "committing acts of robbery and threatening to . . . do other acts of violence." They reportedly harbored runaway slaves and intimidated and plundered pro-Confederate neighbors.

The governor dispatched troops to break them up, scoring some successes in that effort. By March, the threat appeared to have been suppressed. But in June an army commander was again reporting "considerable trouble" in the hill districts. In one county, residents loyal to the Confederacy had arrested a group of deserters. Allies of those arrested, however, had then attacked the loyalists, freeing the prisoners and killing or wounding several of their captors. By the fall, a state official was describing a neighboring county, too, as "overrun" with deserters, unionists, and "rogues."[102] A number of groups commonly referred to collectively as "the Peace Society"[103] worked to attract Georgia's civilians and soldiers to antiadministration candidates for office and to compel the government to sue for peace.[104] In February 1864, a correspondent "mingling freely with the common people" in the up-country informed the governor that "among that class generally there is a strong Union feeling" and a belief "that the people could not fare any worse under Lincoln than [they] are fairing under Jeff [Davis]."[105]

The same or similar organizations began to grow in both up-country and "piney woods" sections of Alabama and Mississippi.[106] (The "piney woods" regions of southwest Alabama and southeast Mississippi were cursed with pine forests and wire grass that were difficult to clear, and thin topsoil not conducive to cotton cultivation. They contained comparatively few slaveholders.)

By the fall of 1863, deserters in three Mississippi counties (Jones, Smith, and Greene) had begun to form into bands that, for mutual protection, maintained communication with one another.[107] The leader of the group in Jones County was named Newton Knight. Born into a slaveless family, he seems to have opposed secession and definitely opposed the draft law's planter exemption. Deserting the Confederate army after Iuka and Corinth, Knight was soon captured but in May 1863 managed to escape once again.[108] Between the fall of 1863 and the beginning of 1865, Knight's band fought Confederate forces more than a dozen times. Women cooked for and sheltered the tired and wounded deserters and warned them when soldiers approached. Slaves brought them food and information.[109]

A captain in a Mississippi regiment who visited the area reported that groups of "deserters and conscripts" were in such close contact with one another that within "a few hours large bodies of them can be collected at any given point prepared to attempt almost anything," including "deeds of violence, bloodshed, and outlawry" throughout southern and southeastern parts of the state. "Gin-houses, dwelling-houses, and barns, and the court-house of Greene County have been destroyed by fire," the captain noted. "Bridges have been burned and ferry-boats sunk on almost every stream and at almost every ferry to obstruct the passage of troops." One party of deserters surprised and captured one Confederate officer and then debated whether to hang him. At length deciding on leniency, they granted him parole on condition "that he would never again enter the county as a Confederate officer under orders or authority, or in any way aid or assist in molesting them." Other Confederate soldiers and officials received similar treatment. Newton Knight's band made a special target of the tax in kind and those who collected it. Early in 1864 they raided a tax depot in Paulding (the county seat of Jasper, just north of Jones) and made off with five wagonloads of corn, distributing some of it to the local poor.[110]

To hunt down these anti-Rebel rebels, Confederate general Leonidas Polk sent first a cavalry and then an infantry regiment into the area in March and April 1864.[111] His troops caught several, sometimes by holding their family members as hostages. Some of those prisoners were hanged, others forced back into the Confederate army.[112] But though seriously reduced in numbers, deserter bands continued to plague government forces.

In North Carolina, the anti-Confederate Heroes of America, which first appeared in 1861, began to grow rapidly in number and geographical reach after enactment of conscription in the spring of 1862. During that summer, increasing numbers of soldiers from the state's central counties began to desert and return to their homes. The Heroes welcomed them, and the deserters—along with those evading the draft—joined its ranks. This group's leaders included prominent professionals of various kinds, but whites with little or no property in both the countryside and urban centers supplied most of its grassroots support. By 1864, the Heroes were openly recruiting among Raleigh's white working class and among those who labored in Wilmington's saltworks, many of whom were unionists and conscientious objectors sent there by the Confederate government. By one estimate, the Heroes eventually commanded the loyalty of some ten thousand people in the Tar Heel State.[113]

The Heroes also provided intelligence about southern troop movements to Union forces and helped persecuted unionists to escape into Union-held territory, especially Kentucky and parts of Tennessee. Like the Newton Knight group in Mississippi, Tar Heel bands associated with the Heroes were clashing more and more frequently and violently with militia forces by the end of 1863, with considerable losses on both sides.[114] Meanwhile, draft agents, government officials, and army officers found that similar groups had ensconced themselves elsewhere in North Carolina—in the hills along the borders with both Tennessee and South Carolina. These groups already numbered more than a thousand, and they were "augmenting their number every day."[115]

North Carolina's Zebulon Vance set out to destroy these bands of armed resisters. He instructed his militia and a newly formed Guard for Home Defense to root them out.

But Vance soon discovered that the militia and guard units were themselves intimidated by the resisters; others, he found, sympathized too strongly with deserters to act against them.[116] Perhaps, Vance now suggested, the Army of Northern Virginia could spare a few brigades "or a good strong regiment" to deal with this internal danger. "Something of this kind *must* be done," he stressed. Robert E. Lee dispatched two infantry regiments and a cavalry squadron in early September 1863 to impose order.[117]

During the next few months, those soldiers and home guard units who supported them resorted to severe measures. To force Heroes to surrender, or at least to discover their whereabouts, soldiers tortured their family members. Those methods led to the capture of thousands. But they failed fully to pacify the region, while spreading and deepening popular disaffection.[118] When the Confederate troops eventually departed in mid-February 1864, outlaws who had evaded capture emerged from their hiding places and took vengeance on pro-Confederate residents.[119]

Defeatism and open defiance of the Confederacy was much weaker in the armies than in the civilian population, partly because the men who were the most dedicated to the Confederacy had most readily put on uniforms and taken up arms to repel the Yankee abolitionists. And among the soldiery, Lee's Army of Northern Virginia maintained the highest level of morale, in large part because Lee had led it from victory to victory ever since he assumed command in the spring of 1862.[120]

The experience of the Army of Tennessee (formerly dubbed the Army of Mississippi) had been quite different. As the Confederacy's principal military force in the western war theater, it had witnessed and suffered one defeat after another ever since the fall of Tennessee's Forts Henry and Donelson in early 1862. Those accumulating blows had inevitably taken a heavy toll on its morale.

After the shattering reversal outside Chattanooga late in 1863, where Union troops had rolled over the Army of Tennessee's seemingly impregnable positions, the Confederate troops regrouped in winter quarters outside the town of Dalton in the hills of northern Georgia. At that point, it seems, the Peace Society began to recruit among them. Some soldiers vowed never to fight again.[121] W. A. Stephens of the Forty-Sixth Alabama regiment had decided that the South's defeat had become inevitable and that therefore "the lives that is lost in this war now is for no good." B. L. Wyman, another member of the Forty-Sixth, recorded that "a large number are for going back into the 'Union.' "[122]

But these sentiments were not confined to the ill-starred Army of

Tennessee. As early as August 1863, a company in the Twenty-Fourth North Carolina regiment, then stationed in Virginia, announced that it was "opposed to any more shedding of blood in this war" and was "unanimously in favor of peace on the best terms that can be obtained."[123] A private in the Fifty-Seventh North Carolina claimed that "most of the solegers" in his regiment were "for peese" in the nearly unconditional manner championed in William W. Holden's newspaper.[124]

Certain Alabama units displayed even more advanced symptoms of decay. Just after Christmas 1863, the commander of the Fifty-Ninth Alabama regiment discovered that many of his troops—and especially those who were immigrants, paid substitutes, or of "the poorer class of men"—believed that "they have but little to fight for." They showed "a general disposition" to "lay down their arms, yieldup the cause and accept the best terms the Yankee Government will grant."[125] A similar report came that same day from the colonel of the Fifty-Seventh Alabama. His men displayed a "considerable manifestation of revolutionary spirit . . . on account of the tax in kind law and the impressment system." Determined to "protect their families from supposed injustice and wrong on the part of the [Confederate] Government," they declared themselves ready to surrender themselves to Union forces.[126]

Shortly afterward, on January 5, 1864, sixty Alabama soldiers stationed just across the border from the Florida panhandle mutinied, refusing to take any further part in the war. They were promptly arrested. More than a hundred of their comrades "acknowledged themselves members" of the Peace Society but now recanted that membership in hopes of pardon.

These regiments formed part of a brigade that had been recruited in Alabama's nearby piney woods counties. According to the department commander, the whole brigade was "full of this disaffection." Upon investigating, he found that "an organized opposition to the war exists in our midst" that stood for "peace on any terms" and swore "never to fight against the enemy; to desert the service of the Confederacy; to encourage and protect deserters, and to do all other things in their power to end the war and break down the Government and the so-called Southern Confederacy."[127] Richmond disbanded the brigade.[128]

Less sensational but more important militarily than these eruptions in Confederate ranks was the fact that thousands of white residents of the Confederacy, especially from the up-country, enlisted and fought in the Union army. Some were Confederate soldiers who volunteered for Union service after surrendering to U.S. troops. Some left their homes and made their way to Union recruiting offices. Others joined Union armies as they moved through their home districts. In November 1863, Zebulon Vance learned that "several men who recently figured in 'peace meetings' have gone off and taken arms with the enemy." At least two-thirds of the men in one Union regiment, he added in embarrassment, hailed from his own state.[129]

In fact, about five thousand white North Carolinians served in Union uniforms over the course of the war. Three thousand white Alabamians did the same thing, as did seven thousand white Louisianans and ten thousand white Arkansans. Virginia alone (especially its western counties) supplied some thirty thousand recruits. The largest single contingent hailed from Tennessee—some forty-two thousand in number. The grand total exceeded one hundred thousand, most of them serving under officers from their states and in federal units that bore their states' names.[130]

Elite Confederates disparaged these southern-born Union soldiers as human trash. Plantation mistress Catherine Edmondston sneered that they were "people who can neither read or write & who never had a decent suit of clothes until they [the Yankees] gave it to them, poor ignorant wretches who cannot resist a fine uniform and the choice of the horses in the country & liberty to help themselves without check to their neighbors belongings."[131] But such words, redolent of aristocratic condescension, could not offset the practical significance of those defections. The white residents of Confederate states who served under the Union flag would together have filled out an army larger than any that Richmond fielded throughout the war.

The second calendar year of war, 1863, had dawned brightly for the slaveholders' republic. Lee's breathtaking Virginia victories at the end of 1862 and in the spring of 1863 lifted spirits and kindled hopes for an early end to the conflict on Richmond's terms. But the slaughter at Gettysburg, the disaster at Vicksburg, and then the rout at Chattanooga brought a chill of foreboding to Confederate leaders and followers alike. Desperate longings for peace began to replace triumphalist dreams, especially in sectors of the slaveless white population, which bore most of the burdens of the war but whose immediate interests were less bound up with its outcome.

Even now, however, most Confederates (and especially those serving in Lee's Army of Northern Virginia) remained committed to a southern victory. And in 1864, just as at the start of the preceding year, military developments would once again buoy the hopes of those committed to preserving the slaveholders' republic.

Chapter Eight

_____

A RAY OF LIGHT SHINES BRIEFLY
THROUGH THE RAFTERS

May through December 1864

From the Union's point of view, the start of 1864 seemed to brim over with military promise. During the previous six months, victories at Vicksburg and Port Hudson had completed the conquest of the strategic Mississippi River and its fertile valley. That had divided the Confederacy along a North-South axis, effectively isolating its eastern and western regions from each other. More recently, the stunning victory outside Chattanooga had overwhelmed and driven the Confederate Army of Tennessee out of the state whose name it bore. Meanwhile, the Union navy's blockade of the Confederate coast tightened, as did the Union army's grip on portions of it.

The United States was also making strides in identifying and empowering effective military leadership. In February and March, Congress revived the rank of lieutenant general—previously held only by George Washington and Winfield Scott (the latter on an honorary basis). Lincoln conferred the full rank on Ulysses S. Grant and then made him general in chief of all Union armies. Grant, in turn, handed over command of all forces in the West to William Tecumseh Sherman.

In June, Lincoln's party affirmed its commitment to him and his war program. The Republican national convention in Baltimore renominated Lincoln for the presidency on a platform promising "to prosecute the war with the utmost possible vigor to the complete suppression of the Rebellion." To help attract the broad political support that it now sought, the party rechristened itself the National Union party and gave its vice presidential nomination to Andrew Johnson, a War Democrat whom Lincoln had appointed as war governor of Tennessee and who had by now reconciled himself to emancipation.

The 1864 platform also called for amending the U.S. Constitution to "terminate and forever prohibit the existence of Slavery" not only within the rebellious states but everywhere "within the limits of the jurisdiction of the United States."[1] Abolitionists and radical Republicans had begun to press for such an amendment in the spring of 1863, partly to protect Lincoln's proclamation against judicial attempts to nullify it as unconstitutional. But they also wanted to extend liberty to many legally unaffected by the proclamation or any other emancipatory measure. The destruction of slavery throughout the United States, they asserted, was essential to building a just society in the restored Union.[2] By mid-1864, teams of northern women and men had collected almost four hundred thousand signatures on petitions supporting nationwide abolition.

The Republicans' promise to support the amendment represented a major radicalization of the party program since 1860, when it had pledged only to prevent slavery's expansion into the territories while promising solemnly not to touch the institution within any of the states. Two confiscation acts, an emancipation proclamation, the large-scale recruitment of black soldiers, and a series of other state and federal actions marked the road along which public (but especially Republican) opinion had traveled during the ensuing years of war.

The Democratic Party as a whole set itself determinedly against the proposed amendment, and in June that opposition deprived it of the two-thirds majority it needed to pass the U.S. House of Representatives.[3] But events and much popular sentiment continued to press toward emancipation. Abolition was steadily advancing in border states and Union-occupied parts of the Confederacy where civilian antislavery forces had taken political power. By the summer of 1864, constitutional conventions had outlawed slavery in Maryland, Arkansas, and Louisiana; emancipation came to the new state of West Virginia and to occupied parts of Virginia proper through statute and decree.[4]

Lincoln's own views about emancipation's place in Union war policy were also evolving. Having initially depicted it strictly as a means to save the Union, Lincoln had now come to regard it as a war aim in its own right. He was thus asked in mid-1864 under what conditions he would consider negotiating with the Confederacy. Only, he replied, when Jefferson Davis consented in advance to both "the restoration of the Union" and the "abandonment of slavery." In accepting his party's renomination for the presidency, Lincoln endorsed the proposed amendment "in the joint names of Liberty and Union."[5] Undoubtedly influencing this change was the Union president's growing appreciation for those thousands of "black men who . . . with silent tongue, and clenched teeth, and steady eye, and well-poised bayonet" were serving in the Union army and navy.[6]

In private, Lincoln was going even further. Representatives of African American communities in both the North and Union-occupied parts of the South were pressing to make freedom for black people mean the same thing that it did for whites. That meant granting them the full rights of citizenship. In October 1864, a national convention of black men held in Syracuse, New York, called not only for the abolition of slavery throughout the United States, but also for equality before the law and voting rights for adult black males.[7] Earlier that year, Lincoln had met with two black residents of New Orleans who urged that they and other black men in Louisiana be given the suffrage. A day after that meeting Lincoln gently and privately suggested that those attempting to erect a Union-loyal government in conquered portions of Louisiana grant the franchise to "the very intelligent, and especially those who have fought gallantly in our ranks."[8]

As the Union's military strength and commitment to emancipation grew, Robert E. Lee revised his strategic plans in light of the Confederacy's weakened condition. The Army of Northern Virginia's depleted ranks would no longer allow the kind of strategic offensives launched earlier, most notably in Kentucky, Maryland, and Pennsylvania. Lee would now depend more heavily on the advantage of defensive postures to inflict as many casualties on Union forces as possible, hoping thereby to demoralize the northern population into sending a Democrat to the White House in November—a man more pliable than Lincoln and open to a negotiated peace that would leave the slaveholders' republic intact and independent. "Every bullet we can send against the Yankees," explained a Georgia newspaper at the start of the year, "is the best ballot that can be deposited against Lincoln's election."[9]

Lincoln's new general in chief was planning a series of changes in the Union's military effort as well. Like Lincoln, Grant had concluded early that Confederate forces were profiting from a lack of coordination among the larger Union armies. That failing had allowed Davis to take advantage of his interior lines to shuttle troops to whichever front was under the greatest pressure.

Confederate forces also benefited from the fact that combat had occurred only intermittently. Nearly all the fighting took place between early spring and late autumn, with both sides using the winter to rest, recuperate, and regroup. Even in good weather major battles were generally followed by more or less prolonged periods of quiescence. Grant understood that such disengagement took the pressure off Confederate forces and minimized the impact of the North's numerical advantage, allowing the Confederacy to "furlough large numbers to go to their homes and do the work of producing for the support of their armies."[10]

Grant therefore proposed to alter both patterns. He would initiate the "active and continuous operations of all the troops that could be brought into the field, regardless of season and weather." In this way he aimed "to hammer continuously against the armed force of the enemy and his resources until, by mere attrition, if in no other way, there should be nothing left to him" but surrender.

To these two guidelines, Grant added a third: Whenever possible, systematically destroy the material resources—the potential sources of supply—that enemy armies depended upon and crack the morale of the secessionist population.[11]

Grant intended to implement these new policies in campaigns against the Confederacy's Army of Tennessee in Georgia and its Army of Northern Virginia in the Old Dominion. Still formally under the command of George Gordon Meade, who had led it to victory at Gettysburg, the Union Army of the Potomac would run Robert E. Lee's army to the ground and subdue it. Ulysses S. Grant's headquarters would travel with Meade's army and, in fact, direct its operations. In the meantime, Sherman's army, then camped in southeastern Tennessee, would link up with two other smaller ones and then move against the Confederate Army of Tennessee, by now led by Joseph Johnston, pulverize it, and then proceed farther southward into Georgia. Grant assigned supporting roles to smaller Union armies in western and eastern Virginia and Louisiana (under the commands of Generals Franz Sigel, Benjamin Butler, and Nathaniel Banks, respectively) to keep up the pressure, thereby preventing the Confederacy from concentrating all its forces against the two biggest Union armies.[12]

The North now pinned on Grant the kind of extravagant hopes that it had placed upon George B. McClellan a few years earlier. And at first, those expectations seemed on the verge of fulfillment. By May 1864 northern newspapers were cheering that "the Virginia campaign approaches a Glorious consummation" and even that "Lee's army as an effective force has practically ceased to exist."[13]

Once again, however, military events dispelled illusions that the end of the war was nigh. Instead, Confederate officers and men managed to stall Union progress for crucial months.

Sherman's men began their march through the hills of southeastern Tennessee and northwestern Georgia in May 1864. They were bound for Atlanta, a rail hub linking together much of the Confederacy east of the Mississippi and a key administrative and logistical supply center that produced or stored ammunition, firearms, cannons, saddles, flour, railroad rails, and other key items. Robert E. Lee believed that the safety of all Confederate forces "on the Atlantic" depended upon holding Georgia.[14]

To hold it, General Joseph E. Johnston had resupplied, reimposed discipline upon, and raised the esprit of the Confederate Army of Tennessee from the depths to which it had fallen after Chattanooga. One of its soldiers now told his sister that he "never saw the army in such fine spirits"; all were now "hopeful and confident."[15]

As Sherman's troops headed southward, Johnston repeatedly placed his army across their path, dug in, and dared the Union force to attack. But the Union commander, determined to avoid the costly losses that frontal assault had usually incurred, instead launched a series of flanking attacks. In response to each of these, Johnston pulled his men back just far enough southward along the tracks of the Western and Atlantic Railroad to protect that supply line and avoid encirclement. And the same dance steps would then repeat.

Johnston's delaying tactics, plus difficult terrain and weather, slowed Sherman's progress toward Atlanta considerably. "If we can keep this up," a Confederate captain assayed in early July, "we win."[16] The *Richmond Sentinel* thought so, too: "Time is victory to us and death to our enemies."[17]

In the third week of June, Sherman's patience gave out. Frustrated at the slow pace of his advance and his failure to deal a mortal blow to the Army of Tennessee, Sherman sent his men on a frontal assault across a third of a mile against a strong Confederate position on the seven-hundred-foot-high Kennesaw Mountain.[18] The assault failed bloodily, at the cost of three thousand casualties while imposing only a sixth as many upon the Confederates. Atlanta applauded. Sherman, announced one newspaper there, "has been successfully halted in his mad career and Gen. Johnston has said to him, 'Thus far shall thou come, and no further.' "[19]

In the meantime, Grant, Meade, and their Army of the Potomac had crossed the Rapidan River in northern Virginia and in May 1864 entered a dense, fifteen-to-twenty-mile-deep forest near Chancellorsville known as the Wilderness. Lee's men pounced on Union troops before they could make their way out of the woods, relying upon the thicket to slow the enemy down and thin out his lines. Federal casualties in that battle were 50 percent higher than Confederate.

Instead of disengaging and pulling back, however, this time the Army of the Potomac resumed the offensive, moving around Lee's right flank toward Richmond. The two armies clashed again at Spotsylvania Court House in nearly two weeks of bloody combat. Grant pushed Lee's lines back but could not break them, and Union casualties were once more half again as great as those of the enemy. Mistakenly believing that the Army of Northern Virginia was by now not only weakened but demoralized as well, on June 3 Grant tried simply throwing three corps of Union infantry directly at Confederate defenses at Cold Harbor. The result was a calamitous repulse, and Union losses were this time almost five times those of the Confederacy.

Grant's steady pressure had nonetheless brought both armies to the outskirts of Richmond. Grant now sought to surprise Lee with a strategic flanking maneuver, keeping his foe preoccupied with a distracting demonstration on the north side of the James River while leading the bulk of his army on a long swing around Lee's right flank and across the river to its southern bank. Grant would then catch Lee unawares by thrusting northward through Richmond's neighboring city of Petersburg, striking the unsuspecting Army of Northern Virginia from the rear.

Much went according to plan. Grant successfully flanked Lee and crossed the James undetected on June 12, 1864. Benjamin Butler's army then joined Grant's on the outskirts of Petersburg. But the subsequent attacks on the Petersburg defenses were poorly coordinated, and the Union troops—badly shaken by the enormous losses sustained to date in the campaign—demonstrated little ardor. The relatively small force that Lee had placed in Petersburg under the command of P.G.T. Beauregard therefore managed to hold off Grant's advance guard long enough for reinforcements to arrive from the main army at Richmond.

Union hopes for a dramatic, decisive breakthrough in Virginia had thus been disappointed once again. Magnifying that disappointment was the huge number of casualties that Grant's forces had sustained. While Lee had lost more than 30,000 men in these clashes, Grant's army lost anywhere from 55,000 to 65,000.[20]

Such was the bleak news for the Union that newspapers carried northward in mid-1864. In both Georgia and Virginia, federal armies were bleeding badly while making little dramatic progress against the enemy. Public spirits in the North collapsed back into the depths they had plumbed a year earlier, before the victories at Gettysburg and Vicksburg. Reciprocally, a new surge of Confederate optimism carried North Carolina governor Zebulon Vance to a lopsided reelection victory in midsummer over his opponent, the newspaper editor and peace candidate William W. Holden. Vance garnered about four-fifths of the civilian vote, leaving Holden with a majority only in three of the state's most consistently anti-secessionist counties.[21] Vance owed his triumph not only to the revival of Confederate military fortunes that season. As a persistent critic of the Richmond government, he could evade blame for the Confederacy's failures and impositions on its citizens—and even associate himself with popular resentment of them. At the same time, his racially charged campaign shrilly warned the voters that reunification with the North would bring emancipation, and emancipation would surely mean black equality.[22]

By summer's end, Confederate triumphalists were in full cry. "Who [is] so blind," one Virginian demanded, "as not to be able to see the hand of a merciful and protective God" in accomplishing this "wonderful deliverance of our army and people from the most powerful conflagrations ever planned for our destruction!"[23] A Richmond editor assured readers that within six months "the armies of Grant, Sherman, and Sheridan" might well be "almost annihilated." Indeed, the journalist enthused, "six weeks hence, instead of waging defensive warfare, we may be invading the enemy's soil, and carrying out offensive warfare."[24] More sober-minded slaveholders and their allies began once again to hope that the Union's military problems in Virginia and Georgia would at least discourage the North enough to doom Lincoln's reelection campaign that fall and place a more pliable man in the White House.

Having failed to outflank Lee's army at Petersburg, Ulysses S. Grant settled down into a siege of that city and the Confederate capital—a siege that would last a full ten months. The grisliest moment of the campaign occurred in its first phase. During June and July of 1864, Pittsburgh hard-coal miners serving in the Forty-Eighth Pennsylvania regiment dug a five-hundred-foot-long tunnel that began behind Union lines and ended under those of Lee's army. At the end of the tunnel they planted four tons of gunpowder. Just before 5 A.M. on July 30, 1864, they detonated the mine.

The explosion was terrific. It blew tons of dirt and timber into the air and killed or wounded some 350 men. Union commanders then ordered three divisions of unprepared and badly led troops to charge through the breach torn in the Confederate defenses. The blue-clad soldiers did so but haplessly headed straight into the crater that the explosion had dug. Unable to climb out of it, they clawed futilely at its walls and milled about helplessly while Confederate troops recovered from the shock, regrouped, and counterattacked. The trapped Union troops died like fish in a barrel.

One of the units on the Union siege lines was the Twenty-Eighth Regiment of the United States Colored Troops (USCT), in which Garland White then served as chaplain. When the crater swallowed the first wave of Union troops ordered forward that day, commanders could think of nothing else to do but order White's regiment and thousands of other black soldiers in after them. Those men had by then seen enough to guess what lay in store. Before the assault, a number requested that chaplain White write to their families and assure them that their relatives had died bravely.[25] The black troops then dutifully charged forward, but many of them, too, were soon driven into the crater.

What followed was probably the worst massacre of African American soldiers to occur during the war. Claiming that the black infantrymen had proclaimed "no quarter" during their initial charge, Confederate troops from Virginia, Georgia, and Alabama now butchered them by the score. John S. Wise, ex-governor Henry Wise's son, was a young Confederate soldier in Petersburg that day. "It was the first time Lee's army had encountered negroes," he wrote later, "and their presence excited in the troops indignant malice. . . . Inflamed," they "disregarded the rules of warfare which restrained them in battle with their own race, and brained and butchered the blacks until the slaughter was sickening."[26] "As soon as we got upon them," Confederate artillery colonel William Pegram recalled, "they threw down their arms in surrender, but were not allowed to do so. . . . This was perfectly right, as a matter of policy," Pegram declared, and had "a splendid effect on our men."

A conservative estimate holds that almost a thousand black soldiers were killed that day, perhaps half of them after surrendering or while trying to surrender.[27]

Northern Peace Democrats were hardly bothered by the killing of black Union troops, but they hammered away at the apparent lack of military success on the Petersburg front and the high price being paid in the blood of northern white soldiers. The Confederacy was obviously unbeatable, they trumpeted, and the Republican government was prolonging the war simply "to serve its own unrighteous ends"—that is, emancipation.[28] The South stands upon the verge of victory, declared one Democratic newspaper, while Lincoln stands "between the people and an honorable peace."[29]

The Democratic Party held its national convention in Chicago in the last days of August, nearly two months after the Republicans' gathering. Democratic delegates, like their party, were divided into "War" and "Peace" wings—divided, that is, over whether or not to prosecute the war until the Confederacy was destroyed. The convention tried to bridge the rift by emphasizing a shared opposition to emancipation.

Members of the Peace wing wrote the party platform. It demanded "immediate efforts" to stop the fighting in the expectation that "an ultimate convention of the States, or other peaceable means" could then reunite the country "at the earliest practicable moment."[30] A cease-fire first, in other words, to be followed eventually by negotiations of some sort to restore the Union peacefully.

That platform pleased Alexander Stephens. He was confident, and rightly so, that during any such armistice, the Union population's commitment to the war would drain away. In negotiations conducted after fighting had ceased, Confederates would make it clear that reunion was "out of the question." So the talks would break down and Confederate independence would become permanent. No wonder Stephens's brother called the Peace Democrats' platform "a ray of light."[31]

War Democrats, in contrast, recognized that only military defeat could compel Confederate leaders to give up the rebellion, and they therefore opposed that platform. To placate them, the convention gave the party's presidential nomination to one of their number—ex-general George B. McClellan, who promised to prosecute the war until reunion was achieved but without wielding the weapon of emancipation.

What would a McClellan victory in November 1864 mean? What effect would the electoral triumph of a man who vociferously denounced emancipation and who was publicly identified as the "peace candidate" have on the morale of Republican-minded troops and civilians, the most dedicated and unswerving supporters of the Union war effort? What impact would it have on the Union's ability and willingness to continue that effort into the winter of 1864–65 and beyond?

Such questions weighed on Abraham Lincoln's mind. By the end of the summer, flagging war spirit in the Union populace had led him to doubt that he would be reelected in November; a great number of his friends and advisers concurred. The worried president reviewed his apparently dwindling options. A McClellan triumph, Lincoln felt sure, would have grave consequences for the Union. For if his Democratic opponent should conquer at the polls, Lincoln believed, "he will have secured his election on such ground that he can not possibly save [the Union] afterwards."[32]

But Lincoln would not seek to avoid electoral defeat by sacrificing his party's platform. He would not offer peace on any terms other than reunion and emancipation. As he had instructed his secretary of state to say some months earlier, there were now two conditions for peace: "The Union must be maintained," and "African slavery must cease to exist."[33] Were he to renege on the Emancipation Proclamation, he wrote in August, he could not "escape the curse of Heaven, or of any good man." More practically, such an announcement would kill all recruitment of black soldiers and lead those already in the ranks to desert. "And rightfully, too," Lincoln judged. For "why should they give their lives for us, with full notice of our purpose to betray them?" That path led, Lincoln believed, to the Union's military defeat. "Take from us, and give to the enemy, the hundred and thirty, forty, or fifty thousand colored persons now serving us as soldiers, seamen, and laborers," he said, "and we can not longer maintain the contest."[34]

The Confederacy did all it could to bring on the Republican electoral defeat that Lincoln feared. Everything hung on its armies' ability to protract the summer's seeming stalemates until the Union's election day arrived. Lee was able to do that at Petersburg. But things went differently in Georgia.

After the costly frontal assaults he ordered at Kennesaw Mountain, a chastened William Tecumseh Sherman abandoned those aggressive tactics and returned to flanking maneuvers. And with them he continued to press Joseph E. Johnston and the Army of Tennessee steadily southward. On July 10, 1864, his soldiers began to cross the Chattahoochee River, the last natural barrier between them and Atlanta, now only some five miles away.[35]

Johnston's deliberate, cautious defensive tactics had slowed Sherman's advance, but they had won him no points in Richmond. Jefferson Davis disliked and distrusted Johnston and had given him command of the Army of Tennessee only with the greatest reluctance. The Confederate president and cabinet were now sure that much more could have been accomplished in Georgia by a more aggressive commander. Davis decided to remove Johnston on July 17, 1864, replacing him with John Bell Hood, a general with a well-earned reputation as a tough and hard-charging fighter.

But Hood's elevation to command proved a bad mistake. His penchant for aggressive tactics regardless of circumstances swiftly yielded severe and costly defeats for his army. In nine days Sherman soundly defeated Hood three times in head-to-head combat, in the process inflicting terrible casualties upon Hood's forces. Desertion once again grew rampant in the Army of Tennessee.[36] And then, in the last week of August, as Lincoln contemplated defeat in the coming election, Sherman's men cut Hood's supply lines and threatened him with encirclement. The Army of Tennessee fled Atlanta on the night of September 1 and 2, 1864, after torching part of the city to deny its use to the Yankees. Sherman's troops marched in on September 3.[37]

The consequences of Atlanta's fall transcended even the city's considerable military importance. Newspapers in both North and South had focused public attention on the fate of that important center, and many people on both sides had come to see the contest as a microcosm of the war as a whole and a harbinger of its likely outcome. Charles Colcock Jones's son John judged the loss of Atlanta to be "the greatest blow of the war," adding that "without special divine interposition we are a ruined people."[38] Mary Chesnut, following developments from Charleston, concluded, "We are going to be wiped off the face of the earth."[39]

In hopes of restoring calm and élan, Jefferson Davis boarded a train for Georgia in late September. Union control of Atlanta forced him to take a circuitous route, along which he addressed supporters seeking reassurance.[40] He promised listeners in Macon that the Union army in Georgia would soon overextend its supply lines. And when that welcome day arrived, Sherman, just like Napoléon in Russia in 1812, would begin a terrible retreat from which he would "escape with only a bodyguard."[41]

Davis finally reached the headquarters of Hood's army, twenty miles to Atlanta's southwest, on September 25, 1864. This was his third visit to the Army of Tennessee since 1862. In both 1862 and 1863, the soldiers he reviewed had cheered him lustily. This time they saluted him somberly and in silence.[42]

On the surface, however, much of the Confederate elite seemed blissfully untroubled. "Never," according to a letter published in a Montgomery, Alabama, newspaper, "were parties more numerous" among the First Families than in the winter of 1864–65. And "never were the theaters and places of public amusement so resorted to." After a "brief abstinence," moreover, "the love of dress, the display of jewelry and costly attire, the extravagance and folly" now seemed greater than ever.[43] No matter the disasters occurring without, recorded Mary Chesnut, "we are—in this house—like the outsiders at the time of the Flood. We care for nothing of these things. We eat, drink, laugh, dance, in lightness of heart!!"[44] In Richmond, Sallie Putnam saw "a reckless expenditure of money, and a disposition to indulge in extravagances at whatever cost."[45]

To Virginia's Sara Agnes Rice Pryor, this "disposition to revel in times of danger and suffering" seemed "passing strange."[46] But South Carolina's Grace Elmore understood that "utter abandonment to the pleasure of the present" allowed "shutting out for the moment the horrors that surround us."[47] In fact, the splendid balls and other social events that members of the elite threw for themselves looked like nothing so much as tableaus out of another Edgar Allan Poe tale—"The Masque of the Red Death," in which the wealthiest residents of a plague-ridden land seek desperately to keep their terror at bay with expensive entertainments and fabulous food and drink. More than one witness drew the same parallel. "Florence was never so gay," noted Sarah Pryor, "as during the Plague!"[48] In Texas, a displaced Katherine Stone observed, "The refugees remind me of the description of the life of the nobility of France lived during the days of the French Revolution—thrusting all the cares and tragedies of life aside and drinking deep of life's joys while it lasted."[49]

Stunning the white South, Sherman's victory at Atlanta transformed the political atmosphere in the North as well. "The political skies begin to brighten," reported a relieved *New York Times*. "The clouds that lowered over the Union cause a month ago are breaking away."[50] Helping to brighten the skies was good news arriving from other fronts. A week before the taking of Atlanta, Union naval and land forces had closed the blockade-running port of Mobile, Alabama. And in September and October, Philip H. Sheridan's troops repeatedly overwhelmed Jubal A. Early's in Virginia's Shenandoah Valley, ultimately sending the enemy troops into what a Confederate observer considered "one of the most shameful and disgraceful stampedes on record." A Louisiana captain thought it "equal to the First Manassa stampede," but with men in gray now doing the running.[51]

Even in Virginia, the Union's situation was far more favorable than most northerners had recognized. In driving the Army of Northern Virginia back into the Richmond and Petersburg defenses in June, Grant had placed Lee's army under siege, a position that the southern general had long dreaded. During the summer and fall of 1864, Lee's position deteriorated. As the Union's Army of the Potomac slowly grew in numbers, Grant was able to steadily lengthen his siege lines around Richmond and Petersburg, compelling Lee's smaller army to match him yard by yard, mile by mile, stretching its thin lines ever thinner.

With their confidence in Republican leadership restored, especially by Sherman's success in Georgia, Union voters reelected Abraham Lincoln by a comfortable margin that November. The official count gave him an edge of about four hundred thousand votes over McClellan, or a majority of 55 percent. McClellan carried only one free state (New Jersey) and two loyal slave states (Delaware and Kentucky). Allowing for ballot irregularities, the Republicans probably garnered about the same share of the vote in the free states that they had won in 1860.

Considering the amount of blood and treasure that the war effort had cost—and especially how the administration's war program had radicalized—over the intervening four years, this outcome registered an important set of changes in the northern population's sentiments.[52] In 1864, a majority of northern voters endorsed and strengthened the hand of the party that was bent on the Confederacy's unconditional surrender, the party of the Emancipation Proclamation, the party now committed to freedom for all slaves throughout the United States. With that election, Secretary of State William H. Seward observed, "the country has safely passed the turning-point in the revolutionary movement against slavery."[53] Lincoln also proved to have long coattails: As a result of those elections, the Republican Party controlled about four out of every five seats in both houses of Congress, regained all the state legislatures it lost in 1862, and controlled the governor's office in every Union state but New Jersey.

Southern hopes of securing Confederate independence electorally, by going around Lincoln and his party, vanished. "There is no use in disguising the fact," sighed Confederate ordnance chief Josiah Gorgas, "that our subjugation is popular at the North."[54]

During Jefferson Davis's visit to Georgia two months earlier, in September 1864, General John Bell Hood had outlined the grandiose plans he had formulated for his badly weakened army. He would move north and west into Alabama and Tennessee, threatening Sherman's railroad link to his supply base in Chattanooga, and hoping thereby to pull Sherman's army after him and away from its intended line of march (to Georgia's coast and then northward toward Robert E. Lee in Richmond and Petersburg). Hood would recruit additional troops in Tennessee and then turn eastward in order to rendezvous with and reinforce Lee's Army of Northern Virginia.

At first, in early October, it looked as though at least part of that plan would succeed. Sherman did begin to turn and pursue the retreating Hood. But the Union general then reconsidered. He didn't need a supply line, he decided. He and his men could plow ahead into Georgia, living off the rich low-country land much as both he and Grant had done in Mississippi the previous year. His army would "cripple their resources" and "make Georgia howl"[55]—both deprive the Confederacy of the state's war-making resources and drive home to civilians that continuing the rebellion would carry a big price tag.

Sherman dispatched a portion of his command under General George H. Thomas to deal with the Army of Tennessee. At the end of November, Hood clashed with part of Thomas's force at the town of Franklin. The Confederate commander ordered a grand charge against the Union works across a half mile of open ground. The result was a predictable disaster for the South. Confederate casualties exceeded six thousand, including five generals wounded, one captured, and six (including Patrick Cleburne) killed. Federal losses were only about a third as large. About two weeks later, Thomas attacked Hood's army at Nashville and smashed it. What was left of it—some eighteen thousand beaten and demoralized men—retreated farther westward into Mississippi.

In the middle of November 1864, meanwhile, Sherman and the bulk of his army began their long and destructive march to Savannah and the Georgia coast. Before leaving Atlanta, however, they emptied it of

its civilian population and deliberately destroyed much of what the retreating Army of Tennessee had left standing, determined to leave behind as little as possible to whatever Confederate force might later
return. As Sherman's troops filed out of the burning city, the general
later recalled in his memoirs, "some band, by accident, struck up the
anthem of 'John Brown's soul goes marching on.' " Soldiers "caught up
the strain," their commander recalled, "and never before or since have I
heard the chorus of 'Glory, glory, hallelujah!' done with more spirit, or
in better harmony of time and place."[56]

Sherman's army proceeded to cut a wide swath through the lower
two-thirds of Georgia. Marching along four parallel roads, his men
began to lay waste to a strip of countryside sixty miles wide and eventually three hundred miles long. They destroyed buildings, farm equipment, wagons, crops—anything that might aid the Confederate war
effort. With the Army of Tennessee out of the way, there was little to
impede them. Georgia's state militia tried feebly, as did Joseph Wheeler's cavalry and small groups of Confederate infantry. Sherman's army
accepted the surrender of Savannah, on the Atlantic coast, on December 21, 1864.

Today Sherman's march is remembered almost solely for the physical
destruction it wrought. But those Union soldiers destroyed more than
buildings, crops, and farm implements. Wherever they went they broke
the power of the secessionist government, the slaveholders' social order,
and most of whatever fighting spirit remained among Confederate partisans.[57] One Georgia farmer reported to Jefferson Davis that "if the
question were put to the people of this state, whether to continue the
war or return to the union, a large majority would vote for a return"—and
would do so even "if *emancipation* was the *condition*."[58]

As Confederate loyalists in Georgia lowered their heads, white
unionists—silenced or in hiding for more than three years—raised
theirs. And black people who had known only bondage since birth saw
a road to freedom open before their eyes.

The process had begun as soon as Sherman's troops entered northern Georgia back in the spring of 1864. Unionists rushed to them from
the surrounding hills, almost a thousand strong in the town of Jasper
alone, where they formed a loyal home guard unit and prepared for the

arrival of hundreds more recruits from surrounding counties.[59] Other hill-country unionists took advantage of the collapse of Confederate power to make their way to the rear, to the more secure Union bastions of eastern Tennessee, taking with them as much of their property as they could carry.[60]

Slaves also greeted Sherman's soldiers as they entered the state—and in steadily larger numbers as the army moved south toward the low country.[61] They came on foot or on horses, cows, wagons, carts, and whatever other type of vehicle could be found or taken from their masters. By the time the army reached Atlanta, somewhere between ten thousand and twenty thousand refugees were following behind it.[62]

That army's commander felt little affection for them, however. William Tecumseh Sherman despised black people and felt no distaste for slavery. He had lived much of his adult life in the South, where he had owned slaves himself. He believed implicitly in "the strong attachment between master and slave,"[63] and was still claiming in the summer of 1862 that "not one nigger in ten wants to run off."[64] Though the general's loyalty to the Union was absolute, he had strongly opposed the Second Confiscation Act as well as Lincoln's proclamation of freedom.

Sherman had eventually come to accept emancipation as a war measure, but his racial animus remained. He was happy to make use of black labor, and about a thousand men, most of them recently emancipated field slaves, performed a range of tasks for his army as it pushed toward Atlanta.[65] Other black refugees served as guides, foraged, cooked, cleaned, and brought intelligence and whatever foodstuffs they could from their masters' larders.[66] But Sherman refused to enlist such men as soldiers or to allow black men already in Union ranks to serve with him. He stubbornly resisted attempts by Halleck, Grant, and even Lincoln to permit black recruitment along his line of march through Georgia.[67] He could not, he said, "bring myself to trust negroes with arms in positions of danger and trust."[68] They were not brave and were incapable of the kind of independent initiative that soldiers needed.[69]

Sherman's concerns went far beyond the soldierly capabilities of black men. He also worried about the social consequences of placing them in uniform. The general declared himself reconciled to the fact that "we are in a Revolution" and to the notion that "the negro should be a free man."[70] But black people did not deserve "an equality with whites."[71]

Sherman made no secret of his views, a fact that encouraged those of his men who shared them. Not all did, of course. Many appreciated the welcome that black Georgians gave them and former slaves' evident love for and support of the Union cause. They also admired fugitives' willingness to endure great hardship in pursuit of freedom. But others freely and loudly announced their hatred for blacks—a hatred that fostered callousness and sometimes brutality. As Sherman's army cut through Georgia between Atlanta and the Atlantic coast, many of his soldiers plundered or destroyed the meager belongings of slaves as readily as they did the far greater wealth of the masters. Few helped infirm or older black refugees struggling to match the army's pace.

In early December, the Fourteenth Corps crossed a deep and fast-moving creek near Savannah by marching over portable pontoon bridges. After reaching the other side, the Union commander ordered his troops to immediately pull up the bridges. That trapped most of the refugees who had been following them alone and unarmed on the other bank, vulnerable to vengeful rebel cavalry and militia. Terrified, men, women, and children threw themselves into the icy water, desperately trying to escape. Some of them drowned. Others were apparently killed by pursuing Confederates.[72] "The waters of the Ogeechee and Ebenezer Creek can account for hundreds . . . abandoned . . . after being encouraged 'to gwine along,' " according to a Union captain. Others "died in the bayous and lagoons of Georgia."[73]

And occasionally Union soldiers did worse. One tired and resentful soldier, seeing a freedman asleep by the side of the road, shot the man and cursed, "Take that you damned Niger and see if you'll sleep again while I have to march." Later, when they reached Beaufort, South Carolina, some of Sherman's troops attacked a group of black soldiers and civilians, leaving two or three dead and more wounded.[74]

To put it mildly, Sherman's army sent out mixed signals to their black would-be friends and companions. But still they came. "Although the Negroes have suffered every form of injury from the enemy in their persons and property," Georgia plantation mistress Mary Jones noted in bemusement, "yet they regard them as their best friends."[75] Warned by masters that the Yankees would kill them, some blacks told Union troops that they "preferred death by Yanks than longer to live with their cruel masters, in slavery."[76]

Decisions like these shocked some masters, including Savannah's

Mrs. H. J. Wayne. As Sherman approached, she tried to refugee her slaves, many of whom had promised to accompany her wherever she went. Unlike the Old Testament's Ruth, however, they did not make good on that pledge. As Wayne hastily departed the city, "every one of my negroes left me," she wrote.[77] Her experience was not unusual.[78] Although some house servants helped owners to hide valuables from Sherman's soldiers, others proved just as eager to reveal them.[79]

At the end of November, one of Gertrude Thomas's slaves, a man named Henry, left her plantation. The next morning Henry, now wearing a Union uniform, returned with federal troops "and showed them the place in which Uncle Sykes (our Negro driver) had concealed the Horses and mules." Thomas consoled herself that of all her servants only Henry had turned on her. But soon she learned that her heretofore faithful coachman had vanished, too.[80] A month later she was wondering if she would "have any servants . . . when another Christmas comes around."[81]

Many Atlanta masters would have envied Thomas's small servant problem. According to a disapproving Union soldier, black people in Atlanta celebrated the first night after Sherman's arrival with a rampage through the city, "smashing the windows, doors, and furniture of every description." They "broke the china-ware, smashed the pianos, and annihilated the chairs, tables and bedsteads. They cut open the beds, and emptied the contents into the streets. They dashed into the cellars, and drank all the liquors."

Captain George Pepper disdained the conduct of this "drunken and furious mob."[82] He could not identify with the pent-up resentment and fury of people forced to wait hand and foot, day after day, year after year, on those who owned them, beat them, and held over them the power of life and death. A house servant named Louisa would have understood better. Her master's house, she told another Union officer just outside Savannah, "*ought* to be burned" because "there has been so much devilment here, whipping niggers most to death to make 'em work."[83]

The path of Sherman's army, as another of its generals noted accurately, led through a part of the Confederacy "never before visited by a Union soldier."[84] But everywhere that army went, Georgia slaves made it clear that they understood exactly why the war was occurring and what was at stake in it, sometimes down to the smallest political details.[85] An elderly couple was determined to leave their owner, despite his entreaties and attempts by Union soldiers to dissuade them. "We must go," the two insisted, for "freedom is as sweet to us as it is to you."[86]

Sherman personally encountered evidence of that knowledge and understanding. After leaving Atlanta, he came across an elderly black man in the town of Covington. As Sherman recalled in his memoirs, he asked the man "if he understood about the war and its progress." The freedman replied that even though the Yankees "professed to be fighting for the Union, he supposed that slavery was the cause, and that our success was to be his freedom." He assured Sherman that all the slaves he knew held the same view of things.[87] Two hundred miles to the south, in Savannah, Sherman would hear similar things from a spokesman for that city's black population, who also proved strikingly well informed about the war's origins and the policies of both sides.[88]

Sherman's opinion of black people—and even the way some of his soldiers treated them—was less important in shaping their decisions than what they knew his army meant to their future. But the general's contempt for blacks and his refusal to enlist them in his army deeply dismayed sections of the Republican Party. Union cabinet member Salmon P. Chase, a fellow Ohioan who had previously sought to advance Sherman's career, advised the general that his racial views and "the apparent harshness of your actions towards the blacks" were becoming a scandal.[89] General Henry W. Halleck, who sympathized with Sherman's opinions, suggested the general disarm Republican critics by giving "escaped slaves . . . at least a partial supply of food in the rice-fields about Savannah, and cotton plantations on the coast."[90]

On January 7, 1865, Secretary of War Edwin M. Stanton boarded the ship *Nevada* and sailed down to Georgia to confer with the general about his relations with the freedpeople. Stanton's own views had evolved over time from those of a typical War Democrat to those of a radical Republican. In Savannah he asked Sherman to arrange a meeting with leaders of the black population to discuss their fate and that of the thousands of refugees who had followed Sherman's forces.[91]

On Thursday evening, January 12, 1865, at 8 P.M., the two men and some other officers met at Sherman's headquarters with twenty black men, fifteen of whom were former slaves. Nine of those fifteen had obtained their freedom only with the arrival of Sherman's army. According to General Oliver O. Howard, the men included barbers, ships' pilots, sailors, ministers, and some that he called plantation "overseers" (but who were more likely drivers). Nearly all were connected with one or another black church. One of those was William Gaines, a Methodist preacher who, like Garland White, had been owned by Robert Toombs's family until the Union army freed him.[92]

As the meeting began, the twenty black men distributed themselves around the room. Sherman stood near the fireplace, and Stanton sat at a table and began to take notes.[93] The general and secretary had a list of questions for the men and asked them to select a spokesman who would reply. They chose Garrison Frazier, a Baptist minister. Sixty-seven years of age, the North Carolina–born Frazier had been a slave until eight years before, when he managed to buy freedom for himself and his wife.

For the two northerners, the most important question of the day was what to do with the thousands of refugees who had followed Sherman's army to Savannah and the coast. What would it take to detach them from the general's moving columns? Rev. Frazier answered clearly and concisely. "The way we can best take care of ourselves," he said, "is to have land, and turn in and till it by our own labor . . . and we can soon maintain ourselves and have something to spare."[94]

After the meeting ended, Stanton and Sherman produced Special Field Orders No. 15, which set aside abandoned cotton and rice plantations of coastal South Carolina and Georgia—from Charleston southward to Jacksonville and along the rivers for thirty miles inland—for the exclusive occupation of black people.[95] It also established procedures by which those people might acquire "possessory" (which proved to mean "temporary") title to forty-acre plots. As a result, some twenty thousand freedpeople came for a time into possession of some one hundred thousand acres by the end of the war.[96] Once again, the logic of events had induced an unlikely individual to advance the interests of the former slaves.

Elsewhere in the Confederacy, meanwhile, the direct struggle between masters and bondspeople escalated. South Carolina's Adele Petigru Allston learned from her overseer in mid-July 1864 that a slave named Stephen had taken his family and fled by boat from her coastal Chicora

Wood rice plantation. Their successful escape, the overseer added, was now encouraging "a goodeal of obstanetry in Some of the People." Allston decided to respond harshly. She ordered Stephen's aged parents, Mary and James, to be confined in "some secure jail in the interior and held as hostages for the conduct of their children." The same should be done to all "the old people whose children have deserted." Only when they learn "that they will be held responsible for the behavior of their children" would "the older negroes" try "to influence the younger ones to order and subordination while this war lasts."[97]

But plantation discipline continued nonetheless to erode. A few months later, Allston's overseer again informed her that her slaves "doant seem to care to obay orders." It was the job of the enslaved driver, a man named Jack, to help the overseer to enforce compliance. But Jack had now become part of the problem. In the overseer's words, Jack was "not behaveing write. . . . He doant talk write among the People."[98]

Slavery was showing signs of decay even in distant Texas. Southern masters had refugeed an estimated 150,000 slaves into the state by the end of 1864.[99] The Union's seizure of the Mississippi River in mid-1863 had isolated Texas from the bulk of the Confederacy and spared it most of the ravages of war since then. It had also redirected Texans' trade from the rest of the South to Mexico—and especially to the city of Matamoros, which was both close to the Gulf coast and just a mile south of Brownsville.[100] At the end of 1864, a Galveston newspaper noted that many Texas "planters and traders" regularly visited Matamoros, taking with them "their trusty negroes"—those slaves they considered "too faithful and trustworthy, too much attached to his master to quit him under any circumstances."

But slavery was illegal in Mexico, a fact that made Matamoros a dangerous influence on the Texans' human property, no matter how apparently loyal and trustworthy they appeared. Proof of that, said the editor, was the fact that Matamoros's streets were today "overrunning" with such "trusty, now insolent, negroes." Even the slave who did not use the visit to Matamoros simply to slip away from his owner still saw "too much, [heard] too much in Matamoros, and [talked] too much" when he returned to Confederate Texas and thereby sowed "the seeds of Matamoros freedom throughout the nigger neighborhood."[101]

The accumulation of reports like these—and personal experience—compelled even Virginia planter and proslavery ideologue Edmund

Ruffin to revise some of his most long-held views about that subject by the end of 1864. "I had before believed in the general prevalence of much attachment & affection of negro slaves for the families of their masters," he wrote in his diary, "& especially in the more usual circumstances of careful & kind treatment of the slaves." But the war experience had shattered that assumption. "Though some few cases of great attachment & fidelity have been exhibited," he now confessed, "there have been many more of signal ingratitude & treachery of slaves to the most considerate & kind of masters—& the far greater number have merely shown indifference & entire disregard of all such supposed ties of attachment & loyalty."[102]

Plantation mistresses Mary Jones and Mary Chesnut bemoaned more succinctly the advancing collapse of their society amid this second American revolution. "Clouds and darkness are round about us," Jones sighed, and "the hand of the Almighty is laid in sore judgment upon us; we are a desolate and smitten people. . . . At present the foundations of society are broken up; what hereafter is to be our social and civil status we cannot see."[103] An image that filled Mary Chesnut's thoughts seemed to have been plucked from the end of Poe's "House of Usher"— she felt "the deep waters closing over us."[104]

While Confederate slave owners grieved over their loss of mastery, Confederate soldiers were leaving the ranks in greater numbers than ever. During his fall 1864 visit to Georgia, Jefferson Davis publicly complained that "two thirds of our men are absent, some sick, some wounded, but most of them absent without leave."[105] He probably exaggerated a bit, but only a bit. The proportion absent from the Army of Tennessee was about one-half; from Lee's army, perhaps three-fifths.[106]

Like nearly everyone else in the Confederacy, Lee's soldiers in 1864 had one eye on Atlanta and the other on the Union presidential elections in November. Setbacks in both dropped morale to previously unplumbed depths, and desertion rates shot upward.[107] Far more men than ever before, moreover, were deserting the ranks in the conviction that the war was already lost. And a growing number were individually surrendering to Union soldiers. General Meade estimated that, by the middle of September, men abandoning Lee's army were entering his lines at the rate of ten per night.[108]

Things were no better once again even in the faraway, relatively pacific Trans-Mississippi Department. Desertion there had reached dangerous proportions by the summer of 1864 and grew only worse during the fall and winter that followed. In November, department commander E. Kirby Smith began to conduct daily executions of deserters, but even that failed to stem the exodus.[109]

Some deserters surrendered to Union forces. Others managed to return to their own homes unmolested. Still others joined the armed bands that continued to bedevil Confederate officials in a number of states. In North Carolina, the secretive Heroes of America suffered a blow in the summer of 1864 when newspapers published the names of a number of individual members and accused them of treason. That frightened many into confessions and public repudiations of the group.[110] But the failure of William W. Holden's gubernatorial campaign in late July and early August, dashing hopes for a negotiated early end to the war, apparently pushed new recruits and injected new life into the guerrillas.[111] So did the fact, as Governor Vance learned, that "Holdenite" North Carolina troops were deserting from Lee's army and returning to the state's central piedmont region.[112]

In response to the renewed insurgent threat, Vance mobilized eighteen home guard battalions against the armed deserters.[113] He again employed severe tactics to suppress the insurgents, including making hostages of women and children until husbands and fathers turned themselves in. And such tactics once more chalked up successes. By the end of September 1864, perhaps a thousand guerrillas had been caught or induced to surrender.[114] But the popular sentiments that sustained the dissidents remained as strong and widespread as ever. "I can hardly give you an adequate conception," Vance told fellow governor Joseph E. Brown in mid-January 1865, "of the general despondency and gloom which prevails among us."[115] A North Carolinian who signed her letter simply as "A Poor Woman" appealed to her governor in that month to bring a cruel and hopeless war to an end. "You know as well as you have a head that it is impossible to whip they Yankees," she told Vance, and "there fore I beg you for God sake to try to make peace on some terms. . . . I believe slavery is doomed to dy out that god is agoing to liberate niggers and fighting any longer is agoing against God."[116]

Brown was wrestling with even bigger problems in Georgia. Even as Sherman's army cut through that state, "robber bands of deserters" from southern armies were looting plantations, and Confederate cavalrymen were stealing horses and generally wreaking havoc among pro-Confederate citizens.[117] "The time appears rapidly approaching," plantation mistress Gertrude Thomas wrote in her diary, "when we have almost as much to dread from our own demoralized mob as from the public enemy."[118]

The fall of 1864 found Jefferson Davis's home state also overrun with deserters. "At a time when the wants of the country require every man to be at his post," his secretary of war fumed, "the highest military crime, desertion, is committed almost with impunity" in Mississippi. Deserters seemed to have no "difficulty in obtaining shelter in any section" of the state, even from other Confederate army units operating there.[119] The pattern of desertion, moreover, revealed definite class cleavages in Lee's army. Men from families with the weakest economic ties to slavery were leaving much more often than were slaveholders.[120]

For many Confederate soldiers, the burden of defending the South's peculiar institution had simply grown too heavy, especially because they believed that the burden was being borne inequitably. Early in September 1864, "many soldiers" in "the ditches" of Georgia told Jefferson Davis that they were "ask[ing] ourselves what we are fighting for." They were "tired of fighting for this negro aristockracy," tired of fighting "for them that wont fight for themselves."[121] Another man told the war department that "the poor" had "nothing to fight for," and that "the poor will not Stand it much longer nor neither will I." "For my part," he added, "I would not Give my life for all the Blame negroes in the Confederacy."[122] A self-described "mechanic" objected that "Slavery is the cause of the war," and "a poor man with nothing but his trade to live on" had "no interest at stake" in that conflict.[123]

Such words revealed a pattern that the Virginia war widow Cornelia McDonald discerned in 1865. Those who remained most "enthusiastic" about the Confederacy and its war generally came from "the higher classes." But "those who had but their poor homes and little pieces of ground by which they managed to provide little more than bread for their families" manifested a very different attitude. For them "it was oppression to be forced into the army, and not ever to be free from the apprehension that their families were suffering." Especially because they had come to believe that "they would be as well off under one government as another."[124]

But for whatever reasons soldiers deserted, the effect was the same—to weaken southern armies even further. By the end of 1864, the Confederacy had only a quarter as many soldiers in the field as the Union and no sources of reinforcements in sight. Jefferson Davis's chief of conscription had already reported many months earlier that the country no longer contained any potential "fresh material for the armies" and suggested that his bureau simply close down by the end of the year. Robert Garlick Hill Kean, the staunch Virginia secessionist who headed the War Bureau, could not imagine how the South could match the Union armies' next levy of conscripts.[125]

The second American revolution had by now become a seemingly irresistible juggernaut, crushing and rolling over whatever stood in its way. Confederate hopes that the Union might repudiate Lincoln in 1864 and place a more malleable man in the White House had died when Atlanta surrendered. A Republican Party standing on a platform of nationwide emancipation had scored a convincing triumph at the polls. More and more black southerners were gaining their freedom each day, while southern soldiers abandoned their armies in ever-growing numbers.

As the position of the counterrevolutionary Confederacy grew desperate, some of its leaders began to reconsider options that they had previously dismissed as unthinkable.

Chapter Nine

FEELING THE TIMBERS SHUDDER

January through March 1865

It had become clear by the end of 1864 that the steps that slave owners had taken to preserve their cherished "way of life"—secession and war—had instead placed them and their institutions in the gravest peril. The fierce, sanguinary, and protracted war had shaken the masters' world to its foundations. Cracks in the House of Dixie's façade of seamless white unity widened further with each passing year. The house's foundation—the slave-labor system—was in many places crumbling before the masters' eyes. In the first two months of 1865, both Missouri and Tennessee, now in Republican hands, abolished slavery.[1]

Even now, not every Confederate stalwart acknowledged the danger. Some still believed, or hoped, or at least said, that victory lay just over the horizon. That, despite the loss of the Mississippi River and river valley, the fall of Atlanta and the virtual collapse of Confederate spirit in Georgia, the shattering of the Army of Tennessee, and the seemingly inexorable tightening of the noose around Lee's army in Virginia.

In early November 1864, just two months after Atlanta's surrender, Jefferson Davis offered the slave owners' Congress another rosy assessment of their condition and prospects. On one front after another, he reported, southern armies' efforts had been crowned with success. The North's occupation of cities such as Atlanta signified little. In fact, he declaimed, "there is no military success of the enemy which can accomplish" the Confederacy's destruction.[2] The *Richmond Examiner* endorsed that sunny outlook at the end of January. "There was a time," it granted, "when there was a danger that the Southern Confederacy would be overpowered by the violence and superior power of its enemy." Happily, though, "that time is passed."[3] In fact, it added just a few days later, "no former period of the war has contained such elements of encouragement for the South as the present."[4]

But the public did not appear to agree. Atlanta's fall, reported former senator James Phelan, had convinced most white Mississippians of the "hopelessness of success."[5] Robert Toombs expected sunny assurances that "all is right" to continue emanating from official Richmond right "until Lee's defeat or evacuation, and then—chaos."[6] Despairing thoughts haunted the sober and well-informed Mary Chesnut, too. The South had "but two armies," she knew, and "Sherman was between them now." So "what is there to prevent Sherman taking General Lee in the rear?"[7] The effective destruction of the Army of Tennessee in mid-December only made that question more immediate. In January 1865, Zebulon Vance confidentially suggested to fellow governor Joseph E. Brown that their "chief aim" should now simply be "to hold the demoralized and trembling fragments of society and law together and prevent them from dropping to pieces until the rapidly hastening end of our struggle."[8]

Meanwhile, the mounting fears for slavery's future multiplied. A Texas cavalry colonel in January 1865 derided those around him who were "becoming more and more frightened every day" concerning slavery's future. Both "you and your children," he assured a friend, would "be waited upon by slaves as long as you all live."[9] But those at whom the colonel jeered were growing in number and grim conviction. Tennessee planter John H. Bills had concluded by the summer of 1864 that "negro slavery is about played out."[10] Within a few months, former Virginia governor Henry Wise was broadcasting his belief that slavery was dead in his state, too.[11]

Sherman's march immeasurably strengthened that view. "In the foreground of this picture of national military disaster," judged the *Macon Telegraph and Confederate* in January 1865, "we shall not fail to discover, torn up root and branch, the institution of domestic slavery."[12] Mary Akin, wife of a Georgia congressman, agreed. "Slavery," she believed, "is now gone."[13] Even in faraway eastern Texas, planter and jurist John T. Mills came to recognize that truth. Mills predicted in early February that slavery was "doomed" even if the South won the war.[14]

For those who recognized the severity of the crisis, the problem of the hour was what to do about it. Was it possible, at this late date, to rescue the masters and their republic by some change in policy or strategy? Might they yet save slavery itself and the plantation system that it served? Was there any way to salvage something from the wreckage of their prewar life, wealth, and power? Many who would not admit it publicly were asking themselves these questions in private. But different members of the southern establishment offered different answers to those questions.

In the judgment of one group of political and military leaders, at whose head stood Jefferson Davis and his closest associates, the survival of the Confederacy was of paramount importance. Only an independent country, government, and army could adequately safeguard the masters' interests. For the sake of that Confederacy's survival, other things—even crucially important things—could and should be sacrificed if necessary.

On November 7, 1864, Jefferson Davis greeted the reconvening Confederate Congress with a major public message. Nine months earlier, he noted, Congress had passed a law calling for the hiring or impressment of up to twenty thousand slaves to labor in support of the armies. "This act," Davis noted without elaboration, "has produced less result than was anticipated." The existing impressment machinery, he continued, was inadequate to meet current needs. It was designed to make material and slaves available to the army only for limited periods, to complete discreet and time-bound tasks. But the armies now needed to keep such laborers with them for more extended periods, even indefinitely, and to expose those laborers to great hazard on the front lines.

To meet these needs, Davis proposed that the government purchase forty thousand slaves outright and then train and organize them as military laborers. He then opened the door to using those purchased slaves as fully fledged combat soldiers if "our white population shall prove insufficient for the armies we require." It was "unlikely," he immediately reassured the Congress, that such a day would ever arrive. But should the Confederacy "ever" face a choice between destruction and "the employment of the slave as a soldier," there should be "no reason to doubt what should then be our decision."

Whatever he chose to say in public for morale's sake, no one knew better than the Confederate president that this point had, in fact, long since arrived. But because the idea of arming blacks, and especially slaves, remained so repugnant to most whites, he broached the subject with the greatest caution.

What Davis said next was more shocking still to southern white sensibilities. Performing the kind of hazardous frontline labor now called for, he said, not to mention possibly serving as genuine soldiers, would require of slaves not merely obedience but active "loyalty and zeal." To arouse those sentiments, Davis said, the South must promise to "liberate the negro on his discharge after service faithfully rendered."[15] What was recently inconceivable had now become unavoidable.

December 1864 saw Davis make a related radical change in his foreign policy. In a final bid to enlist the active aid of Britain and France, he offered to initiate some plan for the gradual termination of slavery within the Confederacy.

This represented a complete about-face not only in substance but also in form. The Confederate government had begun the war by frankly telling the European powers that it had separated from the United States precisely in order to protect slavery from the North's antislavery electorate.[16] It had also held that, even were it so inclined, it had no constitutional power to touch the institution of slavery within its own states' borders.[17] Davis's government publicly stood by that interpretation of the law for the duration of the war.[18]

Behind the scenes, however, Davis now acted very differently. He dispatched the major Louisiana planter and congressman Duncan F. Kenner to Britain and France to offer them exactly what the Confederate government had previously claimed it would not and could not do.[19] Kenner was to carry a letter from Davis to Confederate diplomats James Mason and John Slidell directing them to tell Paris and London that "the sole object" of the Confederate war effort was "the vindication of our rights to self-government and independence." And that to achieve those goals, "no sacrifice is too great, save that of honor."

European governments had thus far refused assistance to the Confederacy, the note continued. Was that, perhaps, because of some "objections not made known to us?" If so, and if those governments were now ready to specify those objections and their "exact terms or conditions" for recognizing Richmond diplomatically, the Confederate president wished "an opportunity . . . for meeting and overcoming those objections . . . by consenting to such terms" as soon as possible.[20] The intense political sensitivity of the subject at home forbade saying things any more clearly, especially in writing.[21]

Because the Union's blockade of the southern coast significantly delayed Kenner's departure, he didn't reach Europe until February 21, 1865, whereupon he conveyed the new turn in Richmond's diplomacy to Mason and Slidell. The three men then set out to bring Davis's message to Louis Bonaparte, Emperor Napoléon III, and Britain's prime minister, Lord Palmerston.

On March 4, 1865, Louis-Napoléon responded that he was "willing and anxious" to assist the South. He had his own reasons. Bonaparte was at that moment attempting to impose a French puppet emperor upon the people of Mexico. Doing that, he well knew, contravened Washington's long-held policy of excluding European powers from the western hemisphere. The French emperor would much rather have a friendly Confederacy for his Mexican protectorate's northern neighbor than a hostile United States. But, mindful of France's military limitations, he hesitated to square off against the United States without the active collaboration of Britain.

So James Mason proceeded to London. There Lord Palmerston, though "conciliatory and kind," made it very clear that the main obstacle to Britain's aiding the Confederacy was not slavery but the South's weak showing in the war. London had for some time considered the southern cause to be lost; it was not now prepared to wager so much on so poor a hand.[22] As a Richmond editor had anticipated more than a month before, no European power would now "accept the Southern Confederacy even if we should tender them the gift."[23]

Even as these scenes played out, Jefferson Davis was engaged in a second diplomatic maneuver. For many months he had been rejecting pleas from around the Confederacy that he propose peace negotiations to the Union. But now he abruptly changed course and delegated three of his most prominent political critics to meet informally with a Union delegation—as it turned out, with Abraham Lincoln himself and his secretary of state, William H. Seward. On February 3, 1865, Confed-

erate vice president Alexander Stephens, Senate president pro tempore
R.M.T. Hunter, and Assistant Secretary of War John A. Campbell
met the two Union leaders on the U.S. transport *River Queen,* which
was anchored off Fort Monroe in a Virginia inlet called Hampton
Roads.

Both Davis and Lincoln looked upon the meeting as a means to silence or at least outflank those in their own camps who had been clam-
oring for peace. Lincoln fully expected Davis to stand by his oft-stated
refusal to dissolve the Confederacy and rejoin the United States under
any conditions. He counted on Davis to repeat that position and thereby
discredit the Northern Peace Democrats who doubted the need to continue prosecuting the war. And Jefferson Davis felt equally sure that
Lincoln would restate his own position—that hostilities would cease
only when the rebellious states returned to the Union uncondition-
ally.[24] When Stephens, Hunter, and Campbell returned from Hampton
Roads with the news that Davis anticipated, all true southerners would
have to acknowledge that the Confederacy's only remaining option was
continued war.

At the meeting, Lincoln and Seward adhered to a policy memorandum that the Union president had drawn up earlier for guidance. They
made clear to the southern delegation that there would be no formal
treaty between the United States and the Confederacy. Peace would
occur only when the rebels laid down their arms and once again submitted to the "national authority." Nor would Lincoln retreat from any
of his government's measures to date on the subject of slavery. In fact,
he and Seward informed the Confederate leaders, just a few days earlier, on January 31, 1865, the U.S. House of Representatives had approved a constitutional amendment outlawing slavery immediately
throughout the United States. (The 1864 elections had made that possible by increasing the size of the Republican delegation in the House
and by convincing a handful of Democrats that abolition had become
too popular to resist.)[25] The congressionally approved thirteenth
amendment was heading toward the states for ratification even as the
Hampton Roads colloquy began.[26]

The meeting on the *River Queen* broke up on the afternoon of February 3, 1865, without any agreement. Afterward, the South's three-
man delegation reported back to a doubtless satisfied Davis in
Richmond. It had all turned out exactly as he had expected, and he

would now make the most of the result. On the following day, Davis reported to his Congress that "the enemy refused to enter into negotiations with the Confederate States, or any one of them separately, or to give to our people any other terms or guarantees than those which a conqueror may grant," including "unconditional submission to their rule" and the "emancipation of all the negro slaves, and with the right on the part of the Federal Congress to legislate on the subject of the relations between the white and black population of each State."[27] Davis brought the same message to the Confederate public later that day.[28]

As Davis had hoped, Confederate loyalists responded with declarations of renewed commitment to the war effort. "Every one thinks," reported War Department clerk John B. Jones, "the Confederacy will at once gather up its military strength and strike such blows as will astonish the world."[29] Confederate regiments assured their government of continued, last-ditch support.[30] Men such as Charles James, of the Eighth Virginia regiment, were not about to "have our property confiscated, our slaves emancipated, our leaders hung" while "we become serfs in the land of our fathers."[31]

But, as one of the *Richmond Examiner*'s editors later acknowledged, this proved only "a spasmodic revival, or short fever of the public mind." When it passed, all that remained "among the best people" was "a dull, helpless expectation, a blank despondency."[32] Sallie Putnam corroborated that description. By that point in the war, she recalled soon afterward, "despondency rested too heavily on the hearts of many to permit more than a momentary and convulsive effort to shake off the incubus."[33]

The talks in Europe and at Hampton Roads had failed to solve the profound crisis confronting the southern elite. All the more reason, concluded Jefferson Davis and his political allies, to move ahead with the idea of offering freedom to slaves who would take up arms and fight in the ranks of southern armies. The plan received an incalculable boost when Robert E. Lee publicly endorsed it in February and when most of Lee's troops announced their assent in regimental resolutions passed shortly afterward.

Davis's proposal seemed to fly in the face of southern white culture, proslavery ideology, and the Confederacy's very reason for being. It therefore touched off a heated, prolonged, wide-ranging, and very public debate. As the North Carolina legislature's omnibus protest viewed it, Davis's proposal "would be wrong in principle, disastrous in practice, an infringement upon states rights, an endorsement of the principle contained in President Lincoln's emancipation proclamation, an insult to our brave soldiers and an outrage upon humanity."[34]

How can we allow black men to become soldiers, R.M.T. Hunter demanded, when "the condition of the soldier" is one "socially equal to any other in society"?[35] In North America, slavery's justification rested largely on claims that Africans and their descendants were uniquely suited to dull, arduous labor but incapable of assuming the responsibilities of free people, citizens, or soldiers. To recruit black men into Confederate armies now, exclaimed Davis's critics, would mean confessing that slavery was based on a lie. The reigning ideology, furthermore, held that blacks, because incapable of governing themselves, *needed* masters both to discipline and to look after them. Freedom was not only useless to them but positively harmful. How could the masters' government now offer to reward them with something that whites had always said would ruin blacks' lives? Finally, Davis's plan undermined the claim that blacks recognized their inability to thrive in freedom and were therefore satisfied to be slaves. Offering them liberty as a reward implicitly admitted that they longed for freedom.

At least as important as these ideological objections were a number of more practical ones. One of these *acknowledged* that enslaved black men ardently wished to be free, consequently resented both their masters and the Confederacy deeply, and had become unbreakably loyal to the Union cause. If we now arm and train such people, this objection concluded, we will soon find ourselves facing the business end of their muskets.[36]

Expectations that such black soldiers would prove loyal to the Union rather than the Confederacy rested in part on another important fact: The Union was offering slaves a better deal. At most, Jefferson Davis was talking about freedom solely for those military-age males whose masters were prepared to volunteer them. He offered no freedom at all to their parents, children, siblings, friends, and neighbors. Abraham Lincoln, in contrast, had already declared *all* Confederate slaves to be free. Confront slaves with these two competing offers, a Georgia editor predicted, and they "would soon perceive the incentives are unequal." And then "who can doubt which side they will take?"[37]

Of course, a slave might conceivably accept Davis's offer despite its flaws if he thought that Richmond was likely to win the war. In that case, Confederate freedom might be the only one available. But the dramatic turn that the tide of war had taken with Atlanta's fall and Lincoln's reelection made it unlikely that southern blacks would see things that way.

But the most fundamental and most powerful objection to Davis's plan was that, in the words of Mississippi planter and congressman Henry C. Chambers, it would in practice "subvert the labour system, the social system and the political system of our country."[38] Our president seems to have forgotten, he and others cried, why we are at war at all. The South left the Union, formed its own country, and took up arms in order to bar the door to emancipation. But now, the *Charleston Mercury* raged, "the Confederate Government threatens to put upon us all the evils we threw off the dominion of our Yankee enemies to avoid."[39] Davis's proposition, agreed the *Macon Telegraph and Confederate* (and many, many others), constituted "the abandonment of the whole object of the war."[40] It would, Zebulon Vance protested, "surrender the entire question which has ever separated the North from the South," would turn secession and our war effort into "a mere objectless waste of human life."[41]

Some of the measure's champions responded coyly to this most fundamental of objections. The editors of two Richmond papers declared that they and the white South as a whole had been fighting not for the sake of slavery but to secure states' rights and southern independence. "We are told by some horrified individuals," said the *Richmond Sentinel* in affected surprise, "that this is 'giving up the cause.'" But, its editor demanded, just what cause are they referring to? "We thought that *independence* was, just now, the great question."[42] "This war is waged for the liberty, independence, and nationality of these States," the *Enquirer* chimed in, and it was "for this object *only*" that "the people have made the tremendous sacrifices of the last four years." It follows as night the day that "*any* measure which *secures* the liberty, independence and nationality of these States is justified and made our imperative duty."[43]

Davis's opponents found this claim simply laughable. Yes, they retorted, we value states' rights. But the purpose of those rights has always been to protect the southern master from interference by a potentially hostile national government. All southerners knew that "slavery—aggressions upon it by the North, apprehensions for its safety in the South"—was the "cause of Secession" and that "all other questions were subordinate to it," one Georgian now reminded his president. "The principle of State Sovereignty" was "important to the South principally, or solely, as the armor that encased her peculiar institution."[44] They had finally opted for full-scale independence for the same reason—to guarantee slavery's future. "Of what value is 'self-government' to the South," one Texan demanded, once "the very fabric of Southern prosperity" has been lost?[45]

Objections such as these finally cut to the core of the Richmond regime's problem. How could it offer enough to its slaves to attract them to its banner while simultaneously retaining enough of the old South to make the war worth winning?

The most candid reply to this question was rarely heard in public. It held that slavery was already dead, or at least was at death's doorstep. The only real question now was, what will replace it? And that was why southern whites had to be ready to do almost anything to win the war and keep the Confederacy secure. Because only then would *they* be the ones to answer that crucial question. Yes, Davis's plan might well require that all the slaves be formally freed. But if that helped to keep the Confederacy alive, then white southerners (and not northern abolitionists) would define the meaning and set the limits of black freedom. Southern masters would retain not only their own personal freedom and the rest of their considerable property; they would also keep political power in their own hands. And that would allow their politicians in Richmond and the various state capitals to shape an emancipation process that best served the masters' needs. They would dictate the pace as well as the nature and degree of freedom that the former slaves received. So, the *Richmond Sentinel* pointed out, even if Davis's plan left southerners "stripped of property" in human beings "but master of the government," their position would still "be infinitely better than if" they were "despoiled by the enemy" and subjected to his rule.[46]

General Patrick Cleburne had made this very point when he proposed arming and freeing slaves back in the winter of 1863–64. "It is said slaves will not work after they are freed," Cleburne had noted in his memorandum, but that problem could be solved by the combination of economic necessity (their need to make a living) and "wise legislation."[47] The general had explained the point further while talking with a Confederate congressman. "If the Yankees succeed in abolishing slavery," Cleburne said, "equality and amalgamation" between black and white would follow. But "if we take this step now, we can mould the relations, for all time to come, between the white and colored races." This would allow southerners to "control the negroes" and make sure that "they will still be our laborers as much as they now are." The Irish-born Cleburne found an analogy in the way that the British Empire had stripped legally free Catholics in his birthplace of their civic rights in order to dominate them economically. The lesson, Cleburne noted tartly, was that "writing a man 'free' does not make him so."[48]

When Jefferson Davis's government belatedly adopted the substance of Cleburne's proposal in the late fall of 1864, it also accepted his thinking about the place that ex-slaves would occupy in the Confederacy's postwar economy and social structure. In a private letter to an old friend, Confederate secretary of state Judah P. Benjamin explained that if the Richmond regime could survive the war and set the terms of slavery's dissolution, then "ultimate emancipation" would come to members of the "inferior race" only after they first passed through "an intermediate state of serfage or peonage." He did not bother specifying how long that "intermediate state" might last.[49] The main thing right now, said the *Richmond Enquirer,* is "to use negroes as soldiers," even if that requires freeing them. Then, when their aid brings us victory and "quieter times," the South would be in a position to formulate what it delicately termed "the definite arrangements which may thus become needful."[50] If southerners control the emancipation process and direct it in their "own way," agreed the *Lynchburg Virginian,* they would also be the ones to "fix the status of the freedmen" and "regulate their conditions" in society.[51]

Jefferson Davis and his government found their core congressional support for this measure among men whose districts had already been lost to the enemy and therefore had less to fear from radical Confederate measures. Most planters still under Confederate rule, however, continued to oppose placing their slaves in the army.[52] Some simply refused to consider sacrificing their own property, no matter what the reason. One editor described such masters as "Camp Meeting patriots, who ran well, so long as their homes, their property and their persons were safe, but who have grown suddenly lukewarm, when sacrifices were to be made for the country and the cause."[53] Such people, one soldier acidly observed, certainly "would like" to see the Confederacy triumph "and no doubt weary heaven with their prayers for peace and independence." But they prayed at least as fervently "to get through with whole skins and full purses."[54]

Some obstinate masters seemed oblivious to the Confederacy's peril. As War Department clerk John B. Jones put it, "They have not yet awakened to a consciousness that there is danger of losing all."[55] A Florida congressman thus insisted that there was "nothing in the present aspect of our military affairs" to "justify the hazardous experiment" that Davis proposed.[56] Of course, Davis's own assurance in November 1864 that black troops were not yet needed—and would likely *never* be needed—did little to promote public appreciation of the crisis.

And then there were the old South's dead-enders, those "slaveholders on principle" (in Catherine Edmondston's proud self-designation) who preferred defeat and destruction to any infringement on their prerogatives. *"We want no Confederate Government without our institutions,"* the *Charleston Mercury* shouted. "And we will have none."[57] One of Mary Chesnut's acquaintances announced, "If we are to lose our Negroes, we would as soon see Sherman free them as the Confederate government."[58]

Still other Confederates accepted the notion of enlisting black soldiers but rejected the idea of granting them freedom. Since slavery was good for the black man, opined the *Richmond Whig,* "it is right that he should assist in defending the blessings he himself enjoys" in that condition.[59]

But if the last four years had taught such people nothing about the South's black population, Jefferson Davis and his advisers had at least learned something. They had learned that the slaves ardently wished for freedom and would now fight for nothing less. Only the hope of liberty, Davis had pointed out in November, would give the black soldier a sufficient "motive for a zealous discharge of duty."[60] Robert E. Lee later predicted, "Unless their freedom is guaranteed to them [we] shall get no volunteers."[61] Nor, Lee added, would arming slaves without promising them their freedom be "wise."[62] He said no more on the subject, but an anonymous letter in the *Richmond Enquirer* did. It warned against the "dangerous experiment" of "withhold[ing] from the negro soldier his personal freedom" at the same time that freedom is being "freely offered to him in the neighboring hostile camp."[63]

In early February 1865, Jefferson Davis's allies in Congress introduced a number of measures designed to implement the proposal to turn slaves into soldiers. All were tabled or killed. Then, on February 10, Mississippi's Ethelbert Barksdale brought a bill into the House of Representatives that pointedly declined to empower the Confederate government either to conscript or to emancipate a single slave. It would enable the president only "to ask for and accept from the owners of slaves, the services of such number of able-bodied negro men as he may deem expedient." Barksdale's bill went on to promise that "nothing in this act shall be construed to authorize a change in the relation which the said slaves shall bear toward their owners, except by consent of the owners and of the States in which they may reside."[64]

Barksdale celebrated the toothlessness of his bill. It proposed, he boasted, to raise black troops "not by wholesale conscription—not by compulsion—not by exercise of unauthorized power to interfere with the relation of the slave to his owner as property, but by leaving this question, where it properly belongs—to the owners of slaves, by the consent of the States and in pursuance of the laws thereof." Surely this abject surrender in the face of masters' protests would finally allow the bill to become law. Or, Barksdale challenged, "Are gentlemen unwilling to let the people have the privilege of contributing their slaves" even "as a free-will offering?"[65]

In the meantime, the military situation had gone from dire to desperate. In the few months since Davis stunned the South with his November proposal, the battle of Nashville had all but obliterated the Army of Tennessee, Savannah had fallen, and in South Carolina Sherman's forces had taken both Columbia and Charleston. East of the Mississippi River, Confederate military forces now firmly controlled only shrinking islands of territory.

Nevertheless, getting even Barksdale's very weak bill passed required considerable arm-twisting. During the first week of March, the Virginia legislature instructed its two Confederate senators (R.M.T. Hunter and Allen T. Caperton) to swallow their personal objections and vote aye.[66] That permitted the Senate to pass the bill on March 8, 1865, and even then only by a one-vote majority.[67] The Confederate

House assented the next day, and Jefferson Davis signed it into law on the thirteenth.[68]

Ten days later, the army issued orders implementing the new law. Those orders specified that "no slave will be accepted as a recruit unless with his own consent and with the approbation of his master by a written instrument conferring, as far as he may, the rights of a freedman." In other words, any master volunteering a slave had to manumit him first, and any black men offered in that way had first to agree to serve.[69]

Robert E. Lee delegated oversight of the project to his erstwhile corps commander, Lieutenant General Richard S. Ewell, and recruiters were sent to Georgia, South Carolina, Alabama, Florida, and various parts of Virginia.[70]

The new Confederate law authorized raising a total of three hundred thousand black troops, and Confederate leaders and journalists predicted quick success in doing so. But the actual results proved far, far smaller. No black soldiers at all materialized other than in Richmond and Petersburg. Within those two cities, white officials mustered black employees of two local hospitals into a company or two of a local defense corps (not part of the regular Confederate army) alongside convalescing patients.[71] At least some of these men were ordered into the trenches to defend against a mid-March Union raid.[72] But other reports suggest they may have gone there without uniforms or arms.[73]

And what of the main event—the plan to recruit black soldiers directly into the army proper, the point of the government's bill? Richmond newspapers were "glad to report" later that month that "recruiting is going on rapidly" and that "the owners of slaves are coming up heartily." As for the slaves themselves, enthused another paper, they were now in the grip of a veritable "military fever."[74] Other reports, however, disclosed that recruiters had by then managed to enlist only thirty to forty men—and by the war's end, perhaps only twenty more. The Davis regime drilled, fed, and housed those men at military prison facilities under the watchful eyes of military police and prison wardens.[75] That treatment belied all the government's public assurances of good faith and warm welcome. So did reports that white boys threw mud at black soldiers on city streets. General Ewell himself objected that "some of the blk soldiers were whipped they were hooted at and treated generally in a way to nullify the law."[76]

Not surprisingly, some observers found the black soldiers dispirited.

The son of a Virginia legislator watched them drill one day. Their body language told him that they were "engaged in a work not exactly in accord with their notions of self interest" and that "their inclination must have been against engaging on the Southern side."[77] When the troops paraded through the streets, another journalist recorded, black bystanders looked on "with unenvious eyes."[78]

A major reason for the dismally small number of recruits was that most masters refused to cooperate—a response that should have surprised no one. Since the second year of the war, after all, masters had proved less and less willing to allow the army to use their slaves even temporarily, and even as laborers. Now the government was expecting the same people to surrender their slaves permanently and put muskets in their hands. Georgia's leading newspaper, for one, had been "very certain" for months that slave owners would withhold their men.[79]

Masters of all political shadings bore out that prediction. William A. Graham, a major planter and former North Carolina governor, had led the fight in the Senate against the Davis plan. On March 10, 1865, he told his wife about the bill's passage. "It provides, however, that they shall only be taken with the consent of the masters," he noted, "and this I hope no master will yield. Certainly I shall not."[80] Two days later Graham invited a longtime ally back in Raleigh (David Swain, another former governor) to help persuade others to fold their arms as well. "I trust no master in N.C. will volunteer or consent, to begin this process of abolition," he wrote, "as I feel very confident the [state] Gen'l Assembly will not."[81] As Graham well knew, the Tar Heel State's legislature had gone on record more than a month earlier "against the policy of arming slaves."[82]

Graham and Swain had been unionists until the war began. But consistently secessionist fire-eaters such as Catherine Edmondston were no readier to "yield their property & their hopes," much less to "allow a degraded race to be placed at one stroke on a level with them."[83] The same opposition among masters that had so long made a black-soldier law inconceivable now made it unworkable.

While some masters opposed and resisted Davis's scheme reflexively or on principle, others did so because they thought they knew a better method with which to protect their interests. A Lynchburg newspaper reported that "some prominent gentlemen from Virginia" opposed Davis's plan because they were "hoping to save their property" by "fall[ing] back into the arms of Lincoln."[84] Word reached the *Richmond Enquirer* that "certain members of Congress, representing large slaveholding constituencies," had "openly declared their preferences for reconstruction, with Federal guaranty of slavery, to the emancipation of slaves as a means of securing the independence of the Confederate States."[85]

War Department clerk John B. Jones heard much the same thing—as well he might, because the idea was being floated within the department itself.[86] At the end of December 1864, Assistant Secretary of War John A. Campbell told an underling "that the only question now is the *manner*" in which the Union would be "reconstructed"—that is, "whether the South shall be destroyed and subjugated" or whether it could find a way to return not only with its honor but also with its "rights" intact, even if without its many former "advantages of power, influence, or political supremacy."[87] A variation on that theme was the hope that even if slavery were abolished, white landowners would be permitted through state and local laws to impose tight controls over the lives and labors of the freedpeople.

Those who nurtured such hopes included quondam unionists such as Alexander Rives, a prominent Virginia planter and jurist. Rives hoped that southern masters might "be restored to their rights under the Union."[88] So, of course, did North Carolinian William Woods Holden and his supporters, as well as John J. Seibels and others in Alabama who had sought to strike such a deal in the spring of 1864.

Joining these men now (according to War Bureau chief Robert Garlick Hill Kean) was "a large part of the Congress," including powerful members of the planter establishment.[89] Former North Carolina governors David Swain and William Graham and the state's current treasurer, Jonathan Worth, had all opposed peace talk early in 1864 when they feared it could only weaken the Confederacy and encourage the war party in the North. They had then stood, like Zebulon Vance, for holding out so long as they saw any chance of maintaining the independence of the slave states through war. As one planter associated with them put it, "Until it has been *demonstrated* that these means are inadequate to the accomplishment of independence, it is our duty to persist in the struggle for it." But, he then added, "When we have satisfied ourselves, by the exhaustion of these means, that our original aim cannot be attained, we will 'accept the situation' and make the best terms in our power."[90]

For some, this point had arrived in the autumn of 1864 with Atlanta's loss and Lincoln's reelection.[91] The sharp drop in Confederate fortunes that then convinced Jefferson Davis to arm and free slaves had led Graham and his circle to opposite practical conclusions. They were now for seeking the most advantageous possible basis on which to be reintegrated into the Union. In late January, Graham predicted that the North, in order to restore the Union without further bloodletting, would offer them attractive terms—would "guarantee slavery as it now exists, and probably make other concessions" as well.[92]

The abortive meeting with Lincoln and Seward at Hampton Roads did not extinguish those hopes, in part because some leading Confederates refused to read its meaning in the same way that Jefferson Davis reported it. The southern delegation—Vice President Stephens, Assistant Secretary of War Campbell, and Senator Hunter—knew more than the official account had disclosed. While on board the *River Queen*, they had heard Lincoln and Seward say things that offered them a wider choice of options than Davis had conveyed to Congress and the public.[93]

According to privately circulated accounts by Campbell and Stephens (and endorsed years later by Hunter), Lincoln and Seward had noted that federal courts might yet rule the Emancipation Proclamation unconstitutional or, at least, null and void once the war was over. Seward had observed that the prospective Thirteenth Amendment was a war measure and that it, too, might lose public favor with the end of hostilities. Seward had also said that the states of the former Confederacy, upon rejoining the Union, might help deprive the proposed amendment of the supermajority (three-quarters) positive vote it would need for ratification.

It seems doubtful that Lincoln thought this likely, mentioning the ideas to help some proslavery bitter-enders to swallow reunion. Even if reunion did impose general emancipation, the Confederate conferees quoted Lincoln as saying, the federal government might yet compensate masters for their losses. As for other forms of rebel property, Lincoln promised to exercise great "liberality" in implementing the confiscation laws.[94]

The Campbell-Stephens version of what had transpired at Hampton Roads circulated at the time among the members of Graham's circle and very possibly beyond, encouraging masters to hope that the war's prompt cessation would leave them better off both economically and politically than would its continuation.[95] In any case, North Carolina state treasurer Jonathan Worth observed, "this is the only hope of saving anything from the wreck." Only in this way might southerners "avoid further abolition, confiscation, and prosecution for treason."[96]

As Confederate senators dithered over the black-soldier bill in late February 1865, and while more and more planters placed hopes of maintaining their power and property in reunion rather than military victory, the *Richmond Enquirer* pointed frantically at the swiftly deteriorating military situation. Grant was "gradually and perhaps surely extending his lines around Petersburg and Richmond," threatening "every moment" to burst through Richmond's defenses.[97] Meanwhile, Sherman's forces were "rushing through the Carolinas like an avalanche."[98]

In accord with Grant's decision to continue campaigning through the calendar year, Sherman's army moved out of Savannah on the first day of February. Organized as before into four parallel columns, its men began churning a wide path through South Carolina, commandeering or destroying property with even greater thoroughness and enthusiasm than they had displayed in Georgia. For this, they firmly believed, was the state that had caused the war in the first place. "The army burned everything it came near in the State of South Carolina," Union major James Connolly told his wife, "not under orders, but in spite of orders. The men 'had it in' for the State and they took it out in their own way."[99]

Sherman's troops encountered more resistance in South Carolina than in Georgia, and the rain-soaked wintertime terrain was more daunting, too. Though Sherman charted a line of march that led inland from the coast toward drier ground, his soldiers still found themselves slogging through swamps and laboriously fording or bridging rivers. White soldiers and freedmen cut down trees to "corduroy" soggy roads (that is, pave them with logs).

On February 17, 1865, Sherman's troops entered the state capital of Columbia. Slaves and free blacks lined the streets and cheered ecstatically. As a member of Sherman's staff later recalled, a "stranger looking on would have believed that this was a triumphal return of some favorite hero, rather than the entry of the conqueror who had struck another blow at the heart of people who hate him and his."[100] Of course, Sherman was both things simultaneously, though to different parts of the local population.

Nearly two years earlier, in May 1862, Robert E. Lee had ordered the Confederate general then in command at Charleston to defend that symbolically important city "to the last extremity . . . street by street and house by house as long as we have a foot of ground to stand upon."[101] But in seizing Columbia, Sherman had now outflanked and isolated the Charleston garrison, cutting its transportation and communication links to the state's interior. So, one day after Columbia's occupation, Charleston—secession's cradle—meekly surrendered to another Union force that had until then been inconclusively besieging it from the sea.

The first federal unit to enter Charleston was the Twenty-First U.S. Colored Infantry regiment, now incorporating the Third, Fourth, and Fifth South Carolina Volunteer regiments that had been raised in the Department of the South. It was filled with men who had shortly before been slaves in South Carolina, Georgia, and Florida. A few days later, the all-black Fifty-Fifth Massachusetts regiment joined the Twenty-First. A mounted black soldier carrying a banner proclaiming "Liberty" led a column down the main thoroughfare.[102] The regiment's colonel accepted the humbled city's surrender.

As Union soldiers strode through the streets, slaves and free blacks of Charleston and its environs flocked to their side. Two weeks after Union investment of the city, black residents celebrated their liberation with a massive procession, including bands, black Union soldiers, members of many manual occupations, ministers, a large contingent of women, and some 1,800 children who sang that although "John Brown's body lies a moulding in the grave, We go marching on!"[103]

In February, meanwhile, U.S. Marines had occupied the city of Georgetown on the northern coast of South Carolina; a Union admiral declared slavery dead in the surrounding district. On March 1, 1865, troops from both the 54th Massachusetts and the 102nd and 103rd USCT regiments took control of the town.[104] A few days later, groups of soldiers fanned out into the countryside to bring the news of freedom to the area's black population. Those visits touched off additional explosions of joy and retribution. Freedmen burned buildings and made off with furniture, clothing, linens, food, cattle, and other pieces of their former masters' property.

The meaning of such acts now dawned on South Carolina plantation mistress Adele Petigru Allston who, not then at home, was receiving detailed reports from a neighboring planter. It all showed, Allston realized, that "they *think it right* to steal from us, to spoil us, as the Israelites did the Egyptians." Her epiphany no doubt accurately interpreted the sentiments of the freedpeople involved. Field laborers, announcing their refusal ever again to work under drivers, began pulling down fences and "divided out" the land.[105] Allston's neighbor advised her that "if you come here all your servants . . . will immediately leave you." They will prove "more or less impertinent as the humor takes them and in short will do as they choose." Only those blacks with families too large to move easily were staying in place and maintaining a "veneering of fidelity."[106]

Also in February, Union troops under the command of General John Schofield, using recently captured Fort Fisher as a base, began to encircle Confederate forces in and around Wilmington, North Carolina. The gray-clad troops retreated, and on the night of February 21, 1865, they evacuated the city. Union soldiers marched in the following day.

Several days afterward, nearly 1,600 black worshippers filled Wilmington's Front Street Methodist Church, where Rev. L. S. Burkhead, a white minister, had for years presided over the predominantly black congregation. By tradition, the class leaders, all of whom were black, would conduct Sunday's sunrise prayer meeting. But as Rev. Burkhead took his seat near the altar, the mood of the assemblage suggested that this would be a unique service. "The whole congregation was wild with excitement," he recalled years later, "and extravagant beyond all precedent with shouts, groans, amen, and unseemingly demonstrations."

The congregation sang a hymn strikingly appropriate for the occasion, "Sing unto the Lord a New Song," and when it had finished, an unfamiliar black man strode to the pulpit. He was William H. Hunter, the son of a North Carolina slave who had eventually managed to buy freedom for himself and his family and then took them to the North. Hunter was now a chaplain in the U.S. Army, a member of one of the black Union regiments that had entered the city. The church's class leaders had invited him to the service.

"I listened to your prayers," Hunter told the congregation that morning, "but I did not hear a single prayer offered for the President of the United States or for the success of the American Army. But I knew what you meant. You were not quite sure that you were free, therefore a little afraid to say boldly what you felt. I know how it is. I remember how we used to have to employ our dark symbols and obscure figures to cover up our real meaning. The profoundest philosopher could not understand us." From the congregation came affirmations: "Amen! Hallelujah! That's so."

The chaplain warmed to the theme of past and present. "My brethren and friends," he said, "I rise to address you, but I scarcely know what line of thought to pursue. When a thousand thoughts crowd upon my mind it is difficult to select that which will be more appropriate than the rest. A few short years ago I left North Carolina a slave; I now return a man. I have the honor to be a regular minister of the Gospel in the Methodist Episcopal Church of the United States and also a regularly commissioned chaplain in the American Army." He was proud to report, moreover, that just three weeks earlier "as black a man as you ever saw, preached in the city of Washington to the Congress of the United States." That was Rev. Henry Highland Garnet. "And that a short time ago another colored man was admitted to the bar of the Supreme Court of the United States as a lawyer." That was the Boston lawyer John S. Rock. "One week ago you were all slaves; now you are all free. Thank God the armies of the Lord and of Gideon has triumphed and the Rebels have been driven back in confusion and scattered like chaff before the wind."

According to Rev. Burkhead, the black chaplain's words elicited a "tumultuous uproar" from the congregation. Once the service had ended, the shaken white minister retired to his parsonage to consider the implications of what he had just seen and heard. Like so many other whites who had presided over black congregations, he would soon receive a formal demand from his parishioners that he surrender the pulpit and that the church affiliate with the African Methodist Episcopal Church.[107]

William Tecumseh Sherman's army entered North Carolina a week or two later. His soldiers went easier on the residents of that state, whom they considered less responsible for the war than their more southerly neighbors.

Some panicky Tar Heel whites nevertheless found evidence everywhere of intended slave insurrections that would rape and slaughter whites indiscriminately. They reacted violently. Reports told of many blacks being lynched.[108] Just inside the state's southern border, for example, a group of slaves had begun meeting to plan a mass escape to Sherman's column. The home guards who discovered and captured them hanged twenty-five.[109] Thousands of other black people succeeded in leaving farms and plantations and followed in Sherman's wake.[110]

Black North Carolinians received different kinds of treatment from different kinds of Union soldiers. "One Yankee would come along an' give us sumptin'," Fannie Dunn recalled, "an' another would come on behind him an' take it. Dats de way dey done. . . . One give mother a mule," and another "give mother a ham of meat." But a third soldier then "come right on behind him an' took it away from her."[111] John Bectom recalled later that a Union soldier had caught one of his master's shoats, killed and butchered it, and gave one of the hindquarters "to me, and told me to carry and give it to my mother." But another Yankee soldier stole a pair of shoes from the same woman.[112] Such recollections were common.[113]

In the course of their long march, Sherman and his men asked black people they encountered about Confederate hopes to arm them. On the way to Savannah in early December 1864, Sherman told a group of older black men that Jefferson Davis "was talking about arming the negroes." Yes, they already knew that, they replied. "Well," Sherman asked, "what'll you all do—will you fight against us?" "No, *Sir*," came the reply. "De day dey gives us arms, *dat day de war ends!*" Those words, according to the adjutant who recorded the exchange in his diary, were "eagerly spoken—and the rest [of them] as eagerly assented."[114]

In both North and South Carolina, Sherman's aide-de-camp, Major George W. Nichols, heard much the same thing. In Fayetteville he spoke with an older woman as she sat surrounded by her family. "There, sir," she said, pointing, "are my two sons-in-law. Yesterday morning their master tried to take them away, offering them their freedom if they would go into the army voluntarily; but they know better than that. They never would fire a gun against the Federals." One of the young men spoke up for himself. "If they had forced me into the army," he said, "I would have shot the officer they put over me the first time I got a chance." They understood very well why slave owners were offering arms and freedom to their slaves and what it all meant. "They'd never put muskets in the slaves' hands if they were not afeared that their cause was gone up," the matriarch said. They were making this offer because "they are going to be whipped"—and, in fact, "are whipped now." And just "supposing they do free the colored men who fight for them," she said. "What is to become of us, their mothers, wives, and children at home? We are to remain slaves, of course."[115]

Skeptics might discount these words and others like them as simply telling northerners what they wanted to hear. But some staunch Confederates were hearing the same things. Walking the streets of Macon, Georgia, in January 1865, a Confederate editor watched some white boys demand of a black man, "Uncle, why don't you go and fight?" "What I fight for?" the man responded. "For your country," a white shot back. "I have no country to fight for," the man replied.[116]

In South Carolina, the Chesnut family was making similarly disquieting discoveries about their own slaves' feelings on this subject. At the war's start, James Chesnut, Jr., had talked to his most trusted slaves and heard (as his wife later recorded) that "they were keen to go in the army" if by doing so they could obtain freedom and a bounty. But by late 1864 that early inclination had disappeared. "Now they say coolly they don't want freedom if they have to fight for it." Because now "they are pretty sure of having it anyway" with the aid of Union troops.[117]

In late February and early March, Confederate forces made their most powerful and most promising attempt to end Sherman's march, which had now reached North Carolina. On February 22, 1865, Robert E. Lee gave command of that effort to Joseph E. Johnston. Johnston assembled a new Army of the South, about twenty-three thousand strong, composed of a number of smaller units, including remnants of the Army of Tennessee.

About a month later, one of Johnston's generals, William Hardee, engaged Sherman's left wing, commanded by General Henry W. Slocum, at the village of Averasboro. Hardee sought to slow Slocum's advance long enough for Johnston to prepare a bigger and more powerful attack. The accomplishment cost Hardee 25 percent more casualties than his enemy suffered. Three days later, Johnston launched serial assaults upon Slocum's force at Bentonville, some thirty miles to the northeast. But on March 20, 1865, Sherman's right wing (under Oliver O. Howard) arrived on the field, making further Confederate attacks futile. During the night of March 21, 1865, Johnston broke off the engagement after suffering losses 70 percent higher than Sherman's. Sherman moved on toward his intended rendezvous with General John Schofield's forces at Goldsboro on March 24. With those reinforcements, Sherman's army now boasted some ninety thousand men. After pausing to rest and resupply, Sherman planned to head north once again—to the decisive confrontation in eastern Virginia.[118]

At bay in Petersburg and Richmond, Lee's army was already disintegrating. During February and March, an average of more than eight hundred men left its ranks each week.[119] Some deserters took heart from letters from family members, friends, and neighbors promising to support their decision. During the winter of 1864–65, a town in Alabama's wire grass region hosted a dinner that honored fifty-seven deserters. Warrants were issued for their arrest, but the local constable refused to enforce them.[120]

Just as telling as the extent of desertion was the quality of the soldiers now leaving. They included men who had previously seemed the most loyal. They would no longer risk their lives in behalf of a cause that seemed already lost. And as that assessment of the situation spread, those who remained in ranks ceased to view those who departed as cowards or criminals. "The men on the picket line fire off their guns in the air," Captain Benjamin Wesley Justice noted in mid-March, "& will not try to shoot down those who are in the act of deserting to the enemy."[121]

Robert E. Lee knew that "the state of feeling in the country" was taking its toll on his army in Petersburg and Richmond.[122] At the end of February, he informed his War Department that men "from the North Carolina regiments, and especially those from the western part of that State" were hearing from relatives and friends that if they deserted and returned to their families "they will be in no danger of arrest" because "the bands of deserters so far outnumber the home guards" back home.[123]

The advancing disintegration of southern armies was one of the factors that had driven Jefferson Davis to propose arming slaves and free blacks. Perhaps, he had hoped, final military defeat and the radical revolution in southern life that it threatened could be avoided by taking at least one page from the revolutionaries' book. But the attempt had come far too late and foundered on the resistance of masters and slaves alike. There would be no black Confederate army to help Lee and his Army of Northern Virginia break the siege of Petersburg and Richmond.

Chapter Ten

AND THE WALLS GAVE WAY:
RICHMOND, APPOMATTOX, AND AFTER

With the South's Army of Tennessee shattered and great swaths of Confederate territory now controlled by or within the reach of northern forces, the key obstacle to Union victory was the defeat of Robert E. Lee's Army of Northern Virginia, entrenched in Richmond and Petersburg. But that was a big obstacle, indeed. Lee was by far the Confederacy's best field commander. He may well have been the outstanding commander of the war, on either side. The army that Lee led was not only the Confederacy's largest but also its most lethally effective, as a string of Union generals could ruefully attest. So neither Abraham Lincoln nor Ulysses S. Grant was about to underestimate the task that faced them now—not only to defeat Lee and his army in a battle but to force its complete and unconditional surrender. Even as he planned and maneuvered to do that, moreover, Grant struggled with another anxiety—that the wily and unpredictable Lee might find a way to escape the Richmond siege. "I knew he could move much more lightly and more rapidly than I," Grant later recalled, "and that, if he got the start, he would leave me behind so that we would have the same army to fight again farther south—and the war might be prolonged another year."[1]

Lee enjoyed one major advantage in 1865 that Confederate general John C. Pemberton had lacked during the Vicksburg siege two years earlier. The cordon around Richmond and Petersburg, unlike the one that had choked Vicksburg, was not complete enough to seal it off from all outside sources of supply. The extent and nature of the ground to be

covered made it far more difficult for Union forces to completely surround the defenders there. Some supplies therefore continued to reach
Richmond by canal and wagon.[2] Most important, Lee managed to
keep railroad lines open to the west and to Raleigh, successfully repel-
ling some attempted attacks on them and relatively quickly repairing
the damage inflicted upon them by Union raiders. That is why the
confrontation at Petersburg lasted so much longer than did the one at
Vicksburg—more than nine months by late March 1865.[3]

But the closing of the port of Wilmington in mid-January had sev-
ered Raleigh's (and therefore Petersburg-Richmond's) link to the sea,
reducing the amount and kind of material that Lee now received. And
Sherman's drive northward menaced the Raleigh lifeline itself. Johnston's failure at the battle of Bentonville to significantly damage Sherman's army killed any realistic hopes of stopping its northward advance.
If Sherman's army reached Petersburg, Lee knew, the besiegers' combined forces would surely overwhelm his Army of Northern Virginia.

Lee had begun to prepare Jefferson Davis for that eventuality in the
last days of January 1865. If Grant's force grew much stronger, he told
Davis, "I do not see how in our present position he can be prevented
from enveloping Richmond." Before Sherman arrived, therefore, Lee
would have to try to strike a blow against Grant—a decisive blow if
possible, but one strong enough at least to allow Lee to break out of the
Petersburg entrenchments and make his way westward to rail lines that
would carry his army southward toward North Carolina and Joseph
Johnston's force.[4] On March 9, Lee warned the War Department that
he probably could not long "maintain our present position with the
means at the disposal of the Government."[5]

By the last week of March, Lee saw that his position had finally
become indefensible. On March 25, he ordered troops of John B. Gordon's command to attack Union siege lines at Fort Stedman, an earthen
redoubt just east of Petersburg. He aimed either to break through
Grant's lines there or at least compel Grant to reinforce that point at the
expense of others, thereby opening gaps through which Lee's army
could escape the two cities.

The attack at Stedman began well but then stalled and failed in the
face of fierce artillery barrages and massive infantry counterattacks.
"On they came," an awe-struck Confederate soldier recalled of one
Union assault, "shoulder to shoulder, the stars and stripes flying over

their heads. Again the fire broke from our rifle pits, extending to the right and left till the whole line . . . was crackling and sputtering. But forward still swept the line of blue, heeding neither their dead nor their wounded. Forward still, with a rush and a shout, the flag well to the front, and our hearts sink with the fear that they will go over the works at the first charge." Gordon's troops fired another volley, and "the enemy's line falters, appears about to break and flee." Just then, however, "the color bearer runs forward alone with his flag. With a shout that rings again, the blue line follows in a swift charge through our deadliest fire. They reach the works and turning rapidly to the right and left, sweep the line in both directions for a long distance, taking possession of half a mile of rifle pits."[6]

Gordon's promising assault on Fort Stedman had ended in disaster. It proved to be, as one southerner wrote, "only the meteor's flash that illumines for a moment and leaves the night darker than ever."[7] It cost the Army of Northern Virginia thousands of additional casualties and left Union troops closer than ever to Lee's lines.[8]

Grant now dispatched Philip Sheridan and a large force of infantry and cavalry westward, to the far right of Lee's line, aiming to get around it and interdict the Southside Railroad. On April 1, 1865, at a crossroads called Five Forks, Sheridan's troops collided with brigades under George Pickett's command, ultimately smashing them and taking thousands of prisoners.[9]

That victory, in turn, encouraged Grant to order a general advance. Before dawn the next morning, soldiers of the Union's Sixth Corps broke through Confederate lines south of Petersburg at the Boydton Plank Road. Confederate casualties that day exceeded five thousand— perhaps a tenth of Lee's entire army—with many surrendering to the attacking bluecoats.[10]

Lee would afterward attribute much of this Union success to his own troops' sinking morale. Their actions "were not marked by the boldness and decision which formerly characterized them," he reported. "Except in particular instances, they were feeble; and a want of confidence seemed to possess officers and men."[11]

That same morning, Lee informed Jefferson Davis of Grant's breakthrough at the Boydton section of the line. The Confederate president then went to Sabbath services at Saint Paul's Episcopal Church. Before the service concluded, the church sexton came striding up the aisle to bring President Davis another message. This one advised him that Lee was about to evacuate Richmond and Petersburg and urged the government to do the same.[12]

Upon reading those words, Davis arose, walked back down the aisle, and left the church. Cabinet members and other officials followed soon afterward. Other congregants, guessing what was afoot, ignored the pastor's attempts to keep them in their seats and filed out the doors as well. What they saw on the street confirmed their worst fears: government functionaries burning piles of official documents.[13]

Documents were not the only things consigned to flames that day. Confederate soldiers torched tobacco warehouses to deny their contents to the Yankees. The flames then spread into the rest of the city, eventually reaching the arsenal and detonating explosives kept there. Naval vessels, too, were set ablaze or blown up in the harbor. To Sallie Putnam and others, these sounds and scenes seemed to foreshadow "the horrors of the final conflagration, when the earth shall be wrapped in flames and melt with fervent heat."[14]

Panic now seized many of Richmond's white residents.[15] A young woman found her neighbor "running from room to room, wringing her hands, tearing her hair," and bewailing the prospect of soon facing black Union troops. "They say the black wretches are in the very front of Grant's army," she cried, "and will rush into the city before any decent white men are here to restrain them!"[16]

Richmond's black population reacted rather differently to news of Lee's flight. Men and women worshipping at the African Church now came onto the streets, too. When they learned of the impending evacuation, Confederate navy secretary Stephen Mallory observed, they began "shaking hands and exchanging congratulations upon all sides. Many of them walked the streets with eager faces, parted lips, and hurried strides, gazing anxiously into the distance as if to catch the first glimpse of their coming friends."[17]

As southern troops began to leave the two cities, some black residents joined deserters and poor whites in pillaging shops and warehouses.[18] Others disappeared from the streets. Afraid of being forced to accompany fleeing white masters, they spent that night in their churches.[19] Still others took advantage of the evacuation-spawned chaos to escape from their masters across the same bridges over which Confederate soldiers streamed westward toward the Richmond and Danville Railroad line.[20]

Along with members of his cabinet and the Confederate Treasury, Jefferson Davis left the capital that night by train. His newest secretary of war, General John C. Breckinridge, would join them later.[21] Many civilians hurried to leave as well, by horse, on foot, in wagons and carriages, or by rail, often offering extravagant sums for any kind of vehicle.[22] Slave dealer Robert Lumpkin frantically begged for access to crowded railroad cars for himself and fifty black people he held in shackles. Unable to gain passage, he had little choice but to return his human goods to the jail that normally held those destined for sale.[23]

The advance guard of Grant's army marched into Petersburg on the morning of April 2, 1865, and from there continued into Richmond. The capital of the Confederacy had fallen at long last. General Godfrey Weitzel, commander of the all-black Twenty-Fifth Corps of the USCT, accepted the city's formal surrender. As his troops surged into Richmond, well-to-do residents retreated into their homes, bolted their doors, and peered anxiously, indignantly, and incredulously through shuttered windows.[24] Appalled, Sallie Putnam watched as "long lines of negro cavalry" flowed down Broad Street and raised their voices in the ode to John Brown, the man that Robert E. Lee had helped bring to the gallows in that state only six years before. The black horsemen brandished their sabers and shouted in triumph. To Putnam, the sound seemed "savage."[25]

But it was all music to the ears of free blacks and those who were only now freed from slavery. They stood atop shacks and waved their hats, crying, " 'The Lord bless the Yankees, the Lord bless the Yankees.' "[26] Others thronged the victorious cavalrymen in the streets and returned their exultant cheers. "Babylon is fallen, Babylon is fallen," some sang; and "I'm going to occupy the land."[27] Black newspaper correspondent Thomas Morris Chester noted that the crowds included "pious old negroes, male and female" who called out to the black soldiers, "God bless you!," "Jesus has opened the way!," "We've been looking for you these many days!," "You've come at last!"—and, nervously but hopefully, "Have you come to stay?"[28]

Once again, persistent illusions about slave faithfulness to their masters and their masters' cause shattered. Black house servants eagerly informed Union soldiers of where some Confederate troops were still hiding in the city.[29] Mary Fontaine's father and husband were both Confederate generals. She watched in horror as her servants "danced and shouted, men hugged each other, and women kissed."[30] Fontaine herself sank to her knees, "and the bitter, bitter tears came in a torrent."[31] She heard others say "it was like their idea of the judgment day." And, she reflected, "perhaps it may be."[32]

One of the Union soldiers who entered Richmond that day was Garland White, who as a boy had been separated from his mother and sold to a young Georgian named Robert Toombs. Now the chaplain of the Twenty-Eighth U.S. Colored Infantry, White thrilled to "the shouts of ten thousand voices" celebrating liberation on the streets of the former Confederate capital. Black men and women gathered around him, urging him to speak, and so he did; he "proclaimed for the first time in that city freedom to *all* mankind."[33]

As White stood in the street, trying to take it all in, an older woman approached him and asked his name, his birthplace, and the name of his mother. When he had answered all her questions, she quietly informed him that "this *is* your mother, Garland, whom you are now talking to, who has spent twenty years of grief about her son." And so she proved to be, one of so many mothers and fathers that day peering hopefully into the faces of the black soldiers passing by, searching for the remembered features of other "children who had been sold south of this state in tribes" in years and decades past.[34]

The telegraph sent the electrifying news of Richmond's fall flashing across the Union, everywhere provoking rapturous celebration. Flags waved, church bells rang, cannons boomed, crowds cheered. The word spread, too, through still-unoccupied parts of the Confederacy. When it reached the Virginia peninsula, the news reduced one planter family to tears. One of the servants, hearing and understanding the masters' anguished cries, kept a straight face, finished her tasks as quickly as possible, offered an excuse, walked out of the big house, and then ran until she knew she was alone. Only then did she dare "jump up an' scream, 'Glory, glory, hallelujah to Jesus! I's free! Glory to God.' "[35]

"Thank God I have lived to see this," Abraham Lincoln exclaimed upon hearing the same news. "It seems to me that I have been dreaming a horrid dream for four years, and now the nightmare is over."[36] On April 3, 1865, the president visited the occupied city of Petersburg. Encountering Ulysses S. Grant, he pumped the general's hand vigorously and at length. The next day Lincoln proceeded by launch to Richmond. Forty or fifty black laborers on the wharf rushed to welcome him. When word of his presence spread, hundreds more came streaming toward him through the streets. A Boston journalist on the scene described what transpired.

> They gathered round the President, ran ahead, hovered upon the flanks of the little company, and hung like a dark cloud upon the rear. Men, women, and children joined the constantly increasing throng. They came from all the by-streets, running in breathless haste, shouting and hallooing and dancing with delight. The men threw up their hats, the women waved their bonnets and handkerchiefs, clapped their hands, and sang, Glory to God! glory! glory! glory!

An elderly black man took off his hat, bowed, and, with tears running down his cheeks, said, "May de good Lord bless you, President Linkum!" Lincoln replied by removing his own hat and silently returning the bow. That gesture, the northern reporter noted, "upset the forms, laws, customs, and ceremonies of centuries." It represented, he thought, "a death-shock to chivalry, and a mortal wound to caste." (No wonder that a white woman, watching the vignette from a nearby house, turned away "in unspeakable disgust.")[37]

Another man Lincoln encountered in Richmond was Confederate assistant secretary of war John A. Campbell. Still encouraged by what he had heard at Hampton Roads just two months earlier—and now freed by Jefferson Davis's absence to act as he saw fit—Campbell attempted to salvage something of the old South from the Confederacy's ruins.

At Campbell's urging, and in hopes of hastening the end of hostilities, Lincoln handed him a note allowing "the gentlemen who have acted as the Legislature of Virginia, in support of the rebellion," to meet to order an end to that rebellion in the Old Dominion.[38]

Campbell had a far bigger role in mind for the Old Dominion's secessionist lawmakers. He falsely informed members of the rebel state legislature that Lincoln had, in fact, invited them, as "the government of Virginia," now to "administer the laws in connection with the authorities of the United States, and under the Constitution of the United States." Lincoln had assured him, Campbell claimed, that if they (and, by implication, all their counterparts throughout the ex-Confederacy) agreed to do that, "no attempt will be made to establish or sustain any other authority" than theirs within their borders.[39]

As the Union president realized only later, Campbell was trying to transmute what Lincoln thought of as only a small, pragmatic concession (allowing them to meet simply to facilitate the state's surrender) into a formal commitment to treat "the insurgent Legislature of Virginia . . . as the rightful Legislature of the State." That would allow representatives of the Virginia elite to retain their political power and use it to enforce upon the black population either slavery or, failing that, the kind of strict racial subordination and draconian labor discipline that they had been seeking ever since slavery began to disintegrate during the war. It was no accident, thus, that Campbell's brief message to Virginia's Confederate legislature repeatedly suggested that the Emancipation Proclamation might yet be rescinded or pronounced legally invalid in the courts. In any case, Campbell announced, "the condition of the slave population" would now be decided through negotiations between Washington and the several southern state governments.[40]

When the president grasped Campbell's purpose, he swiftly put an end to the maneuver. Lincoln rescinded his original offer to Campbell and ordered General Weitzel to prevent the Confederate state legislators from reassembling.[41] He was not about to let them continue governing Virginia now that their rebellion had collapsed.

On the morning of April 10, 1865, a terrific artillery barrage filled the ears of Richmond's residents. Confederate loyalists hoped the cannons were Robert E. Lee's, come to retake the city. But they were, in fact, Union guns celebrating the capitulation of Lee's army at Appomattox Court House the day before.[42]

As the Army of Northern Virginia had fled westward, General Sheridan's Union cavalry followed it along a parallel route to the south, blocking escape in that direction, and the rest of Grant's army chased after it from the east. Confederate soldiers anxious to lighten their loads abandoned vehicles, equipment, arms, blankets, and clothing. Many of Lee's men, anticipating the end and unwilling to face it, abandoned the army itself along the way.[43]

On April 6, 1865, some fifty miles southwest of Petersburg, advance elements of the Army of the Potomac overtook and attacked Lee's rearguard at Sayler's Creek. In a series of clashes, Union forces killed, wounded, or captured almost eight thousand men, including eight Confederate generals.[44] Observing the rout from high ground nearby, a horrified Robert E. Lee exclaimed, "My God! Has the army been dissolved?"[45]

The next day, Grant sent Lee a message pointing out the "hopelessness" of the latter's situation and urging him to surrender in order to avoid "any further effusion of blood." Lee rejected the suggestion, proposing instead that the two generals meet to end the war on terms more acceptable to the rebels. But Grant, mindful of Lincoln's firm position, was having none of that. If southern soldiers wanted peace, he replied, they knew very well how to get it—by "laying down their arms."[46]

That Lee's position was, indeed, hopeless and that Grant's ultimatum was irresistible became clear the following day. On April 8, 1865, Sheridan's cavalry and infantry forces materialized in front of what remained of the Army of Northern Virginia. There was nothing to do now, Lee recognized, but to capitulate. He did that shortly after noon on April 9, by which time fewer than ten thousand troops remained with him.[47]

Grant's terms, though extremely generous to individuals, were militarily and politically uncompromising. With the exception of the officers' sidearms and the soldiers' mounts and private baggage, all weapons and equipment were to be "parked and stacked, and turned over to the officers appointed by me." Pending exchange with Union soldiers still held as prisoners of war, Confederate officers and men would swear not to again take up arms against the U.S. government. Once they swore, they would be permitted to return to their homes.[48]

As the Army of Northern Virginia died, the train carrying Jefferson Davis, members of his cabinet, and the Confederate Treasury pressed southward. It reached Danville, Virginia, on Monday, April 3, 1865, where Davis attempted to re-form his government. On Tuesday, he issued a proclamation assuring diehard supporters that the catastrophe of Richmond's loss was "not without compensation." For now the Confederacy's armed forces were "relieved from the necessity of guarding cities and particular points, important but not vital to our defense." Its soldiers were "free to move from point to point" and were "operating on the interior of our own country, where supplies are more accessible, and where the foe will be far removed from his own base and cut off from all succor in case of reverse." Surely, therefore, "nothing is now needed to render our triumph certain but the exhibition of our own unquenchable resolve."[49]

Davis's public optimism had scaled new heights of delusion. His government was in full flight and unable to influence events in any part of the South. Members of the Congress had scattered to the four winds. Joseph E. Johnston's patchwork army in North Carolina had proved unable to do more than annoy Sherman's. Most of the Confederacy's supporters were by now exhausted, demoralized, and broken in spirit. So far as Davis then knew, Lee's army remained in the field, but at last report it was desperately trying to elude a better-armed and far larger pursuer.

On the afternoon of April 9, 1865, couriers brought word of Lee's surrender to Davis and his cabinet. Incredibly, according to navy secretary Stephen Mallory, Davis was "wholly unprepared" for this "unexpected blow."[50] On April 10, his train left Danville. Reaching Greensboro, North Carolina, the next day, the Confederate president summoned generals Joseph E. Johnston and P.G.T. Beauregard to confer with him and his advisers about the state's military situation. Davis conducted that two-day meeting in full denial of the obvious. "I think we can whip the enemy yet," he declared, "if our people will turn out."

Johnston refused to feed that fantasy. "Our people" will not turn out, he bluntly told Davis, because they already "feel themselves whipped." His own army, the general added, was even then "melting away like snow before the sun." Every day additional levies deserted, stealing artillery teams to use as mounts. "If I march out of North Carolina," Johnston predicted, all of his soldiers who hailed from that state would instantly abandon him as well. And if he ordered the army still farther south, the South Carolinians and Georgians would abandon him, too.[51] P.G.T. Beauregard seconded Johnston's report. So, moreover, did Robert E. Lee, albeit in absentia. Davis had just received Lee's preliminary report of his army's disintegration and surrender; it noted that during the flight from Richmond "many" of the men "threw away their arms."[52]

Rebuffed by his generals, Jefferson Davis polled his cabinet. Only Judah P. Benjamin endorsed Davis's perspective. Postmaster General John H. Reagan counseled surrender, but surrender with certain conditions. The Confederate government should offer to capitulate *if* all residents of the rebellious states would retain all their political and property rights, and *if* they received immunity for their wartime conduct, and *if* throughout the South the rebel state governments would remain in office following reunion.[53] Here was another try for the kind of deal that John A. Campbell had just sought to wangle from Lincoln. One Davis cabinet member after another endorsed the attempt. Davis remained committed to war, but to appease his advisers and generals, he allowed Johnston to ask Sherman for a cease-fire during which the Union and Confederate governments would formally consult on the terms of peace.[54]

North Carolina governor Zebulon Vance was by now in agreement with Davis's cabinet. After long resisting the idea of seeking a separate peace between North Carolina and the United States, he had now come around to that idea: better to offer to surrender immediately in hopes of softening the terms of reunion than to await outright military defeat and the loss of all remaining bargaining leverage that would bring. To that end, Vance dispatched William A. Graham and David Swain to Sherman's headquarters on April 12, 1865, where they received an encouraging welcome.[55]

Four days later, Sherman and Johnston met about midway between the two armies' lines.[56] Confederate secretary of war John C. Breckinridge joined them the next morning. By the end of that second day, the three men had drafted an agreement that incorporated nearly everything that the Confederate cabinet had hoped to obtain. All residents of the formerly rebellious states would be guaranteed full enjoyment of civil, political, and property rights in the Union. Confederate armies would not surrender to U.S. forces but simply disband on their own initiative. Their soldiers would not hand over their arms to Union troops but would carry them back to their own states' arsenals, to be used thereafter "to maintain peace and order." Who would define the "peace and order" that those arms would "maintain"? The answer to that question could be found in another of the pact's provisions; it stipulated that "the several State governments" of the former Confederacy would continue to rule the southern states after they returned to the Union.[57]

The Union general was offering the mildest peace terms imaginable by this point—an end to the fighting and a return of the Confederate states to the Union with nearly all their political rights and power intact and even with the Confederate-era political leadership still in place at the state level. Preparing copies of this tentative pact for both the Union and Confederate leaderships, Sherman congratulated himself for making possible "peace from the Potomac to the Rio Grande."[58] For good measure, he assured his friend and superior officer, Ulysses S. Grant, that "all the men of substance [of the] south sincerely want peace" and "will in the future be perfectly subordinate to the Laws of the United States."[59]

Sherman later claimed that the agreement he struck with Johnston accorded with Abraham Lincoln's wishes. Unlike Lincoln's Proclamation of Amnesty and Reconstruction of December 1863, however, Sherman's terms required no southern state government to accept the abolition of slavery. In fact, they said nothing about slavery at all. That seemed of little moment to Sherman; he, Johnston, and Breckinridge had informally agreed that slavery had already passed into oblivion; was it really necessary to spell all that out in writing? Sherman privately assured Johnston that if "the South" would simply declare "that slavery is dead," the "Negroes would remain in the South and afford you abundance of cheap labor."[60]

These were, in short, the same terms that John A. Campbell had tried to extract from Lincoln a few days earlier—and that Lincoln had peremptorily dismissed.

While a doubtlessly pleased Johnston returned to his army, Breckinridge brought a copy of the draft agreement to Davis and the cabinet, who were now in Charlotte, North Carolina, traveling by wagon train with a large escort of Confederate cavalrymen. Perusing the document, cabinet members quickly realized what a gift it was. Stephen Mallory could hardly restrain his enthusiasm. Surely these terms were "more favorable . . . than could justly have been anticipated," he pointed out.[61] The pact's total silence on the subject of slavery, John H. Reagan pointed out, was a sheer windfall because it "requires no concession from us in regard to it." The government should quickly accept these terms, Reagan continued, or the individual states would soon be forced to accept others far less agreeable.[62] Even now, Attorney General George Davis added, the people of North Carolina were positively "eager to accept terms far less liberal" than Sherman's.[63] Even Judah Benjamin, who until that point had faithfully seconded his president's defiant stance, now agreed with the others.

But on April 24, 1865, the Union cabinet abruptly shut down the maneuver. It unanimously rejected the Sherman-Johnston pact, ordering Grant to ride to Sherman's headquarters in person and instruct his friend to demand the surrender of Johnston's army immediately on the more stringent terms previously offered to the Army of Northern Virginia. Chastened, Sherman did as he was told.[64]

In response, Jefferson Davis and John C. Breckinridge instructed Joseph E. Johnston to prepare his army to resume fighting. Recognizing the futility of doing so, however, Johnston declined to comply. Instead, he and his army capitulated to Sherman on April 26, 1865.[65] In Alabama one week later, on May 4, Confederate general Richard Taylor surrendered not only his own army of twelve thousand troops then in Alabama but all remaining southern forces east of the Mississippi River, nominally some forty-two thousand in number.

Outraged at Johnston's insubordination, Jefferson Davis pointed his own party farther southward. If no one east of the Mississippi would fight on, he would make his way to Texas and the Trans-Mississippi Department where, with the support of General E. Kirby Smith's army, he would once again prosecute the war.

Smith's army, however, was hardly in a condition to do that. Deserters were already legion in the Trans-Mississippi Department at the start of 1865 and were barely bothering to conceal their intentions. "The state of things now in this Dept.," one soldier marveled in February 1865, "approaches nearer to mutiny than anything I can say." In early April, almost a hundred men in one regiment abruptly defied their officers and began plundering nearby farms. Such things became even more common in the next few days and weeks.[66]

Jefferson Davis's fleeing column was splintering as well. By the time it reached Abbeville, South Carolina, in early May, many of the thousands of cavalrymen in his escort remained with him largely because doing so guaranteed them food. More than a few troopers, according to one witness, had already sold or thrown away their weapons. Others were deserting by the score.[67] "I have the bitterest disappointment in regard to the feeling of our troops," Davis told a secretary, "and would not have any one I love dependent upon their resistance against an equal force."[68]

On May 3, 1865, the Davis party crossed into Georgia. Most of its escort now refused to go any farther. Keenly aware that the cabinet still carried thousands of dollars in gold and silver coin from the Confederate Treasury, the cavalrymen demanded a share of it in back pay. John C. Breckinridge handed the money over, sure (as he later explained to Postmaster Reagan) that otherwise the troopers would take it by force. Over the next two days, all but a few score abandoned the column.[69]

In the early evening of May 9, 1865, Davis and his remaining companions set up a tent camp just north of Irwinville, Georgia, where Davis continued planning to make his way to Texas. But the next day, Michigan and Wisconsin cavalry units discovered and took the president of the Confederate States of America and his party into custody. Within ten days, Davis would find himself charged with treason and imprisoned at Fort Monroe, "Freedom Fort," where he would remain for two years.

The army on which Davis had pinned his last hopes—the troops of E. Kirby Smith's Trans-Mississippi Department—did not remain at large much longer. On May 13, the Confederate governors of Louisiana, Arkansas, Missouri, and Texas resolved to seek terms from the Union reminiscent of those that Joseph E. Johnston had initially managed to wangle out of Sherman, including a provision that "the present State governments in this department, now in arms against the U.S. authority, be recognized" until such time as a final "settling [of] any and all conflicts between the people of the respective States" might occur.[70] But the local Union commander demurred and demanded a simple surrender.[71]

E. Kirby Smith refused and began to prepare for combat. But before he could do much of anything, his army fell to pieces. On May 14,

1865, four hundred soldiers in the Confederate garrison at Galveston attempted an armed desertion en masse. Two days later, a Texas private warned his commander in writing that "if you intend on fighting the Yankey any more you Need Not count me and a thousand more in."[72] The level of desertion and mutiny rose so high that Smith was, by his own account, "compelled to remain 36 hours in Huntsville to escape the mob of disorderly soldiers soldierly thronging the roads." A week later, cursing his soldiers for leaving him "a Commander without an army," Smith belatedly and anticlimactically accepted the reality of Confederate defeat and surrendered what little remained of his command.[73]

"WE SHOULD REJOICE"

The American Civil War was enormously destructive. In four years, it killed more than three-quarters of a million soldiers and wounded hundreds of thousands more. The economic cost was also huge. The war destroyed a third of the South's livestock and halved the value of all its real property. Wherever one looked there were wagons, bridges, railroads and track, ships, factories, shops, warehouses, towns, and cities in ruins.[1]

Why did it occur?

It is often said that the North went to war solely to save the Union and not to abolish slavery. And at one level that is quite true. The war's immediate trigger was secession and the secessionists' attack on Fort Sumter. Only the defense of the republic and its physical integrity could rally the North as a whole to the war effort in 1861.

But it is just as true that a war to save the Union was necessary in 1861 only because a political party that denounced slavery and menaced its future in the Union had won the support of a clear majority of northern voters in 1860. If secession had caused the war, therefore, it was the sharpening conflict over slavery that had caused secession.

No one made that point more succinctly than did Abraham Lincoln in his second inaugural address in March 1865. Four years ago, he reminded his listeners, "one-eighth of the whole population were colored slaves, not distributed generally over the Union, but localized in the southern part of it." The ownership of "these slaves constituted a peculiar and powerful interest," and "all knew that this interest was somehow the cause of the war." The aim of the slave owners and their allies, stated and restated over decades, was "to strengthen, perpetuate, and extend" the system of bound labor. The aim of the young Republican Party and its supporters was "to restrict the territorial enlargement" of that system, something that both slavery's opponents and supporters believed would also eventually kill it within the southern states.[2]

When Lincoln won election to the presidency, slave owners began to pull the United States apart in order to create for themselves a new confederacy in which slavery would be more secure. Loud voices then demanded, in the name of peace and Union, that the Republicans repudiate their antislavery program. The Republican leadership and rank and file refused to comply. Although determined to preserve the Union, they were not willing to do so at any cost. They intended instead (as Lincoln had said a few years earlier and would say again) to save the Union in a way that would leave it "forever worthy of the saving."[3]

Great revolutions rarely happen according to someone's preconceived plan. They commonly occur through the escalation of an initially more limited conflict—when a relatively modest program of reform runs into obstacles too great to overcome without raising the level as well as the stakes of the struggle. In France at the end of the eighteenth century, for example, calls for some changes in policies and practices turned into a republican revolution when the king and aristocracy fought those more modest reforms. In North America a few years earlier, for another example, attempts to modify the way that the British empire treated its colonies confronted imperial authorities unwilling to grant such concessions voluntarily—and too powerful militarily to be forced quickly or easily into capitulating. As a result, petitions for imperial reform gave way to an armed struggle, one that eventually aimed to break the grip of the empire entirely and found a republic without monarchs or aristocrats.

The second American revolution followed a similar trajectory. In the spring of 1861, Abraham Lincoln went to war not to transform southern society but to compel the departed slave states to return to the Union. And he attempted to achieve that goal with only limited, tightly focused military measures while pledging not to interfere with slavery in the seceding states.

But that conservative war policy proved insufficient to the task.

What the former slave Frederick Douglass called "the inexorable logic of events" demonstrated the need to revise that policy fundamentally. By the end of 1862, Lincoln had come to accept that logic. The Union now gave up trying to wage war without angering its enemies; it began instead to target those enemies and strip them of the slave labor that helped make them so formidable. By 1863, the tumult of war and the Union's increasingly revolutionary war policy were enabling black people to escape from their masters' control by the tens of thousands. By 1865, half a million had managed to do so. Even many who remained formally enslaved behind Confederate lines until the war's end had begun to resist (and sometimes openly defy) the commands of owners, supervisors, and foremen.

Most white northerners probably embraced wartime emancipation only because it undermined a foe that had sought to destroy their precious Union. But many others came to see immediate emancipation as an end worthy in its own right. Slaves, free blacks, and abolitionists naturally considered the war necessary and worthy precisely in order to destroy a centuries-old system of bondage that had devoured the lives of many generations of black people. The war was a noble one, in Frederick Douglass's words, for destroying "the gigantic system of American slavery, which had defied the march of time, resisted all the appeals and arguments of the abolitionists, and the humane testimonies of good men of every generation."[4] Had Union armies not begun to dismantle it, Douglass believed, "in all the probabilities of the case, that system of barbarism would have continued its horrors far beyond the limits of the nineteenth century."[5] A Georgian known as Uncle Stephen made much the same point, if in simpler terms. Encountering Stephen on the way to Savannah, William Tecumseh Sherman asked him what he thought about the war. "Well, Sir," Stephen said, "what I think about it, is this—it's mighty distressin' this war, but it 'pears to me like *the right thing couldn't be done without it*."[6]

Over the course of the war, numerous white northerners who had never been abolitionists came to embrace emancipation not only for its practical utility but also as a political and moral necessity. In their ranks stood some War Democrats, including Secretary of War Edwin M. Stanton, and a great many Republicans. Lincoln articulated their opinion when he suggested in his second inaugural address that the war was God's way of punishing the country as a whole for so long indulging in the sin of slavery. If heaven wills, he said, that the fighting and destruction should "continue until all the wealth piled by the bondsman's two hundred and fifty years of unrequited toil shall be sunk, and until every drop of blood drawn with the lash shall be paid by another drawn with the sword," then one could only bow the head and agree with the psalmist that "the judgments of the Lord are true and righteous altogether."[7]

This growing and deepening moral revulsion against slavery invigorated the Republican effort to ratify the Thirteenth Amendment to the U.S. Constitution, abolishing slavery throughout the United States. That effort succeeded in December 1865. That sentiment also strengthened the fight against racial discrimination. During the war and in the next few years, Republicans struggled against some of the laws that imposed second-class status on free black residents of northern states. In 1862, Congress repealed an act passed forty years earlier that forbade black people from carrying the mail. In 1864, Iowa repealed existing laws excluding free blacks from entering that state. Illinois and Ohio repealed kindred laws in 1865. San Francisco, Cleveland, Cincinnati, and New York all desegregated their streetcar systems during the war; Philadelphia did so in 1867. Chicago desegregated its public schools in 1865, as did the state of Rhode Island. Connecticut mandated equal educational rights in 1868. Boston had done that back in 1855; in 1865, the state of Massachusetts outlawed discrimination in a wide range of public accommodations.[8]

Even as the war hammered at the South's central institution, it weakened the social cohesion of the region's dominant race. "History will record," predicted the Mississippi planter and congressman Henry C. Chambers in late 1864, that the Confederacy's white population "rose as one man in defence of their rights, and . . . endured till God crowned their efforts with success."[9] But what history actually records is more complicated than that.

The bonds that held together the white South's diverse elements had proved serviceable enough for most purposes during the preceding decades of peace. By seeking to break up the Union and then engaging in a war against that Union, however, Confederate leaders subjected those bonds to unprecedented stresses and strains.

In some cases, those bonds snapped early. But until the last year of the war or so, Davis, Lee, and their cohorts retained the support of most slaveless white Confederates. Shoring up that support were widespread devotion to slavery as an institution; an even more widespread and deeply ingrained dedication to white supremacy; religious doctrines and clerical exhortations; local, regional, and family ties; outrage at the wounds inflicted by enemy armies; codes of personal pride and honor; and hopes for eventual victory.

But it is also true that as the war lengthened and became bloodier and more destructive, growing numbers of "common whites" found themselves asked—or forced—to sacrifice more and more of their already-limited means and to risk their lives and those of their loved ones. As the demands and dangers increased, some began to ask themselves just how much the survival of slavery and a separate southern republic was worth. Laws that seemed to favor the wealthy, loading a disproportionate share of the war's burdens on non-masters' shoulders, stoked resentment toward "a rich man's war" being waged principally by poorer men and sustained by the privation of their families.

Further inflaming that resentment were masters who repeatedly placed the preservation of their personal property above the needs of a war effort that their own class had organized, led, and made necessary. Even before the fighting began, as a Texan noted in early 1865, there had been a considerable "disposition on the part of the non-slaveholder, to feel a prejudice against the slaveholder." But "since this war commenced, this prejudice has increased." Disloyal elements had "labored to produce the impression among the poor that this is the slaveholders' war," and they had done that "with too much success."[10]

As such disaffection deepened and spread, armed bands of deserters and draft resisters formed in the hill country and elsewhere. Three hundred thousand white men from southern states donned Union uniforms during the war; one in three came from states that adhered to the Confederacy. Less dramatically but just as significantly, a mounting and increasingly desperate popular clamor for peace arose after 1863— a clamor increasingly for peace at almost any price. Battlefield victories by southern armies could quiet that clamor for a time, as could recurring certainties that the North was about to abandon the fight. But disaffection and demoralization reappeared with a vengeance with each new setback and as each bubble of false hope burst.

Confederate civilian and military leaders tried to assuage discontent by relieving some of the burdens on the poorest whites and by reducing or rescinding some of the elite's most objectionable privileges. They could, in theory, have done considerably more. For one thing, they might have offered early in the war to enlist and manumit military-age male slaves. Doing so could have reduced the North's manpower advantage while also reducing the demands upon the Confederate white population. It would also have demonstrated to slaveless whites that members of the southern elite were prepared to make sacrifices for the war's sake that were commensurate with their wealth.

But the Richmond regime steadfastly refused to do that. It refused, first, because the great majority of masters would have no part of such a policy. On the contrary, many of them—including some of the most politically prominent and visible—became ever more reluctant even to lend or rent their slaves temporarily to the army as laborers, let alone give them up entirely and see them freed and armed. Richmond also rejected this option for fear of offending the racial sensitivities of its non-slaveholding majority. Most Confederate soldiers, trained to prize their elevation above blacks, indignantly rejected the idea of serving beside them as equals until the conflict's eleventh hour. Thus did the ideology of white supremacy, which had always provided crucial support for slavery, inhibit the slaveholders' government from doing what it needed to do in order to survive.

A war launched to preserve slavery succeeded instead in abolishing that institution more rapidly and more radically than would have occurred otherwise. No one was more aware of those consequences than the planter families, whose vaunted world of privilege and power had come crashing down around them. "The props that held society up are broken," fretted writer Eliza Frances Andrews, the daughter of one of Georgia's major planters.[11] "Our world has gone to destruction," Mary Chesnut grieved.[12] Those who were "once rich, hospitable, *powerful*," wailed a Mississippi banker and planter, "are now poor, and like 'Samson of old' shorn of their pride and strength."[13] Tomorrow appeared to augur only worse. It seemed to Katherine Edmondston that the "future stands before us dark, forbidding, & stern," full of "all the bitterness of death without the lively hope of Resurrection."[14]

In later years, ex-masters, anxious to deny that the white South had gone to war for the sake of slavery, commonly claimed to have favored emancipation before the war and to have happily embraced it when it came. Robert E. Lee—whose army had made a point of hunting down black people in southern Pennsylvania in 1863 and sending them into slavery back in Virginia—professed after the war to have "always been in favor of emancipation of the negroes" and claimed that now he "rejoiced that slavery is abolished." The same was true, he added, of "the best men of the South" generally. They "have long desired to do away with the institution and were quite willing to see it abolished."[15]

The truth was very different. "This overthrow of the labor system of a whole country," Confederate War Bureau chief R.G.H. Kean declared at the time, was "the greatest social crime ever committed on the earth."[16] Gertrude Clanton Thomas complained bitterly that now everything "is entirely reversed."[17] In her memoirs, Varina Davis angrily denounced Lincoln's presumption, by "a single dash of the pen," to "annihilate four hundred billions of our property, to disrupt the whole social structure of the South, and to pour over the country a flood of evils many times greater than the loss of property."[18] When Katherine Stone published her wartime diary decades later, she claimed never to have regretted slavery's end. But when the Confederacy fell, she recoiled in horror at the prospect of "submission to the Union (how we hate the word!), confiscation, and Negro equality. . . . Truly," Stone exclaimed, "our punishment is greater than we can bear."[19] It was certainly more than the ruined Virginia planter Edmund Ruffin could bear. Contemplating a world with "slaves . . . all lost," the "government overthrown, & the whole property of myself and my family . . . swept away," Ruffin shot himself on June 18, 1865, joining in death the society that in life he had loved above all things.[20]

Having founded the Confederacy boasting of its inherent superiority and invincibility, some now blamed their ruin on the personal failings of one or another individual or group. The Confederate Congress in 1865 accused the soldiers who had left their posts in great numbers.[21] Jefferson Davis faulted "the persistent interference of some of the State Authorities, Legislative, Executive, and Judicial, hindering the action of the Government, obstructing the execution of its laws, denouncing its necessary policy, impairing its hold upon the confidence of the people, and dealing with it rather as if it were the public enemy."[22] Catherine Edmondston indicted the whole political leadership—"our own Congress, our public men, our own President & his imbecile Cabinet. They it is who have beaten us."[23] Yes, agreed Robert Barnwell Rhett, Sr., "the Government of the Confederacy, destroyed the Confederacy."[24] Sallie Putnam laid responsibility at the feet of fair-weather friends who turned on the South in its hour of need—on "a certain class of malcontents, who, when the light of prosperity shone on our arms, were first to hail the Confederacy, but who . . . possessed not moral courage enough to sustain them under the dark clouds and beating winds of adversity."[25]

Masters who had rallied to the Confederacy in 1860–61 against their better tactical judgment now berated those they blamed for pulling them into the maelstrom. "Secession seems not to have produced the results predicted by its sanguine friends," North Carolina senator William A. Graham noted in sarcastic understatement. "There was to be no war, no taxes worth prattling about, but an increase of happiness, boundless prosperity, and entire freedom from all Yankee annoyance." And just "where are we after a 4 years struggle? . . . On the brink of ruin."[26] Henry L. Flash, the editor of Georgia's leading newspaper, ruefully recalled "the amount of nonsense that passed for great truths" at the war's inception, including assurances that "the Yankees wouldn't fight," that cotton was king, and that a slaveholders' government could depend on "the faithfulness of the slaves."[27] The consistent unionist, Natchez planter, and merchant William J. Britton went further a few years later. "I often feel," he said, "that I would like to see some of the political mad caps who have destroyed our once prosperous & happy people Swing at the end of hemp—and I do not think my tears wd flow if our great man Davis was among the number."[28]

But that was a minority view. However they evaluated individual leaders, most southerners mourned the Confederacy's death, sympathized with their former president, and reserved their hottest outrage for the North, the Republican Party, and treacherous freedpeople.

A little vignette that played out in Georgia in May 1865 captured those sentiments. After taking Jefferson Davis into custody, Union troops bearing him northward passed through the city of Augusta. The planters Gertrude and Jefferson Thomas happened to be there at the time. Jefferson sadly doffed his hat in salute when their captured leader's carriage went by. As her husband paid that tribute, Gertrude spied "a crowd of Negroes . . . running and rushing . . . and coming from every direction, all to see the procession." If only, she wished, "a volley of musketry" could be "sent among the Negroes who were holding such a jubilee."[29]

The same sentiments led to Abraham Lincoln's assassination. Soon after Lee's surrender, the Union president addressed a crowd at the White House on the subject of the postwar South. In his remarks, he for the first time voiced publicly a wish previously expressed only in private—that black soldiers and educated black men might be permitted to vote.[30] Lincoln had no intention of imposing this wish; he presented it merely as a suggestion. But that was enough for one Confederate sympathizer standing in the crowd that day. "That means nigger citizenship," spat the Maryland actor John Wilkes Booth. "That is the last speech he will ever make."[31] Three days later, on April 14, 1865, Booth shot the president of the United States as he sat in a theater watching a play. "Sic semper tyrannis," the assassin shouted as he made his escape—"Thus ever to tyrants," the official motto of the state of Virginia. The same night Lewis Powell, a coconspirator, attacked and severely wounded Secretary of State William H. Seward. Seward survived, but Lincoln died the next morning.

Prominent figures in the Confederate pantheon publicly deplored the murder. Some called it morally repulsive. Most feared that such a crime at such a time could only further inflame northern passions against them. No one, Sallie Putnam assured readers of her 1867 memoir, expressed pleasure at Lincoln's death. "In the wonderful charity which buries all quarrels in the grave," she wrote, "Mr. Lincoln, dead, was no longer regarded in the character of an enemy; for with the generosity native to Southern character, all resentment was hidden in his tomb in Springfield. We were satisfied to let the 'dead Past bury its dead.'"[32]

Her words must have surprised many readers in the South, who rejoiced at the death of the man they most identified with the revolutionary destruction of their world. If few had dared to show their satisfaction openly, quite a few did so in private conversations and personal papers. "We hear that Lincoln is dead," Katherine Stone told her diary. She certainly hoped it was true. "All honor to J. Wilkes Booth," the Union president's "brave destroyer." Learning later that Lincoln's assassin had himself been slain, Stone shed a tear for "poor Booth," sure that "many a true heart at the South weeps for his death."[33] "Lincoln the oppressor is dead!" Catherine Edmondston exulted; she regretted only that in deciding to kill him Booth had "delay[ed] it for so long."[34] Edmund Ruffin considered public repudiations of Booth "shameful" and was "sorry" to learn that William H. Seward was recovering from his wounds.[35] To Colonel Louis A. Bringier, scion of a wealthy Louisiana planter family, the news of Lincoln's murder was "cheering," and he named his newborn son after the president's killer.[36]

"Let us leave our land and emigrate to any desert spot of the earth," Louisianan Sarah Morgan wrote in her diary in April 1865, "rather than return to the Union, even as it Was" before war and emancipation.[37] Some ten thousand irreconcilables did leave the United States.[38] John C. Breckinridge fled to Cuba.[39] So did Robert Toombs, who was "much pleased" by what he found on the island. "It is very fertile and boundless in wealth" and blessed "with slave labour." But Toombs worried that England and the United States would soon force the issue of emancipation there, too, and when that happened, he believed, Cuba would be "doomed."[40] According to a northern reporter visiting Cuba, masters in that country believed their bondspeople were "well acquainted with the essential facts in our own great conflict, and the whole slave community is said to be fermenting with ideas engendered by American emancipation."[41]

Thousands of other last-ditch Confederates made their way to Brazil, whose monarch had maintained a stance of formal neutrality during the American Civil War, but one strongly tinged with southern sympathies.[42] Slavery still lived on in Brazil, too, but high slave prices there prevented most of the expatriates from resuming careers as masters.[43]

The largest contingent of Confederate "wild geese" headed for Mexico. Ex-Commodore Matthew Fontaine Maury paved their way by getting himself appointed as Emperor Maximilian's commissioner for colonization in the summer of 1865.[44] Trans-Mississippi commander E. Kirby Smith had begun planning his own departure months earlier, and on May 2, anticipating the Confederacy's collapse, he notified Maximilian that he would seek asylum in Mexico. Facing unemployment and perhaps worse at home, the general suggested that "the services of our troops would be of inestimable value" to the deeply unpopular French-imposed emperor.[45]

When Kirby Smith finally fled southward across the Rio Grande, he did so in the company of some three hundred of his former soldiers plus a gaggle of other ex-generals, ex-colonels, and ex-governors.[46] In their Mexican exile, most ex-Confederates turned to agriculture, often on land that their patron, Maximilian, took from local peasants expressly for that purpose. Even so, however, life in Mexico proved harder than anticipated. Rebuilding a plantation system there would require not only land but also a workforce.[47] But Mexico had outlawed slavery in the 1830s, and Maximilian had not restored it. Confederate exiles who brought slaves with them therefore found themselves without a government prepared to enforce servitude. "All our negroes decided to leave us upon our arrival here," complained former general Thomas C. Hindman, and there seemed no way to stop them.[48] Matthew Fontaine Maury dreamed of instituting some form of forced-labor system in Mexico.[49] But in 1867, insurgent forces led by Benito Juárez, an admirer of Lincoln, put an end to all such fantasies by defeating, capturing, and executing Louis-Napoléon's puppet emperor.

Far fewer Confederates experimented with exile than threatened to do so.[50] And most of those who did go abroad eventually straggled back into the restored Union, where they joined the great mass of former slave owners determined to salvage something from the wreckage of the world they had known and that some had dreamed would last forever.[51] As Katherine Stone sighed after returning from Texas to Brokenburn, "Nothing is left but to endure."[52]

Enduring meant abandoning further hopes for an independent slaveholders' republic. But what else it might mean was less clear. Perhaps, as so many late-war southern peace advocates had hoped, black labor—and black people generally—might yet be kept firmly under whites' control. Mary Greenhow Lee, the daughter of a successful Virginia merchant, landowner, and politician, wrote in her diary in September 1865 that "political reconstruction might be unavoidable now, but social reconstruction we . . . might prevent."[53]

In its crudest form, this goal translated into refusing even the semblance of emancipation. By the spring of 1865, about half a million bound laborers had in one way or another become free of their masters.[54] But the great majority remained formally enslaved. In parts of the South least affected by the war and the immediate postwar occupation, masters kept some slaves in chains well after the Confederacy's collapse. Some slave owners in Texas and remoter parts of Georgia informed their laborers that nothing had changed, and they continued to act on that pretense. An African Methodist Episcopal missionary in Georgia discovered four months after Appomattox that "the people do not know really that they are free, and if they do, their surroundings are such that they would fear to speak of it."[55] A Georgia girl named Charity Austen was twelve years old when the war ended. "Boss tole us Abraham Lincoln wus dead," she recalled many years later, "and we were still slaves. Our boss man bought black cloth and made us wear it for mourning for Abraham Lincoln and tole us that there would not be freedom. We stayed there another year after freedom." At that point "we finally found out we were free and left."[56]

Eventually, as in Austen's case, attempts to preserve slavery sub rosa failed. And the ratification of the Thirteenth Amendment in December 1865 brought legal freedom to Kentucky and Delaware, two loyal slave states not covered by the Emancipation Proclamation and whose legislatures had not yet enacted abolition.

But Mary Greenhow Lee's more general hope—to avoid a radical alteration in southern society—persisted. Even if one human being could no longer legally own another, perhaps the same ends could be accomplished by other means. Maybe a less complete form of servitude could be imposed—some form that, if not as satisfactory to them as old-South slavery, would still prove more profitable for employers than would genuinely free labor. The goal, in other words, was to obtain the same kind of arrangement that masters had tried to secure during the war from Nathaniel Banks and other Union officers in occupied parts of the Confederacy. A number of proslavery peace advocates had hoped to achieve much the same thing in 1863 and afterward, as did several Confederate officials when they sought to trade slavery for black soldiers in 1864–65. Although now confronting forcible reintegration into the Union, Georgia's James Appleton Blackshear anticipated merely replacing slavery with "a system of serfdom."[57] Contemplating the former slaves, a Louisiana planter calculated that "the best we can do is keep 'em as near a state of bondage as possible."[58] One of his colleagues, William J. Minor, looked forward to rejoining the Union with "things as they were, but perhaps under some other name" than slavery.[59] As one Union official reported in September 1865, ex-masters "feel that this kind of slavery will be better than none at all."[60]

In 1865 and 1866, Lincoln's successor, Andrew Johnson, allowed newly elected local and state governments (dominated in many places by former leaders of the Confederacy) to pass laws designed to impose "this kind of slavery"—to herd black people back onto the plantations and to keep them there in a position of semi-servitude. Known as "black codes," the laws denied many personal rights to the freedpeople, including the right to move about freely; to seek new occupations; to select, change, and bargain with employers; and even to enjoy secure custody of their own children.

Congress's Republican majority, African Americans, and the U.S. Army blocked that attempt in a postwar era that became known as "Reconstruction." During it, black people worked to reconstitute families and create schools and religious and secular community institutions, and they instructed and mobilized themselves politically. Congress overturned the black codes and threw out the results of the white-supremacist elections of 1865–66. It would not allow white southerners to enforce a new kind of servile status on the ex-slaves, nor would it tolerate the planters' attempt to retake political control of the South and flex resurgent political muscle in Washington. It would not allow the revolution's conquered enemies to nullify its achievements.

The Republican Party successfully amended the U.S. Constitution in 1868 and 1870 to grant full legal equality and full political rights (including the vote) to yesterday's slaves. Only on that basis, the freedpeople and their allies successfully argued, could they defend their rights and interests. And only extending the vote and the right to hold office to freedpeople could give the Republican Party the kind of electorate that it needed to govern the postwar South. On this basis Republicans proceeded to create radically new kinds of state governments in the South, staffed with southern whites who had come to oppose the Confederacy during the war as well as northerners who had settled in the South in the war's aftermath. Others among the new officeholders were black men, some of whom had been free before the war and others who became free only because of it.

Once again, the dynamic of this revolution—its "inexorable logic"— had revealed and asserted itself. As at every previous stage, accomplishing a relatively limited task demanded taking on a much bigger one. To achieve one goal, it proved necessary to aim for a higher one. Winning the war and suppressing secession required emancipating and arming the slaves. Saving the fruits of that victory had made full citizenship for the freedpeople unavoidable.

But the second American revolution had now reached its apogee. It had gone as far—had become as radical—as circumstances and the human and material resources available to it would allow. And from there it began to slip backward, as Colonel Thomas Wentworth Higginson knew that revolutions sometimes do.[61]

Forces committed to restoring white supremacy launched a ruthless, bloody campaign of terror and intimidation against freedpeople and their white allies in the South. As young southern units of the Republican Party broke under those blows and the Republicans of the North retreated and grew more conservative, Reconstruction collapsed. With it went many of the gains of the second American revolution. A resurgent southern elite once again set about imposing white supremacy and tyrannical labor discipline while stripping freedpeople of many of their civic and political rights. In the 1890s came an even more complete, even more thorough imposition of segregation and subordination—a "Jim Crow" system that would last until well past the middle of the next century. As the great historian W.E.B. Du Bois wrote, "The slave went free; stood a brief moment in the sun; then moved back again toward slavery."[62]

But while forced to retreat from its most advanced positions, the second American revolution was never completely overthrown. This was unmistakable at the national level. The southern elite, which dominated all branches of the federal government throughout most of the prewar era, was now driven into a corner politically and remained there for decades. Half a century would pass before any man born in the South would again sit in the White House or preside over the U.S. Senate. The Supreme Court remained in the hands of non-Southerners, too. Control of the federal government now rested instead in the hands of those who represented the interests of northern-based manufacturing and commerce. Among the early fruits of that profound power shift was a raft of laws designed to encourage industrial development, with protective tariffs, subsidies for railroad construction, a national currency, and national banking and land-grant college systems.

But it was in the South that the Civil War and its aftermath left its deepest enduring imprint. The destruction of slavery—the seizure without compensation of the elite's most valuable property and the emancipation of four million human beings—remained a central, immovable fact of postwar life. On this subject W.E.B. Du Bois chose his words well. Black southerners after Reconstruction were forced to retreat back *toward* slavery, but never back *into* slavery. Millions of black Americans could no longer be bought and sold like furniture or cattle. People such as Jacob Thomas could observe with some peace of mind that "I has got thirteen great-gran' chilluns, an' I knows whar dey ever'one am. In slavery times dey'd have been on de block some time ago."[63]

Black field laborers found themselves saddled with a labor system known as sharecropping that exploited and oppressed them and kept them mired in poverty. But that system never equaled in severity and brutality the work regime of the prewar South. The average living standards of black people rose by half during the fifteen years following the Civil War. And even in the pit of the late nineteenth century, landowners could never compel their laborers to work with the inhuman intensity that slavery had once exacted as a norm.[64]

Just as important, the fruits of emancipation helped advance the cause of greater liberty and equality. The greater freedom of action that slavery's destruction brought enabled black people to forge stronger family ties and build strong organizations, and thereby organize and fight more effectively for equal rights when improved conditions later on made that possible. And for those who experienced or heard or read about what slavery's enemies had achieved during the 1860s, the memory of the second American revolution could provide hope and inspiration in that ongoing struggle.

The war that accomplished all these things was a worthwhile, necessary, and even glorious one. "The world has not seen a nobler and grander war," Frederick Douglass reflected at the time, than the one fought "to put an end to the hell-black cause out of which the Rebellion has risen." Those who waged that war were "writing the statutes of eternal justice and liberty in the blood of the worst of tyrants as a warning to all aftercomers. We should rejoice that there was normal life and health enough in us to stand in our appointed place, and do this great service for mankind."[65]

Acknowledgments

The seed of this book was planted some forty years ago, when I was an undergraduate student at the University of Michigan. Professor William Toll led a wonderful seminar there in African American history, the assigned readings of which included W.E.B. Du Bois's *Black Reconstruction in America* and James M. McPherson's *The Negro's Civil War.* Those two books opened my eyes for the first time to the drama of the wartime struggle against slavery and the slaveholders. During the intervening decades of reading, thinking, and talking about that subject, I have accrued intellectual debts far too big and numerous to be adequately credited in a brief note of acknowledgment or in this book's endnotes (most of which cite sources only for specific quotations or lesser-known facts).

But I would at least like to name and thank some of my most recent creditors.

Eric Foner, Jim Horton, James Oakes, Josh Brown, and Elliott Gorn helped me navigate the choppy waters of fellowship applications. Speaking of which, I express my sincere appreciation to the Illinois Program for Research in the Humanities—and its director and senior associate director, Diane Harris and Christine Catanzarite—for a fellowship that offered both a semester's leave from teaching and the chance to exchange ideas with them and the other fine scholars affiliated with them. And to Tom Bedwell, the irreplaceable business manager of the history department at the University of Illinois, Urbana-Champaign, for arranging the finances that supported that plus another semester of leave. The Newberry Library kindly offered me a National Endowment for the Humanities fellowship to work there; it was my bad luck that other circumstances prevented me from accepting it. Many thanks to history department chairs Antoinette Burton and James Barrett for being considerate of my time when handing out committee assignments during the years when I was teaching full-time.

Sally Heinzel and Martin Smith provided skillful and energetic research assistance. A number of scholars shared their knowledge of specific subjects and the fruits of their own research, including Jonathan Beecher, Victoria Bynum, Lynda Crist, Paul Escott, Gary Gallagher, Mark Grimsley, Daniel Hamilton, James Illingworth, Christopher Morris, Christopher Phillips, Daniel Raymond, Leslie Rowland, William K. Scarborough, J. Mills Thornton, Mark Traugott, and David Williams.

I no longer believe it possible to write a book entirely free of factual or interpretive errors. But my deepest gratitude goes to those who caught at least some of them before this book reached print and who made insightful suggestions about how to write (or rewrite) it. For reading and critiquing the entire manuscript, my effusive thanks to Joshua Brown, John Coski, Gary Gallagher, Joseph Glatthaar, Dan Green, Sally Heinzel, Ruth Hoffman, James M. McPherson, James Oakes, David Roediger, and Scott Ware. O. Vernon Burton, Elliott Gorn, Mark Grimsley, and Erik S. McDuffie kindly read and helpfully responded to sections of the manuscript.

Years ago, friends told me I needed to find a literary agent. Carol Berkin specifically pointed me toward Dan Green of POM, Inc., and Dan has proven simply superb. Thanks, Dan. And thanks to Tim Bartlet at Random House, who offered me the book contract and then showed great consideration and patience as my editor during a difficult first year on the project. When Tim moved on to other pastures, Lindsey Schwoeri took over and has worked very hard to improve the book's clarity and readability. Michelle Daniel did an amazing, meticulous job of copyediting the manuscript as a whole. Nancy Delia, the associate managing editor, couldn't have been more conscientious or cooperative.

A number of longtime friends and companions offered warm encouragement and sustaining friendship. At the top of that list are Josh Brown, Elliott Gorn, and Scott Ware—and especially Ruth Hoffman, who has brightened my life beyond measure. I dedicate this book to her with all my love and the most profound appreciation. I also want to thank Mike and Joey for not allowing me to get so deeply buried in this project that I forgot about them.

Josh Brown—selfless, as always—gave me invaluable help in tracking down, identifying, and obtaining visual images. I'd also like to thank the following individuals and agencies for their assistance in that endeavor: Ed Jackson; Victoria Bynum; Peter H. Wood; William (Bill) H. Brown, Kim Anderson Cumber, and Alan Westmoreland of the State Archives of North Carolina; Judy Bolton of the Louisiana State University Libraries Special Collections; Nicole Joniec of the Library Company of Philadelphia; Eric Seiferth of the Historic New Orleans Collection; and Nicole Contaxis of the New-York Historical Society.

My father died while I was working on this book. My debt to him was the greatest of all. He taught me to read, to write, and to think critically. I've tried to put those skills to worthwhile use. During his last year, he always asked, "How's the book going?" I'm sorry he didn't live to see it completed. I don't know for sure that he would have liked it, but I hope so.

Notes

Introduction

1. *The Life and Writings of Frederick Douglass*, ed. Philip S. Foner (New York, 1950–75), 4:369–70.

2. Mark Twain and Charles Dudley Warner, *The Gilded Age* (1873; reprint, Stillwell, Kans., 2007), 77.

3. *The Memphis Argus*, quoted in Eugene D. Genovese, *Roll, Jordan, Roll: The World the Slaves Made* (New York, 1974), 110.

4. Richard Taylor to Samuel L. M. Barlow, December 13, 1865, in the Samuel Latham Mitchell Barlow Papers, Huntington Library. Barlow was a wealthy New York City attorney influential in the Democratic Party.

5. *The Collected Works of Abraham Lincoln*, ed. Roy P. Basler (New Brunswick, N.J., 1953), 7:51, 23. In subsequent notes, this is abbreviated as *ALCW*.

6. Philip S. Foner and George E. Walker, eds., *Proceedings of the Black State Conventions 1840–1865* (Philadelphia, 1980), 2:302.

7. Elizabeth Hyde Botume, *First Days amongst the Contrabands* (1893; reprint, New York, 1968), 1.

8. Quoted in Allan Nevins, *The War for the Union*, vol. 2, *War Becomes Revolution, 1862–1863* (New York, 1960), 241.

Chapter One. The House of Dixie

1. *Selections from the Letters and Speeches of the Hon. James H. Hammond, of South Carolina* (New York, 1866), 311.

2. The census of 1860 reported that the total population of the slave states was just over 12.2 million. Of those, about 8 million were whites, about a quarter million were free blacks, and more than 3.9 million were slaves.

3. James L. Huston, *Calculating the Value of the Union: Slavery, Property Rights, and the Economic Origins of the Civil War* (Chapel Hill, N.C., 2003), 26–29.

4. James M. McPherson and James K. Hogue, *Ordeal by Fire: The Civil War and Reconstruction*, 4th ed. (New York, 2009), 35; Roger L. Ransom, *Conflict and Compromise: The Political Economy of Slavery, Emancipation, and the American Civil War* (New York, 1989), 67.

5. Lee Soltow, "Economic Inequality in the United States in the Period from 1790 to 1860," *Journal of Economic History* 31 (1971): 838; Soltow, *Men and Wealth in the United States, 1850–1870* (New Haven, Conn., 1975), 157.

6. Lewis Cecil Gray, *History of Agriculture in the United States to 1860* (Gloucester, Mass., 1958), 1:482. In 1860, the South's 8 million white people lived in about 1.5 million family units. About a quarter of those families, or just under 400,000 of them, owned slaves. Stanley Lebergott, "Labor Force and Employment, 1800–1960," in *Output, Employment, and Productivity in the United States after 1800*, ed. Dorothy Brady (New York, 1966), 131; Kenneth M. Stampp, *The Peculiar Institution: Slavery in the Ante-bellum South* (New York, 1966), 30; James Oakes, *The Ruling Race: A History of American Slaveholders* (New York, 1982), 39.

7. Oakes, *Ruling Race*, 39.

8. Ransom, *Conflict and Compromise*, 228.

9. Joseph C. G. Kennedy, *Agriculture of the United States in 1860* (Washington, D.C., 1864), 247; Oakes, *Ruling Race*, 38, 52; Gray, *History of Agriculture*, 1:530; Ransom, *Conflict and Compromise*, 63.

10. Stampp, *Peculiar Institution*, 30; Oakes, *Ruling Race*, 65.

11. Andrew Ward, *The Slaves' War: The Civil War in the Words of Former Slaves* (Boston, 2008), 12.

12. The Edmondstons owned eighty-eight slaves. *"Journal of a Secesh Lady": The Diary of Catherine Ann Devereux Edmondston, 1860–1866*, ed. Beth Gilbert Crabtree and James W. Patton (Raleigh, N.C., 1979), xxxvi, 7n. In subsequent notes, this is abbreviated as *Edmondston Diary*.

13. *The Secret Eye: The Journal of Ella Gertrude Clanton Thomas, 1848–1889* (Chapel Hill, N.C., 1990) 3, 5, 232n, 276. In subsequent notes, this is abbreviated as *Thomas Diary*.

14. Douglas Southall Freeman, *R. E. Lee* (New York, 1934–35), 1:390. See also Emory M. Thomas, *Robert E. Lee: A Biography* (New York, 1995), 173–78, 273.

15. *1860 Census of Agriculture*, 247; Stampp, *Peculiar Institution*, 30–31; Gray, *History of Agriculture*, 1:530.

16. *Brokenburn: The Journal of Kate Stone 1861–1868*, ed. John Q. Anderson (Baton Rouge, 1995), xvii, 6.

17. Janet Sharp Hermann, *The Pursuit of a Dream* (New York, 1981), 6–11; William J. Cooper, *Jefferson Davis, American* (New York, 2000), 82, 243; *The Papers of Jefferson Davis*, ed. Lynda Lasswell Crist, et al. (Baton Rouge, 1971–), 6:666n. In subsequent notes, this is abbreviated as *PJD*.

18. Robert Manson Myers, ed., *The Children of Pride: A True Story of Georgia and the Civil War* (New Haven, Conn., 1972), 17–18.

19. In 1860, Toombs owned 16 slaves in Wilkes County plus 160 slaves on two plantations in Stewart County, for a total of 176. Thanks to Professor William K. Scarborough for this data.

20. William Kauffman Scarborough, *Masters of the Big House: Elite Slaveholders of the Mid-Nineteenth-Century South* (Baton Rouge, 2003), 6, 476.

21. *A Fire-Eater Remembers: The Confederate Memoir of Robert Barnwell Rhett*, ed. William C. Davis (Columbia, S.C., 2000), 140n32; Scarborough, *Masters of the Big House*, 452.

22. Scarborough, *Masters of the Big House*, 3.

23. Ibid., 304.

24. James Bagwell, *Rice Gold: James Hamilton Couper and Plantation Life on the Georgia Coast* (Macon, Ga., 2000), 120.

25. *Thomas Diary*, 184.

26. Ulrich B. Phillips, *Life and Labor in the Old South* (1929; reprint, Boston, 1963), 232–33; Robert A. Lancaster, Jr., "Westover," in *Homes and Gardens in Old Virginia*, ed. Frances Archer Christian and Susanne Massie (Richmond, Va., 1931).

27. Scarborough, *Masters of the Big House*, 153.

28. Stone, *Brokenburn*, 4.

29. Bagwell, *Rice Gold*, 146; *Mary Chesnut's Civil War*, ed. C. Vann Woodward (New Haven, Conn., 1981), xxiv.

30. Scarborough, *Masters of the Big House*, 29–44.

31. *Lee's Aide-de-Camp, Being the Papers of Colonel Charles Marshall, Sometime Aide-de-Camp, Military Secretary, and Assistant Adjutant General of Robert E. Lee, 1862–1865*, ed. Frederick Maurice (1927; reprint, Lincoln, Neb., 2000), 41.

32. Ralph A. Wooster, *Politicians, Planters, and Plain Folk: Courthouse and Statehouse in the Upper South, 1850–1860* (Knoxville, Tenn., 1975), 163–69; Wooster, *The People in Power: Courthouse and Statehouse in the Lower South, 1850–1860* (Knoxville, Tenn., 1969), 125, 128, 133, 138, 143, 148, 153.

33. Steven Hahn, "Class and State in Postemancipation Societies: Southern Planters in Comparative Perspective," *American Historical Review* 95 (1990): 81–83.

34. Charles Colcock Jones, *The Religious Instruction of the Negroes: An Address Delivered before the General Assembly of the Presbyterian Church, At Augusta, Ga., December 10, 1861* (Richmond, Va., n.d.), 7–8.

35. Ibid.

36. *Selections from the Letters and Speeches of the Hon. James H. Hammond of South Carolina* (New York, 1866), 140–41.

37. Stone, *Brokenburn*, 4–5.

38. Ibid.

39. A modern historian not inclined to exaggerate such things notes that it was "the enormous, almost unconstrained degree of force available to masters" that caused the slaves to work as hard as they did. Robert W. Fogel, *Without Consent or Contract: The Rise and Fall of American Slavery* (New York, 1989), 34, 162.

40. Willie Lee Rose, *Rehearsal for Reconstruction: The Port Royal Experiment* (New York, 1964), 126.

41. Frederick Law Olmsted, *A Journey in the Back Country, 1853–1854* (1860; reprint, New York, 1970), 84–87.

42. William Harper, "Memoir on Slavery," in *The Ideology of Slavery: Proslavery Thought in the Antebellum South, 1830–1860*, ed. Drew Gilpin Faust (Baton Rouge, 1981), 100.

43. Daniel R. Hundley, *Social Relations in Our Southern States*, ed. William J. Cooper (1860; reprint, Baton Rouge, 1979), 132.

44. Elizabeth Brown Pryor, *Reading the Man: A Portrait of Robert E. Lee through His Private Letters* (New York, 2007), 260–61.

45. Harper, "Memoir on Slavery," 127.

46. Ibid., 128.

47. Stone, *Brokenburn,* 8; Paul David, et al., *Reckoning with Slavery* (New York, 1976), 356.

48. *Edmondston Diary,* 242.

49. Stampp, *Peculiar Institution,* 202.

50. Richard H. Steckel, "Birth Weights and Infant Mortality among American Slaves," *Explorations in Economic History* (1986): 174; Steckel, "A Dreadful Childhood: The Excess Mortality of American Slaves," *Social Science History* 10 (1986): 449–52.

51. Richard Follett, *The Sugar Masters: Planters and Slaves in Louisiana's Cane World, 1820–1860* (Baton Rouge, 2005), 78.

52. William Dusinberre, *Them Dark Days: Slavery in the American Rice Swamps* (Athens, Ga., 1996), 237–38, 414–16.

53. Stone, *Brokenburn,* 86.

54. Michael Tadman, *Speculators and Slaves: Masters, Traders, and Slaves in the Old South* (Madison, Wis., 1989), 5.

55. Ibid., 45, 71–77.

56. John W. Blassingame, ed., *Slave Testimony: Two Centuries of Letters, Speeches, Interviews, and Autobiographies* (Baton Rouge, 1977), 616.

57. Botume, *First Days amongst the Contrabands,* 163–64.

58. *Thomas Diary,* 216–17.

59. *Letters and Speeches of Hammond,* 137.

60. Drew Gilpin Faust, *James Henry Hammond: A Design for Mastery* (Baton Rouge, 1982), 86–87.

61. *Thomas Diary,* 59.

62. *Mary Chesnut's Civil War,* 29–31.

63. Scarborough, *Masters of the Big House,* 213–16.

64. Robert A. Toombs, *Lecture Delivered in the Tremont Temple, Boston, Massachusetts, on the 26th January, 1856* (Washington, D.C., 1856), 18–19.

65. *The Diary of Edmund Ruffin,* ed. William Kauffman Scarborough (Baton Rouge, 1972–89), 2:477. In subsequent notes, this is abbreviated as *Ruffin Diary.*

66. Toombs, *Lecture Delivered in the Tremont Temple,* 18–19.

67. Edward A. Miller, Jr., "Garland H. White, Black Army Chaplain," *Civil War History* 43 (1997): 201–18; Garland White, Compiled Military Service Record, National Archives (NA), Washington, D.C. These are the sources used to chart Garland White's experiences during the war, along with his letters published in the African Methodist Episcopal Church's *Christian Recorder,* many of which are reprinted in *A Grand Army of Black Men: Letters from African-American Soldiers in the Union Army, 1861–1865,* ed. Edwin S. Redkey (Cambridge, UK, 1992).

68. Ulrich B. Phillips, *American Negro Slavery* (1918; reprint, Baton Rouge, 1966), 401.

69. *Montgomery Mail,* December 3, 1864.

70. Abel P. Upshur, "Domestic Slavery, as It Exists in Our Southern States," *Southern Literary Messenger* 5 (1839): 677.

71. Rev. B. M. Palmer, "Thanksgiving Sermon," *DeBow's Review* 30, no. 2 (February 1861): 327–28.

72. *The Works of John C. Calhoun,* ed. Richard K. Crallé (Charleston, S.C., 1851–70), 2:631.

73. Harper, "Memoir on Slavery," 81.

74. Upshur, "Domestic Slavery," 677, 685.

75. Harper, "Memoir on Slavery," 101.

76. *Letters and Speeches of Hammond,* 318.

77. Ibid., 127.

78. Ibid.

79. *Thomas Diary,* 195; *Edmondston Diary,* 652.

80. Joseph Jones, *Agricultural Resources of Georgia: Address before the Cotton Planters Convention of Georgia at Macon, December 13, 1860* (Augusta, Ga., 1861), 6.

81. Myers, *Children of Pride,* 1244.

82. Robert E. Lee to Andrew Hunter, January 11, 1865, in *The War of the Rebellion: A Compilation of the Official Records of the Union and Confederate Armies* (Washington, D.C., 1880–1901), ser. 4, 3:1012–13. In subsequent notes, this is abbreviated as *OR.*

83. Jefferson Davis, *The Rise and Fall of the Confederate Government* (1881; reprint, New York, 1990), 2:161–62.

84. Harper, "Memoir on Slavery," 130.

85. Breeden, *Advice among Masters*, 58.

86. Maurice D. McInnis, *The Politics of Taste in Antebellum Charleston* (Chapel Hill, N.C., 2005), 29.

87. Stone, *Brokenburn*, 110.

88. Thomas Jefferson, *Notes on the State of Virginia*, ed. William Peden (1787; reprint, New York, 1972), 162–63.

89. *Mary Chesnut's Civil War*, xxxiv–xxxv.

90. McInnis, *Politics of Taste*, 29.

91. Steven M. Stowe, *Intimacy and Power in the Old South: Rituals in the Lives of the Planters* (Baltimore, 1987), 6; Edward L. Ayers, *Vengeance and Justice: Crime and Punishment in the 19th-Century American South* (New York, 1984), 11–21.

92. Thomas Roderick Dew, "Abolition of Slavery," in Faust, *Ideology of Slavery*, 65.

93. Frederick Adolphus Porcher, "Southern and Northern Civilization Contrasted," *Russell's Magazine*, 1 (1857): 100.

94. *Mary Chesnut's Civil War*, 234.

95. *Edmondston Diary*, 653.

96. Harper, "Memoir on Slavery," 128.

97. *Letters and Speeches of Hammond*, 31–32.

98. Ibid., 145.

99. Porcher, "Southern and Northern Civilization Contrasted," 106.

100. Howell Cobb, *A Scriptural Examination of the Institution of Slavery in the United States; with Its Objects and Purposes* ([Perry?] Ga., 1856), 24.

101. In Freeman, *R. E. Lee*, 1:371–73.

102. Ira Berlin, *Slaves without Masters: The Free Negro in the Antebellum South* (New York, 1974), 270–73; Michael P. Johnson and James L. Roark, *Black Masters: A Free Family of Color in the Old South* (New York, 1984), 37.

103. Gavin Wright, *The Political Economy of the Cotton South: Households, Markets, and Wealth in the Nineteenth Century* (New York, 1978), 35.

104. Sally E. Hadden, *Slave Patrols: Law and Violence in Virginia and the Carolinas* (Cambridge, Mass., 2001), 99–104.

105. Martin Crawford, *Ashe County's Civil War: Community and Society in the Appalachian South* (Charlottesville, Va., 2001), 65.

106. *North Carolina Yeoman: The Diary of Basil Armstrong Thomasson, 1853–1862*, ed. Paul D. Escott (Athens, Ga., 1996), 29.

107. Olmsted, *Journey in the Back Country*, 202–3, 239.

108. *PJD*, 6:280–81.

109. Joseph H. Parks, *Joseph E. Brown of Georgia* (Baton Rouge, 1911), 1–11; *Journal of the Senate of the State of Georgia, at the Annual Session of the General Assembly, Begun and Held in Milledgeville, the Seat of Government, in 1861* (Milledgeville, Ga., 1861), 37, 39.

110. John C. Inscoe and Gordon B. McKinney, *The Heart of Confederate Appalachia: Western North Carolina in the Civil War* (Chapel Hill, N.C., 2000), 49–50.

111. J. William Harris, *The Making of the American South: A Short History, 1500–1877* (Malden, Mass., 2006), 137; Inscoe and McKinney, *Heart of Confederate Appalachia*, 49.

112. Siler was a nephew of the state's quondam governor, David L. Swain. Inscoe and McKinney, *Heart of Confederate Appalachia*, 223; John C. Inscoe, *Mountain Masters, Slavery, and the Sectional Crisis in Western North Carolina* (Knoxville, Tenn., 1989), 292n30; *The Papers of Zebulon Baird Vance*, ed. Frontis W. Johnston and Joe A. Mobley (Raleigh, N.C., 1963–), 2:301n38 (in subsequent notes, this is abbreviated as *Vance Papers*); John H. Wheeler, *Historical Sketches of North Carolina: From 1584 to 1851, Compiled from Original Records, Official Documents and Traditional Statements: With Biographical Sketches of Her Distinguished Statesmen, Jurists, Lawyers, Soldiers, Divines, Etc.* (Philadelphia, 1851), 250.

113. *The Papers of Andrew Johnson*, ed. LeRoy P. Graf, et al. (Knoxville, Tenn., 1967–2000), 2:354–55, 477. In subsequent notes, this is abbreviated as *Johnson Papers*.

114. Toombs, *Lecture Delivered in the Tremont Temple*, 16.

115. J.D.B. DeBow, *The Industrial Resources, Statistics, Etc. of the United States*, 3rd. ed. (New York, 1854), 1:151.

Chapter Two. Securing the Mansion: The Slaveholder Revolt and Its Origins

1. J. H. Hammond, Speech on the Admission of Kansas, U.S. Senate, March 4, 1858, in *Letters and Speeches of Hammond*, 320.

2. Frank Moore, ed., *The Rebellion Record: A Diary of American Events, with Documents, Narratives, Illustrative Incidents, Poetry, Etc.* (New York, 1861–68), 1:418.

3. James L. Huston, *Calculating the Value of the Union* (Chapel Hill, N.C., 2003), 45.

4. Frederick Douglass, *The Life and Times of Frederick Douglass*, rev. ed. (1892; reprint, London, 1962), 327.

5. Oliver P. Temple, *East Tennessee and the Civil War* (Johnson City, Tenn., 1899), 120n.

6. Steven A. Channing, *Crisis of Fear: Secession in South Carolina* (New York, 1970), 93.

7. Robin Blackburn, *The Overthrow of Colonial Slavery, 1776–1848* (London, 1988), chap. 9.

8. Channing, *Crisis of Fear*, 266.

9. Robert Pierce Forbes, *The Missouri Compromise and Its Aftermath: Slavery and the Meaning of America* (Chapel Hill, N.C., 2007); Bruce Levine, *Half Slave and Half Free: The Roots of Civil War*, rev. ed. (New York, 2005), 136–38.

10. *The Diary of John Quincy Adams, 1794–1845*, ed. Allan Nevins (New York, 1951), 231–32.

11. *Letters and Speeches of Hammond*, 145.

12. Douglass, *Life and Times*, 292–93.

13. Leonard L. Richards, *Slave Power: The Free North and Southern Domination, 1780–1860* (Baton Rouge, 2000), 153.

14. The leaders of both political parties in Virginia (Democratic and Whig) stood behind that threat for the next decade and a half—right down to the Civil War's actual outbreak. Herman V. Ames, ed., *State Documents on Federal Relations: The States and the United States* (Philadelphia, 1906), 246; Henry T. Shanks, *The Secession Movement in Virginia* (1934; reprint, New York, 1970), 23.

15. James Brewer Stewart, *Holy Warriors: The Abolitionists and American Slavery*, rev. ed. (New York, 1977), 122.

16. Cooper, *Jefferson Davis, American*, 211.

17. *Jefferson Davis, Constitutionalist: His Letters, Papers, and Speeches*, ed. Dunbar F. Rowland (Jackson, Miss., 1923), 1:484–85.

18. Thelma Jennings, *The Nashville Convention: Southern Movement for Unity, 1848–1850* (Memphis, Tenn., 1980), 192–95, 231; Mark Ren-

fred Cheathem, *Old Hickory's Nephew: The Political and Private Struggles of Andrew Jackson Donelson* (Baton Rouge, 2007), 256.

19. These included *Charleston Mercury* publisher Robert Barnwell Rhett, Sr.; Alabama politician and renowned orator William L. Yancey; Virginia jurist and prolific writer Nathaniel Beverley Tucker; and Mississippi governor John A. Quitman. See Richard H. Sewell, *Ballots for Freedom: Antislavery Politics in the United States, 1837–1860* (New York, 1976), 231.

20. Pleasant A. Stovall, *Robert Toombs: Statesman, Speaker, Soldier, Sage* (New York, 1892), 84.

21. Allan Nevins, *Ordeal of the Union* (New York, 1947), 1:366, 374–77.

22. Ibid., 440–46.

23. Horace Greeley and John F. Cleveland, eds., *Political Text-Book for 1860* ([1860]; reprint, New York, 1969), 26–27.

24. *ALCW,* 2:453.

25. Ibid., 3:16, 4:160, 263.

26. Dwight Lowell Dumond, *Southern Editorials on Secession* (1931; reprint, Gloucester, Mass., 1964), 204.

27. *Mary Chesnut's Civil War,* 3–4; *The Private Mary Chesnut: The Unpublished Civil War Diaries,* ed. C. Vann Woodward and Elisabeth Muhlenfeld (New York, 1984), 3–4.

28. Channing, *Crisis of Fear,* 284–85; Charles Edward Cauthen, *South Carolina Goes to War, 1860–1865* (1950; reprint, Columbia, S.C., 2005), 70–71.

29. Joseph Carlyle Sitterson, *The Secession Movement in North Carolina* (Chapel Hill, N.C., 1939), 224.

30. Channing, *Crisis of Fear,* 222.

31. Those who saw things similarly included John Bell and John H. Bills of Tennessee; Jonathan Worth, William A. Graham, Congressman Zebulon B. Vance, and Thomas P. and Catherine Ann Devereux of North Carolina; James Lusk Alcorn, William J. Minor, and Stephen Duncan of Mississippi; and Sam Houston of Texas.

32. North Carolina's Jonathan Worth, for example, was a textile manufacturer. Tennessean John Bell worked many of his slaves in his coal mine and ironworks, selling much of what they produced to northern manufacturers. Mississippi's Stephen Duncan boasted a portfolio that included shares in railroads and banks as well as U.S. bonds. Duncan's

fellow planter William Newton Mercer also owned stock in northern railroads, steamships, and mining companies. Michael Wayne, *The Reshaping of Plantation Society: The Natchez District* (Urbana, Ill., 1990), 36–38.

33. Dumond, *Southern Editorials*, 388.

34. Dumond, *Southern Editorials*, 227, 254.

35. *Mary Chesnut's Civil War*, 241.

36. *The Correspondence of Robert Toombs, Alexander H. Stephens, and Howell Cobb*, ed. Ulrich Bonnell Phillips (Washington, D.C., 1913), 487.

37. *The Papers of William Alexander Graham*, ed. Joseph Grégoire de Roulhac Hamilton (Raleigh, N.C.: 1957–92), 5:219. In subsequent notes, this is abbreviated as *Graham Papers*.

38. Roark, *Masters without Slaves*, 3. Original emphasis.

39. Jonathan Atkins, *Parties, Politics, and Sectional Conflict: Tennessee 1832–1861* (Memphis, Tenn., 1997), 241–42.

40. *Vance Papers*, 1:87.

41. Alexander Stephens, *A Constitutional View of the Late War between the States* (Philadelphia, 1868–70), 2:676–77.

42. Channing, *Crisis of Fear*, 161.

43. Ibid., 257.

44. Toombs, Stephens, and Cobb, *Correspondence*, 520.

45. Ibid., 521.

46. Ibid., 450.

47. Erskine Clarke, *Dwelling Place: A Plantation Epic* (New Haven, Conn., 2005), 397–99.

48. Jones, *Agricultural Resources of Georgia*, 10.

49. Scarborough, *Masters of the Big House*, 282.

50. Cooper, *Jefferson Davis, American*, 317.

51. *PJD*, 6:364–66.

52. Ibid., 6:369; William C. Davis, *Jefferson Davis: The Man and His Hour* (Baton Rouge, 1991), 285.

53. Cooper, *Jefferson Davis, American*, 342–43.

54. *PJD*, 6:377. Against his better judgment, Davis was then persuaded to participate in further compromise negotiations, which collapsed by the end of the month. Cooper, *Jefferson Davis, American*, 342–43.

55. Richard E. Beringer, "A Profile of the Members of the Confederate Congress," *Journal of Southern History* 32 (1967): 518–41.

56. *Jefferson Davis, Constitutionalist*, 5:47–48; Cooper, *Jefferson Davis, American*, 352–53.

57. *Jefferson Davis, Constitutionalist*, 5:48.

58. *PJD*, 7:47–49. He returned to the theme in a major address the following February. "To save ourselves from a revolution," he and his supporters had left the Union "to make a new association, composed of States homogeneous in interest, in policy, and in feeling." *Jefferson Davis, Constitutionalist*, 5:200.

59. Charles B. Dew, *Apostles of Disunion: Southern Secession Commissioners and the Causes of the Civil War* (Baton Rouge, 2001), 15.

60. *Official Records of the Union and Confederate Navies in the War of the Rebellion* (Washington, D.C., 1894–1922), ser. 2, 3:257. In subsequent notes, this is abbreviated as *OR/Navies*.

61. *OR*, ser. 2, 2:1208.

62. Emory M. Thomas, *The Confederate Nation: 1861–1865* (New York, 1979), 313.

63. Andrew Torget, "Unions of Slavery: Slavery, Politics, and Secession in the Valley of Virginia," in *Crucible of the Civil War: Virginia from Secession to Commemoration*, ed. Edward L. Ayers, Gary W. Gallagher, and Andrew J. Torget (Charlottesville, Va., 2006), 9–34.

64. Sitterson, *Secession Movement in North Carolina*, 222–23; Atkins, *Parties, Politics, and Sectional Conflict*, 241.

65. Dumond, *Southern Editorials*, 254.

66. Ibid., 286. See also Atkins, *Parties, Politics, and Sectional Conflict*, 231–32.

67. Inscoe and McKinney, *Heart of Confederate Appalachia*, 44.

68. The Civil War aborted the ratification process, and Corwin's proposed amendment became a dead letter.

69. *ALCW*, 4:150, 172.

70. James M. Woods, *Rebellion and Realignment: Arkansas's Road to Secession* (Fayetteville, Ark., 1987), 139, 143–44; *Journal of Both Sessions of the Convention of the State of Arkansas* (Little Rock, Ark., 1861), 51–54.

71. Orville J. Victor, *The Comprehensive History of the Southern Rebellion and the War for the Union* (New York, 1862), 1:250; Atkins, *Parties, Politics, and Sectional Conflict*, 238.

72. Shanks, *Secession Movement in Virginia*, 252n; *OR*, ser. 4, 1:77.

73. Shanks, *Secession Movement in Virginia*, 263n3; George H. Reese, ed., *Proceedings of the Virginia State Convention of 1861, February 13–May 1* (Richmond, Va., 1965), 2:35–37.

74. *Proceedings of the Virginia State Convention*, 1:228.

75. Ibid., 3:63, 72–76.

76. Douglass, *Life and Writings*, 3:127.

77. Kenneth M. Stampp, "Comment on 'Why the Republicans Rejected Both Compromise and Secession,'" in *The Crisis of the Union, 1860–61*, ed. George Harmon Knoles (Baton Rouge, 1965), 107–113.

78. Myers, *Children of Pride*, 666–67.

79. *Proceedings of the Virginia State Convention*, 3:61–62.

80. The letter is appended to Frederic Bancroft, *The Life of William H. Seward*, 2 vols. (New York, 1900), 2:546–47.

81. Channing, *Crisis of Fear*, 263–64.

82. Ruffin, Roger Pryor, and others called on South Carolina and the lower-South Confederacy to do just this. See Shanks, *Secession Movement in Virginia*, 266n5, 198; *OR*, ser. 1, 1:264.

83. *Letters and Speeches of Hammond*, 313.

84. [George Fitzhugh], "The Message, the Constitution, and the Times," *DeBow's Review* 30 (February 1861): 162, 164.

85. *Edmondston Diary*, 72.

86. Andrew Ward, *The Slaves' War: The Civil War in the Words of Former Slaves* (Boston, 2008), 4.

87. Bell Irvin Wiley, *The Plain People of the Confederacy* (Columbia, S.C., 2000), 56–57.

88. Jon L. Wakelyn, ed., *Southern Pamphlets on Secession, November 1860–April 1861* (Chapel Hill, N.C., 1996), 276.

89. John H. Reagan, *Memoirs: With Special Reference to Secession and the Civil War*, ed. Walter Flavius McCaleb (New York, 1906), 117.

90. [Fitzhugh], "The Message, the Constitution, and the Times," 166.

91. Sitterson, *Secession Movement in North Carolina*, 218.

92. Nevins, *War for the Union*, 1:95–96.

93. Stone, *Brokenburn*, 13.

94. Varina Davis, *Jefferson Davis: A Memoir by His Wife* (1890; reprint, Baltimore, 1990), 2:5, 8.

95. Stone, *Brokenburn*, 79.

96. Roark, *Masters without Slaves*, 27.

97. *Edmondston Diary*, 30.

98. Beringer, "Profile of Members of the Confederate Congress" (November 1967): 528, 535.

99. Scarborough, *Masters of the Big House*, 317–19.

100. Ibid., 330–33.

101. Drew Gilpin Faust, *Mothers of Invention: Women in the Slaveholding South in the American Civil War* (New York, 1996), 24–26.

102. Drew Gilpin Faust, "Confederate Women and Narratives of War," in *Divided Houses: Gender and the Civil War*, ed. Catherine Clinton and Nina Silber (New York, 1992), 182.

103. Bell Irvin Wiley, *Southern Negroes, 1861–1865* (1938; reprint, Baton Rouge, 1965), 130–33; James H. Brewer, *The Confederate Negro: Virginia's Craftsmen and Military Laborers, 1861–1865* (Durham, N.C., 1969).

104. Joseph T. Glatthaar, *General Lee's Army: From Victory to Collapse* (New York, 2008), 17–21.

105. *OR*, ser. 4, 1:318.

106. W. Todd Groce, *Mountain Rebels: East Tennessee Confederates and the Civil War, 1860–1870* (Knoxville, Tenn., 1999), 68–76; Inscoe and McKinney, *Heart of Confederate Appalachia*, 73–74.

107. [J.D.B. DeBow], "The Non-Slaveholders of the South," *DeBow's Review* 30 (1861): 69.

108. W. S. Oldham, "True Cause and Issues of the Civil War," *DeBow's Review* 6 (1869): 678–79.

109. *OR*, ser. 4, 1:318.

110. Cauthen, *South Carolina Goes to War*, 72.

111. James M. McPherson, *For Causes and Comrades: Why Men Fought in the Civil War* (New York, 1997), 33.

112. Shelby Foote, *Civil War, a Narrative* (1958; reprint, New York, 1986), 1:65.

113. J. D. Stapp to Dear Mother, March 6, 1864, Jos. D. Stapp Letters, 1864–1865, Virginia Historical Society (VHS).

114. Sitterson, *Secession Movement in North Carolina*, 221.

115. Donald E. Reynolds, *Editors Make War: Southern Newspapers in the Se-*

cession Crisis (1970; reprint, Carbondale, Ill., 2006), 125–26; Channing, *Crisis of Fear,* 287.

116. David W. Siler to Governor Vance, November 3, 1862, Adjutant and Inspector General's Office, Letters Received, entry 12, N-525 (1862), *War Department Collection of Confederate Records,* Record Group (RG) 109, NA.

117. John Cimprich, *Slavery's End in Tennessee, 1861–1865* (University, Ala., 1985), 13–14.

118. Clarke, *Dwelling Place,* 305, 309.

119. *Edmondston Diary,* 23.

120. Ibid., 115.

121. Stone, *Brokenburn,* 18; *Thomas Diary,* 190.

122. Davis, *Jefferson Davis: A Memoir by His Wife,* 2:18–19.

123. Bell Irvin Wiley, *The Life of Johnny Reb: The Common Soldier of the Confederacy* (1943; reprint, Baton Rouge, 1978), 327–28.

124. James Dinkins, *1861 to 1865, by an Old Johnnie: Personal Recollections and Experiences in the Confederate Army* (Cincinnati, 1897), 62–63.

125. [Fitzhugh], "Message, the Constitution, and the Times," 162.

126. Edward McPherson, ed., *The Political History of the United States of America during the Great Rebellion* (Washington, D.C., 1865), 281.

127. Ash, *Middle Tennessee Society Transformed,* 81.

128. Johnson and Roark, *Black Masters,* 293.

129. McPherson, *Political History,* 281.

130. *OR,* ser. 1, 15:556–57; James G. Hollandsworth, Jr., *The Louisiana Native Guards: The Black Military Experience during the Civil War* (Baton Rouge, 1995), 2–9.

131. *OR,* ser. 4, 1:1020.

132. Arthur W. Bergeron, *Confederate Mobile* (Baton Rouge, 1991), 105.

133. Wiley Sword, *Southern Invincibility: A History of the Confederate Heart* (New York, 2000), 29.

134. Stone, *Brokenburn,* 14.

135. Anne Sarah Rubin, *A Shattered Nation: The Rise and Fall of the Confederacy, 1861–1868* (Chapel Hill, N.C., 2005), 40.

136. Clarke, *Dwelling Place,* 409.

137. *Edmondston Diary,* 56.

138. C. C. Coffin, "Late Scenes in Richmond," *Atlantic Monthly* (1865): 745; Nevins, *War for the Union*, 1:93.

139. *New York Evening Post*, April 23, 1861.

Chapter Three. Early Portents: The First Phases of War

1. Archer Jones, *Civil War Command and Strategy: The Process of Victory and Defeat* (New York, 1992), chap. 3.

2. *PJD*, 7:260–62.

3. Stephen W. Sears, *To the Gates of Richmond: The Peninsula Campaign* (Boston, 1992), 338, 342–43.

4. *The Journals of Josiah Gorgas, 1857–1858*, ed. Sarah Woolfolk Williams (Tuscaloosa, Ala., 1995), 52. In subsequent notes, this appears as *Gorgas Journals*.

5. *OR*, ser. 1, 16:753.

6. James H. McPherson, *Crossroads of Freedom: Antietam* (New York, 2002), 91.

7. Ibid., 89.

8. Stone, *Brokenburn*, 142.

9. Toombs, Stephens, and Cobb, *Correspondence*, 561.

10. *The New York Times*, April 15, 1861.

11. Russell McClintock, *Lincoln and the Decision for War: The Northern Response to Secession* (Chapel Hill, N.C., 2008), 256–73.

12. Phillip Shaw Paludan, *"A People's Contest": The Union and the Civil War, 1861–1865* (New York, 1988), 18.

13. Kenneth M. Stampp, *And the War Came: The North and the Secession Crisis, 1860–61* (1950; reprint, Baton Rouge, 1970).

14. Chandra Manning, *What This Cruel War Was Over: Soldiers, Slavery, and the Civil War* (New York, 2007), 44.

15. Bell Irvin Wiley, *The Life of Billy Yank: The Common Soldier of the Union* (1952; reprint, Baton Rouge, 1981), 41.

16. Kenneth M. Stampp, ed. *The Causes of the Civil War*, rev. ed. (New York, 1992), 193.

17. *ALCW*, 4:426.

18. Manning, *What This Cruel War Was Over*, 40.

19. James M. McPherson, *What They Fought For* (New York, 1995), 33.

20. *The New York Times,* September 16, 1861.

21. Friedrich Kapp, *Geschichte der Sklaverei in den Vereinigten Staaten von Amerika* (Hamburg, 1861), xi–xii.

22. Walter D. Kamphoefner, Wolfgang Helbich, and Ulrike Sommer, eds., *News from the Land of Freedom: German Immigrants Write Home* (Ithaca, N.Y., 1991), 402.

23. Wiley, *Life of Billy Yank,* 39.

24. Reagan, *Memoirs,* 116–17.

25. Wiley, *Life of Johnny Reb,* 313.

26. *Congressional Globe,* 37th Cong., 1st sess., July 26, 1861, 258–65.

27. See, for example, the March 26, 1861, speech of Kentucky's senator John J. Crittenden before his state's legislature in (Mrs.) Chapman Coleman, ed., *The Life of John J. Crittenden: With Selections from His Correspondence and Speeches* (Philadelphia, 1871), 2:299–316.

28. Eugene Morrow Violette, *A History of Missouri* (Boston, 1918), 369.

29. James L. Abrahamson, *The Men of Secession and Civil War, 1859–1861* (Wilmington, Del., 2000), 160.

30. Stone, *Brokenburn,* 90.

31. Davis to Braxton Bragg, October 17, 1862, in *PJD,* 8:48.

32. *Edmondston Diary,* 72.

33. Ibid., 286.

34. Robert E. Lee, *The Wartime Papers of R. E. Lee,* ed. Clifford Dowdey (Boston, 1961), 298.

35. Stone, *Brokenburn,* 146.

36. James M. McPherson, *Battle Cry of Freedom: The Civil War Era* (New York, 2008), 284, 293.

37. Craig L. Symonds, *Lincoln and His Admirals: Abraham Lincoln, the U.S. Navy, and the Civil War* (New York, 2008), 117–20; Toombs, Stephens, and Cobb, *Correspondence,* 588.

38. William Freehling, *The South vs. the South: How Anti-Confederate Southerners Shaped the Course of the Civil War* (New York, 2001), 79–80.

39. Ira Berlin, et al., *The Destruction of Slavery* (Cambridge, UK, 1986), 259; *OR,* ser. 1, 13:524–25; Carl H. Moneyhon, *The Impact of the Civil War and Reconstruction on Arkansas: Persistence in the Midst of Ruin* (Baton Rouge, 1994), 138.

40. James M. McPherson, *Tried by War: Abraham Lincoln as Commander in Chief* (New York, 2008), 70–71, 268–69.

41. George W. Cable, "New Orleans before the Capture," in *Battles and Leaders of the Civil War*, ed. Robert Johnson and Clarence Buel (1887–1888; reprint, Edison, N.J., n.d.), 2:15.

42. See Chester G. Hearn, *The Capture of New Orleans, 1862* (Baton Rouge, 1995).

43. David D. Porter, "The Opening of the Lower Mississippi," in *Battles and Leaders of the Civil War*, 2:47.

44. *OR*, ser. 1, 6:531–32.

45. Stone, *Brokenburn*, 100.

46. *OR*, ser. 4, 1:1101–2.

47. *Edmondston Diary*, 164.

48. T. Conn Bryan, ed., *Confederate Georgia* (Athens, Ga., 1953), 139.

49. Paul D. Escott, *After Secession: Jefferson Davis and the Failure of Confederate Nationalism* (Baton Rouge, 1978), 95.

50. Hugh C. Bailey, "Disloyalty in Early Confederate Alabama," *Journal of Southern History* 23 (1957): 525. See also Bailey, "Disaffection in the Alabama Hill Country, 1861," *Civil War History* 4 (1958): 183–94.

51. *OR*, ser. 4, 1:318.

52. Laurence Shore, *Southern Capitalists: The Ideological Leadership of an Elite, 1832–1885* (Chapel Hill, N.C., 1986), 78.

53. *The Papers of Thomas Ruffin*, ed. Joseph Grégoire de Roulhac Hamilton (Raleigh, N.C., 1920), 3:109.

54. Thomas Goode Tucker to Ellis, May 7, 1961, in John Willis Ellis, *Papers*, ed. Noble J. Tolbert (Raleigh, N.C., 1964), 2:728; George Brown Goode, *Virginia Cousins: A Study of the Ancestry and Posterity of John Goode of Whitby* (Richmond, Va., 1887), 125.

55. Escott, *North Carolina Yeoman*, 351.

56. Ellis, *Papers*, 2:766. Emphasis added.

57. Inscoe and McKinney, *Heart of Confederate Appalachia*, 76.

58. Sitterson, *Secession Movement in North Carolina*, 5, 11–12.

59. On slaveholding, see the map in Sitterson, *Secession Movement in North Carolina*, 2.

60. Ellis, *Papers*, 2:867–68.

61. William Thomas Auman, "Neighbor against Neighbor: The Inner

Civil War in the Central Counties of Confederate North Carolina" (PhD diss., University of North Carolina at Chapel Hill, 1988), 90.

62. *Vance Papers*, 1:374–75. Coltrane was from Randolph County.

63. Nevins, *War for the Union*, 1:139.

64. Those counties opposed secession by more than three to one. Richard Orr Curry, *A House Divided: A Study of Statehood Politics and the Copperhead Movement in West Virginia* (Pittsburgh, 1964), 143; Crofts, *Reluctant Confederates*, 341.

65. *OR*, ser. 1, 2:630.

66. Ibid.

67. Ibid., 2:827.

68. Ibid., 2:239.

69. Ibid., 2:291.

70. Ibid., 2:112–13.

71. Ibid., 2:630.

72. Ibid., 2:827, 855, 239, 863.

73. Ibid., 2:1012. Emphasis added.

74. Ibid., 2:158.

75. Richard Nelson Current, *Lincoln's Loyalists: Union Soldiers from the Confederacy* (Boston, 1992), 6–8.

76. *OR*, ser. 1, 2:1012.

77. Herman Hattaway and Archer Jones, *How the North Won: A Military History of the Civil War* (Urbana, Ill., 1991), 36–39.

78. *OR*, ser. 1, 2:70–71.

79. Groce, *Mountain Rebels*, 27–34, 54; Temple, *East Tennessee and the Civil War*, 195.

80. Temple, *East Tennessee and the Civil War*, 548.

81. Noel C. Fisher, *War at Every Door: Partisan Politics and Guerrilla Violence in East Tennessee, 1860–1869* (Chapel Hill, N.C., 1997), 32.

82. Ibid., 35; Atkins, *Parties, Politics, and Sectional Conflict*, 240–41, 247–49.

83. Fisher, *War at Every Door*, 39.

84. Ibid., 42.

85. Ibid., 50–51.

86. Temple, *East Tennessee and the Civil War*, 381–87.

87. *OR*, ser. 1, 4:239. Quotes on 237, 239.

88. Fisher, *War at Every Door*, 53, 56–57.

89. Ibid., 58; Temple, *East Tennessee and the Civil War*, 408.

90. Fisher, *War at Every Door*, 71.

91. Groce, *Mountain Rebels*, 88, 95.

92. *OR*, ser. 1, 4:239.

93. Temple, *East Tennessee and the Civil War*, 203; Fisher, *War at Every Door*, 92–93.

94. Wiley, *Southern Negroes*, 45; Wilfred Buck Years, *The Confederate Congress* (Athens, Ga., 1960), 131.

95. Judah P. Benjamin, until then attorney general, replaced Toombs as secretary of state.

96. William Y. Thompson, *Robert Toombs of Georgia* (Baton Rouge, 1966), 185–87.

97. Stone, *Brokenburn*, 100–101.

98. *OR*, ser. 1, vol. 10, pt. 2, 451.

99. Harold D. Woodman, *King Cotton and His Retainers: Financing and Marketing the Cotton Crop of the South* (Lexington, Ky., 1968), 219–22.

100. Jefferson Davis subsequently lodged a claim with the Confederate Treasury for the loss of those cotton bales. James Garfield Randall, *The Confiscation of Property during the Civil War* (Indianapolis, 1913), 41n; Christopher Morris, *Becoming Southern: The Evolution of a Way of Life, Warren County and Vicksburg, Mississippi, 1770–1860* (New York, 1995), 184; James Allen plantation book, typescript, entries from May 6 through June 21, 1862, 77–82, Mississippi Department of Archives and History. Thanks to Professor Morris for generously sending me copies of these plantation records kept by Allen, who was a neighbor of Joseph Davis.

101. Woodman, *King Cotton and His Retainers*, 223.

102. John K. Bettersworth, ed., *Mississippi in the Confederacy as They Saw It* (1961; reprint, New York, 1970), 227–28.

103. Berlin, *Destruction of Slavery*, 667, 688.

104. *OR*, ser. 1, vol. 51, pt. 2, 456.

105. Berlin, *Destruction of Slavery*, 691.

106. Harrison A. Trexler, "The Opposition of Planters to the Employment of Slaves as Laborers by the Confederacy," *Mississippi Valley Historical Review* 27 (1940): 211–12.

107. William Preston Johnston, *The Life of Albert Sidney Johnston* (New York, 1878), 410, 416; Berlin, *Destruction of Slavery*, 696.

108. Johnston, *Life of Albert Sidney Johnston*, 552–53.

109. Thompson, *Robert Toombs of Georgia*, 185–87.

110. Toombs, Stephens, and Cobb, *Correspondence*, 591.

111. Faust, *James Henry Hammond*, 369.

112. *Edmondston Diary*, 233.

113. Ibid., 351.

114. McPherson, *Political History*, 282.

115. Stone, *Brokenburn*, 95.

116. Hattaway and Jones, *How the North Won*, 114.; E. B. Long, with Barbara Long, *The Civil War Day by Day: An Almanac, 1861–1865* (Garden City, N.Y., 1971), 706.

117. Scarborough, *Masters of the Big House*, 352.

118. Thomas E. Schott, *Alexander H. Stephens of Georgia: A Biography* (Baton Rouge, 1988), 354–55.

119. Allen D. Candler, ed., *The Confederate Records of the State of Georgia*, vol. 3, *Official Correspondence of Governor Joseph E. Brown, 1860–1865* (Atlanta, 1910), 301; Toombs, Stephens, and Cobb, *Correspondence*, 598.

120. Joseph H. Parks, *Joseph E. Brown of Georgia* (Baton Rouge, 1977), 213.

121. Albert Burton Moore, *Conscription and Conflict in the Confederacy* (1924; reprint, Columbia, S.C., 1996), 27.

122. *OR*, ser. 4, 2:162, 553, 3:179. William Blair found that in Virginia the law of February 1864 was implemented in a way that extended exemptions to many masters who owned considerably fewer than fifteen slaves, while "in the Deep South, large slave-holders benefited the most from this same law." Blair, *Virginia's Private War: Feeding Body and Soul in the Confederacy, 1861–1865* (Oxford, UK, 1998), 105.

123. *OR*, ser. 1, vol. 19, pt. 2, 790.

125. Stephen V. Ash, *When the Yankees Came: Conflict and Chaos in the Occupied South, 1861–1865* (Chapel Hill, N.C., 1995), 178.

125. Ira Berlin, Joseph P. Reidy, and Leslie Rowland, eds., *The Black Military Experience* (Cambridge, UK, 1982), 290.

126. Marshall, *Lee's Aide-de-Camp*, 42.

127. W. Buck Yearns and John G. Barrett, eds., *North Carolina Civil War Documentary* (Chapel Hill, N.C., 1980), 98.

128. Clement Dowd, *Life of Zebulon B. Vance* (Charlotte, N.C., 1897), 447.

129. *OR,* ser. 1, 21:776.

130. See William W. Freehling, *The Reintegration of American History: Slavery and the Civil War* (New York, 1994), 5; Freehling, *South vs. the South,* xii–xiii; Christopher Leslie Brown and Philip D. Morgan, eds., *Arming Slaves: From Classical Time to the Modern Age* (New Haven, Conn., 2006).

131. Benjamin Quarles, *The Negro in the American Revolution* (1961; reprint, New York, 1973); Woody Holton, *Forced Founders: Indians, Debtors, Slaves, and the Making of the American Revolution in Virginia* (Chapel Hill, N.C., 1999), 133–63.

132. *Mary Chesnut's Civil War,* 256.

133. Tasker Gantt to Henry Hunt, May 19, 1886, Hunt Jackson Papers, Library of Congress (LC); Jefferson Davis to Campbell Brown, June 14, 1886, George Washington Campbell Brown Papers, LC.

134. James A. Seddon to Hon. E. S. Dargan, December 18, 1863, RG 109, NA.

135. Judah P. Benjamin to Benjamin H. Micou, August 18, 1863, Letterbook, Confederate States of America records, LC.

136. William R. Blair, et al., to Major P. H. Nelson, n.d., and accompanying notations, copy in Eleanor S. Brockenbrough Library, the Museum of the Confederacy, Richmond, Va. See also Arthur W. Bergeron, Jr., "Free Men of Color in Grey," *Civil War History* 32 (1996): 250–53.

137. *Thomas Diary,* 190, 166.

138. Charles Colcock Jones, *Religious Instruction of the Negroes: An Address . . . December 10, 1861,* 5.

139. Myers, *Children of Pride,* 805.

140. Davis, *Jefferson Davis: A Memoir by His Wife,* 2:11.

141. Ash, *When the Yankees Came,* 11, 15, 22.

142. Wiley, *Southern Negroes,* 11, 33–35; J. M. Beasley, et al., to Secretary of War, August 18, 1862, WD-1113–1862, RG 109, NA.

143. William Howard Russell, *My Diary North and South,* ed. Eugene H. Berwanger (New York, 1988), 98.

144. *OR,* ser. 4, 1:998–1000.

145. Marshall served as Lee's military secretary from March 1862 to the war's end. He argued in his memoirs that concerns about maintaining control over slaves "contributed as much as any single cause to the unfortunate dispersion of the Confederate troops during the first year of the war," a dispersion that "permanently impaired" the Confederate war effort. Marshall, *Lee's Aide-de-Camp,* 63–65.

146. Bryan, *Confederate Georgia,* 82–83.

147. Ibid., 83–84.

148. Charles Colcock Jones, *The Religious Instruction of the Negroes in the United States* (1842; reprint, Manchester, N.H., 1971), 110.

149. *Mary Chesnut's Civil War,* 48.

150. W.E.B. Du Bois, *Black Reconstruction in America: An Essay Toward a History of the Part Which Black Folk Played in the Attempt to Reconstruct Democracy in America, 1860–1880* (1935; reprint, Cleveland, 1968), 30.

151. Frederick Douglass pointed to this fact in addressing black men later in the war: "You have to some extent rated your value by the estimate of your enemies and hence have counted yourself less than you are." Douglass, *Life and Writings,* 3:342–43.

152. Norman R. Yetman, ed., *When I Was a Slave: Memoirs from the Slave Narrative Collection* (New York, 2002), 70.

153. Dinkins, *1861 to 1865,* 62–63.

154. Robert F. Durden, *The Gray and the Black: The Confederate Debate on Emancipation* (Baton Rouge, 2000), 32.

155. Glatthaar, *General Lee's Army,* 313.

156. Andrea Sutcliffe, ed., *Mighty Rough Times, I Tell You: Personal Accounts of Slavery in Tennessee* (Winston-Salem, 2000), 30.

157. Douglass, *Life and Times,* 39.

158. Steven Hahn, *A Nation under Our Feet: Black Political Struggles in the Rural South from Slavery to the Great Migration* (Cambridge, Mass., 2003), 65.

159. Merton L. Dillon, *Slavery Attacked: Southern Slaves and Their Allies, 1619–1865* (Baton Rouge, 1990), 240.

160. Morris, *Becoming Southern,* 174–75.

161. *A Voice of Thunder: The Civil War Letters of George E. Stephens,* ed. Donald Yacavone (Urbana, Ill., 1997), 15, 151.

162. Susie King Taylor, *Reminiscences of My Life: A Black Woman's Civil War Memoirs* (New York, 1998), 32.

163. Charlotte Forten, "Life on the Sea Islands," *Atlantic Monthly* 13 (1864): 593.

164. *Mary Chesnut's Civil War*, 234.

165. *OR*, ser. 2, 1:750; Leon F. Litwack, *Been in the Storm So Long: The Aftermath of Slavery* (New York, 1979), 54.

166. Andrew Ward, *Dark Midnight When I Rise: The Story of the Jubilee Singers Who Introduced the World to the Music of Black America* (New York, 2000), 24.

167. Winthrop Jordan, *Tumult and Silence at Second Creek: An Inquiry into a Civil War Slave Conspiracy* (Baton Rouge, 1993), 14–15.

168. John J. Cheatham to L. P. Walker, May 4, 1861, War Department, Letters Received (WD/LR) C-605-1861, Record Group (RG) 109, NA.

169. Stone, *Brokenburn*, 37.

170. Ibid., 39, 53.

171. *Edmondston Diary*, 173.

172. Jordan, *Tumult and Silence*, 18, 315.

173. Albert J. Raboteau, *Slave Religion: The "Invisible Institution" in the Antebellum South* (New York, 1978), 248; Susan King Taylor, *Reminiscences of My Life: A Black Woman's Civil War Memoirs* (New York, 1998), 32; Thomas Wentworth Higginson, *Army Life in a Black Regiment* (1869; reprint, Boston, 1970), 34.

174. *Harper's Weekly*, October 18, 1862, 658.

175. Cimprich, *Slavery's End in Tennessee*, 20.

176. Ira Berlin, et al., eds., *The Wartime Genesis of Free Labor: The Lower South* (Cambridge, UK, 1986), 723.

177. Wiley, *Southern Negroes*, 19.

178. Johnson and Roark, *Black Masters*, 293; Bergeron, "Free Men of Color in Grey," 247–55.

179. Hollandsworth, *Louisiana Native Guards*, 16.

180. *OR*, ser. 2, 1:750; Litwack, *Been in the Storm So Long*, 54.

181. Edward L. Pierce, "The Contrabands at Fortress Monroe," *Atlantic Monthly* 8 (1861): 626–40; Berlin, *Destruction of Slavery*, 67.

182. Edward L. Pierce to Salmon P. Chase, February 8, 1862, in Moore, *Rebellion Record*, 3:308.

183. *OR*, ser. 1, vol. 51, pt. 2, 279.

184. Ibid., 9:477.

185. *Edmondston Diary,* 273.

186. Rose, *Rehearsal for Reconstruction,* 9–10.

187. Ibid., 11–12; *OR,* ser. 1, 6:3–13.

188. Ibid., 12; George P. Rawick, ed., *The American Slave: A Composite Auto-biography* vol. 3 (Westport, Conn., 1973), 200, 202–4.

189. *OR/Navies,* ser. 1, 12:773.

190. Symonds, *Lincoln and His Admirals,* 160.

191. *The South Carolina Rice Plantation as Revealed in the Papers of Robert F. W. Allston,* ed. J. H. Easterby (Chicago, 1945), 190.

192. Myers, *Children of Pride,* 925.

193. Clarke, *Dwelling Place,* 415.

194. Albert V. House, Jr., "Deterioration of a Georgia Rice Plantation during Four Years of Civil War," *Journal of Southern History* 9 (1943): 100–107.

195. Ash, *When the Yankees Came,* 223.

196. George L. Wood, *The Seventh Regiment: A Record* (New York, 1865), 77.

197. Katherine M. Jones, *Heroines of Dixie: Confederate Women Tell Their Story of the War* (Indianapolis, 1955), 118–19.

198. Berlin, *Destruction of Slavery,* 24.

199. David F. Allmendinger, *Ruffin: Family and Reform in the Old South* (New York, 1990), 165; *The Diary of Edmund Ruffin,* ed. William Kauffman Scarborough (Baton Rouge, 1972–89), 2:317, 350. In subsequent notes, this is abbreviated as *Ruffin Diary.*

200. *Ruffin Diary,* 2:307, 317, 409–10.

201. *The Westover Journal of John A. Selden, Esq., 1858–1862,* ed. John Spencer Bassett and Sidney Bradshaw Fay (Northampton, Mass., 1921), 322, 325, 329.

202. Brooks D. Simpson, *Let Us Have Peace: Ulysses S. Grant and the Politics of War & Reconstruction, 1861–1868* (Chapel Hill, N.C., 1991), 27.

203. Ebenezer Hannaford, *The Story of a Regiment: A History of the Campaigns, and Associations in the Field, of the Sixth Regiment Ohio Volunteer Infantry* (Cincinnati, 1868), 227.

204. John Beatty, *The Citizen-soldier: Or, Memoirs of a Volunteer* (Cincinnati, 1879), 119.

205. Simpson, *Let Us Have Peace,* 27.

206. John Eaton, *Grant, Lincoln, and the Freedmen: Reminiscences of the Civil War* (1907; reprint, New York, 1969), 1–2.

207. Berlin, *Destruction of Slavery,* 254.

208. John Cimprich, "Slave Behavior during the Federal Occupation of Tennessee, 1862–1865," *The Historian* 44, no. 3 (1982): 340.

209. James T. Currie, *Enclave: Vicksburg and Her Plantations, 1863–1870* (Jackson, Miss., 1980), 88.

210. Hermann, *Pursuit of a Dream,* 38–39; William C. Davis, *Jefferson Davis: The Man and His Hour,* 409, 505; Cooper, *Jefferson Davis, American,* 243–56.

211. Wiley, *Southern Negroes,* 74–75.

212. Joseph Carlyle Sitterson, *Sugar Country: The Cane Sugar Industry in the South, 1753–1950* ([Lexington, Ky.], 1953), 209.

213. Wiley, *Southern Negroes,* 66.

214. William F. Messner, "Black Violence and White Response: Louisiana, 1862," *Journal of Southern History* 41 (1975): 20–21.

215. *OR,* ser. 1, 15:164–66, 170–72; Benjamin F. Butler, *Butler's Book: Autobiography and Personal Reminiscences of Major Benjamin F. Butler* (Boston, 1892), 1:496–500.

216. Stone, *Brokenburn,* 125.

217. Ibid., 127.

218. Ibid., 134–35.

219. [Ruffin], *Anticipations of the Future,* 130, 149–50, 220, 234–35, 242.

220. Clarke, *Dwelling Place,* 415.

221. Myers, *Children of Pride,* 929–30.

222. *Ruffin Diary,* 351–53.

223. Wiley, *Southern Negroes,* 10–11; Cimprich, *Slavery's End in Tennessee,* 29–30.

224. A. K. Farrar to Governor Pettus, July 17, 1862, quoted in Herbert Aptheker, "Notes on Slave Conspiracies in Confederate Mississippi," *Journal of Negro History* 29 (1944): 76.

225. Scarborough, *Masters of the Big House,* 362.

226. *Edmondston Diary,* 220.

227. Litwack, *Been in the Storm So Long,* 13.

Chapter Four. Recognizing the "Logic of Events": Union War Policy Evolves, 1861–63

1. Stephens, *Voice of Thunder,* 150.

2. *ALCW,* 4:160.

3. Ibid., 4:332.

4. He went on record with that view almost a quarter of a century before he entered the White House (1837). Abraham Lincoln, Protest in Illinois Legislature on Slavery, March 3, 1837, in *ALCW,* 1:75.

5. Abraham Lincoln, annual message to Congress, December 3, 1861, in *ALCW,* 5:48.

6. McPherson, *Tried by War,* 34.

7. *ALCW,* 4:532.

8. McPherson, *Political History,* 286.

9. Johnson at this point shared his constituents' hostility to emancipation. See, for example, *The Papers of Andrew Johnson,* ed. LeRoy P. Graf and Ralph W. Haskins (Knoxville, Tenn., 1972), 3:495–96.

10. *Congressional Globe,* 37th Cong., 1st sess., July 22, 1861, 222–23; ibid., July 25, 1861, 258–65.

11. Douglass, *Life and Writings,* 3:113, 114–15, 123.

12. James M. McPherson, *The Struggle for Equality: Abolitionists and the Negro in the Civil War and Reconstruction* (Princeton, N.J., 1964), 63.

13. Douglass, *Life and Writings,* 3:99.

14. Owen Lovejoy, *His Brother's Blood: Speeches and Writings, 1838–64,* ed. William F. Moore and Jane Ann Moore (Urbana, Ill., 2004), 193.

15. Hans L. Trefousse, *The Radical Republicans: Lincoln's Vanguard for Racial Justice* (New York, 1968), 204; McPherson, *Struggle for Equality,* chap. 3.

16. McPherson, *Struggle for Equality,* 90–91.

17. Ibid., 82–84.

18. Ibid., 93, 95.

19. Ibid., 114–15.

20. Ibid., 111.

21. McPherson, *Political History,* 244; *OR,* ser. 1, 2:48–48, 593, 661–62, 750.

22. Butler, *Butler's Book,* 1:256–58; *Private and Official Correspondence of Gen. Benjamin F. Butler during the Period of the Civil War* (Norwood,

Mass., 1917), 1:116; McPherson, *Political History*, 244; *OR*, ser. 1, 2:648–52; ibid., ser. 3, 1:243.

23. Butler, *Private and Official Correspondence*, 1:185–88.

24. Bruce Levine, *The Spirit of 1848: German Immigrants, Labor Conflict, and the Coming of the Civil War* (Urbana, Ill., 1992).

25. Berlin, *Destruction of Slavery*, 253.

26. McPherson, *Political History*, 246–47, 250–51.

27. *ALCW*, 5:532.

28. Ibid., 5:506.

29. McPherson, *Political History*, 246–47, 250–51.

30. Ibid., 245–51; Berlin, *Destruction of Slavery*, 256–57.

31. Stephens, *Voice of Thunder*, 138.

32. After the fall of Forts Henry and Donelson, for example, Ulysses S. Grant's headquarters declared both "the great necessity of keeping out fugitives" and that "such slaves as were within the lines at the time of the capture of Fort Donelson and such as have been used by the enemy in building the fortifications or in any way hostile to the Government will not be released or permitted to return to their masters but will be employed in the quartermaster's department for the benefit of Government." *OR*, ser. 2, 1:808.

33. McPherson, *Tried by War*, 58.

34. *ALCW*, 5:318.

35. Michael Burlingame, *Abraham Lincoln: A Life* (Baltimore, 2008), 2:229.

36. Abraham Lincoln, Appeal to Border State Representatives to Favor Compensated Emancipation, July 12, 1862, in *ALCW*, 5:317.

37. See, for example, LaWanda Cox, *Lincoln and Black Freedom: A Study in Presidential Leadership* (Urbana, Ill., 1985), 9.

38. McPherson, *Political History*, 210.

39. *New York Tribune*, July 19, 1862.

40. William A. Blair, "The Seven Days and the Radical Persuasion: Convincing Moderates in the North of the Need for a Hard War," in *The Richmond Campaign of 1862: The Peninsula and the Seven Days*, ed. Gary W. Gallagher (Chapel Hill, N.C., 2000), 153–80.

41. Quoted in chap. 3.

42. Mark Grimsley, *The Hard Hand of War: Union Military Policy toward*

Southern Civilians, 1861–1865 (Cambridge, UK, 1995), 112–19; Simpson, *Let Us Have Peace,* 23–34.

43. Blair, "Seven Days and the Radical Persuasion," 153–80.

44. James M. McPherson, *The Negro's Civil War: How the American Negroes Felt and Acted during the War for the Union* (New York, 1965), 237–38, 195, 286–87, 44; James G. Blaine, *Twenty Years of Congress: From Lincoln to Garfield* (Norwich, Conn., 1884), 1:354.

45. It offered up to $300 per lost slave.

46. McPherson, *Political History,* 196, 211–12, 239, 254.

47. *OR,* ser. 3, 2:275–76.

48. Burlingame, *Abraham Lincoln: A Life,* 2:357.

49. Berlin, *Destruction of Slavery,* 193, 208–21.

50. *ALCW,* 5:343n1.

51. Ibid., 5:342–46.

52. Ibid.

53. *Diary of Gideon Welles, Secretary of the Navy under Lincoln and Johnson* (Boston: Houghton Mifflin, 1911), 1:70–71. In subsequent notes, this is abbreviated as *Welles Diary.*

54. The Adjutant General's Office sent the order out (as General Orders No. 109) on August 16, 1862. *OR,* ser. 3, 2:397.

55. *Inside Lincoln's Cabinet: The Civil War Diaries of Salmon P. Chase,* ed. David Donald (New York, 1954), 95–99. In subsequent notes, this is abbreviated as *Chase Diary.*

56. *ALCW,* 5:434.

57. Allen C. Guelzo, *Lincoln's Emancipation Proclamation: The End of Slavery in America* (New York, 2004), 207–9.

58. Ibid., 211.

59. Ibid., 180, 187, 213.

60. Quoted in *Blackwood's Edinburgh Magazine* 92 (November 1862): 644.

61. McPherson, *Tried by War,* 128.

62. Guelzo, *Lincoln's Emancipation Proclamation,* 213.

63. Victor B. Howard, *Black Liberation in Kentucky: Emancipation and Freedom, 1862–1884* (Lexington, Ky., 1983), 32–34; Christopher Phillips, " 'The Chrysalis State': Slavery, Confederate Identity, and the Creation of the Border South," in *Inside the Confederate Nation,* ed. Lesley J. Gordon and John C. Inscoe (Baton Rouge, 2005), 147–55.

64. John G. Barrett, *The Civil War in North Carolina* (Chapel Hill, N.C., 1963), 173.

65. *The Civil War Papers of George B. McClellan: Selected Correspondence, 1860–1865*, ed. Stephen W. Sears (New York, 1992), 344–45. This was not the first time McClellan had expressed such views to the government. In the fall of 1861, as Salmon P. Chase later learned, the general told an assistant secretary of war that "we should conduct the war so as to avoid offence as far as possible" and that if McClellan thought that an appreciably harder kind of war was necessary to save the Union "he should feel obliged to lay down his arms." *Chase Diary*, 101–2.

66. McClellan, *Civil War Papers*, 481–82.

67. Jacob Dolson Cox, *Military Reminiscences of the Civil War* (New York, 1900), 1:209.

68. McClellan, *Civil War Papers*, 351.

69. Nevins, *War for the Union*, 2:231n.

70. Ibid., 375; *Inside Lincoln's White House: The Complete Civil War Diary of John Hay*, ed. Michael Burlingame and John R. Turner Ettlinger (Carbondale, Ill., 1997), 41; McPherson, *Tried by War*, 133–34.

71. *Abraham Lincoln: The Observations of John G. Nicolay and John Hay*, ed. Michael Burlingame (Carbondale, Ill., 2007), 108.

72. Guelzo, *Lincoln's Emancipation Proclamation*, 182–86, 190–91; McPherson, *Tried by War*, 115, 137.

73. *OR*, ser. 1, vol. 16, pt. 2, 421.

74. Adam J. P. Smith, *No Party Now: Politics in the Civil War North* (New York, 2006), 57.

75. Ibid., 56; Josiah Henry Benton, *Voting in the Field: A Forgotten Chapter of the Civil War* (Boston, 1915), 26, 306–8; and Oscar Osburn Winther, "The Soldier Vote in the Election of 1864," *New York History* 25 (1944): 440–48.

76. McPherson, *For Causes and Comrades*, 121.

77. Wiley, *Life of Billy Yank*, 42.

78. McPherson, *Tried by War*, 127.

79. *Ruffin Diary*, 2:609.

80. McPherson, *For Causes and Comrades*, 118.

81. Frank L. Byrne and Jean Powers Soman, eds., *Your True Marcus: The Civil War Letters of a Jewish Colonel* (Kent, Ohio, 1985), 316.

82. Manning, *What This Cruel War Was Over*, 118–19, 268n33.

83. Earl J. Hess, *Liberty, Virtue, and Progress: Northerners and Their War for the Union* (New York, 1997), 97.

84. McPherson, *What They Fought For*, 59.

85. Stephens, *Voice of Thunder*, 161, 170.

86. *A Wisconsin Boy in Dixie: Civil War Letters of James K. Newton*, ed. Stephen E. Ambrose (Madison, Wis., 1995), 28.

87. William E. Gienapp, ed., *The Civil War and Reconstruction: A Documentary Collection* (New York, 2001), 242–45.

88. Manning, *What This Cruel War Was Over*, 89, 93.

89. Allan Nevins, *The War for the Union*, vol. 3, *The Organized War, 1863–1864* (New York, 1971), 154–58, 167–72, 177–79.

90. *The Works of James Abram Garfield*, ed. Burke A. Hinsdale (Boston, 1882–83), 13.

91. Georges Clemenceau, *American Reconstruction, 1865–1870* (New York, 1928), 165; *Congressional Globe*, 37th Cong., 1st sess., August 2, 1861, 415.

92. Frederick Douglass, "How to End the War" (May 1861), in Douglass, *Life and Writings*, 3:94–95.

93. McPherson, *The Negro's Civil War*, 19–22.

94. Berlin, *Black Military Experience*, 82–83.

95. *OR*, ser. 3, 1:133; McPherson, *Negro's Civil War*, 22; Peter H. Clark, *Black Brigade of Cincinnati: Being a Report of Its Labors and a Muster-Roll of Its Members etc.* (Cincinnati, 1864), 6. The government seems simply to have ignored Garland White's offer.

96. Dudley Taylor Cornish, *The Sable Arm: Black Troops in the Union Army, 1861–1865* (1956; reprint, Lawrence, Kans., 1987), 21–22; McPherson, *Political History*, 249.

97. *ALCW*, 5:356–57.

98. *OR*, ser. 1, vol. 10, pt. 2, 162.

99. Ibid., 14:375.

100. Ibid., ser. 3, 2:198.

101. Cornish, *Sable Arm*, 52–53.

102. Ibid., 58–64.

103. *Chase Diary*, 96–100, 105.

104. Stephen V. Ash, *Firebrand of Liberty: The Story of Two Black Regiments That Changed the Course of the Civil War* (New York, 2008), 52–53.

105. *OR*, ser. 1, 14:374.

106. Salmon P. Chase to General Butler, July 31, 1862, in Butler, *Private and Official Correspondence*, 2:131–38.

107. *OR*, ser. 1, 14: 377–78.

108. Cornish, *Sable Arm*, 88.

109. Ash, *Firebrand of Liberty*, 33.

110. Ibid., 38.

111. *OR*, ser. 1, 14:377.

112. *OR*, ser. 1, 15:556–57; Hollandsworth, *Louisiana Native Guards*, 2–9.

113. They had first made this offer to Phelps, who then referred them to Butler. Berlin, *Black Military Experience*, 64.

114. Butler, *Butler's Book*, 1:492–93.

115. Salmon P. Chase to General Butler, July 31, 1862, in Butler, *Private and Official Correspondence*, 2:131–38. In fact, Chase had entrusted to Butler the sharply worded letters from Lincoln to Reverdy Johnson and Cuthbert Bullitt for delivery to those two southern unionists.

116. *OR*, ser. 3, 2:437–38.

117. Cornish, *Sable Arm*, 67.

118. George S. Denison to Salmon P. Chase, September 9, 1862, in *Diary and Correspondence of Salmon P. Chase* (Washington, D.C., 1903), 313; Hollandsworth, *Louisiana Native Guards*, 18, 21.

119. [W. C. Corsan], *Two Months in the Confederate States: Including a Visit to New Orleans under the Domination of General Butler* (London, 1863), 40.

120. Cornish, *Sable Arm*, 70–78.

121. Ibid., 105–11.

122. Frank Freidel, "The Loyal Publication Society: A Pro-Union Propaganda Agency," *Mississippi Valley Historical Review* 26 (1939): 366.

123. Lee to Seddon, January 10, 1863, in *OR*, ser. 1, 21:1086.

124. *Thomas Diary*, 195–96.

125. *Mobile Register and Advertiser*, November 26, 1863.

126. The Confederate Congress thought this story of Napoléon's enlightened self-restraint compelling enough to repeat it a year later. *OR*, ser. 1, vol. 28, pt. 2, 11–13; ser. 4, 3:133.

127. Eugene Tarle, *Napoleon's Invasion of Russia, 1812* (New York, 1942), 256–67; Hugh Seton-Watson, *The Russian Empire, 1801–1917* (New York, 1988), 129.

128. *ALCW*, 6:29–30; 5:537.

129. Robin Blackburn, *The Overthrow of Colonial Slavery, 1776–1848* (London, 1988), 340–59. See also Paul Verna, *Petion y Bolívar* (Caracas, 1980), 150–72; J. L. Salcedo-Bastardo, *Bolívar: A Continent and Its Destiny* (Richmond, UK, 1977), 103–12; and especially Peter Blanchard, *Under the Flags of Freedom: Slave Soldiers and the Wars of Independence in Spanish South America* (Pittsburgh, 2008).

130. Karl Marx and Frederick Engels, *Collected Works* (Moscow, 1975–2005), 19:178, 248, 41:364.

Chapter Five. "The Clouds Are Dark over Us": The Convulsions of 1863

1. Carl Sandburg, *Abraham Lincoln: The Prairie Years and the War Years* (New York, 1954), 346.

2. McPherson, *Struggle for Equality*, 122.

3. Berlin, *Destruction of Slavery*, 31–32; Grimsley, *Hard Hand of War*, 78.

4. Jaime Amanda Martinez, "The Slave Market in Civil War Virginia," in *Crucible of the Civil War: Virginia from Secession to Commemoration*, ed. Edward L. Ayers, Gary W. Gallagher, and Andrew J. Torget (Charlottesville, Va., 2006), 116.

5. *Richmond Dispatch*, reprinted in the *New York Tribune*, January 12, 1863.

6. Stone, *Brokenburn*, 146.

7. John B. Jones, *A Rebel War Clerk's Diary at the Confederate States Capital* (Philadelphia, 1866), 1:233. This is abbreviated in subsequent notes as *Jones Diary*.

8. James D. Richardson, ed., *A Compilation of the Messages and Papers of the Confederacy, Including Diplomatic Correspondence, 1861–1865* (Nashville, Tenn., 1905), 1:277.

9. George H. Washburn, *A Complete Military History and Record of the 108th Regiment N.Y. Volunteers* (Rochester, N.Y., 1894), 36.

10. Noah Brooks, *Abraham Lincoln* (New York, 1894), 358.

11. *OR*, ser. 1, vol. 24, pt. 1, 22.

12. *OR*, ser. 1, vol. 17, pt. 1, 613.

13. McPherson, *Tried by War*, 167–69.

14. Levine, *Spirit of 1848*, 258.

15. Paludan, *People's Contest*, 113.

16. *Edmondston Diary*, 440.

17. Gordon B. McKinney, *Zeb Vance: North Carolina's Civil War Governor and Gilded Age Political Leader* (Chapel Hill, N.C., 2004), 168.

18. David G. Smith, "Race and Retaliation: The Capture of African-Americans during the Gettysburg Campaign," in *Virginia's Civil War*, ed. Peter Wallenstein and Bertram Wyatt-Brown (Charlottesville, Va., 2005), 137–51; Margaret Creighton, *The Colors of Courage: Gettysburg's Forgotten History: Immigrants, Women, and African Americans in the Civil War's Defining Battle* (New York, 2005), 50–51.

19. Stone, *Brokenburn*, 215, 227.

20. *OR*, ser. 1, vol. 24, pt. 2, 680.

21. Thomas B. Alexander, *Thomas A. R. Nelson of East Tennessee* (Nashville, Tenn., 1956), 98–103; *OR*, ser. 1, vol. 16, pt. 2, 909–10.

22. Fisher, *War at Every Door*, 113–14; Inscoe and McKinney, *Heart of Confederate Appalachia*, 222.

23. John Watson Foster, *War Stories for My Grandchildren* (Washington, D.C, 1918), 123–25. The quotations come from Foster's contemporaneous letter to his wife, reproduced in this volume.

24. Groce, *Mountain Rebels*, 121–26.

25. *OR*, ser. 1, vol. 23, pt. 2, 55.

26. Larry J. Daniel, *Soldiering in the Army of Tennessee: A Portrait of Life in a Confederate Army* (Chapel Hill, N.C., 1991), 136.

27. *OR*, ser. 4, 2:993–94.

28. Thomas Lawrence Connelly, *Autumn of Glory: The Army of Tennessee, 1862–1865* (Baton Rouge, 1971), 274–77; *Personal Memoirs of U. S. Grant* (1885; reprint, New York, n.d.), 383–84; James Cooper Nisbet, *Four Years on the Firing Line* (1914; reprint, Jackson, Tenn., 1963), 158–59.

29. Many accounts of subsequent combat in Georgia between Sherman's army group and the Army of Tennessee continue to speak of it as occurring in the western theater of war.

30. *Mobile Register and Advertiser,* December 1, 1863.

31. Connelly, *Autumn of Glory,* 273.

32. Daniel, *Soldiering in the Army of Tennessee,* 155–56.

33. *OR,* ser. 4, 2:991.

34. Glatthaar, *General Lee's Army,* 283, 412–14; *Inside the Confederate Government: The Diary of Robert Garlick Hill Kean, Head of the Bureau of War,* ed. Edward Younger (New York, 1957), 86, abbreviated in subsequent notes as *Kean Diary; Gorgas Journals,* 136.

35. Ibid.; *Gorgas Journals,* 136.

36. Jefferson Davis to Lieutenant General T. H. Holmes, July 15, 1863, and Davis to Hon. R. W. Johnson, July 14, 1863, in *PJD,* 9:276, 281.

37. *Jones Diary,* 1:374, 378, 2:16; see also *Kean Diary,* 119.

38. Richard Taylor, *Destruction and Reconstruction: Personal Experiences of the Late War* (1879; reprint, New York, 1955), 281.

39. Reagan, *Memoirs,* 161.

40. Ibid., 86.

41. Connelly, *Autumn of Glory,* 276–77; Daniel, *Soldiering in the Army of Tennessee,* 137–38, 155–56; Diane Neal and Thomas W. Kremm, *Lion of the South: General Thomas C. Hindman* (Macon, Ga., 1993), 184.

42. *Mary Chesnut's Civil War,* 551.

43. *Jones Diary,* 1:374, 378, 2:16.

44. Daniel, *Soldiering in the Army of Tennessee,* 137; Connelly, *Autumn of Glory,* 291.

45. Toombs, Stephens, and Cobb, *Correspondence,* 621.

46. *PJD,* 9:339.

47. Eugene D. Genovese, *A Consuming Fire: The Fall of the Confederacy in the Mind of the Christian South* (Athens, Ga., 1998), 47–51.

48. Rubin, *Shattered Nation,* 37.

49. Steven E. Woodworth, *While God Is Marching On: The Religious World of Civil War Soldiers* (Lawrence, Kans., 2001), 271.

50. W. J. Worsham, *The Old Nineteenth Tennessee Regiment, C.S.A. June, 1861–April, 1865* (Knoxville, Tenn., 1902), 104, 108–9.

51. Quoted in Genovese, *Consuming Fire,* 48.

52. Cimprich, *Slavery's End in Tennessee,* 27.

53. Bettersworth, *Mississippi in the Confederacy,* 241.

54. James Freeman Clarke, *Autobiography, Diary and Correspondence*, ed. Edward Everett Hale (Boston, 1892), 286.

55. Peter Cooper, *The Death of Slavery* (New York, 1863), 4.

56. Litwack, *Been in the Storm So Long*, 21.

57. Wilbert L. Jenkins, *Climbing Up to Glory: A Short History of African Americans During the Civil War and Reconstruction* (Wilmington, Del., 2002), 18.

58. Captain C. B. Wilder before the American Freedmen's Inquiry Commission, in David Stephen Heidler, Jeanne T. Heidler, and David J. Coles, eds., *Encyclopedia of the American Civil War: A Political, Social, and Military History* (New York, 2002), 2429.

59. Davis, *Jefferson Davis: A Memoir by His Wife*, 2:217.

60. *Mary Chesnut's Civil War*, 535; Emory M. Thomas, *The Confederate State of Richmond: A Biography of the Capital* (1971; reprint, Baton Rouge, 1998), 155.

61. Stone, *Brokenburn*, 178.

62. Ibid., 184.

63. Ibid.

64. Telegram from Colonel J. Thompson to Lieutenant General Pemberton, January 18, 1863, Records of Military Commands, Papers of Various Confederate Notables, Gen. John C. Pemberton, Telegrams Received, January–February 1863, entry 131, RG 109, NA.

65. Stone, *Brokenburn*, 171, 175.

66. Ibid., 185.

67. Ibid., 184.

68. Ibid., 198.

69. Ibid.

70. Ibid., 191.

71. Robert L. Kerby, *Kirby Smith's Confederacy: The Trans-Mississippi South, 1863–1865* (Tuscaloosa, Ala., 1972), 255.

72. Stone, *Brokenburn*, 198–99.

73. Bettersworth, *Mississippi in the Confederacy*, 241.

74. *Ruffin Diary*, 2:661.

75. Currie, *Enclave*, 33.

76. Toombs, Stephens, and Cobb, *Correspondence*, 629.

77. *OR*, ser. 1, vol. 24, pt. 2, 681.

78. Currie, *Enclave*, 73.

79. Ibid., 74.

80. Berlin, *Destruction of Slavery*, 676.

81. William J. Minor, Plantation Diary 35, entry for January 3, 1863, William J. Minor and Family Papers, Ms. 519, Louisiana and Lower Mississippi Valley Collection, Special Collections, Louisiana State University Libraries, abbreviated in subsequent notes as Minor Papers; J. Carlyle Sitterson, "The William J. Minor Plantations: A Study in Ante-Bellum Absentee Ownership," *Journal of Southern History* 9 (February 1943): 61.

82. Minor, Plantation Diary 35, entry for February 26, 1863, Minor Papers.

83. Ibid., entry for June 8, 1863. There were innumerable stories like this one. See, for example, Wiley, *Plain People of the Confederacy*, 74–82.

84. Ludwell H. Johnson, *Red River Campaign: Politics and Cotton in the Civil War* (Kent, Ohio, 1993), 112.

85. Scarborough, *Masters of the Big House*, 362.

86. *Edmondston Diary*, 463–64.

87. Wiley, *Southern Negroes*, 19.

88. Berlin, *Destruction of Slavery*, 263; Nevins, *War for the Union*, 3:430.

89. *Sherman's Civil War: Selected Correspondence of William T. Sherman, 1860–1865*, ed. Brooks D. Simpson and Jean V. Berlin (Chapel Hill, N.C., 1999), 591.

90. Wiley, *Southern Negroes*, 40.

91. Scarborough, *Masters of the Big House*, 355.

92. Berlin, *Destruction of Slavery*, 778–79; *OR*, ser. 4, 3:41–42.

93. Berlin, *Wartime Genesis: Lower South*, 671–73; Berlin, *Destruction of Slavery*, 327, 674, 679–80.

94. *Edmondston Diary*, 463–64.

95. Ibid.

96. Ash, *When the Yankees Came*, 187.

97. Stone, *Brokenburn*, 173.

98. *Memoirs and Selected Letters: Personal Memoirs of U. S. Grant, Selected Letters 1839–1865,* ed. Mary Drake McFeeley and William McFeeley (New York, 1990), 1033.

99. *Graham Papers,* 5:530. This is a summary of Graham's views recorded by a colleague following a meeting with him.

100. Wiley, *Confederate Women,* 154.

101. Smith to Stephens, August 20, 1863, in Schott, *Alexander H. Stephens of Georgia,* 384.

102. James D. Waddell, *Biographical Sketch of Linton Stephens* (Atlanta, 1877), 263.

103. Ash, *Firebrand of Liberty,* 200–204.

104. See, for example, Rose, *Rehearsal for Reconstruction,* 146–47, 192, 267–69, 329.

105. *Douglass's Monthly,* March 21, 1863, quoted in Douglass, *Life and Times,* 340.

106. Berlin, *Black Military Experience,* 117; *OR,* ser. 3, 3:1189–90.

107. Berlin, *Destruction of Slavery,* 96–97.

108. Stephens, *Voice of Thunder,* 31–34.

109. Ibid., 31.

110. *Edmondston Diary,* 270.

111. Ibid., 328.

112. *Jones Diary,* 1:213.

113. Hollandsworth, *Louisiana Native Guards,* 30.

114. Even decades later, ex–Confederate general Edward Porter Alexander sniffed that although the Union's raising of black units "was supposed to be a war measure," in fact "nothing could have been more [de]void of effect." See E. P. Alexander, *Military Memoirs of a Confederate: A Critical Narrative* (New York, 1907), 276.

115. Richard Lowe, "Battle on the Levee: The Fight at Milliken's Bend," in *Black Soldiers in Blue: African American Troops in the Civil War Era,* ed. John David Smith (Chapel Hill, N.C., 2002), 107–35; *OR,* ser. 1, vol. 24, pt. 2, 467.

116. Stone, *Brokenburn,* 218.

117. McPherson, *Negro's Civil War,* 185.

118. *OR,* ser. 1, vol. 26, pt. 1, 45.

119. McPherson, *Negro's Civil War,* 185.

120. Stephens, *Voice of Thunder*, 39–40.

121. This assault climaxed the film *Glory* (1989).

122. Union forces drove Confederate troops out of Battery Wagner in September 1863.

123. Stephens, *Voice of Thunder*, 45.

124. Luis F. Emilio, *A Brave Black Regiment: The History of the 54th Massachusetts, 1863–1865* (1891; reprint, New York, 1995), 67–104.

125. Cornish, *Sable Arm*, 146, 152–56; Joseph T. Glatthaar, *Forged in Battle: The Civil War Alliance of Black Soldiers and White Officers* (New York, 1991), 136–42; Mark A. Lause, *Race and Radicalism in the Union Army* (Urbana, Ill., 2009), 97–102.

126. Moore, *Rebellion Record*, 7:381.

127. See, for example, Lincoln to General John A. Schofield, October 1, 1863, in *ALCW*, 6:492–93.

128. Such loyal masters were to be compensated for their resulting losses, but the compensation offered was nominal ($300 per slave). *OR*, ser. 3, 3:860–61.

129. Berlin, *Black Military Experience*, chap. 4.

130. *OR*, ser. 3, 3:1034–36, 4:733–34; Berlin, *Black Military Experience*, 183–93.

131. Glatthaar, *Forged in Battle*, 79.

132. William Wells Brown, *The Negro in the American Rebellion: His Heroism and His Fidelity*, ed. John David Smith (1867; reprint, Athens, Ohio, 2003), 162.

133. Botume, *First Days amongst the Contrabands*, 206–7.

134. *OR*, ser. 1, vol. 52, pt. 2, 586–90.

135. James H. McNeilly, "In Winter Quarters at Dalton, Ga.," *Confederate Veteran* 28 (1920): 130–31; Nisbet, *Four Years on the Firing Line*, 171.

136. William B. Bate to W. H. T. Walker, January 9, 1864, Civil War Collection, Huntington Library.

137. *OR*, ser. 1, 15:907.

138. Wiley, *Southern Negroes*, 37, 40; *OR*, ser. 1, vol. 17, pt. 2, 740.

139. Carrington Examinations, Entry 445, PI-101, misfiled with Records Concerning Prisoners of War, RG 109, NA; *Marching with Sherman: Passages from the Letters and Campaign Diaries of Henry Hitchcock, Major and Assistant Adjutant General of Volunteers, November 1864–May 1865,*

ed. M. A. DeWolfe Howe (1927; reprint, Lincoln, Neb., 1995), 84. See also Botume, *First Days amongst the Contrabands*, 55; *Two Diaries From Middle St. John's, Berkeley, South Carolina, February–May, 1865: Journals Kept by Miss Susan R. Jervey and Miss Charlotte St. J. Ravenel, at Northampton and Pooshee Plantations, and Reminiscences of Mrs. (Waring) Henagan with Two Contemporary Reports from Federal Officials* ([Pinopolis, S.C.], 1921), 18.

140. *Graham Papers*, 6:43.

141. John Cimprich, *Fort Pillow, a Civil War Massacre, and Public Memory* (Baton Rouge, 2005), 81.

142. Jason Phillips, *Diehard Rebels: The Confederate Culture of Invincibility* (Athens, Ga., 2007), 67.

143. *OR*, ser. 1, vol. 39, pt. 1, 229.

144. Cimprich, *Fort Pillow*, 73, 81–85; Albert Castel, "The Fort Pillow Massacre: An Examination of the Evidence," originally published in 1958, reprinted in *Black Flag over Dixie: Racial Atrocities and Reprisals in the Civil War*, ed. Gregory J. W. Urwin (Carbondale, Ill., 2004), 89–103.

145. Cimprich, *Fort Pillow*, 95–96; Kerby, *Kirby Smith's Confederacy*, 312.

146. Rose, *Rehearsal for Reconstruction*, 263.

147. David J. Coles, " 'Shooting Niggers Sir': Confederate Mistreatment of Union Black Soldiers at the Battle of Olustee," in Urwin, *Black Flag over Dixie*, 64–88.

Chapter Six. Bound for "A Land They Knew Not": After Slavery, What?

1. Benjamin Quarles, *The Negro in the Civil War* (1953; reprint, New York, 1968), 176; S. Emma Edmonds, *The Female Spy of the Union Army* (Boston, 1864), 340; Dena J. Epstein, *Sinful Tunes and Spirituals: Black Folk Music to the Civil War* (Urbana, Ill., 2003), 257–58.

2. Mary A. Livermore, *My Story of the War: A Woman's Narrative of Four Years Personal Experience* (Hartford, Conn., 1892), 341–45.

3. Berlin, *Wartime Genesis: Lower South*, 31.

4. Philip S. Foner and George E. Walker, eds., *Proceedings of the Black State Conventions* (Philadelphia, 1979–80).

5. Peter Winthrop Bardaglio, *Reconstructing the Household: Families, Sex,*

and the Law in the Nineteenth-Century South (Chapel Hill, N.C., 1995), 116.

6. Botume, *First Days amongst the Contrabands,* 156.

7. Ibid., 143.

8. Quarles, *Negro in the Civil War,* 289.

9. James A. Evans to William Smith, December 14, 1864, Virginia Governor's Office, William Smith Executive Papers, 1864–1865, RG 3, Accession 36916, State Records Collection, Library of Virginia, Richmond. For a similar encounter in North Carolina in January 1863, see Berlin, *Destruction of Slavery,* 87–88.

10. Quarles, *Negro in the Civil War,* 289.

11. Botume, *First Days amongst the Contrabands,* 158.

12. Raboteau, *Slave Religion,* 154.

13. Ibid., 151.

14. Blassingame, *Slave Testimony,* 642.

15. Lawrence W. Levine, *Black Culture and Black Consciousness: Afro-American Folk Thought from Slavery to Freedom* (New York, 1997), 45.

16. Blassingame, *Slave Testimony,* 642.

17. Wiley, *Southern Negroes,* 108f.

18. Janet Duitsman Cornelius, *When I Can Read My Title Clear: Literacy, Slavery, and Religion in the Antebellum South* (Columbia, S.C., 1992), 86.

19. Rawick, *American Slave: Composite Autobiography,* 2:284.

20. Wiley, *Southern Negroes,* 108–9.

21. David Macrae, *Americans at Home: Pen-and-Ink Sketches of American Men, Manners, and Institutions* (Edinburgh, 1870), 2:100.

22. Botume, *First Days amongst the Contrabands,* 100.

23. *A Woman's Life-Work: Labors and Experiences of Laura S. Haviland* (Chicago, 1887), 321.

24. *Friends' Intelligencer* 9, no. 22 (August 9, 1862): 350.

25. Maria Waterbury, *Seven Years among the Freedmen,* 3rd ed. (Chicago, 1893), 81.

26. Rose, *Rehearsal for Reconstruction,* 86, 88.

27. Blassingame, *Slave Testimony,* 598. Original emphasis.

28. John Richard Dennett, *The South as It Is: 1865–1866,* ed. Henry M.

Christman (New York, 1965), 322. These were originally dispatches published in *The Nation* magazine.

29. Cornelius, *When I Can Read My Title Clear*, 144–47.

30. Ira Berlin, et al., eds., *The Wartime Genesis of Free Labor: The Upper South* (Cambridge, UK, 1993), 212.

31. Ibid., 217.

32. Botume, *First Days amongst the Contrabands*, 112.

33. Blassingame, *Slave Testimony*, 174.

34. Berlin, *Wartime Genesis: Upper South*, 152.

35. Botume, *First Days amongst the Contrabands*, 87.

36. Berlin, *Wartime Genesis: Upper South*, 211.

37. Botume, *First Days amongst the Contrabands*, 92.

38. Cornelius, *When I Can Read My Title Clear*, 142.

39. Eaton, *Grant, Lincoln, and the Freedmen*, 208.

40. Botume, *First Days amongst the Contrabands*, 151.

41. Eaton, *Grant, Lincoln, and the Freedmen*, 105.

42. McPherson, *Negro's Civil War*, 294.

43. Berlin, *Wartime Genesis: Lower South*, 233n.

44. Stanton appointed to it three ardent opponents of slavery—its chairman, James McKaye, a self-made millionaire in telegraphy; physician, educator, and internationalist Samuel Gridley Howe; and utopian socialist, women's rights advocate, and sometime congressman and diplomat Robert Dale Owen—all three of whom served from the creation of the committee in 1863 until their submission of its final report in May 1864.

45. *OR*, ser. 3, 3:437.

46. Rose, *Rehearsal for Reconstruction*, 282. Emphasis added.

47. John Townsend Trowbridge, *The South: A Tour of Its Battlefields and Ruined Cities, a Journey through the Desolated States, and Talks with the People, Being a Description of the Present State of the Country—Its Agriculture—Railroads—Business and Finance* (Hartford, Conn., 1866), 151.

48. *The New York Times*, quoted in Eric Foner, *Politics and Ideology in the Age of the Civil War* (New York, 1974), 144.

49. Helene Sarah Zahler, *Eastern Workingmen and National Land Policy, 1829–1862* (New York, 1941); Mark A. Lause, *Young America: Land, Labor, and the Republican Community* (Urbana, Ill., 2005).

50. *The Papers of Alexander Hamilton*, ed. Harold C. Syrett (New York, 1961–79), 1:106; Max Farrand, ed., *Records of the Federal Convention* (New Haven, Conn., 1966), 2:203–4; Susan P. Castillo, ed., *The Literatures of Colonial America: An Anthology* (Malden, Mass., 2001), 488.

51. Thomas Jefferson, *Notes on the State of Virginia* (1787; reprint New York, 1972), 165.

52. Whitelaw Reid, *After the War: A Tour of the Southern States, 1865–66* (1866; reprint, New York, 1965), 59.

53. McPherson, *Negro's Civil War*, 295.

54. Berlin, *Wartime Genesis: Lower South*, 195; James S. Allen, *Reconstruction: The Battle for Democracy, 1865–1876* (New York, 1937), 44.

55. Sidney Andrews, *The South since the War* (1866; reprint, 1971), 233.

56. Sitterson, *Sugar Country*, 210; Hahn, *Nation under Our Feet*, 81–82; Litwack, *Been in the Storm So Long*, 438; Berlin, *Wartime Genesis: Lower South*, 438–39, 460.

57. Hermann, *Pursuit of a Dream*, 42–43; Currie, *Enclave*, 90–91.

58. Stone, *Brokenburn*, 209–10.

59. Berlin, *Destruction of Slavery*, 221n.

60. Berlin, *Wartime Genesis: Lower South*, 409.

61. Ibid., 50, 187, 406, 808–9.

62. These "insurgent Negroes" were later recaptured by the Confederate army and marched into Jackson. Allen, *Reconstruction*, 43.

63. Charles L. Perdue, Jr., Thomas E. Barden, and Robert K. Phillips, eds., *Weevils in the Wheat: Interviews with Virginia Ex-Slaves* (Charlottesville, Va., 1976), 291.

64. Garfield, *Works*, 1:11.

65. Berlin, *Wartime Genesis: Lower South*, 532–34.

66. Rose, *Rehearsal for Reconstruction*, 239.

67. McPherson, *Struggle for Equality*, 252.

68. Louis S. Gerteis, *From Contraband to Freedman: Federal Policy toward Southern Blacks, 1861–1865* (Westport, Conn., 1973), 169.

69. *OR*, ser. 3, 2:276–77.

70. *ALCW*, 5:329–31.

71. Rose, *Rehearsal for Reconstruction*, 225.

72. Ibid., 211; Berlin, *Wartime Genesis: Lower South*, 37.

73. Rose, *Rehearsal for Reconstruction*, 217–18.

74. Berlin, *Wartime Genesis: Lower South*, 15, 290.

75. Ibid., 726.

76. Rose, *Rehearsal for Reconstruction*, 214.

77. Ibid., 215.

78. Berlin, *Wartime Genesis: Lower South*, 300.

79. Ibid., 37, 306; Elizabeth Ware Pearson, *Letters from Port Royal 1862–1868* (New York, 1969), 220. Emphasis added.

80. Rose, *Rehearsal for Reconstruction*, 274–75; Berlin, *Wartime Genesis: Lower South*, 60; *A Digest of the Military Laws of the United States: From 1860 to the Second Session of the Fortieth Congress, 1867, Relating to the Army, Volunteers, Militia, and the Rebellion and Reconstruction of the Southern States* (Boston, 1868), 84; *ALCW*, 6:457.

81. Rose, *Rehearsal for Reconstruction*, 273–74; *ALCW*, 7:98–99.

82. Rose, *Rehearsal for Reconstruction*, 286–87; Berlin, *Wartime Genesis: Lower South*, 282–83.

83. Berlin, *Wartime Genesis: Lower South*, 276–77; *OR*, ser. 3, 4:119.

84. *The Salmon P. Chase Papers*, ed. John Niven (Kent, Ohio, 1993–98), 4:293.

85. Eric Foner, "Thaddeus Stevens, Confiscation, and Reconstruction," in Foner, *Politics and Ideology*, 131–32.

86. *ALCW*, 5:329–31.

87. Berlin, *Wartime Genesis: Lower South*, 36.

88. Rose, *Rehearsal for Reconstruction*, 287–90.

89. Edward Royce, *The Origins of Southern Sharecropping* (Philadelphia, 1993), 89; Berlin, *Wartime Genesis: Lower South*, 310. Chase's biographer, who is also the editor of his papers, concludes that Lincoln's Treasury secretary had "finally capitulated to what he saw as the political imperatives of private enterprise." John Niven, *Salmon P. Chase: A Biography* (New York, 1995), 329.

90. *Letters and Diary of Laura M. Towne; Written from the Sea Islands of South Carolina 1862–1864*, ed. Rupert Sargent Holland (Cambridge, Mass., 1912), 101; Berlin, *Wartime Genesis: Lower South*, 297–98, 302.

91. Pearson, *Letters from Port Royal*, 276–77.

92. Ibid.

93. Berlin, *Wartime Genesis: Lower South*, 291.

94. Ibid., 298–99.

95. McPherson, *Negro's Civil War*, 298.

96. Berlin, *Wartime Genesis: Lower South*, 307.

97. Steven Joseph Ross, "Freed Soil, Freed Labor, Freed Men: John Eaton and the Davis Bend Experiment," *Journal of Southern History* 44 (1978): 218; Gerteis, *From Contraband to Freedman*, 175.

98. Eaton, *Grant, Lincoln, and the Freedmen*, 86.

99. Hermann, *Pursuit of a Dream*, 42–43; Eaton, *Grant, Lincoln, and the Freedmen*, 163–64; Currie, *Enclave*, 94.

100. Ross, "Freed Soil," 219.

101. Ibid., 222.

102. Eaton, *Grant, Lincoln, and the Freedmen*, 165; Hermann, *Pursuit of a Dream*, 48–62.

103. Berlin, *Wartime Genesis: Lower South*, 497.

104. Ibid., 47.

105. *OR*, ser. 1, 15:667.

106. Peyton McCrary, *Abraham Lincoln and Reconstruction: The Louisiana Experiment* (Princeton, N.J., 1978), 115–19, 154–55.

107. Ibid., 119–21, 154–55; Berlin, *Wartime Genesis: Lower South*, 364–66.

108. Eaton, *Grant, Lincoln, and the Freedmen*, 134; *OR*, ser. 3, 4:166–70; Berlin, *Wartime Genesis: Lower South*, 643.

109. Gerteis, *From Contraband to Freedman*, 171; Berlin, *Wartime Genesis: Upper South*, 120–21, 208–9, 214; Berlin, *Wartime Genesis: Lower South*, 24–25, 39, 70–71, 660–64.

110. Eaton, *Grant, Lincoln, and the Freedmen*, 163; Berlin, *Wartime Genesis: Lower South*, 645f.

111. Gerteis, *From Contraband to Freedman*, 170.

112. Berlin, *Wartime Genesis: Lower South*, 632.

113. Ibid., 683. Original emphasis.

114. Ibid., 632.

115. Ibid., 147–48, 633.

116. Ibid., 743–44.

117. *ALCW*, 7:54.

118. McPherson, *Political History*, 148.

119. Berlin, *Wartime Genesis: Lower South*, 66.

120. Rose, *Rehearsal for Reconstruction*, 298.

121. Ibid., 313.

122. Botume, *First Days with the Contrabands*, 169.

123. Berlin, *Wartime Genesis: Lower South*, 455.

124. Ibid., 426–27.

125. Ibid., 455.

126. Ibid., 356–58, 367.

127. Berlin, *Wartime Genesis: Upper South*, 68.

128. Berlin, *Wartime Genesis: Lower South*, 69.

129. Pearson, *Letters from Port Royal*, 275.

130. Sitterson, *Sugar Country*, 221.

131. Berlin, *Wartime Genesis: Lower South*, 52, 353.

132. Ash, *When the Yankees Came*, 167; Martha Jane Brazy, *An American Planter: Stephen Duncan of Antebellum Natchez and New York* (Baton Rouge, 2006).

133. Sitterson, *Sugar Country*, 221.

134. Berlin, *Wartime Genesis: Lower South*, 423.

135. Ibid., 761.

136. *ALCW*, 7:54–55.

137. Ibid., 7:1–2.

138. Chase, *Papers*, 4:203–4.

139. *ALCW*, 7:145, 51.

140. *OR*, ser. 3, 4:169.

141. Berlin, *Wartime Genesis: Lower South*, 638.

142. Ibid., 779. Original emphasis.

143. Ibid., 58.

Chapter Seven. Cracks in the Walls Widen

1. Gary W. Gallagher, *The Confederate War* (Cambridge, Mass., 1997), 56–57.

2. See especially Aaron Sheehan-Dean, *Why Confederates Fought: Family and Nation in Civil War Virginia* (Chapel Hill, N.C., 2007); Rubin, *Shattered Nation*; and Gary W. Gallagher, "Disaffection, Persistence,

and Nation: Some Directions in Recent Scholarship on the Confederacy," *Civil War History* 55 (2009): 329–53.

3. Bernard Nelson, "Confederate Slave Impressment Legislation, 1861–1865," *Journal of Negro History* 31 (1946): 394–400; Wiley, *Southern Negroes*, 116.

4. Thomas, *Confederate Nation*, 196; Thomas B. Alexander and Richard E. Beringer, *The Anatomy of the Confederate Congress* (Nashville, 1972), 139.

5. *Mobile Register and Advertiser*, November 6, 1863; Blair, *Virginia's Private War*, 121–22.

6. *Mobile Register and Advertiser*, November 11, 1863.

7. *Secret and Sacred: The Diaries of James Henry Hammond, a Southern Slaveholder*, ed. Carol Bleser (New York, 1988), 296–97.

8. The Alabama Department of Archives and History, in Montgomery, holds the original diary of Sarah Espy. Its text can be found online at http://files.usgwarchives.org/al/cherokee/history/espy_diary_4.txt.

9. General W. L. Walker to General Thomas Jordan, November 18, 1862, Records of Military Commands, Department of Ga., S.C., and Fla., series 12, Letters Received, W-86, RG 109, NA.

10. *OR,* ser. 4, 2:999.

11. Berlin, *Destruction of Slavery,* 778–79; *OR,* ser. 4, 3:41–42.

12. *OR,* ser. 1, vol. 331, pt. 3, 707, 712, 746. That the Richmond regime never enforced a policy of removing slaves from the path of Union armies is reflected in the urgent call by a group of Confederate governors in October 1864 to do just that. See *OR,* ser. 4, 3:735–36.

13. Berlin, *Destruction of Slavery,* 710–11; *OR,* ser. 1, vol. 28, pt. 2, 533.

14. *OR,* ser. 4, 2:421.

15. Ibid., 998.

16. *Edmondston Diary,* 529.

17. Wiley, *Southern Negroes,* 125.

18. *OR,* ser. 1, 14:915.

19. Ibid., vol. 28, pt. 2, 532.

20. Berlin, *Destruction of Slavery,* 705.

21. *Letters of Warren Akin, Confederate Congressman,* ed. Bell Irvin Wiley (Athens, Ga., 1959), 33.

22. Gary W. Gallagher, ed., *The Wilderness Campaign* (Chapel Hill, N.C., 2006), 37.

23. *Mobile Register and Advertiser,* November 6, 1863.

24. *Memphis Appeal,* November 18, 1863.

25. Toombs, Stephens, and Cobb, *Correspondence,* 629.

26. Ibid., 618–19.

27. Thomas, *Confederate Nation,* 198.

28. Escott, *After Secession,* 153; Confederate States of America, Department of the Treasury, *Documents Accompanying Report of Secretary of the Treasury,* http://www.ebooksread.com/authors-eng/confederate-states-of-america-dept-of-the-treasu/documents-accompanying-report-of-secretary-of-the-treasury-fno/page-2-documents-accompanying-report-of-secretary-of-the-treasury-fno.shtml.

29. Manning, *What This Cruel War Was Over,* 133.

30. Chandra Manning, "The Order of Nature Would be Reversed: Soldiers, Slavery, and the North Carolina Gubernatorial Election of 1864," in *North Carolinians in the Era of Civil War and Reconstruction,* ed. Paul D. Escott (Chapel Hill, N.C., 2008), 108.

31. John Christopher Schwab, *The Confederate States of America, 1861–1865* (New York, 1901), 295–96. The Confederate Congress later amended the law to allow payment in cash to substitute for payment in kind.

32. Blair, *Virginia's Private War,* 121.

33. Mark Thornton and Robert B. Ekelund, Jr., *Tariffs, Blockades, and Inflation: The Economics of the Civil War* (Wilmington, Del., 2004), 72–73.

34. Cooper, *Jefferson Davis,* 482; William C. Davis, *Jefferson Davis: The Man and His Hour,* 496.

35. Sara Agnes Rice Pryor, *Reminiscences of Peace and War* (New York, 1904), 238.

36. Thomas, *Confederate Nation,* 202–4; E. Merton Coulter, *The Confederate States of America* (Baton Rouge, 1950), 422–23; *Jones Diary,* 1:284–86; Mary Elizabeth Massey, *Ersatz in the Confederacy: Shortages and Substitutes on the Southern Homefront* (1952; reprint, Columbia, S.C., 1993), 165–66; Davis, *Jefferson Davis: A Memoir by His Wife,* 2:373–76; The quoted words come from Jefferson Davis's unfinished draft autobiography, which Varina cited frequently in her own volumes.

37. Thomas, *Confederate Nation,* 204–5; Coulter, *Confederate States of America,* 423; *Jones Diary,* 2:101.

38. *Edmondston Diary,* 378.

39. Barrett, *Civil War in North Carolina,* 166; *Edmondston Diary,* 378n; McKinney, *Zeb Vance,* 163.

40. Blair, *Virginia's Private War,* 100.

41. *Jones Diary,* 1:381, 2:48, 66–68, 90; Thomas, *Confederate Nation,* 234–35.

42. Ash, *When the Yankees Came,* 191.

43. Blair, *Virginia's Private War,* 100.

44. Bessie Martin, *A Rich Man's War, A Poor Man's Fight: Desertion of Alabama Troops from the Confederate Army* (1932; reprint, Tuscaloosa, Ala., 2003), 128, 163–65, 185; Joe A. Mobley, *Weary of War: Life on the Confederate Home Front* (Westport, Conn., 2008), 43–48; Blair, *Virginia's Private War,* 70–76, 93–104; Escott, *After Secession,* 128–29.

45. Thomas Auman, "Neighbor against Neighbor," 200; Glatthaar, *General Lee's Army,* 255–56, 302.

46. Auman, "Neighbor against Neighbor," 307–8.

47. McKinney, *Zeb Vance,* 174–77.

48. Auman, "Neighbor against Neighbor," 302–4.

49. *Vance Papers,* 2:181.

50. Auman, "Neighbor against Neighbor," 206.

51. Ibid., 213.

52. Ibid., 223.

53. Ibid., 270–71.

54. McKinney, *Zeb Vance,* 170.

55. *The Correspondence of Jonathan Worth,* ed. Joseph Grégoire de Roulhac Hamilton (Raleigh, N.C., 1909), 1:247.

56. McPherson, *Tried by War,* 171–72.

57. Rubin, *Shattered Nation,* 83.

58. Glatthaar, *General Lee's Army,* 295.

59. McKinney, *Zeb Vance,* 176.

60. *OR,* ser. 1, vol. 29, pt. 2, 710; ser. 1, vol. 51, pt. 2, 763–65, 777–78; *The Papers of William Woods Holden,* ed. Horace W. Raper and Thornton W. Mitchell (Raleigh, N.C., 2000–), 1:140–44; Barrett, *Civil War in North Carolina,* 195.

61. *OR,* ser. 1, vol. 51, pt. 2, 765.

62. Ibid., vol. 29, pt. 2, 710; vol. 51, pt. 2, 763–65, 777–78; Holden, *Papers,* 1:140–44; Barrett, *Civil War in North Carolina,* 195.

63. *OR,* ser. 1, vol. 51, pt. 2, 765.

64. Ibid., vol. 51, pt. 2, 740.

65. *Vance Papers,* 2:318–19.

66. McKinney, *Zeb Vance,* 200.

67. *OR,* ser. 1, vol. 51, pt. 2, 807.

68. Gordon B. McKinney, "Layers of Loyalty: Confederate Nationalism and Amnesty Letters from Western North Carolina," *Civil War History* (2005): 5; also McKinney, *Zeb Vance,* 261–62.

69. *OR,* ser. 1, vol. 24, pt. 3, 549.

70. The words come from a summary of that letter in *Jones Diary,* 2:16.

71. Once a Stephen Douglas supporter, he had later become an active secessionist. Eventually judging the war to be lost, however, Humphreys changed his allegiance once again. Fleming, "The Peace Movement in Alabama," *South Atlantic Quarterly* 2 (1903): 122.

72. *The New York Times,* March 24, 1864.

73. *OR,* ser. 4, 3:393–98; Georgia Lee Tatum, *Disloyalty in the Confederacy* (1934; reprint, Lincoln, Neb., 2000), 26–32, 43–44, 66–67; Walter L. Fleming, *Civil War and Reconstruction in Alabama* (New York, 1905), 15, 143, 146–47, 342–43; Fleming, "Peace Movement," 259.

74. Such was evidently the case in Georgia. See Rod Andrew, Jr., "The Essential Nationalism of the People: Georgia's Confederate Congressional Elections of 1863," in Gordon and Inscoe, *Inside the Confederate Nation,* 128–46.

75. George C. Rable, *The Confederate Republic: A Revolution against Politics* (Chapel Hill, N.C., 1994), 219.

76. James Graham Ramsey (a former Whig-unionist who owned five slaves) opposed the tax in kind, impressment, the draft, the "twenty negro" draft exemption, and the suspension of habeas corpus. Josiah Turner had resisted secession even after the firing on Fort Sumter. George W. Logan was a consistent opponent of secession who declared in 1863 that peace was "the only practical issue now before the people" and the one "upon which the election must turn." Planter James T. Leach had also opposed disunion in 1860–61 and later rejected the tax in kind, impressment, and the planter exemption. Just a few months before his elec-

tion, he publicly called for peace through reunion, provided that the southern states could retain slavery. As a Confederate congressman, he called on North Carolina to seek a separate peace with the Union on the best terms possible. Samuel H. Christian was a textile manufacturer and planter who owned more than forty slaves. Declaring the southern war effort to be hopeless, he called on the seceded states to meet in convention to consider seeking an armistice and a negotiated peace with the Union. Christian's opponent was the incumbent, Thomas S. Ashe, another onetime unionist who had metamorphosed into a firm Confederate. In the election, Christian swamped Ashe, winning almost two-thirds of all the ballots cast. See Rable, *Confederate Republic*, 97, 227, 230, 233; McKinney, *Zeb Vance*, 192; Auman, "Neighbor against Neighbor," 205, 229–31; and Joseph Grégoire de Roulhac Hamilton, *Reconstruction in North Carolina* (New York, 1914), 55.

77. Parks, *Joseph E. Brown*, 257, 269.

78. Rable, *Confederate Republic*, 216.

79. Ibid., 216–18; Steven Hahn, *The Roots of Southern Populism: Yeoman Farmers and the Transformation of the Georgia Upcountry* (New York, 1983), 130; Louise Biles Hill, *Joseph E. Brown and the Confederacy* (Chapel Hill, N.C., 1939), 137.

80. Benjamin H. Micou to Judah P. Benjamin, August 10, 1863, Confederate States of America records, Manuscript Division, LC; Robert Douthat Meade, *Judah P. Benjamin, Confederate Statesman* (New York, 1943), 66, 289.

81. Watts received three times as many votes as Shorter. Malcolm Cook McMillan, *Disintegration of a Confederate State: Three Governors and Alabama's Wartime Home Front, 1861–1865* (Macon, Ga., 1986), 55.

82. Ibid., 68–70.

83. Rable, *Confederate Republic*, 220–21; McMillan, *Disintegration of a Confederate State*, 52–55, 67–70; Malcolm C. McMillan, *Alabama Confederate Reader* (1963; reprint, Tuscaloosa, Ala., 1992), 236–37.

84. McMillan, *Disintegration of a Confederate State*, 65. Thanks to Professor Mills Thornton for information about the process by which the 1861 legislature made its decisions concerning the Confederate Senate.

85. Curry lost the election by a margin of two to one. Rable, *Confederate Republic*, 228–29; *Rise and Fall of the Confederacy: The Memoir of Senator William S. Oldham, C.S.A.*, ed. Clayton E. Jewett (Columbia, Mo., 2006), 57.

86. *OR,* ser. 4, 2:726–27.

87. Rable, *Confederate Republic,* 348n33; McMillan, *Alabama Confederate Reader,* 236, 239.

88. Fleming, "Peace Movement in Alabama," 246n. Sarah Woolfolk Wiggins, *The Scalawag in Alabama Politics, 1865–1881* (Tuscaloosa, Ala., 1977), 6; Willis Brewer, *Alabama, Her History, Resources, War Record, and Public Men: From 1540 to 1872* (Montgomery, Ala., 1872), 286–87; Wilfred Buck Yearns, *The Confederate Congress* (Athens, Ga., 1960), 251n.

89. Benjamin H. Micou to Judah P. Benjamin, August 10, 1863, Confederate States of America records, Manuscript Division, LC; Meade, *Judah P. Benjamin,* 66, 289.

90. *Kean Diary,* 177; Alexander and Beringer, *Anatomy of the Confederate Congress,* 133, 163, 336–37.

91. Ella Lonn, *Desertion during the Civil War* (1928; reprint, Lincoln, Neb., 1998), 29; *American Annual Cyclopedia and Register of Important Events of the Year 1863* (New York, 1864), 18–19.

92. Drew Faust, "Altars of Sacrifice: Confederate Women and the Narratives of War," *Journal of American History* 76 (1990): 1200–28.

93. *Mobile Register and Advertiser,* November 21, 1963.

94. Peter S. Carmichael, *The Last Generation: Young Virginians in Peace, War, and Reunion* (Chapel Hill, N.C., 2005), 154–61; Gallagher, *Confederate War,* 31–32; Lonn, *Desertion during the Civil War,* 232.

95. Glatthaar, *General Lee's Army,* 412.

96. Martin, *Rich Man's War,* 126–27.

97. *OR,* ser. 1, vol. 25, pt. 2, 814; Auman, "Neighbor against Neighbor," 196.

98. Wiley, *Southern Negroes,* 49.

99. The quoted words are a paraphrase of Caperton's message that War Department clerk John B. Jones confided to his diary. *Jones Diary,* 2:30.

100. Blair, *Virginia's Private War,* 59.

101. *OR,* ser. 4, 2:786.

102. Bryan, *Confederate Georgia,* 144–46.

103. Martin, *Rich Man's War,* 114.

104. Bryan, *Confederate Georgia,* 147.

105. Hahn, *Roots of Southern Populism,* 131.

106. Martin, *Rich Man's War*, 114.

107. Victoria Bynum, *The Free State of Jones: Mississippi's Longest Civil War* (Chapel Hill, N.C., 2001), 100, 103.

108. Ibid., 84, 98–99, 104.

109. Ibid., 106–8.

110. *OR*, ser. 1, vol. 32, pt. 3, 711–14.

111. Ibid., vol. 32, pt. 3, 662–63.

112. Bynum, *Free State of Jones*, 124.

113. William T. Auman and David D. Scarboro, "The Heroes of America in Civil War North Carolina," *North Carolina Historical Review* 58 (1981): 327, 350–51; *OR*, ser. 1, vol. 51, pt. 2, 840, 881; 33:1303.

114. Auman, "Neighbor against Neighbor," 125–27, 151, 154–56, 163, 168–69; *Vance Papers*, 1:386, 393, 398–99, 445.

115. *OR*, ser. 4, 2:783–85.

116. Auman, "Neighbor against Neighbor," 238.

117. *OR*, ser. 4, 2:674, 731–34; *Vance Papers*, 2:249–55.

118. Barrett, *Civil War in North Carolina*, 192–94.

119. Auman, "Neighbor against Neighbor," 290–91.

120. Lisa Laskin, " 'The Army Is Not Near So Much Demoralized as the Country Is': Soldiers in the Army of Northern Virginia and the Confederate Home Front," in *The View from the Ground: Experiences of Civil War Soldiers*, ed. Aaron Sheehan-Dean (Lexington, Ky., 2007), 91–120.

121. Bryan, *Confederate Georgia*, 149–50.

122. Daniel, *Soldiering in the Army of Tennessee*, 137.

123. McKinney, *Zeb Vance*, 176–77.

124. Manning, "Order of Nature Would Be Reversed," 108.

125. *OR*, ser. 1, vol. 26, pt. 2, 550.

126. Ibid.

127. Ibid., 548–58.

128. Martin, *Rich Man's War*, 117.

129. *Vance Papers*, 2:318–19.

130. Ash, *When the Yankees Came*, 128; Current, *Lincoln's Loyalists*, 213–18.

131. *Edmondston Diary*, 242–43. Edmondston seemed quite unaware that her words implicitly conceded the existence of big pockets of poverty in the Confederacy.

Chapter Eight. A Ray of Light Shines Briefly through the Rafters

1. Donald Bruce Johnson, comp., *National Party Platforms,* rev. ed. (Urbana, Ill., 1978), 1:35–36.

2. Eric Foner, *The Fiery Trial: Abraham Lincoln and American Slavery* (New York, 2010), 293.

3. Ibid., 290–94; Michael Vorenberg, *Final Freedom: The Civil War, the Abolition of Slavery, and the Thirteenth Amendment* (Cambridge, UK, 2001), 94–102, 137–38; McPherson, *Struggle for Equality,* 125–27.

4. Foner, *Fiery Trial,* 274–79.

5. *ALCW,* 7:380, 435, 440–42, 451; McPherson, *Tried by War,* 234–35.

6. *ALCW,* 7:410.

7. *Proceedings of the National Convention of Colored Men Held in the City of Syracuse, N. Y., October 4, 5, 6, and 7, 1864; with the Bill of Wrongs and Rights, and the Address to the American People* (Boston, 1864).

8. *ALCW,* 7:243. Lincoln's recommendation was ignored.

9. Albert Castel, *Decision in the West: The Atlanta Campaign of 1864* (Lawrence, Kans., 1995), 26.

10. *OR,* ser. 1, vol. 38, pt. 1, 1–2.

11. McPherson, *Tried by War,* 209–14.

12. Castel, *Decision in the West,* 111, 350; McPherson, *Tried by War,* 213–14.

13. McPherson, *Tried by War,* 219.

14. *OR,* ser. 1, vol. 29, pt. 2, 859.

15. Gallagher, *Confederate War,* 39.

16. Castel, *Decision in the West,* 365, 453.

17. Ibid., 479.

18. Ibid., 321.

19. Ibid., 327.

20. Mark Grimsley, *And Keep Moving On: The Virginia Campaign, May–June 1864* (Lincoln, Neb., 2002), 224.

21. McKinney, *Zeb Vance,* 215, 229; Auman, "Neighbor against Neighbor," 334–35.

22. McKinney, *Zeb Vance,* 217–22; Manning, "Order of Nature Would Be Reversed," 101–28.

23. Rubin, *Shattered Nation,* 34.

24. Castel, *Decision in the West*, 479.

25. Redkey, *A Grand Army of Black Men*, 111.

26. John S. Wise, *The End of an Era* (Boston, 1899), 366.

27. Confederate artillery officer Edward Porter Alexander confirmed all this in his memoirs: "Some of the Negro prisoners who were originally allowed to surrender by some soldiers, were afterward shot by others, & there was, without doubt, a great deal of unnecessary killing of them." Alexander, *Military Memoirs*, 462; James I. Robertson, ed., " 'The Boy Artillerist': Letters of Colonel William Pegram, C.S.A.," *Virginia Magazine of History and Biography* 98 (1990): 243; Bryce A. Suderow, "The Battle of the Crater," in Urwin, *Black Flag over Dixie*, 203–9. An officer in the Ninth Alabama regiment was embarrassed to admit that his men "took some of the negroes prisoner." But he firmly denied this proved his men too easygoing, considering "the numbers we had already slain." George S. Burkhardt, *Confederate Rage, Yankee Wrath: No Quarter in the Civil War* (Carbondale, Ill., 2007), 159–74.

28. Castel, *Decision in the West*, 476.

29. Ibid., 444–45.

30. Johnson, *National Party Platforms*, 1:34–35.

31. Schott, *Alexander H. Stephens of Georgia*, 425. Robert E. Lee had expressed a similar view a year earlier. Lee to Davis, June 10, 1863, in Dowdey, *Wartime Papers of R. E. Lee*, 507–9.

32. *ALCW*, 7:514.

33. Glyndon Van Deusen, *William Henry Seward* (New York, 1967), 306.

34. *ALCW*, 7:500.

35. Bryan, *Confederate Georgia*, 159.

36. Castel, *Decision in the West*, 483.

37. Ibid., 389, 527.

38. Myers, *Children of Pride*, 1203.

39. *Mary Chesnut's Civil War*, 645.

40. *PJD*, 11:58–60.

41. William C. Davis, *Jefferson Davis: The Man and His Hour*, 565–67; *Jefferson Davis, Constitutionalist*, 6:341–42.

42. Cooper, *Jefferson Davis, American*, 525–26.

43. Faust, *Mothers of Invention*, 244.

44. *Mary Chesnut's Civil War*, 694.

45. Sallie A. Brock Putnam, *Richmond during the War: Four Years of Personal Observation* (Lincoln, Neb., 1997), 345.

46. Sara Agnes Rice Pryor, *Reminiscences of Peace and War,* rev. ed. (New York, 1905), 325.

47. Faust, *Mothers of Invention,* 244.

48. Pryor, *Reminiscences of Peace and War,* 326.

49. Stone, *Brokenburn,* 293.

50. Castel, *Decision in the West,* 543.

51. Glatthaar, *General Lee's Army,* 429–33.

52. According to Michael Vorenberg, by this point even Democratic Party leaders recognized that taking "a proslavery position meant political suicide" for them. Vorenberg, *Final Freedom,* 165.

53. *Papers Relating to Foreign Affairs, Accompanying the Annual Message of the President to the Second Session Thirty-Eighth Congress,* pt. 2 (Washington, 1865), 368.

54. *Gorgas Journals,* 139; J. Tracy Power, *Lee's Miserables: Life in the Army of Northern Virginia from the Wilderness to Appomattox* (Chapel Hill, N.C., 1998), 218–19.

55. William T. Sherman, *Memoirs* (New York, 1875), 2:152.

56. Ibid., 179.

57. According to one estimate, only a third of Georgia's military-age white men were under arms by October. Bryan, *Confederate Georgia,* 150.

58. F. Kendall to Jefferson Davis, September 16, 1864, K-73-1864, WD/LR, RG 109, NA. Original emphasis.

59. *OR,* ser. 1, vol. 38, pt. 5, 299.

60. Governor Joseph E. Brown, message to the General Assembly of Ga., March 10, 1864, in *The Confederate Records of the State of Georgia,* ed. Allen D. Candler (Athens, Ga., 1909), 2:594–95.

61. Joseph P. Reidy, *From Slavery to Agrarian Capitalism in the Cotton Plantation South: Central Georgia, 1800–1880* (Chapel Hill, N.C., 1992), 128–35.

62. Sherman, *Sherman's Civil War,* 794; Clarence L. Mohr, *On the Threshold of Freedom: Masters and Slaves in Civil War Georgia* (Athens, Ga., 1986), 95.

63. John E. Marszalek, *Sherman: A Soldier's Passion for Order* (New York, 1993), 45–46.

64. Sherman, *Sherman's Civil War*, 293.

65. Clarence L. Mohr, "The Atlanta Campaign and the African American Experience in Civil War Georgia," in Gordon and Inscoe, *Inside the Confederate Nation*, 280–81.

66. Joseph T. Glatthaar, *The March to the Sea and Beyond: Sherman's Troops in the Savannah and Carolina Campaigns* (New York, 1985), 63.

67. *OR*, ser. 1, vol. 38, pt. 5, 136–37, 210; ser. 3, 4:433–34, 454–55; *ALCW*, 7:448–49.

68. Sherman, *Sherman's Civil War*, 454.

69. Ibid., 700.

70. Ibid., 454.

71. Sherman "like[d] niggers *well enough* as niggers," but to make them equal to whites would encourage intermarriage, the doleful results of which he thought were on display for all to see in "the Mixed race in Mexico and South America." If truth be told, for that matter, blacks were not even "qualified for utter and complete freedom." Before they would be, they should first "pass through a probationary state." Sherman evidently had in mind the kind of subordinate caste status imposed upon technically free blacks in the prewar South as well as many parts of the North. But if the Union were to arm black men now, Sherman fretted, they would afterward reject the probationary stage. "If negroes are to fight," he told the secretary of war, they will "not be content with sliding back into the status of slave or free negro." *OR*, ser. 1, vol. 39, pt. 2, 132; Sherman, *Sherman's Civil War*, 727–28, 740.

72. Nathaniel Cheairs Hughes, Jr., and Gordon D. Whitney, *Jefferson Davis in Blue: The Life of Sherman's Relentless Warrior* (Baton Rouge, 2006), 308–14; Glatthaar, *March to the Sea and Beyond*, 64.

73. Bryan, *Confederate Georgia*, 128; Jacqueline Jones, *Saving Savannah: The City and the Civil War* (New York, 2008), 202.

74. Glatthaar, *March to the Sea and Beyond*, 54–58.

75. Clarke, *Dwelling Place*, 440.

76. Mohr, "Atlanta Campaign," 283.

77. Mohr, *On the Threshold of Freedom*, 111.

78. Castel, *Decision in the West*, 549.

79. George W. Pepper, *Personal Recollections of Sherman's Campaigns in Georgia and the Carolinas* (Zanesville, Ohio, 1866), 248.

80. *Thomas Diary*, 247.

81. Ibid., 249.

82. Pepper, *Personal Recollections*, 172.

83. Hitchcock, *Marching with Sherman*, 122–23.

84. Harry W. Slocum, "Sherman's March from Savannah to Bentonville," *Battles and Leaders*, 4:688–690.

85. Botume, *First Days amongst the Contrabands*, 169.

86. Glatthaar, *March to the Sea and Beyond*, 61.

87. Sherman, *Memoirs*, 2:180–81.

88. Berlin, *Wartime Genesis: Lower South*, 2:331–38.

89. Marszalek, *Sherman*, 313; Benjamin P. Thomas and Harold Hyman, *Stanton: The Life and Times of Lincoln's Secretary of War* (New York, 1962), 343; *OR*, ser. 1, vol. 39, pt. 3, 428.

90. *OR*, ser. 1, 44:836–37.

91. Thomas and Hyman, *Stanton*, 343–44.

92. Josef C. James, "Sherman at Savannah," *Journal of Negro History* 39 (1954): 127–37; *Autobiography of Oliver Otis Howard* (New York, 1907), 189; Berlin, *Wartime Genesis: Lower South*, vol. 2, 331–38.

93. George Ward Nichols, *The Story of the Great March from the Diary of a Staff Officer* (New York, 1865), 102.

94. Berlin, *Wartime Genesis: Lower South*, 331–38.

95. Marszalek, *Sherman*, 314–15.

96. The testimony of General Rufus Saxton, in *Report of the Joint Committee on Reconstruction* (Washington, D.C., 1866), pt. 2, 221; *ALCW*, 7:54–55.

97. Allston, *South Carolina Rice Plantation*, 199–200, 291–92, 292–93.

98. Ibid., 310.

99. Kerby, *Kirby Smith's Confederacy*, 255.

100. Ibid., 168, 371.

101. *Galveston Tri-Weekly News*, December 30, 1864.

102. *Ruffin Diary*, 3:692.

103. Myers, *Children of Pride*, 1244.

104. *Mary Chesnut's Civil War*, 694.

105. *Jefferson Davis, Constitutionalist*, 6:341–43.

106. *PJD*, 11:66n.

107. Power, *Lee's Miserables*, 228.

108. Glatthaar, *General Lee's Army*, 415, 440; Power, *Lee's Miserables*, 212, 227.

109. Kerby, *Kirby Smith's Confederacy*, 398–99.

110. Auman, "Neighbor against Neighbor," 325–27.

111. Ibid., 347, 377–79.

112. Ibid., 372.

113. Ibid., 375–80.

114. McKinney, *Zeb Vance*, 236; Auman, "Neighbor against Neighbor," 385–409.

115. *OR*, ser. 1, 53:391.

116. Wiley, *Plain People of the Confederacy*, 67.

117. *Macon Telegraph and Confederate*, November 5, December 13, 1864; Bryan, *Confederate Georgia*, 171.

118. *Thomas Diary*, 252.

119. *OR*, ser. 4, 3:707, 710.

120. Glatthaar, *General Lee's Army*, 409.

121. Anonymous to Jefferson Davis, September 16, 1864, A-198-1864, WD/LR, RG 109, NA. See also Anonymous to Secretary of War, November 17, 1865 [misfiled: probably 1864], A-7-1865, WD/LR, RG 109, NA.

122. Anonymous to Secretary of War, November 17, 1865, A-7-1865, WD/LR, RG 109, NA.

123. W. A. Chrica, Kingston, S.C., to Seddon, n.d., but marked received October 18, 1864, WD/LR, C-534, RG 109, NA.

124. Cornelia Peake McDonald, *A Woman's Civil War: A Diary with Reminiscences of the War from March 1862* (Madison, Wis., 1992), 224.

125. *OR*, ser. 4, 3:354.

Chapter Nine. Feeling the Timbers Shudder

1. Harrison Anthony Trexler, *Slavery in Missouri, 1804–1865* (Baltimore, 1914), 208–33; Cimprich, *Slavery's End in Tennessee*, 116; Foner, *Fiery Trial*, 278–80; Vorenberg, *Final Freedom*, 171–72.

2. *Jefferson Davis, Constitutionalist*, 6:384–87.

3. *Richmond Examiner,* January 28, 1865.

4. Ibid., February 1, 1865.

5. *OR,* ser. 4, 3:707, 710.

6. Toombs, Stephens, and Cobb, *Correspondence,* 661.

7. *Mary Chesnut's Civil War,* 645.

8. *OR,* ser. 1, 53:392.

9. Colonel Geo. W. Guess to Mrs. Sarah H. Cockrell, January 5, 1865, George W. Guess Letters, Mss. 793, Louisiana and Lower Mississippi Valley Collection, Special Collections, Louisiana State University Libraries.

10. Litwack, *Been in the Storm So Long,* 126.

11. *Green Mount, A Virginia Plantation Family during the Civil War: Being the Journal of Benjamin Robert Fleet and Letters of His Family,* ed. Betsy Fleet and John D. P. Fuller (Lexington, Ky., 1962), 349; Craig M. Simpson, *A Good Southerner: The Life of Henry A. Wise of Virginia* (Chapel Hill, N.C., 1985), 281.

12. *Macon Telegraph and Confederate,* January 5, 1865.

13. Akin, *Letters,* 117.

14. *Galveston Tri-Weekly News,* February 5, 1865.

15. *Jefferson Davis, Constitutionalist,* 11:394–97.

16. See chapter 2, 44.

17. *OR,* ser. 2, 3:653.

18. Ibid., ser. 4, 3:1160.

19. Thomas Donaldson, Notes of a Conversation with Duncan Farrar Kenner, New York City, October 19, 1882, Duncan Farrar Kenner Collection, Manuscript Division, LC; Craig A. Bauer, *A Leader among Peers: The Life and Times of Duncan Farrar Kenner* (Lafayette, La., 1993), 216–35; Frank Lawrence Owsley, *King Cotton Diplomacy: Foreign Relations of the Confederate States of America* ([Chicago], 1959), 532–34.

20. Richardson, *Compilation of the Messages and Papers,* 2:694–97; William Wirt Henry, "Kenner's Mission to Europe," *William and Mary Quarterly* 25 (1916), 9–12.

21. For the same reason, Kenner's mission began in strict secrecy. But word of its existence soon leaked out. And when John Forsyth, the editor of the *Mobile Register and Advertiser,* wrote Davis to urge such a diplo-

matic overture, the president tipped his hand. "You will appreciate the obligation of reticence imposed upon me in these matters," he replied in late February, but he could "perceive no discordance" between them about the suggestion and even asked the editor's help in preparing public opinion for it. *Richmond Dispatch,* December 30, 1864; Howard Jones, *Blue and Gray Diplomacy: A History of Union and Confederate Foreign Relations* (Chapel Hill, N.C., 2010), 318; *PJD,* 11:266, 413.

22. Richardson, *Compilation of the Messages and Papers,* 233–37; Owsley, *King Cotton Diplomacy,* 536–41.

23. *Richmond Dispatch,* February 6, 1865.

24. If the Confederate leader had really expected Lincoln to modify that stance at the forthcoming meeting, he would surely have sent to it men he agreed with and trusted, not three who were all by then identified with Richmond's own peace faction.

25. Allen C. Guelzo, *Abraham Lincoln: Redeemer President* (Grand Rapids, Mich., 1999), 400–401; Foner, *Fiery Trial,* 310–14.

26. Cooper, *Jefferson Davis, American,* 550–51; McPherson, *Battle Cry of Freedom,* 822–23; *ALCW,* 8:279; Grant, *Personal Memoirs,* 2:591.

27. McPherson, *Political History,* 571.

28. *Richmond Enquirer,* February 9, 1865.

29. Ernest B. Furguson, *Ashes of Glory: Richmond at War* (New York, 1996), 292.

30. *Richmond Sentinel,* February 22, 1865.

31. Sheehan-Dean, *Why Confederates Fought,* 184.

32. Edward A. Pollard, *Life of Jefferson Davis* (Philadelphia, [1869]), 473.

33. Putnam, *Richmond during the War,* 350.

34. North Carolina General Assembly, *Resolutions against the Policy of Arming Slaves* (Richmond, Va., 1865). The resolutions were ratified on February 3, 1865.

35. Furguson, *Ashes of Glory,* 308.

36. *The Charleston Mercury,* January 26, 1865.

37. *Macon Telegraph and Confederate,* October 29, 1864.

38. *Richmond Whig,* November 12, 1864.

39. *The Charleston Mercury,* November 19, 1864.

40. *Macon Telegraph and Confederate,* January 6, 1865.

41. McKinney, *Zeb Vance,* 237–38.

42. *Richmond Sentinel*, November 24, 1864.

43. *Richmond Enquirer*, January 12, 1865.

44. *Macon Daily Telegraph and Confederate*, January 6, 1865.

45. Letter, signed "H.," *Galveston Tri-Weekly News*, February 13, 1865.

46. *Richmond Sentinel*, December 28, 1864.

47. *OR*, ser. 1, vol. 52, pt. 2, 591.

48. A. S. Colyar to Colonel A. S. Marks, January 30, 1864, in "General Cleburne's Views on Slavery," *The Annals of the Army of Tennessee and Early Western History* 1 (1978): 50–52.

49. *OR* ser. 4, 3:959–60. Emphasis added.

50. *Richmond Examiner*, February 25, 1865.

51. *Lynchburg Virginian*, February 18, March 24, 1865.

52. *Jones Diary*, 2:353–54.

53. *The Daily Confederate*, April 5, 1865.

54. *Richmond Sentinel*, January 4, 1865.

55. *Jones Diary*, 2:353–54.

56. Confederate States of America, House of Representatives, Select Committee on Increase of Military Force, Mr. Rogers' Minority Report (Richmond, Va., 1865).

57. *The Charleston Mercury*, January 13, 1865.

58. *Mary Chesnut's Civil War*, 696.

59. *Richmond Whig*, November 8, 1864.

60. *OR*, ser. 4, 3:798.

61. Robert E. Lee to John C. Breckinridge, March 14, 1865, Army of Northern Virginia Headquarters Papers, Robert E. Lee Papers, VHS.

62. Lee to Barksdale, February 18, 1865, as published in the *Richmond Sentinel*, February 23, 1865.

63. *Richmond Enquirer*, November 12, 1864.

64. Frank Vandiver, "Proceedings of the Second Confederate Congress," Southern Historical Society Papers (SHSP), n.s., 52:329.

65. Ibid., 52:330.

66. The Virginia legislature also overrode state laws that forbade black people to bear arms. *OR*, ser. 1, vol. 51, pt. 2, 1068; vol. 46, pt. 3, 1315.

67. Vandiver, "Proceedings of the Second Confederate Congress," SHSP, 52:464–65.

68. Ibid., 52:470; *PJD*, 11:460.

69. *OR*, ser. 4, 3:1161–62.

70. Ibid., 3:1193–94, 1144; *Lynchburg Virginian*, March 18, 1865. Evidently no recruiters were sent to North Carolina, perhaps because its legislature had so firmly rejected the whole idea.

71. *Richmond Examiner*, March 9, 1865.

72. *OR*, ser. 1, vol. 46, pt. 2, 1237–38.

73. *Richmond Examiner*, March 21, 1865; *Richmond Dispatch*, March 22 and 24, 1865; *Lynchburg Virginian*, March 23, 1865.

74. *Richmond Examiner*, March 22, 1865; *Lynchburg Virginian*, March 24, 1865.

75. *Richmond Examiner*, March 27, 1865; *Richmond Whig*, April 29, 1865; *Richmond Times-Dispatch*, April 30, 1910; *OR*, ser. 2, 6:852–53.

76. Richard L. Maury Diary, entry for March 23, 1865, Manuscript Division, VHS; Nelson Lankford, *Richmond Burning: The Last Days of the Confederate Capital* (New York, 2002), 34; Pollard, *Life of Jefferson Davis*, 456; Richard S. Ewell to L. C. [Lizinka Campbell Brown] Ewell, May 12, 1865, Brown-Ewell Family Papers, Filson Historical Society.

77. Thomas Hughes, *A Boy's Experience in the Civil War, 1860–1865* (Baltimore, 1904), 12–13.

78. Pollard, *Life of Jefferson Davis*, 456.

79. *Macon Telegraph and Confederate*, November 2, 1864.

80. *Graham Papers*, 6:274.

81. Ibid., 6:284.

82. North Carolina General Assembly, *Resolutions Against the Policy of Arming Slaves* (Richmond, Va. 1865).

83. *Edmondston Diary*, 653.

84. *Lynchburg Virginian*, March 16, 1865.

85. *Richmond Enquirer*, January 28, 1865.

86. *Jones Diary*, 2:416.

87. *Kean Diary*, 183.

88. *Graham Papers*, 6:216.

89. Putnam, *Richmond during the War*, 350; *Kean Diary*, 202–3.

90. *Graham Papers*, 6:46.

91. Ibid., 6:224–25.

92. Ibid.

93. *Kean Diary,* 194–98.

94. As Hunter detailed in 1870, he had heard the same things at Hampton Roads that Campbell and Stephens did. Even if surrender and abolition were "inevitable," he had therefore wondered, wasn't it "worth the effort to save as much as possible from the wreck?" He believed that the South should explore further the terms of reunion. Surely the North, for its own reasons, would strive "to make them as tolerable as possible." But when Hunter expressed this opinion to Jefferson Davis following the Hampton Roads conference, Davis stonewalled him. Hunter then (unlike Campbell and Stephens) agreed to help the Confederate president prepare the public to continue the war. See Hunter's 1870 letter to James M. Mason, published in Virginia Mason, ed., *The Public Life and Diplomatic Correspondence of James M. Mason, with Some Personal History* (New York, 1906), 596. The former jurist John A. Campbell appended his own opinion that the U.S. Constitution gave its president the power to grant amnesties, and such amnesties would likely secure those who received them in their landed property and even nullify the sales of confiscated real estate that had already taken place. *Graham Papers,* 6:255.

95. *Graham Papers,* 6:232.

96. Worth, *Correspondence,* 1:373.

97. *Richmond Enquirer,* February 25, 1865.

98. Ibid.

99. James Austin Connolly, "Major Connolly's Letters to His Wife, 1862–1865," *Transactions of the Illinois State Historical Society* 35 (1928): 379.

100. Nichols, *Story of the Great March,* 161.

101. *OR,* ser. 1, 14:523–24.

102. Wilbert L. Jenkins, *Seizing the New Day: African Americans in Post–Civil War Charleston* (Bloomington, Ind., 2003), 31.

103. Dorothy Sterling, ed., *The Trouble They Seen: Black People Tell the Story of Reconstruction* (Garden City, N.Y., 1976), 2–3.

104. Dusinberre, *Them Dark Days,* 375.

105. Allston, *South Carolina Rice Plantation,* 206–7.

106. Ibid., 210.

107. Rev. L. S. Burkhead, "History of the Difficulties of the Pastorate of the

Front Street Methodist Church, Wilmington, N. C., for the Year 1865," in *Historical Papers of the Trinity College Historical Society* (Durham, N.C., 1900): 41–43.

108. John G. Barrett, *Sherman's March through the Carolinas* (Chapel Hill, N.C., 1996), 137n; Jacqueline Glass Campbell, *When Sherman Marched North from the Sea: Resistance on the Confederate Home Front* (Chapel Hill, N.C., 2003), 85–86.

109. David P. Conyngham, *Sherman's March through the South* (New York, 1865), 355.

110. Campbell, *When Sherman Marched North from the Sea*, 86.

111. Rawick, *American Slave: Composite Autobiography*, vol. 14, parts 1 and 2, 270–71.

112. Ibid., 96–97.

113. Campbell, *When Sherman Marched North*, 86.

114. Hitchcock, *Marching with Sherman*, 128.

115. Nichols, *The Story of the Great March*, 237–38.

116. *Southern Confederacy*, January 20, 1865.

117. *Mary Chesnut's Civil War*, 678–79.

118. Glatthaar, *March to the Sea and Beyond*, 12–13, 169, 172.

119. Glatthaar, *General Lee's Army*, 451.

120. Martin, *Rich Man's War*, 233.

121. Power, *Lee's Miserables*, 261.

122. Lee, *Wartime Papers*, 938–39.

123. *OR*, ser. 1, vol. 46, pt. 2, 1254.

Chapter Ten. And the Walls Gave Way: Richmond, Appomattox, and After

1. Grant, *Personal Memoirs*, 592.

2. Furguson, *Ashes of Glory*, 286.

3. Bruce Catton, *Grant Takes Command* (Boston, 1969), 296–301.

4. Wilson Greene, *The Final Battles of the Petersburg Campaign: Breaking the Backbone of the Rebellion* (Knoxville, Tenn., 2008), 106.

5. Lee, *Wartime Papers*, 912.

6. Greene, *Final Battles*, 125.

7. Furguson, *Ashes of Glory*, 312.

8. Brooks D. Simpson, "Facilitating Defeat: The Union High Command and the Collapse of the Confederacy," in *The Collapse of the Confederacy*, ed. Mark Grimsley and Brooks D. Simpson (Lincoln, Neb., 2001), 93–95; Greene, *Final Battles*, 112–141.

9. *Personal Memoirs of P. H. Sheridan* (New York, 1888), 2:165.

10. Greene, *Final Battles*, 348.

11. Lee, *Wartime Papers*, 938–39.

12. *Kean Diary*, 205.

13. William C. Davis, *An Honorable Defeat: The Last Days of the Confederate Government* (New York, 2001), 57.

14. Putnam, *Richmond during the War*, 366.

15. Ibid., 364.

16. *"Our Women in the War": The Lives They Lived; The Deaths They Died* (Charleston, S.C., 1885), 100.

17. Stephen R. Mallory, "Last Days of the Confederate Government," *McClure's Magazine* 16 (1900): 101–2.

18. *Thomas Morris Chester Black Civil War Correspondent: His Dispatches from the Virginia Front*, ed. R.J.M. Blackett (New York, 1991), 292.

19. Ibid., 314.

20. Greene, *Final Battles*, 344.

21. Furguson, *Ashes of Glory*, 325.

22. Putnam, *Richmond during the War*, 363.

23. C. C. Coffin, "Late Scenes in Richmond," *Atlantic Monthly* 15 (1865): 751–52.

24. Blackett, *Thomas Morris Chester*, 289.

25. Putnam, *Richmond during the War*, 367.

26. Greene, *Final Battles*, 355.

27. Noah Andre Trudeau, *Like Men of War: Black Troops in the Civil War, 1862–1865* (Boston, 1998), 428.

28. Blackett, *Thomas Morris Chester*, 290.

29. Greene, *Final Battles*, 355–56.

30. Furguson, *Ashes of Glory*, 338.

31. Ibid., 336.

32. Douglas Southall Freeman, ed., *A Calendar of Confederate Papers, with a*

Bibliography of Some Confederate Publications (Richmond, Va., 1908), 251–52.

33. Redkey, *Grand Army of Black Men*, 175. Emphasis added.

34. Ibid., 175–78. Emphasis added.

35. Litwack, *Been in the Storm So Long*, 183.

36. McPherson, *Tried by War*, 261.

37. Coffin, "Late Scenes in Richmond," 753–55.

38. *ALCW*, 8:389.

39. *OR*, ser. 1, vol. 46, pt. 3, 656.

40. To impress General Weitzel with the importance of permitting this to happen, Campbell warned him—contrary to what he knew to be true—that while "the armies of the Confederacy are diminished in point of numbers . . . the spirit of the people is not broken and the resources of the country allow of a prolonged and embarrassing resistance." *OR*, ser. 1, vol. 46, pt. 3, 656–57.

41. *ALCW*, 8:406–7.

42. Chester, *Thomas Morris Chester*, 300.

43. Edward A. Pollard, *Southern History of the War* (1866; reprint, New York, 1990), 2:507–8.

44. Thomas, *Robert E. Lee*, 358–59; Sheridan, *Memoirs*, 2:180–84.

45. Thomas, *Robert E. Lee*, 358.

46. *OR*, ser. 1, vol. 34, pt. 1, 54–55; Davis, *Honorable Defeat*, 108.

47. Over the next few days, a total of some twenty-six thousand Confederate soldiers straggled into Appomattox to accept the parole. Lee, *Wartime Papers*, 937–38; Glatthaar, *General Lee's Army*, 470.

48. *OR*, ser. 1, vol. 34, pt. 1, 56.

49. *Jefferson Davis, Constitutionalist*, 6:530.

50. Mallory, "Last Days," 106–7.

51. Ibid., 240.

52. Lee, *Wartime Papers*, 936.

53. *Jefferson Davis, Constitutionalist*, 8:535–39.

54. Joseph E. Johnston, *Narrative of Military Operations* (New York, 1874), 400.

55. *OR*, ser. 1, vol. 47, pt. 3, 178; Barrett, *Civil War in North Carolina*, 373.

56. Johnston, *Narrative of Military Operations*, 401.

57. Ibid., 405–7.

58. Ibid.

59. Simpson and Berlin, *Sherman's Civil War*, 864.

60. *OR*, ser. 1, vol. 47, pt. 3, 266.

61. Ibid., 832–33.

62. Ibid., 823–24.

63. Ibid., 828.

64. Ibid., 294; *Welles Diary*, 2:294–96.

65. *OR*, ser. 1, vol. 47, pt. 3, 835–38.

66. Kerby, *Kirby Smith's Confederacy*, 398–400, 410, 414.

67. Davis, *Honorable Defeat*, 221.

68. *PJD*, 11:580.

69. Davis, *Honorable Defeat*, 214, 248–54, 278.

70. *OR*, ser. 1, vol. 48, pt. 1, 190–91. Unable to attend the letter's signing, the governor of Texas expressed his endorsement through a representative.

71. Kerby, *Kirby Smith's Confederacy*, 418.

72. Ibid., 421.

73. Ibid., 419–26.

Conclusion: "We Should Rejoice"

1. William J. Cooper and Thomas E. Terrill, *The American South: A History* (Lanham, Md., 2009), 411; J. David Hacker, "A Census-Based Count of the Civil War Dead," *Civil War History* 57 (2011): 306–47.

2. *ALCW*, 8:332–33.

3. Lincoln, speech in Peoria, Ill., October 16, 1854, *ALCW*, 2:276.

4. Douglass, *Life and Times*, 373.

5. Douglass, *Life and Writings*, 4:200.

6. Hitchcock, *Marching with Sherman*, 71. Original emphasis.

7. *ALCW*, 8:332–33.

8. McPherson, *Struggle for Equality*, 227–30; Leslie A. Schwalm, *Emancipation's Diaspora: Race and Reconstruction in the Upper Midwest* (Chapel Hill, N.C., 2009), 104; Arthur Charles Cole, *The Era of the Civil War*

(1919; reprint, Urbana, Ill., 1987), 388; Eric Foner, *Reconstruction: America's Unfinished Revolution* (New York, 1988), 28.

9. *Richmond Whig,* November 26, 1864.

10. Letter in the *Galveston Tri-Weekly News,* February 22, 1865.

11. Eliza Frances Andrews, *The War-Time Journal of a Georgia Girl, 1864–1865* (New York, 1908), 198.

12. *Mary Chesnut's Civil War,* 735.

13. Wayne, *Reshaping of Plantation Society,* 39.

14. *Edmondston Diary,* 712–13.

15. John Leyburn, "An Interview with Gen. Robert E. Lee," *Century Magazine,* May 1885, 166–67; Alan T. Nolan, *Lee Considered: General Robert E. Lee and Civil War History* (Chapel Hill, N.C., 1991), 24–25; and Myrta Lockett Avary, *Dixie after the War: An Exposition of Social Conditions Existing in the South, during the Twelve Years Succeeding the Fall of Richmond* (New York, 1906), 72.

16. *Kean Diary,* 208, 210.

17. *Thomas Diary,* 275.

18. Davis, *Jefferson Davis: A Memoir,* 2:215.

19. Stone, *Brokenburn,* 8, 340–41.

20. *Ruffin Diary,* 3:895, 950.

21. *Richmond Dispatch,* March 21, 1865.

22. *PJD,* 11:229.

23. *Edmondston Diary,* 712.

24. Rhett, *Fire-Eater Remembers,* 88.

25. Putnam, *Richmond during the War,* 344.

26. *Graham Papers,* 6:289–91.

27. *Macon Telegraph and Confederate,* March 22, 1865.

28. Scarborough, *Masters of the Big House,* 344.

29. *Thomas Diary,* 268–69.

30. *ALCW,* 8:403.

31. Burlingame, *Abraham Lincoln,* 2:803.

32. Putnam, *Richmond during the War,* 381.

33. Stone, *Brokenburn,* 333, 341.

34. *Edmondston Diary,* 702–3.

35. *Ruffin Diary,* 3:852–53.

36. Phillips, *Diehard Rebels,* 174; Scarborough, *Masters of the Big House,* 372.

37. Sarah Morgan Dawson, *A Confederate Girl's Diary* (Boston, 1913), 436.

38. Roark, *Masters without Slaves,* 121.

39. Furguson, *Ashes of Glory,* 364.

40. Toombs, Stephens, and Cobb, *Correspondence,* 675; Roark, *Masters without Slaves,* 123.

41. Reid, *After the War,* 195–96.

42. Cyrus B. Dawsey and James M. Dawsey, eds., *The Confederados: Old South Immigrants in Brazil* (Tuscaloosa, Ala., 1995), 86, 161.

43. Ibid., 69, 241n.

44. Furguson, *Ashes of Glory,* 363.

45. Kerby, *Kirby Smith's Confederacy,* 415.

46. Ibid., 428.

47. Andrew Rolle, *The Lost Cause: The Confederate Exodus to Mexico* (Norman, Okla., 1965), 94–95, 120, 174–75, 184.

48. Ted R. Worley, ed., "A Letter Written by General Thomas C. Hindman in Mexico," *Arkansas Historical Quarterly* 15, no. 4 (1956): 366–67.

49. Rolle, *Lost Cause,* 184.

50. Scarborough, *Masters of the Big House,* chap. 10.

51. Ibid., 372.

52. Stone, *Brokenburn,* 364.

53. Faust, *Mothers of Invention,* 248.

54. Berlin, *Wartime Genesis: Lower South,* 77–78, 78n.

55. Litwack, *Been in the Storm So Long,* 199–200.

56. Rawick, *American Slave: Composite Autobiography,* 14:60–61.

57. Dan T. Carter, *When the War Was Over: The Failure of Self-Reconstruction in the South, 1865–1867* (Baton Rouge, 1985), 82–83.

58. Trowbridge, *South,* 392.

59. Berlin, *Wartime Genesis: Lower South,* 603.

60. *Message of the President of the United States, Communicating, in Compliance with a Resolution of the Senate of the 12th Instant, Information in Relation to the States of the Union Lately in Rebellion, Accompanied by a Report of Carl Schurz on the States of South Carolina, Georgia, Alabama,*

Mississippi, and Louisiana; also a Report of Lieutenant General Grant, on the Same Subject (Washington, D.C., 1865), 82.

61. Higginson, *Army Life in a Black Regiment*, 47.

62. Du Bois, *Black Reconstruction in America*, 30.

63. Litwack, *Been in the Storm So Long*, 249.

64. Fogel, *Without Consent or Contract*, 100; Roger L. Ransom and Richard Sutch, *One Kind of Freedom: The Economic Consequences of Emancipation* (Cambridge, UK, 1977), 4–5; James M. McPherson, *Abraham Lincoln and the Second American Revolution* (New York, 1990), 16–19.

65. Douglass, *Life and Writings*, 3:390.

Works Cited

Primary Sources

Published Books, Essays, Speeches, Memoirs, Diaries, Papers, and Government Documents

Adams, John Quincy. *The Diary of John Quincy Adams, 1794–1845*. Ed. Allan Nevins. New York, 1951.

Akin, Warren. *Letters of Warren Akin, Confederate Congressman*. Ed. Bell Irvin Wiley. Athens, Ga., 1959.

Alexander, E. P. *Military Memoirs of a Confederate: A Critical Narrative*. New York, 1907.

Allston, Robert F. W. *The South Carolina Rice Plantation as Revealed in the Papers of Robert F. W. Allston*. Ed. J. H. Easterby. Chicago, 1945.

American Annual Cyclopedia and Register of Important Events of the Year 1863. New York, 1864.

Ames, Herman V., ed. *State Documents on Federal Relations: The States and the United States*. Philadelphia, 1906.

Andrews, Eliza Frances. *The War-Time Journal of a Georgia Girl, 1864–1865*. New York, 1908.

Andrews, Sidney. *The South Since the War*. 1866; reprint, Boston, 1971.

Avary, Myrta Lockett. *Dixie after the War: An Exposition of Social Conditions Existing in the South, during the Twelve Years Succeeding the Fall of Richmond.* New York, 1906.

Beatty, John. *The Citizen-soldier: Or, Memoirs of a Volunteer.* Cincinnati, Ohio, 1879.

Berlin, Ira, et al., eds. *The Destruction of Slavery.* Cambridge, UK, 1986.

———. *The Wartime Genesis of Free Labor: The Lower South.* Cambridge, UK, 1990.

———. *The Wartime Genesis of Free Labor: The Upper South.* Cambridge, UK, 1993.

Berlin, Ira, Joseph P. Reidy, and Leslie S. Rowland, eds. *The Black Military Experience.* Cambridge, UK, 1982.

Bettersworth, John K., ed. *Mississippi in the Confederacy as They Saw It.* 1961; reprint, New York, 1970.

Blaine, James G. *Twenty Years of Congress: From Lincoln to Garfield.* 2 vols. Norwich, Conn., 1884.

Blassingame, John W., ed. *Slave Testimony: Two Centuries of Letters, Speeches, Interviews, and Autobiographies.* Baton Rouge, 1977.

Botume, Elizabeth Hyde. *First Days amongst the Contrabands.* 1893; reprint, New York, 1968.

Brown, William Wells. *The Negro in the American Rebellion: His Heroism and His Fidelity.* Ed. John David Smith. 1867; reprint, Athens, Ohio, 2003.

Bryan, T. Conn, ed. *Confederate Georgia.* Athens, Ga., 1953.

Burkhead, Rev. L. S. "History of the Difficulties of the Pastorate of the Front Street Methodist Church, Wilmington, N. C., for the Year 1865." *Historical Papers of the Trinity College Historical Society* (Durham, N.C., 1900): 35–118.

Butler, Benjamin F. *Butler's Book: Autobiography and Personal Reminiscences of Major Benjamin F. Butler.* 2 vols. Boston, 1892.

————. *Private and Official Correspondence of Gen. Benjamin F. Butler during the Period of the Civil War.* 5 vols. Norwood, Mass., 1917.

Byrne, Frank L., and Jean Powers Soman, eds. *Your True Marcus: The Civil War Letters of a Jewish Colonel.* Kent, Ohio, 1985.

Cable, George W. "New Orleans before the Capture." In *Battles and Leaders of the Civil War,* ed. Robert Johnson and Clarence Buel, 2: 14–21.

Calhoun, John C. *The Works of John C. Calhoun.* 6 vols. Ed. Richard K. Crallé. Charleston, S.C., 1851–70.

Candler, Allen D., ed. *The Confederate Records of the State of Georgia.* Vol. 3, *Official Correspondence of Governor Joseph E. Brown, 1860–1865, Inclusive.* Atlanta, Ga., 1910.

Castillo, Susan P., ed. *The Literatures of Colonial America: An Anthology.* Malden, Mass., 2001.

Chase, Salmon P. *Inside Lincoln's Cabinet: The Civil War Diaries of Salmon P. Chase.* Ed. David Donald. New York, 1954.

————. *The Salmon P. Chase Papers.* 5 vols. Ed. John Niven, et al. Kent, Ohio, 1993–98.

Chester, Thomas Morris. *Thomas Morris Chester, Black Civil War Correspondent: His Dispatches from the Virginia Front.* Ed. R.J.M. Blackett. New York, 1991.

Chesnut, Mary Boykin Miller. *Mary Chesnut's Civil War.* Ed. C. Vann Woodward. New Haven, Conn., 1981.

————. *The Private Mary Chesnut: The Unpublished Civil War Diaries.* Ed. C. Vann Woodward and Elisabeth Muhlenfeld. New York, 1984.

Clark, Peter H. *Black Brigade of Cincinnati: Being a Report of Its Labors and a Muster-Roll of Its Members etc.* Cincinnati, 1864.

Clarke, James Freeman. *Autobiography, Diary and Correspondence.* Ed. Edward Everett Hale. Boston, 1892.

Clemenceau, Georges. *American Reconstruction, 1865–1870.* New York, 1928.

Cobb, Howell. *A Scriptural Examination of the Institution of Slavery in the United States; with its Objects and Purposes.* [Perry?] Ga., 1856.

Coffin, C. C. "Late Scenes in Richmond." *Atlantic Monthly* 15 (1865): 744–56.

Coleman, Mrs. Chapman, ed. *The Life of John J. Crittenden: With Selections from His Correspondence and Speeches.* 2 vols. Philadelphia, 1871.

Confederate States of America. Congress. House. Select Committee on Increase of Military Force. "Mr. Rogers' Minority Report." Richmond, Va., 1865.

Connolly, James Austin. "Major Connolly's Letters to His Wife, 1862–1865." *Transactions of the Illinois State Historical Society* 35 (1928): 215–438.

Conyngham, David P. *Sherman's March through the South.* New York, 1865.

Cooper, Peter. *The Death of Slavery.* New York, 1863.

[Corsan, W. C.]. *Two Months in the Confederate States: Including a Visit to New Orleans under the Domination of General Butler.* London, 1863.

Davis, Jefferson. *Jefferson Davis, Constitutionalist: His Letters, Papers and Speeches.* 10 vols. Ed. Dunbar F. Rowland. Jackson, Miss., 1923.

———. *The Papers of Jefferson Davis.* 12 vols. Ed. Linda Lasswell Crist, et al. Baton Rouge, 1971–.

———. *The Rise and Fall of the Confederate Government.* 2 vols. 1881; reprint, New York, 1990.

Davis, Varina. *Jefferson Davis: A Memoir by His Wife.* 2 vols. 1890; reprint, Baltimore, 1990.

Dawson, Sarah Morgan. *A Confederate Girl's Diary.* Boston, 1913.

[DeBow, J.D.B.]. "The Non-Slaveholders of the South." *DeBow's Review* 30 (1861): 67–77.

DeBow, J.D.B. *The Industrial Resources, Statistics, Etc. of the United States.* 3rd ed. 3 vols. New York, 1854.

Dennett, John Richard. *The South as It Is: 1865–1866*, ed. Henry M. Christman. New York, 1965.

A Digest of the Military Laws of the United States: From 1860 to the Second Session of the Fortieth Congress, 1867, Relating to the Army, Volunteers, Militia, and the Rebellion and Reconstruction of the Southern States. Boston, 1868.

Dinkins, James. *1861 to 1865, by an Old Johnnie: Personal Recollections and Experiences in the Confederate Army.* Cincinnati, 1897.

Douglass, Frederick. *The Life and Times of Frederick Douglass.* Rev. ed., 1892; reprint, London, 1962.

———. *The Life and Writings of Frederick Douglass.* 5 vols. Ed. Philip S. Foner. New York, 1950–75.

Dumond, Dwight Lowell, ed. *Southern Editorials on Secession.* 1931; reprint, Gloucester, Mass., 1964.

Durden, Robert F. *The Gray and the Black: The Confederate Debate on Emancipation.* Baton Rouge, 2000.

Early, Jubal Anderson. *Autobiographical Sketch and Narrative of the War between the States.* Philadelphia, 1912.

Edmonds, S. Emma. *The Female Spy of the Union Army.* Boston, 1864.

Edmondston, Catherine Devereux. *"Journal of a Secesh Lady": The Diary of Catherine Ann Devereux Edmondston, 1860–1866.* Ed. Beth Gilbert Crabtree and James W. Patton. Raleigh, N.C., 1979.

Ellis, John Willis. *Papers.* 2 vols. Ed. Noble J. Tolbert. Raleigh, N.C., 1964.

Farrand, Max, ed. *Records of the Federal Convention.* 4 vols. New Haven, 1966.

Faust, Drew Gilpin, ed. *The Ideology of Slavery: Proslavery Thought in the Antebellum South, 1830–1860.* Baton Rouge, 1981.

[Fitzhugh, George]. "The Message, the Constitution, and the Times." *DeBow's Review* 30 (1861): 156–67.

Fleet, Benjamin Robert. *Green Mount; a Virginia Plantation Family during the Civil War: Being the Journal of Benjamin Robert Fleet and Letters of His Family.* Ed. Betsy Fleet and John D. P. Fuller. Lexington, Ky., 1962.

Foner, Philip S., and George E. Walker, eds. *Proceedings of the Black State Conventions.* 2 vols. Philadelphia, 1979–80.

Forbes, John Murray. *Letters and Recollections of John Murray Forbes.* Ed. Sarah Forbes Hughes. Boston, 1899.

Forten, Charlotte. "Life on the Sea Islands." *Atlantic Monthly* 13 (1864): 587–96.

Freeman, Douglas Southall, ed. *A Calendar of Confederate Papers, with a Bibliography of Some Confederate Publications.* Richmond, Va., 1908.

Garfield, James A. *The Works of James Abram Garfield.* 2 vols. Ed. Burke A. Hinsdale. Boston, 1882–83.

"General Cleburne's Views on Slavery." *Annals of the Army of Tennessee and Early Western History* 1 (1978): 50–52.

Gienapp, William, ed. *The Civil War and Reconstruction: A Documentary Collection.* New York, 2001.

Goode, George Brown. *Virginia Cousins: A Study of the Ancestry and Posterity of John Goode of Whitby.* Richmond, Va., 1887.

Gorgas, Josiah. *The Journals of Josiah Gorgas, 1857–1878.* Ed. Sarah Woolfolk Wiggins. Tuscaloosa, Ala., 1995.

Graham, William Alexander. *The Papers of William Alexander Graham.* 8 vols. Ed. Joseph Grégoire de Roulhac Hamilton. Raleigh, N.C., 1957–73.

Grant, Ulysses S. *Memoirs and Selected Letters: Personal Memoirs of U. S. Grant, Selected Letters 1839–1865.* Ed. Mary Drake McFeeley and William S. McFeeley. New York, 1990.

———. *Personal Memoirs of U. S. Grant.* Two volumes in one. 1885; reprint, New York, n.d.

Greeley, Horace, and John F. Cleveland, eds. *Political Text-Book for 1860.* [1860]; reprint, New York, 1969.

Hamilton, Alexander. *The Papers of Alexander Hamilton.* 27 vols. Ed. Harold C. Syrett. New York, 1961–79.

Hammond, James Henry. *Secret and Sacred: The Diaries of James Henry Hammond, a Southern Slaveholder.* Ed. Carol Bleser. New York, 1988.

———. *Selections from the Letters and Speeches of the Hon. James H. Hammond, of South Carolina.* New York, 1866.

Hannaford, Ebenezer. *The Story of a Regiment: A History of the Campaigns, and Associations in the Field, of the Sixth Regiment Ohio Volunteer Infantry.* Cincinnati, 1868.

Haviland, Laura S. *A Woman's Life-Work: Labors and Experiences of Laura S. Haviland.* Chicago, 1887.

Hay, John. *Inside Lincoln's White House: The Complete Civil War Diary of John Hay.* Ed. Michael Burlingame and John Turner Ettlinger. Carbondale, Ill., 1997.

Hay, John, and John G. Nicolay. *Abraham Lincoln: The Observations of John G. Nicolay and John Hay.* Ed. Michael Burlingame. Carbondale, Ill., 2007.

Higginson, Thomas Wentworth. *Army Life in a Black Regiment.* 1869; reprint, Boston, 1970.

Hitchcock, Henry. *Marching with Sherman: Passages from the Letters and Campaign Diaries of Henry Hitchcock, Major and Assistant Adjutant General of Volunteers, November 1864–May 1865.* Ed. M. A. DeWolfe Howe. 1927; reprint, Lincoln, Neb., 1995.

Holden, William Woods. *The Papers of William Woods Holden.* One vol. to date. Ed. Horace W. Raper and Thornton W. Mitchell. Raleigh, N.C., 2000–.

House, Albert V., Jr., ed. "Deterioration of a Georgia Rice Plantation during Four Years of Civil War." *Journal of Southern History* 9 (1943): 100–107.

Howard, Oliver Otis. *Autobiography of Oliver Otis Howard.* 2 vols. New York, 1907.

Hughes, Thomas. *A Boy's Experience in the Civil War, 1860–1865.* Baltimore, 1904.

Hundley, Daniel R. *Social Relations in Our Southern States.* Ed. William J. Cooper. 1860; reprint, Baton Rouge, 1979.

Jefferson, Thomas. *Notes on the State of Virginia.* Ed. William Peden. 1787; reprint, New York, 1972.

Johnson, Andrew. *The Papers of Andrew Johnson.* 16 vols. Ed. LeRoy P. Graf, et al. Knoxville, Tenn., 1967–2000.

Johnson, Donald Bruce, comp. *National Party Platforms.* 2 vols. Rev. ed., Urbana, Ill., 1978.

Johnson, Robert, and Clarence Buel, ed. *Battles and Leaders of the Civil War: Being for the Most Part Contributions by Union and Confederate Officers.* 4 vols. 1884–88; reprint, Edison, N.J., n.d.

Johnston, Joseph E. *Narrative of Military Operations.* New York, 1874.

Jones, Charles Colcock. *The Religious Instruction of the Negroes: An Address Delivered before the General Assembly of the Presbyterian Church, at Augusta, Ga., December 10, 1861.* Richmond, Va., n.d.

———. *The Religious Instruction of the Negroes in the United States.* 1842; reprint, Manchester, N.H., 1971.

Jones, John B. *A Rebel War Clerk's Diary at the Confederate States Capital.* 2 vols. Philadelphia, 1866.

Jones, Joseph. *Agricultural Resources of Georgia: Address before the Cotton Planters Convention of Georgia at Macon, December 13, 1860.* Augusta, Ga., 1861.

Jones, J. William, ed. *Personal Reminiscences, Anecdotes, and Letters of Gen. Robert E. Lee.* New York, 1875.

Journal of Both Sessions of the Convention of the State of Arkansas. Little Rock, Ark., 1861.

Journal of the Congress of the Confederate States of America, 1861–1865. 7 vols. Washington, D.C., 1905.

Journal of the Senate of the State of Georgia, at the Annual Session of the General Assembly, Begun and Held in Milledgeville, the Seat of Government, in 1861. Milledgeville, Ga., 1861.

Kamphoefner, Walter D., Wolfgang Helbich, and Ulrike Sommer, eds. *News from the Land of Freedom: German Immigrants Write Home.* Ithaca, N.Y., 1991.

Kapp, Friedrich. *Geschichte der Sklaverei in den Vereinigten Staaten von Amerika.* Hamburg, 1861.

Kean, Robert Garlick Hill. *Inside the Confederate Government: The Diary of Robert Garlick Hill Kean, Head of the Bureau of War.* Ed. Edward Younger. Baton Rouge, 1957.

Kennedy, Joseph C. G. *Agriculture of the United States in 1860; Compiled from the Original Returns of the Eighth Census.* Washington, D.C., 1864.

Lee, Robert E. *The Wartime Papers of R. E. Lee.* Ed. Clifford Dowdey. Boston, 1961.

Leyburn, John. "An Interview with Gen. Robert E. Lee." *Century Magazine* 30 (1885): 166–67.

Lincoln, Abraham. *The Collected Works of Abraham Lincoln.* 9 vols. Ed. Roy P. Basler. New Brunswick, N.J., 1953.

Livermore, Mary A. *My Story of the War: A Woman's Narrative of Four Years Personal Experience.* Hartford, Conn., 1892.

Lovejoy, Owen. *His Brother's Blood: Speeches and Writings, 1838–64.* Ed. William F. Moore and Jane Ann Moore. Urbana, Ill., 2004.

Macrae, David. *Americans at Home: Pen-and-Ink Sketches of American Men, Manners, and Institutions.* 2 vols. Edinburgh, 1870.

Mallory, Stephen R. "Last Days of the Confederate Government." *McClure's Magazine* 16 (1900): 99–107, 239–48.

Marshall, Charles. *Lee's Aide-de-Camp, Being the Papers of Colonel Charles Marshall Sometime Aide-de-Camp, Military Secretary, and Assistant Adjutant General of*

Robert E. Lee, 1862–1865. Ed. Frederick Maurice. 1927; reprint, Lincoln, Neb., 2000.

Marx, Karl, and Frederick Engels. *Collected Works.* 50 vols. Moscow, 1975–2005.

Mason, Virginia, ed. *The Public Life and Diplomatic Correspondence of James M. Mason, with Some Personal History.* New York, 1906.

McClellan, George B. *The Civil War Papers of George B. McClellan: Selected Correspondence, 1860–1865.* Ed. Stephen W. Sears. New York, 1992.

McDonald, Cornelia Peake. *A Woman's Civil War: A Diary with Reminiscences of the War from March 1862.* Madison, Wis., 1992.

McMillan, Malcolm C., ed. *The Alabama Confederate Reader.* Tuscaloosa, Ala., 1963; reprint, 1992.

McNeilly, James H. "In Winter Quarters at Dalton, Ga." *Confederate Veteran* 28 (1920): 130–32, 157.

McPherson, Edward, ed. The *Political History of the United States of America during the Great Rebellion.* Washington, D.C., 1865.

Message of the President of the United States, Communicating, in Compliance with a Resolution of the Senate of the 12th Instant, Information in Relation to the States of the Union Lately in Rebellion, Accompanied by a Report of Carl Schurz on the States of South Carolina, Georgia, Alabama, Mississippi, and Louisiana; also a Report of Lieutenant General Grant, on the Same Subject. Washington, D.C., 1865.

Moore, Frank, ed. *The Rebellion Record: A Diary of American Events, with Documents, Narratives, Illustrative Incidents, Poetry, Etc.* 11 vols. New York, 1861–68.

Myers, Robert Manson, ed. *The Children of Pride: A True Story of Georgia and the Civil War.* New Haven, Conn., 1972.

Newton, James K. *A Wisconsin Boy in Dixie: Civil War Letters of James K. Newton.* Ed. Stephen E. Ambrose. Madison, Wis., 1995.

Nichols, George Ward. *The Story of the Great March from the Diary of a Staff Officer.* New York, 1865.

Nisbet, James Cooper. *Four Years on the Firing Line*. 1914; reprint, Jackson, Tenn., 1963.

North Carolina General Assembly. *Resolutions Against the Policy of Arming Slaves*. Richmond, Va., 1865.

Official Records of the Union and Confederate Navies in the War of the Rebellion. 30 vols. Washington, D.C., 1894–1922.

Oldham, William S. *Rise and Fall of the Confederacy: The Memoir of Senator William S. Oldham, C.S.A.* Ed. Clayton E. Jewett. Columbia, Mo., 2006.

———. "True Cause and Issues of the Civil War." *DeBow's Review* 6 (1869): 678–79.

Olmsted, Frederick Law. *A Journey in the Back Country, 1853–1854*. 1860; reprint, New York, 1970.

"Our Women in the War": The Lives They Lived; the Deaths They Died. Charleston, S.C., 1885.

Palmer, Rev. B. M. "Thanksgiving Sermon, Delivered at the First Presbyterian Church, New Orleans, on Thursday, Nov. 29." *DeBow's Review* 30 (1861): 324–36.

Papers Relating to Foreign Affairs, Accompanying the Annual Message of the President to the Second Session Thirty-Eighth Congress. Part 2. Washington, D.C., 1865.

Pearson, Elizabeth Ware, ed. *Letters from Port Royal, 1862–1868*. New York, 1969.

Pepper, George W. *Personal Recollections of Sherman's Campaigns in Georgia and the Carolinas*. Zanesville, Ohio, 1866.

Perdue, Charles L., Jr., Thomas E. Barden, and Robert K. Phillips, eds. *Weevils in the Wheat: Interviews with Virginia Ex-Slaves*. Charlottesville, Va., 1976.

Pierce, Edward L. "The Contrabands at Fortress Monroe." *Atlantic Monthly* 8 (1861): 626–40.

Pollard, Edward A. *Life of Jefferson Davis*. Philadelphia, [1869].

————. *Southern History of the War.* 1866; reprint, New York, 1990.

Porcher, Frederick Adolphus. "Southern and Northern Civilization Contrasted." *Russell's Magazine* 1 (1857): 97–107.

Porter, David D. "The Opening of the Lower Mississippi." In *Battles and Leaders of the Civil War,* ed. Robert Johnson and Clarence Buel, 2: 22–55.

Proceedings of the National Convention of Colored Men Held in the City of Syracuse, N. Y., October 4, 5, 6, and 7, 1864; with the Bill of Wrongs and Rights, and the Address to the American People. Boston, 1864.

"Progress of Education in Virginia." *Southern Literary Messenger* 24 (1857): 241–47.

Pryor, Sara Agnes Rice. *Reminiscences of Peace and War.* New York, 1904.

Putnam, Sallie A. Brock. *Richmond during the War: Four Years of Personal Observation.* Lincoln, Neb., 1997.

Rawick, George P., ed. *The American Slave: A Composite Autobiography.* 19 vols. Westport, Conn., 1972–79.

Reagan, John H. *Memoirs: With Special Reference to Secession and the Civil War.* Ed. Walter Flavius McCaleb. New York, 1906.

Redkey, Edwin S., ed. *A Grand Army of Black Men: Letters from African-American Soldiers in the Union Army, 1861–1865.* Cambridge, UK, 1992.

Reese, George H., ed. *Proceedings of the Virginia State Convention of 1861, February 13–May 1.* 4 vols. Richmond, Va., 1965.

Reid, Whitelaw. *After the War: A Tour of the Southern States, 1865–66.* 1866; reprint, New York, 1965.

Rhett, Robert Barnwell. *A Fire-Eater Remembers: The Confederate Memoir of Robert Barnwell Rhett.* Ed. William C. Davis. Columbia, S.C., 2000.

Richardson, James D., ed. *A Compilation of the Messages and Papers of the Confederacy, Including the Diplomatic Correspondence, 1861–1865.* Nashville, 1905.

Robertson, James I., ed. " 'The Boy Artillerist': Letters of Colonel William Pegram, C.S.A." *Virginia Magazine of History and Biography* 98 (1990): 221–60.

[Ruffin, Edmund]. *Anticipations of the Future, to Serve as Lessons for the Present Time.* Richmond, Va., 1860.

Ruffin, Edmund. *The Diary of Edmund Ruffin.* 3 vols. Ed. William Kaufman Scarborough. Baton Rouge, 1972–89.

Ruffin, Thomas. *The Papers of Thomas Ruffin.* 4 vols. Ed. Joseph Grégoire de Roulhac Hamilton. Raleigh, N.C., 1920.

Russell, William Howard. *My Diary North and South.* Ed. Eugene H. Berwanger. New York, 1988.

Selden, John A. *The Westover Journal of John A. Selden, Esq., 1858–1862.* Ed. John Spencer Bassett and Sidney Bradshaw Fay. Northampton, Mass., 1921.

Sheridan, Philip Henry. *Personal Memoirs of P. H. Sheridan.* 2 vols. New York, 1888.

Sherman, William T. *Memoirs.* 2 vols. New York, 1875.

———. *Sherman's Civil War: Selected Correspondence of William T. Sherman.* Ed. Brooks D. Simpson and Jean V. Berlin. Chapel Hill, N.C., 1999.

Sitterson, J. Carlyle. "The William J. Minor Plantations: A Study in Ante-Bellum Absentee Ownership." *Journal of Southern History* 9 (1943): 59–74.

Slocum, Henry W. "Sherman's March from Savannah to Bentonville." In *Battles and Leaders of the Civil War,* ed. Robert Johnson and Clarence Buel, 4: 688–90.

Smith, James L. *Autobiography of James L. Smith, Including, Also, Reminiscences of Slave Life, Recollections of the War, Education of Freedmen, Causes of the Exodus, Etc.* Norwich, Conn., 1881.

Stampp, Kenneth M., ed. *The Causes of the Civil War.* Rev. ed., New York, 1992.

Stephens, Alexander. *A Constitutional View of the Late War between the States.* 2 vols. Philadelphia, 1868–70.

Stephens, George E. *A Voice of Thunder: The Civil War Letters of George E. Stephens.* Ed. Donald Yacavone. Urbana, Ill., 1997.

Sterling, Dorothy, ed. *The Trouble They Seen: Black People Tell the Story of Reconstruction.* Garden City, N.Y., 1976.

Stone, Kate. *Brokenburn: The Journal of Kate Stone, 1861–1868.* Ed. John Q. Anderson. Baton Rouge, 1995.

Sutcliffe, Andrea, ed. *Mighty Rough Times, I Tell You: Personal Accounts of Slavery in Tennessee.* Winston-Salem, N.C., 2000.

Taylor, Richard. *Destruction and Reconstruction: Personal Experiences of the Late War.* 1879; reprint, New York, 1955.

Taylor, Susie King. *Reminiscences of My Life: A Black Woman's Civil War Memoirs.* New York, 1998.

Temple, Oliver P. *East Tennessee and the Civil War.* Johnson City, Tenn., 1899.

Thomas, Ella Gertrude Clanton. *The Secret Eye: The Journal of Ella Gertrude Clanton Thomas, 1848–1889.* Ed. Virginia Ingraham Burr. Chapel Hill, N.C., 1990.

Thomasson, Basil Armstrong. *North Carolina Yeoman: The Diary of Basil Armstrong Thomasson, 1853–1862.* Ed. Paul D. Escott. Athens, Ga., 1996.

Toombs, Robert A. *Lecture Delivered in the Tremont Temple, Boston, Massachusetts, on the 26th January, 1856, by Robert Toombs.* Washington, D.C., 1856.

Toombs, Robert A., Alexander Hamilton Stephens, and Howell Cobb. *The Correspondence of Robert Toombs, Alexander H. Stephens, and Howell Cobb.* Ed. Ulrich Bonnell Phillips. Washington, D.C., 1913.

Towne, Laura M. *Letters and Diary of Laura M. Towne; Written from the Sea Islands of South Carolina, 1862–1864.* Ed. Rupert Sargent Holland. Cambridge, Mass., 1912.

Trowbridge, John Townsend. *The South: A Tour of Its Battlefields and Ruined Cities, a Journey through the Desolated States, and Talks with the People: Being a Descrip-*

tion of the Present State of the Country—Its Agriculture—Railroads—Business and Finance. Hartford, Conn., 1866.

Twain, Mark, and Charles Dudley Warner. *The Gilded Age.* 1873; reprint, Stillwell, Kans., 2007.

Two Diaries: From Middle St. John's, Berkeley, South Carolina, February–May, 1865: Journals Kept by Miss Susan R. Jervey and Miss Charlotte St. J. Ravenel, at Northampton and Pooshee Plantations, and Reminiscences of Mrs. (Waring) Henagan with Two Contemporary Reports from Federal Officials. [Pinopolis, S.C.], 1921.

United States Congress. *Report of the Joint Committee on Reconstruction.* Washington, D.C., 1866.

Upshur, Abel P. "Domestic Slavery, as It Exists in Our Southern States." *Southern Literary Messenger* 5 (1839): 677–87.

Vance, Zebulon Baird. *The Papers of Zebulon Baird Vance.* 2 vols. to date. Ed. Frontis W. Johnston and Joe A. Mobley. Raleigh, N.C., 1963–.

Vandiver, Frank, ed. "Proceedings of the Second Confederate Congress." *Southern Historical Society Papers,* n.s., 51–52. Richmond, Va., 1958–59.

Victor, Orville J. *The Comprehensive History of the Southern Rebellion and the War for the Union.* New York, 1862.

Violette, Eugene Morrow. *A History of Missouri.* Boston, 1918.

Wakelyn, Jon L., ed. *Southern Pamphlets on Secession, November 1860–April 1861.* Chapel Hill, N.C., 1996.

The War of the Rebellion: A Compilation of the Official Records of the Union and Confederate Armies. 128 vols. Washington, D.C., 1880–1901.

Washburn, George H. *A Complete Military History and Record of the 108th Regiment N.Y. Volunteers.* Rochester, N.Y., 1894.

Waterbury, Maria. *Seven Years among the Freedmen.* 3rd ed. Chicago, 1893.

Welles, Gideon. *Diary of Gideon Welles, Secretary of the Navy under Lincoln and Johnson.* 2 vols. Boston, 1911.

Wheeler, John H. *Historical Sketches of North Carolina: From 1584 to 1851, Compiled from Original Records, Official Documents and Traditional Statements: With Biographical Sketches of Her Distinguished Statesmen, Jurists, Lawyers, Soldiers, Divines, Etc.* Philadelphia, 1851.

Wise, John S. *The End of an Era.* Boston, 1899.

Wood, George L. *The Seventh Regiment: A Record.* New York, 1865.

Worley, Ted R. "A Letter Written by General Thomas C. Hindman in Mexico." *Arkansas Historical Quarterly* 15 (1956): 365–68.

Worsham, W. J. *The Old Nineteenth Tennessee Regiment, C.S.A. June, 1861–April, 1865.* Knoxville, Tenn., 1902.

Worth, Jonathan. *The Correspondence of Jonathan Worth.* 2 vols. Ed. Joseph Grégoire de Roulhac Hamilton. Raleigh, N.C., 1909.

Yearns, W. Buck, and John G. Barrett, eds. *North Carolina Civil War Documentary.* Chapel Hill, N.C., 1980.

Yetman, Norman R., ed. *When I Was a Slave: Memoirs from the Slave Narrative Collection.* New York, 2002.

Newspapers

The Anti-Slavery Reporter

Congressional Globe

The Charleston Mercury

The Daily Confederate (Raleigh, N.C.)

Friends' Intelligencer

Galveston Tri-Weekly News

Harper's Weekly

Lynchburg Virginian

Macon Daily Telegraph and Confederate

Mobile Register and Advertiser

Montgomery Mail

New York Evening Post

The New York Times

New York Tribune

Richmond Dispatch

Richmond Enquirer

Richmond Examiner

Richmond Whig

The Sentinel (Richmond, Va.)

Southern Confederacy (Atlanta, Ga.)

The Times-Dispatch (Richmond, Va.)

Unpublished Papers and Manuscripts

Allen, James. Plantation Book, 1860–63. Mississippi Department of Archives and History, Jackson, Miss. (MDAH).

Army of Northern Virginia Headquarters Papers. Virginia Historical Society, Richmond, Va. (VHS).

Barlow, Samuel Latham Mitchell. Papers. Huntington Library, San Marino, Calif. (HL).

Brown, George Washington Campbell. Papers. Manuscript Division, Library of Congress (LC).

Brown-Ewell Family Papers. Filson Historical Society, Louisville, Ky.

Civil War Collection. HL.

Confederate States of America records. Manuscript Division, LC.

Guess, George W. Letters. Louisiana and Lower Mississippi Valley Collection, Special Collections, Louisiana State University Libraries, Baton Rouge, La. (LSU).

Jackson, Hunt Papers, Manuscript Division, LC.

Kenner, Duncan Farrar. Collection. Manuscript Division, LC.

Lee, R. E. Papers. VHS.

Maury, Richard L. Diary. Manuscripts Division, VHS.

Minor, William J., and Family. Papers. Louisiana and Lower Mississippi Valley Collection, Special Collections, LSU.

Pettus, John J. Papers. MDAH.

Smith, William. Executive Papers, 1864–65. State Records Collection, Library of Virginia, Richmond, Va.

Stapp, Joseph D. Letters, 1864–65. VHS.

War Department Collection of Confederate Records. National Archives and Records Administration, Washington, D.C. (NARA).

White, Garland. Compiled Military Service Record, NARA.

Secondary Works

Books

Abrahamson, James L. *The Men of Secession and Civil War, 1859–1861*. Wilmington, Del., 2000.

Alexander, Thomas B. *Thomas A. R. Nelson of East Tennessee*. Nashville, 1956.

Alexander, Thomas B., and Richard E. Beringer. *The Anatomy of the Confederate Congress*. Nashville, 1972.

Allen, James S. *Reconstruction: The Battle for Democracy, 1865–1876*. New York, 1937.

Allmendinger, David F. *Ruffin: Family and Reform in the Old South*. New York, 1990.

Ash, Stephen V. *Firebrand of Liberty: The Story of Two Black Regiments That Changed the Course of the Civil War*. New York, 2008.

———. *Middle Tennessee Society Transformed, 1860–1870: War and Peace in the Upper South*. Baton Rouge, 1988.

———. *When the Yankees Came: Conflict and Chaos in the Occupied South, 1861–1865*. Chapel Hill, N.C., 1995.

Atkins, Jonathan. *Parties, Politics, and Sectional Conflict: Tennessee 1832–1861*. Memphis, Tenn., 1997.

Auman, William Thomas. "Neighbor against Neighbor: The Inner Civil War in the Central Counties of Confederate North Carolina." PhD diss., University of North Carolina at Chapel Hill, 1988.

Ayers, Edward L. *Vengeance and Justice: Crime and Punishment in the 19th-Century American South*. New York, 1984.

Bagwell, James. *Rice Gold: James Hamilton Couper and Plantation Life on the Georgia Coast*. Macon, Ga., 2000.

Bailey, Hugh C. "Disaffection in the Alabama Hill Country, 1861." *Civil War History* 4 (1958): 183–94.

———. "Disloyalty in Early Confederate Alabama." *Journal of Southern History* 23 (1957): 522–28.

Bancroft, Frederic. *The Life of William H. Seward*. 2 vols. New York, 1900.

Bardaglio, Peter Winthrop. *Reconstructing the Household: Families, Sex, and the Law in the Nineteenth-Century South*. Chapel Hill, N.C., 1995.

Barrett, John G. *The Civil War in North Carolina*. Chapel Hill, N.C., 1963.

————. *Sherman's March through the Carolinas*. Chapel Hill, N.C., 1996.

Bauer, Craig A. *A Leader among Peers: The Life and Times of Duncan Farrar Kenner*. Lafayette, La., 1993.

Benton, Josiah Henry. *Voting in the Field: A Forgotten Chapter of the Civil War*. Boston, 1915.

Bergeron, Arthur W. *Confederate Mobile*. Baton Rouge, 1991.

Berlin, Ira. *Slaves without Masters: The Free Negro in the Antebellum South*. New York, 1974.

Blackburn, Robin. *The Overthrow of Colonial Slavery, 1776–1848*. London, 1988.

Blair, William. *Virginia's Private War: Feeding Body and Soul in the Confederacy, 1861–1865*. Oxford, UK, 1998.

Blanchard, Peter. *Under the Flags of Freedom: Slave Soldiers and the Wars of Independence in Spanish South America*. Pittsburgh, 2008.

Brazy, Martha Jane. *An American Planter: Stephen Duncan of Antebellum Natchez and New York*. Baton Rouge, 2006.

Brewer, James H. *The Confederate Negro: Virginia's Craftsmen and Military Laborers, 1861–1865*. Durham, N.C., 1969.

Brewer, Willis. *Alabama, Her History, Resources, War Record, and Public Men: From 1540 to 1872*. Montgomery, Ala., 1872.

Brooks, Noah. *Abraham Lincoln*. New York, 1894.

Brown, Christopher Leslie, and Philip D. Morgan, eds. *Arming Slaves: From Classical Time to the Modern Age*. New Haven, Conn., 2006.

Burkhardt, George S. *Confederate Rage, Yankee Wrath: No Quarter in the Civil War*. Carbondale, Ill., 2007.

Burlingame, Michael. *Abraham Lincoln: A Life*. 2 vols. Baltimore, 2008.

Bynum, Victoria. *The Free State of Jones: Mississippi's Longest Civil War.* Chapel Hill, N.C., 2001.

Campbell, Jacqueline Glass. *When Sherman Marched North from the Sea: Resistance on the Confederate Home Front.* Chapel Hill, N.C., 2003.

Carmichael, Peter S. *The Last Generation: Young Virginians in Peace, War, and Reunion.* Chapel Hill, N.C., 2005.

Carter, Dan T. *When the War Was Over: The Failure of Self-Reconstruction in the South, 1865–1867.* Baton Rouge, 1985.

Cash, W. J. *The Mind of the South.* 1941; reprint, New York, 1991.

Castel, Albert. *Decision in the West: The Atlanta Campaign of 1864.* Lawrence, Kans., 1995.

Catton, Bruce. *Grant Takes Command.* Boston, 1969.

Cauthen, Charles Edward. *South Carolina Goes to War, 1860–1865.* 1950; reprint, Columbia, S.C., 2005.

Channing, Steven A. *Crisis of Fear: Secession in South Carolina.* New York, 1970.

Cheatham, Mark Renfred. *Old Hickory's Nephew: The Political and Private Struggles of Andrew Jackson Donelson.* Baton Rouge, 2007.

Christian, Frances Archer, and Susanne Massie, eds. *Homes and Gardens in Old Virginia.* Richmond, Va., 1931.

Cimprich, John. *Fort Pillow, a Civil War Massacre, and Public Memory.* Baton Rouge, 2005.

———. *Slavery's End in Tennessee, 1861–1865.* University, Ala., 1985.

Clarke, Erskine. *Dwelling Place: A Plantation Epic.* New Haven, Conn., 2005.

Cole, Arthur Charles. *The Era of the Civil War.* 1919; reprint, Urbana, Ill., 1987.

Connelly, Thomas Lawrence. *Autumn of Glory: The Army of Tennessee, 1862–1865.* Baton Rouge, 1971.

Connor, R.D.W. *North Carolina: Rebuilding an Ancient Commonwealth, 1584–1925*. 2 vols. Spartanburg, S.C., 1973.

Cooper, William J. *Jefferson Davis, American*. New York, 2000.

Cooper, William J., and Thomas E. Terrill, *The American South: A History*. Lanham, Md., 2009.

Cornelius, Janet Duitsman. *When I Can Read My Title Clear: Literacy, Slavery, and Religion in the Antebellum South*. Columbia, S.C., 1992.

Cornish, Dudley Taylor. *The Sable Arm: Black Troops in the Union Army, 1861–1865*. 1956; reprint, Lawrence, Kans., 1987.

Coulter, E. Merton. *The Confederate States of America*. Baton Rouge, 1950.

Cox, LaWanda. *Lincoln and Black Freedom: A Study in Presidential Leadership*. Columbia, S.C., 1981.

Crawford, Martin. *Ashe County's Civil War: Community and Society in the Appalachian South*. Charlottesville, Va., 2001.

Creighton, Margaret. *The Colors of Courage: Gettysburg's Forgotten History: Immigrants, Women, and African Americans in the Civil War's Defining Battle*. New York, 2005.

Crofts, Daniel W. *Reluctant Confederates: Upper South Unionists in the Secession Crisis*. Chapel Hill, N.C., 1989.

Current, Richard Nelson. *Lincoln's Loyalists: Union Soldiers from the Confederacy*. Boston, 1992.

Currie, James T. *Enclave: Vicksburg and Her Plantations, 1863–1870*. Jackson, Miss., 1980.

Curry, Richard Orr. *A House Divided: A Study of Statehood Politics and the Copperhead Movement in West Virginia*. Pittsburgh, 1964.

Daniel, Larry J. *Soldiering in the Army of Tennessee: A Portrait of Life in a Confederate Army*. Chapel Hill, N.C., 1991.

David, Paul, et al. *Reckoning with Slavery*. New York, 1976.

Davis, William C. *An Honorable Defeat: The Last Days of the Confederate Government*. New York, 2001.

———. *Jefferson Davis: The Man and His Hour*. Baton Rouge, 1991.

Dawsey, Cyrus B., and James M. Dawsey, eds. *The Confederados: Old South Immigrants in Brazil*. Tuscaloosa, Ala., 1995.

Dew, Charles B. *Apostles of Disunion: Southern Secession Commissioners and the Causes of the Civil War*. Baton Rouge, 2001.

Dillon, Merton L. *Slavery Attacked: Southern Slaves and Their Allies, 1619–1865*. Baton Rouge, 1990.

Dowd, Clement. *Life of Zebulon B. Vance*. Charlotte, N.C., 1897.

Du Bois, W.E.B. *Black Reconstruction in America: An Essay Toward a History of the Part Which Black Folk Played in the Attempt to Reconstruct Democracy in America, 1860–1880*. 1935; reprint, Cleveland, 1968.

Dusinberre, William. *Them Dark Days: Slavery in the American Rice Swamps*. Athens, Ga., 1996.

Emilio, Luis F. *A Brave Black Regiment: The History of the 54th Massachusetts, 1863–1865*. 1891; reprint, New York, 1995.

Epstein, Dena J. *Sinful Tunes and Spirituals: Black Folk Music to the Civil War*. Urbana, Ill., 2003.

Escott, Paul D. *After Secession: Jefferson Davis and the Failure of Confederate Nationalism*. Baton Rouge, 1978.

Faust, Drew Gilpin. *James Henry Hammond: A Design for Mastery*. Baton Rouge, 1982.

———. *Mothers of Invention: Women in the Slaveholding South in the American Civil War*. New York, 1996.

Fisher, Noel C. *War at Every Door: Partisan Politics and Guerrilla Violence in East Tennessee, 1860–1869.* Chapel Hill, N.C., 1997.

Fleming, Walter L. *Civil War and Reconstruction in Alabama.* New York, 1905.

Fogel, Robert W. *Without Consent or Contract: The Rise and Fall of American Slavery.* New York, 1989.

Follett, Richard. *The Sugar Masters: Planters and Slaves in Louisiana's Cane World, 1820–1860.* Baton Rouge, 2005.

Foner, Eric. *The Fiery Trial: Abraham Lincoln and American Slavery.* New York, 2010.

———. *Reconstruction: America's Unfinished Revolution, 1863–1877.* New York, 1988.

Foote, Shelby. *Civil War, a Narrative.* 3 vols. 1958; reprint, New York, 1986.

Forbes, Robert Pierce. *The Missouri Compromise and Its Aftermath: Slavery and the Meaning of America.* Chapel Hill, N.C., 2007.

Freehling, William W. *The Reintegration of American History: Slavery and the Civil War.* New York, 1994.

———. *The Road to Disunion: Secessionists Triumphant, 1854–1861.* Oxford, UK, 2007.

———. *The South vs. the South: How Anti-Confederate Southerners Shaped the Course of the Civil War.* New York, 2001.

Freeman, Douglas Southall. *R. E. Lee.* 4 vols. New York, 1934–35.

Furguson, Ernest B. *Ashes of Glory: Richmond at War.* New York, 1996.

Gallagher, Gary W. *The Confederate War.* Cambridge, Mass., 1997.

———, ed. *The Wilderness Campaign.* Chapel Hill, N.C., 2006.

Genovese, Eugene D. *A Consuming Fire: The Fall of the Confederacy in the Mind of the Christian South.* Athens, Ga., 1998.

————. *Roll, Jordan, Roll: The World the Slaves Made.* New York, 1974.

Gerteis, Louis S. *From Contraband to Freedman: Federal Policy toward Southern Blacks, 1861–1865.* Westport, Conn., 1973.

Glatthaar, Joseph T. *Forged in Battle: The Civil War Alliance of Black Soldiers and White Officers.* New York, 1991.

————. *General Lee's Army: From Victory to Collapse.* New York, 2008.

————. *The March to the Sea and Beyond: Sherman's Troops in the Savannah and Carolinas Campaigns.* New York, 1985.

Gordon, Lesley J., and John C. Insco, eds. *Inside the Confederate Nation: Essays in Honor of Emory M. Thomas.* Baton Rouge, 2005.

Gray, Lewis Cecil. *History of Agriculture in the United States to 1860.* 2 vols. Gloucester, Mass., 1958.

Greene, A. Wilson. *The Final Battles of the Petersburg Campaign: Breaking the Backbone of the Rebellion.* Knoxville, Tenn., 2008.

Grimsley, Mark. *And Keep Moving On: The Virginia Campaign, May–June 1864.* Lincoln, Neb., 2002.

————. *The Hard Hand of War: Union Military Policy toward Southern Civilians, 1861–1865.* Cambridge, UK, 1995.

Grimsley, Mark, and Brooks D. Simpson, eds. *The Collapse of the Confederacy.* Lincoln, Neb., 2001.

Groce, W. Todd. *Mountain Rebels: East Tennessee Confederates and the Civil War, 1860–1870.* Knoxville, Tenn., 1999.

Guelzo, Allen C. *Lincoln's Emancipation Proclamation: The End of Slavery in America.* New York, 2004.

Hadden, Sally E. *Slave Patrols: Law and Violence in Virginia and the Carolinas.* Cambridge, Mass., 2001.

Hahn, Steven. *A Nation under Our Feet: Black Political Struggle in the Rural South from Slavery to the Great Migration*. Cambridge, Mass., 2003.

———. *The Roots of Southern Populism: Yeoman Farmers and the Transformation of the Georgia Upcountry, 1850–1890*. New York, 1983.

Hamilton, Joseph Grégoire de Roulhac. *Reconstruction in North Carolina*. New York, 1914.

Harris, J. William. *The Making of the American South: A Short History, 1500–1877*. Malden, Mass., 2006.

Hattaway, Herman, and Archer Jones. *How the North Won: A Military History of the Civil War*. Urbana, Ill., 1991.

Hearn, Chester G. *The Capture of New Orleans, 1862*. Baton Rouge, 1995.

Heidler, David Stephen, Jeanne T. Heidler, and David J. Coles, eds. *Encyclopedia of the American Civil War: A Political, Social, and Military History*. New York, 2002.

Hermann, Janet Sharp. *The Pursuit of a Dream*. New York, 1981.

Hess, Earl J. *Liberty, Virtue, and Progress: Northerners and Their War for the Union*. New York, 1997.

Hill, Louise Biles. *Joseph E. Brown and the Confederacy*. Chapel Hill, N.C., 1939.

Hollandsworth, James G., Jr. *The Louisiana Native Guards: The Black Military Experience during the Civil War*. Baton Rouge, 1995.

Holton, Woody. *Forced Founders: Indians, Debtors, Slaves, and the Making of the American Revolution in Virginia*. Chapel Hill, N.C., 1999.

Howard, Victor B. *Black Liberation in Kentucky: Emancipation and Freedom, 1862–1884*. Lexington, Ky., 1983.

Hughes, Nathaniel Cheairs, Jr., and Gordon D. Whitney. *Jefferson Davis in Blue: The Life of Sherman's Relentless Warrior*. Baton Rouge, 2006.

Huston, James L. *Calculating the Value of the Union: Slavery, Property Rights, and the Economic Origins of the Civil War.* Chapel Hill, N.C., 2003.

Inscoe, John C. *Mountain Masters, Slavery, and the Sectional Crisis in Western North Carolina.* Knoxville, Tenn., 1989.

Inscoe, John C., and Gordon B. McKinney. *The Heart of Confederate Appalachia: Western North Carolina in the Civil War.* Chapel Hill, N.C., 2000.

Jenkins, Wilbert L. *Climbing Up to Glory: A Short History of African Americans during the Civil War and Reconstruction.* Wilmington, Del., 2002.

————. *Seizing the New Day: African Americans in Post–Civil War Charleston.* Bloomington, Ind., 2003.

Jennings, Thelma. *The Nashville Convention: Southern Movement for Unity, 1848–1850.* Memphis, Tenn., 1980.

Johnson, Ludwell H. *Red River Campaign: Politics and Cotton in the Civil War.* Kent, Ohio, 1993.

Johnson, Michael P., and James L. Roark. *Black Masters: A Free Family of Color in the Old South.* New York, 1984.

Johnston, William Preston. *The Life of Albert Sidney Johnston.* New York, 1878.

Jones, Archer. *Civil War Command and Strategy: The Process of Victory and Defeat.* New York, 1992.

Jones, Howard. *Blue and Gray Diplomacy: A History of Union and Confederate Foreign Relations.* Chapel Hill, N.C., 2010.

Jones, Jacqueline. *Saving Savannah: The City and the Civil War.* New York, 2008.

Jones, Katherine M. *Heroines of Dixie: Confederate Women Tell Their Story of the War.* Indianapolis, 1955.

Jordan, Winthrop. *Tumult and Silence at Second Creek: An Inquiry into a Civil War Slave Conspiracy.* Baton Rouge, 1993.

Kerby, Robert L. *Kirby Smith's Confederacy: The Trans-Mississippi South, 1863–1865.* Tuscaloosa, Ala., 1972.

Lankford, Nelson. *Richmond Burning: The Last Days of the Confederate Capital.* New York, 2002.

Lause, Mark A. *Race and Radicalism in the Union Army.* Urbana, Ill., 2009.

———. *Young America: Land, Labor, and the Republican Community.* Urbana, Ill., 2005.

Levine, Bruce. *Confederate Emancipation: Southern Plans to Free and Arm Slaves during the Civil War.* New York, 2005.

———. *Half Slave and Half Free: The Roots of Civil War.* Rev. ed., New York, 2005.

———. *The Spirit of 1848: German Immigrants, Labor Conflict, and the Coming of the Civil War.* Urbana, Ill., 1992.

Levine, Lawrence W. *Black Culture and Black Consciousness: Afro-American Folk Thought from Slavery to Freedom.* New York, 1977.

Litwack, Leon F. *Been in the Storm So Long: The Aftermath of Slavery.* New York, 1979.

Long, E. B., with Barbara Long. *The Civil War Day by Day: An Almanac, 1861–1865.* Garden City, N.Y., 1971.

Lonn, Ella. *Desertion during the Civil War.* 1928; reprint, Lincoln, Neb., 1998.

Manning, Chandra. *What This Cruel War Was Over: Soldiers, Slavery, and the Civil War.* New York, 2007.

Marszalek, John E. *Sherman: A Soldier's Passion for Order.* New York, 1993.

Martin, Bessie. *A Rich Man's War, a Poor Man's Fight: Desertion of Alabama Troops from the Confederate Army.* 1932; reprint, Tuscaloosa, Ala., 2003.

Massey, Mary Elizabeth. *Ersatz in the Confederacy: Shortages and Substitutes on the Southern Homefront.* 1952; reprint, Columbia, S.C., 1993.

McClintock, Russell. *Lincoln and the Decision for War: The Northern Response to Secession*. Chapel Hill, N.C., 2008.

McCrary, Peyton. *Abraham Lincoln and Reconstruction: The Louisiana Experiment*. Princeton, N.J., 1978.

McInnis, Maurice D. *The Politics of Taste in Antebellum Charleston*. Chapel Hill, N.C., 2005.

McKinney, Gordon B. *Zeb Vance: North Carolina's Civil War Governor and Gilded Age Political Leader*. Chapel Hill, N.C., 2004.

McMillan, Malcolm Cook. *Disintegration of a Confederate State: Three Governors and Alabama's Wartime Home Front, 1861–1865*. Macon, Ga., 1986.

McPherson, James M. *Abraham Lincoln and the Second American Revolution*. New York, 1990.

———. *Battle Cry of Freedom: The Civil War Era*. New York, 1988.

———. *For Causes and Comrades: Why Men Fought in the Civil War*. New York, 1997.

———. *Crossroads of Freedom: Antietam*. New York, 2002.

———. *The Negro's Civil War: How the American Negroes Felt and Acted during the War for the Union*. New York, 1965.

———. *The Struggle for Equality: Abolitionists and the Negro in the Civil War and Reconstruction*. Princeton, N.J., 1964.

———. *Tried by War: Abraham Lincoln as Commander in Chief*. New York, 2008.

———. *What They Fought For*. New York, 1995.

McPherson, James M., and James K. Hogue. *Ordeal by Fire: The Civil War and Reconstruction*. 4th ed. New York, 2009.

Meade, Robert Douthat. *Judah P. Benjamin: Confederate Statesman*. New York, 1943.

Mohr, Clarence L. *On the Threshold of Freedom: Masters and Slaves in Civil War Georgia*. Athens, Ga., 1986.

Moneyhon, Carl H. *The Impact of the Civil War and Reconstruction on Arkansas: Persistence in the Midst of Ruin*. Baton Rouge, 1994.

Moore, Albert Burton. *Conscription and Conflict in the Confederacy*. 1924; reprint, Columbia, S.C., 1996.

Morris, Christopher. *Becoming Southern: The Evolution of a Way of Life, Warren County and Vicksburg, Mississippi, 1770–1860*. New York, 1995.

Neal, Diane, and Thomas W. Kremm. *Lion of the South: General Thomas C. Hindman*. Macon, Ga., 1993.

Nevins, Allan. *Ordeal of the Union*. 2 vols. New York, 1947.

———. *The War for the Union*. 4 vols. New York, 1959–71.

———. *Salmon P. Chase: A Biography*. New York, 1995.

Nolan, Alan T. *Lee Considered: General Robert E. Lee and Civil War History*. Chapel Hill, N.C., 1991.

Oakes, James. *The Ruling Race: A History of American Slaveholders*. New York, 1982.

Owsley, Frank Lawrence. *King Cotton Diplomacy: Foreign Relations of the Confederate States of America*. [Chicago], 1959.

Paludan, Phillip Shaw. *"A People's Contest": The Union and the Civil War, 1861–1865*. New York, 1988.

Parks, Joseph H. *Joseph E. Brown of Georgia*. Baton Rouge, 1911.

Phillips, Jason. *Diehard Rebels: The Confederate Culture of Invincibility*. Athens, Ga., 2007.

Phillips, Ulrich B. *American Negro Slavery*. 1918; reprint, Baton Rouge, 1966.

———. *Life and Labor in the Old South*. 1929; reprint, Boston, 1963.

Power, J. Tracy. *Lee's Miserables: Life in the Army of Northern Virginia from the Wilderness to Appomattox.* Chapel Hill, N.C., 1998.

Pryor, Elizabeth Brown. *Reading the Man: A Portrait of Robert E. Lee through His Private Letters.* New York, 2007.

Quarles, Benjamin. *The Negro in the American Revolution.* 1961; reprint, New York, 1973.

———. *The Negro in the Civil War.* 1953; reprint, New York, 1968.

Rable, George C. *The Confederate Republic: A Revolution against Politics.* Chapel Hill, N.C., 1994.

Raboteau, Albert J. *Slave Religion: The "Invisible Institution" in the Antebellum South.* New York, 1978.

Randall, James Garfield. *The Confiscation of Property during the Civil War.* Indianapolis, 1913.

Ransom, Roger L. *Conflict and Compromise: The Political Economy of Slavery, Emancipation, and the American Civil War.* New York, 1989.

Ransom, Roger L., and Richard Sutch. *One Kind of Freedom: The Economic Consequences of Emancipation.* Cambridge, UK, 1977.

Reidy, Joseph P. *From Slavery to Agrarian Capitalism in the Cotton Plantation South: Central Georgia, 1800–1880.* Chapel Hill, N.C., 1992.

Reynolds, Donald E. *Editors Make War: Southern Newspapers in the Secession Crisis.* 1970; reprint, Carbondale, Ill., 2006.

Richards, Leonard L. *Slave Power: The Free North and Southern Domination, 1780–1860.* Baton Rouge, 2000.

Roark, James L. *Masters without Slaves: Southern Planters in the Civil War and Reconstruction.* New York, 1977.

Rolle, Andrew. *The Lost Cause: The Confederate Exodus to Mexico.* Norman, Okla., 1965.

Rose, Willie Lee. *Rehearsal for Reconstruction: The Port Royal Experiment.* New York, 1964.

Royce, Edward. *The Origins of Southern Sharecropping.* Philadelphia, 1993.

Rubin, Anne Sarah. *A Shattered Nation: The Rise and Fall of the Confederacy, 1861–1868.* Chapel Hill, N.C., 2005.

Salcedo-Bastardo, J. L. *Bolívar: A Continent and Its Destiny.* Richmond, Va., 1977.

Sandburg, Carl. *Abraham Lincoln: The Prairie Years and the War Years.* New York, 1954.

Scarborough, William Kauffman. *Masters of the Big House: Elite Slaveholders of the Mid-Nineteenth-Century South.* Baton Rouge, 2003.

Schott, Thomas E. *Alexander H. Stephens of Georgia: A Biography.* Baton Rouge, 1988.

Schwab, John Christopher. *The Confederate States of America, 1861–1865.* New York, 1901.

Schwalm, Leslie A. *Emancipation's Diaspora: Race and Reconstruction in the Upper Midwest.* Chapel Hill, N.C., 2009.

Sears, Stephen W. *To the Gates of Richmond: The Peninsula Campaign.* Boston, 1992.

Seton-Watson, Hugh. *The Russian Empire, 1801–1917.* New York, 1988.

Sewell, Richard H. *Ballots for Freedom: Antislavery Politics in the United States, 1837–1860.* New York, 1976.

Shanks, Henry T. *The Secession Movement in Virginia.* 1934; reprint, New York, 1970.

Sheehan-Dean, Aaron. *Why Confederates Fought: Family and Nation in Civil War Virginia.* Chapel Hill, N.C., 2007.

Shore, Laurence. *Southern Capitalists: The Ideological Leadership of an Elite, 1832–1885.* Chapel Hill, N.C., 1986.

Simpson, Brooks D. *Let Us Have Peace: Ulysses S. Grant and the Politics of War & Reconstruction, 1861–1868*. Chapel Hill, N.C., 1991.

Simpson, Craig M. *A Good Southerner: The Life of Henry A. Wise of Virginia*. Chapel Hill, N.C., 1985.

Sitterson, Joseph Carlyle. *The Secession Movement in North Carolina*. Chapel Hill, N.C., 1939.

———. *Sugar Country: The Cane Sugar Industry in the South, 1753–1950*. [Lexington, Ky.], 1953.

Smith, Adam J. P. *No Party Now: Politics in the Civil War North*. New York, 2006.

Soltow, Lee. *Men and Wealth in the United States, 1850–1870*. New Haven, Conn., 1975.

Stampp, Kenneth M. *And the War Came: The North and the Secession Crisis, 1860–1861*. 1950; reprint, Baton Rouge, 1970.

———. *The Peculiar Institution: Slavery in the Ante-bellum South*. New York, 1956.

Stewart, James Brewer. *Holy Warriors: The Abolitionists and American Slavery*. Rev. ed., New York, 1977.

Stovall, Pleasant A. *Robert Toombs: Statesman, Speaker, Soldier, Sage*. New York, 1892.

Stowe, Steven M. *Intimacy and Power in the Old South: Ritual in the Lives of the Planters*. Baltimore, 1987.

Sword, Wiley. *Southern Invincibility: A History of the Confederate Heart*. New York, 2000.

Symonds, Craig L. *Lincoln and His Admirals: Abraham Lincoln, the U.S. Navy, and the Civil War*. New York, 2008.

Tadman, Michael. *Speculators and Slaves: Masters, Traders, and Slaves in the Old South*. Madison, Wis., 1989.

Tarle, Eugene. *Napoleon's Invasion of Russia, 1812*. New York, 1942.

Tatum, Georgia Lee. *Disloyalty in the Confederacy.* 1934; reprint, Lincoln, Neb., 2000.

Thomas, Benjamin P., and Harold Hyman. *Stanton: The Life and Times of Lincoln's Secretary of War.* New York, 1962.

Thomas, Emory M. *The Confederate Nation: 1861–1865.* New York, 1979.

———. *The Confederate State of Richmond: A Biography of the Capital.* 1971; reprint, Baton Rouge, 1998.

———. *Robert E. Lee: A Biography.* New York, 1995.

Thompson, William Y. *Robert Toombs of Georgia.* Baton Rouge, 1966.

Thornton, Mark, and Robert B. Ekelund, Jr. *Tariffs, Blockades, and Inflation: The Economics of the Civil War.* Wilmington, Del., 2004.

Trefousse, Hans L. *The Radical Republicans: Lincoln's Vanguard for Racial Justice.* New York, 1968.

Trexler, Harrison Anthony. *Slavery in Missouri, 1804–1865.* Baltimore, 1914.

Trudeau, Noah Andre. *Like Men of War: Black Troops in the Civil War, 1862–1865.* Boston, 1998.

Urwin, Gregory J. W., ed. *Black Flag over Dixie: Racial Atrocities and Reprisals in the Civil War.* Carbondale, Ill., 2004.

Van Deusen, Glyndon. *William Henry Seward.* New York, 1967.

Verna, Paul. *Petion y Bolívar.* Caracas, 1980.

Vorenberg, Michael. *Final Freedom: The Civil War, the Abolition of Slavery, and the Thirteenth Amendment.* Cambridge, UK, 2001.

Waddell, James D. *Biographical Sketch of Linton Stephens.* Atlanta, Ga., 1877.

Ward, Andrew. *Dark Midnight When I Rise: The Story of the Jubilee Singers Who Introduced the World to the Music of Black America.* New York, 2000.

———. *The Slaves' War: The Civil War in the Words of Former Slaves.* Boston, 2008.

Wayne, Michael. *The Reshaping of Plantation Society: The Natchez District, 1860–80.* Urbana, Ill., 1990.

Wiggins, Sarah Woolfolk. *The Scalawag in Alabama Politics, 1865–1881.* Tuscaloosa, Ala., 1977.

Wiley, Bell Irvin. *Confederate Women.* Westport, Conn., 1975.

———. *The Life of Billy Yank: The Common Soldier of the Union.* 1952; reprint, Baton Rouge, 1981.

———. *The Life of Johnny Reb: The Common Soldier of the Confederacy.* 1943; reprint, Baton Rouge, 1978.

———. *The Plain People of the Confederacy.* Columbia, S.C., 2000.

———. *Southern Negroes, 1861–1865.* 1938; reprint, Baton Rouge, 1965.

Woodman, Harold D. *King Cotton and His Retainers: Financing and Marketing the Cotton Crop of the South, 1800–1925.* Lexington, Ky., 1968.

Woods, James M. *Rebellion and Realignment: Arkansas's Road to Secession.* Fayetteville, Ark., 1987.

Woodworth, Steven E. *While God Is Marching On: The Religious World of Civil War Soldiers.* Lawrence, Kans., 2001.

Wooster, Ralph A. *The People in Power: Courthouse and Statehouse in the Lower South, 1850–1860.* Knoxville, Tenn., 1969.

———. *Politicians, Planters, and Plain Folk: Courthouse and Statehouse in the Upper South, 1850–1860.* Knoxville, Tenn., 1975.

Wright, Gavin. *The Political Economy of the Cotton South: Households, Markets, and Wealth in the Nineteenth Century.* New York, 1978.

Yearns, Wilfred Buck. *The Confederate Congress.* Athens, Ga., 1960.

Zahler, Helene Sarah. *Eastern Workingmen and National Land Policy, 1829–1862.* New York, 1941.

Articles and Book Chapters

Andrew, Rod, Jr. "The Essential Nationalism of the People: Georgia's Confederate Congressional Elections of 1863." In Gordon and Inscoe, *Inside the Confederate Nation.*

Aptheker, Herbert. "Notes on Slave Conspiracies in Confederate Mississippi." *Journal of Negro History* 29 (1944): 75–79.

Auman, William T., and David D. Scarboro. "The Heroes of America in Civil War North Carolina." *North Carolina Historical Review* 58 (1981): 327–63.

Bergeron, Arthur W. "Free Men of Color in Grey." *Civil War History* 32 (1986): 247–55.

Beringer, Richard E. "A Profile of the Members of the Confederate Congress." *Journal of Southern History* 32 (1967): 518–41.

Blair, William A. "The Seven Days and the Radical Persuasion: Convincing Moderates in the North of the Need for a Hard War." In *The Richmond Campaign of 1862: The Peninsula and the Seven Days,* ed. Gary W. Gallagher. Chapel Hill, N.C., 2000.

Cimprich, John. "Slave Behavior during the Federal Occupation of Tennessee, 1862–1865." *The Historian* 44 (1982): 335–46.

Faust, Drew Gilpin. "Altars of Sacrifice: Confederate Women and the Narratives of War." *Journal of American History* 76 (1990): 1200–1228.

———. "Confederate Women and Narratives of War." In *Divided Houses: Gender and the Civil War,* ed. Catherine Clinton and Nina Silber. New York, 1992.

Fleming, Walter L. "The Peace Movement in Alabama." *South Atlantic Quarterly* 2 (1903): 246–60.

Foner, Eric. "Thaddeus Stevens, Confiscation, and Reconstruction." In *Politics and Ideology in the Age of the Civil War,* by Eric Foner. New York, 1980.

Freidel, Frank. "The Loyal Publication Society: A Pro-Union Propaganda Agency." *Mississippi Valley Historical Review* 26 (1939): 359–76.

Gallagher, Gary W. "Disaffection, Persistence, and Nation: Some Directions in Recent Scholarship on the Confederacy." *Civil War History* 55 (2009): 329–53.

Hahn, Steven. "Class and State in Postemancipation Societies: Southern Planters in Comparative Perspective." *American Historical Review* 95 (1990): 75–98.

Henry, William Wirt. "Kenner's Mission to Europe." *William and Mary Quarterly* 25 (1916): 9–12.

James, Josef C. "Sherman at Savannah." *Journal of Negro History* 39 (1954): 127–37.

Laskin, Lisa. " 'The Army Is Not Near So Much Demoralized as the Country Is': Soldiers in the Army of Northern Virginia and the Confederate Home Front." In *The View from the Ground: Experiences of Civil War Soldiers,* ed. Aaron Sheehan-Dean. Lexington, Ky., 2007.

Lebergott, Stanley. "Labor Force and Employment, 1800–1960." In *Output, Employment, and Productivity in the United States after 1800,* ed. Dorothy Brady. New York, 1966.

Lowe, Richard. "Battle on the Levee: The Fight at Milliken's Bend." In *Black Soldiers in Blue: African American Troops in the Civil War Era,* ed. John David Smith. Chapel Hill, N.C., 2002.

Manning, Chandra. "The Order of Nature Would Be Reversed: Soldiers, Slavery, and the North Carolina Gubernatorial Election of 1864." In *North Carolinians in the Era of Civil War and Reconstruction,* ed. Paul D. Escott. Chapel Hill, N.C., 2008.

Martinez, Jaime Amanda. "The Slave Market in Civil War Virginia." In *Crucible of the Civil War: Virginia from Secession to Commemoration,* ed. Edward L. Ayers, Gary W. Gallagher, and Andrew J. Torget. Charlottesville, Va., 2006.

McKinney, Gordon B. "Layers of Loyalty: Confederate Nationalism and Amnesty Letters from Western North Carolina." *Civil War History* 51 (2005): 5–22.

Messner, William F. "Black Violence and White Response: Louisiana, 1862." *Journal of Southern History* 41 (1975): 19–38.

Miller, Edward A., Jr. "Garland H. White, Black Army Chaplain." *Civil War History* 43 (1997): 201–18.

Mohr, Clarence L. "The Atlanta Campaign and the African American Experience in Civil War Georgia." In Gordon and Inscoe, *Inside the Confederate Nation.*

Nelson, Bernard. "Confederate Slave Impressment Legislation, 1861–1865." *Journal of Negro History* 31 (1946): 394–400.

Phillips, Christopher. " 'The Chrysalis State': Slavery, Confederate Identity, and the Creation of the Border South." In Gordon and Inscoe, *Inside the Confederate Nation.*

Ross, Steven Joseph. "Freed Soil, Freed Labor, Freed Men: John Eaton and the Davis Bend Experiment." *Journal of Southern History* 44 (1978): 213–32.

Simpson, Brooks D. "Facilitating Defeat: The Union High Command and the Collapse of the Confederacy." In Grimsley and Simpson, *Collapse of the Confederacy.*

Soltow, Lee. "Economic Inequality in the United States in the Period from 1790 to 1860." *Journal of Economic History* 31 (1971): 822–39.

Stampp, Kenneth M. "Comment on 'Why the Republicans Rejected Both Compromise and Secession.' " In *The Crisis of the Union, 1860–61,* ed. George Harmon Knoles. Baton Rouge, 1965.

Steckel, Richard H. "Birth Weights and Infant Mortality among American Slaves." *Explorations in Economic History* 23 (1986): 173–98.

———. "A Dreadful Childhood: The Excess Mortality of American Slaves." *Social Science History* 10 (1986): 427–65.

Suderow, Bryce A. "The Battle of the Crater." In Urwin, *Black Flag over Dixie.*

Torget, Andrew. "Unions of Slavery: Slavery, Politics and Secession in the Valley of Virginia." In Ayers, Gallagher, and Torget, *Crucible of the Civil War.*

Trexler, Harrison A. "The Opposition of Planters to the Employment of Slaves as Laborers by the Confederacy." *Mississippi Valley Historical Review* 27 (1940): 211–24.

Whittington, G. P., ed. "Concerning the Loyalty of Slaves in North Louisiana in 1863." *Louisiana Historical Quarterly* 14 (1931): 467–502.

Winther, Oscar Osburn. "The Soldier Vote in the Election of 1864." *New York History* 25 (1944): 440–48.

Index

Spottsylvania Court House, battle of, 223

Stanton, Edwin M., 133, 237–38, 286–87

Stapp, Joseph D., 55

state sovereignty, 252–53

Stephens, Alexander, 35, 38–39, 108, 227
  on conscription, 84, 199
  peace talks and, 249–50, 260–61
  vice presidency of, 43–44, 53, 151

Stephens, George E., 93, 107, 164
  on fugitive slaves, 117–18, 129
  recruitment of black Union soldiers by, 161

Stephens, Linton, 159

Stephens, W. A., 150, 214

Stephen (slave), 238–39

Stevens, Thaddeus, 112, 121, 130

Stiles, B. E., 66

Stillwell, William, 152

Stone, Amanda, 103–4, 154

Stone, Katherine, ix–x, 5, 57
  on black Union soldiers, 163
  on burning of cotton crops, 80
  on Confederate defeat, 290, 294
  on Confederate revelry, 230
  on Confederate victories, 62
  on division of slave families, 13
  on the Emancipation Proclamation, 142
  on the fall of New Orleans, 70
  on Lee's Maryland campaign, 68
  on Lincoln's assassination, 293
  on personal power of planters, 20
  on resistance to military service, 83
  on slave labor, 9–10, 12
  on slave's response to the Civil War, 94–95

on the unity of the Confederacy, 53, 59
on unraveling of slavery, 154–55, 159

Stone, William R., 52

Stone family, ix, 6, 7, 103–4

Sullivan, J. A., 210

Sumner, Charles, 36, 112, 113

Swain, David, 258, 259, 279

Sydney (slave), 13

Tamar (freedwoman), 176

Taylor, Richard, xviii, 151, 281

Taylor, Susie King, 94

Taylor, Zachary, 8, 151

Temple, Oliver P., 29, 76

Tennessee, 3, 148
  abolition of slavery in, 244
  Confederate volunteers from, 54
  free blacks in, 58
  peace campaign in, 214–15
  secession of, 44, 46–47, 49–50, 77
  Union advances in, 68–70, 82, 102–3, 116–17, 148–49
  unionist sentiment in, 76–78, 105, 148–49
  Union soldiers from, 216

Texas, 3, 33
  elections of 1863 in, 206
  emigration to Mexico from, 294
  physical isolation from the Confederacy after 1863 of, 144, 155, 239
  refugeeing of slaves to, 239
  secession of, 39, 43–44
  unraveling of slavery in, 239

Third South Carolina Volunteers, 262

Thirteenth Amendment of the U.S. Constitution, 219–20, 249, 260, 287, 295

About the Author

Bruce Levine is the J. G. Randall Distinguished Professor of History at the University of Illinois at Urbana-Champaign. An associate editor of the Civil War magazine *North and South,* he has published three books on the Civil War era. The most recent of these, *Confederate Emancipation: South-ern Plans to Free and Arm Slaves during the Civil War,* re-ceived the Peter Seaborg Award for Civil War Scholarship and was named one of the ten best nonfiction books of the year by *The Washington Post.*

About the Type

This book was set in Caslon, a typeface first designed in 1722 by William Caslon. Its widespread use by most English printers in the early eighteenth century soon supplanted the Dutch typefaces that had formerly prevailed. The roman is considered a "workhorse" typeface due to its pleasant, open appearance, while the italic is exceedingly decorative.